# WordPerfect
# Suite 8

## The Comprehensive Guide

VENTANA

Winston Steward
Gail Perry

# WordPerfect Suite 8

## The Comprehensive Guide

Windows 95/NT

**WordPerfect Suite 8: The Comprehensive Guide**
Copyright © 1997 by Winston Steward and Gail Perry

**Library of Congress Cataloging-in-Publication Data**
Steward, Winston
    Corel WordPerfect Suite 8: The Comprehensive Guide / Winston Steward, Gail Perry. -- 1st ed.
       p        cm
    ISBN 1-56604-652-1
    1. Integrated software.  2. Corel WordPerfect Suite.  I. Perry, Gail.  II. Title
    QA76.76.I57S75  1997
    005.369--dc21                      97-9067
                                    CIP

First Edition 9 8 7 6 5 4 3 2 1

Printed in the United States of America

Ventana Communications Group
P.O. Box 13964
Research Triangle Park, NC 27709-3964
919.544.9404
FAX 919.544.9472
http://www.vmedia.com

Ventana Communications Group is a division of International Thomson Publishing.

**Limits of Liability & Disclaimer of Warranty**
The authors and publisher of this book have used their best efforts in preparing the book and the programs contained in it. These efforts include the development, research, and testing of the theories and programs to determine their effectiveness. The authors and publisher make no warranty of any kind, expressed or implied, with regard to these programs or the documentation contained in this book.

    The authors and publisher shall not be liable in the event of incidental or consequential damages in connection with, or arising out of, the furnishing, performance or use of the programs, associated instructions and/or claims of productivity gains.

**Trademarks**
Trademarked names appear throughout this book and on the accompanying compact disk, if applicable. Rather than list the names and entities that own the trademarks or insert a trademark symbol with each mention of the trademarked name, the publisher states that it is using the names only for editorial purposes and to the benefit of the trademark owner with no intention of infringing upon that trademark.

**President**
Michael E. Moran

**Vice President of
Content Development**
Karen A. Bluestein

**Director of Acquisitions
and Development**
Robert Kern

**Editorial Operations Manager**
Kerry L. B. Foster

**Production Manager**
John Cotterman

**Brand Manager**
Jamie Jaeger Fiocco

**Art Director**
Marcia Webb

**Creative Services Manager**
Diane Lennox

**Acquisitions Editor**
Christopher D. Grams

**Project Editor**
Rachel Pearce Anderson

**Development Editor**
Michelle Corbin Nichols

**Copy Editor**
Sarah O'Keefe

**Technical Reviewer**
Brian Little

**Desktop Publisher**
Jaimie Livingston

**Proofreader**
Tom Collins

**Indexer**
Sherry Massey

**Interior Designer**
Patrick Berry

**Cover Illustrator**
Lisa Gill

## About the Authors

**Winston Steward** is a writer, computer teacher, and consultant for nonprofit organizations. Author of *Every Family's Guide to Computers*, he is also coauthor of *CorelDRAW 7 Secrets*, and *Web Publishing with Macromedia Backstage Internet Studio 2*. Host of *Insights* on *National Public Radio*, he answers computer questions and reviews products.

**Gail Perry** is a Certified Public Accountant (CPA) and WordPerfect Certified Instructor who teaches computer classes at the Indiana CPA Society. Author of several computer- and tax-related books, she co-wrote Ventana's *Quicken 5 on the Internet*.

## Acknowledgments

I would like to thank Michelle Murphy-Croteau at Corel for being so helpful, Michelle Nichols and everybody at Ventana for their hard work, Margot Maley at Waterside, and MegaImage Computers, Pomona, California.

—W.S.

I'd like to thank Rachel Anderson, Michelle Nichols, and Becky Steele at Ventana for their help, guidance, patience, and insight. Thanks to Sarah O'Keefe for helping to blend the voices of the two authors, and to Brian Little for helping to make sure everything works just as we explained it. Thanks also to Michelle Murphy-Croteau at Corel for fielding our questions throughout the entire beta process, and a special thanks to Bill Lauman of Corel Quattro Pro technical support who made helping us a personal quest rather than just a job. Thanks also to Margot Maley who thought of me for this assignment, and to Winston, who is a great writing partner.

—G.A.P.

## Dedication

This book is dedicated to my ever-patient family, with a long-overdue thanks to Irma. Without her, very little I tried to accomplish in the last 10 years would have been possible. And to Colleen, for making everything new again.

—W.S.

To Georgia and Katherine, who are the two best reasons in the world for working from home.

—G.A.P.

# Contents

**PART II**

**Corel WordPerfect 8**

## PART III

# Presentations

**PART IV**
**Quattro Pro 8**

## PART V

# Bonus Applications

PART VII
# Appendices

# Introduction

WordPerfect Suite 8 is the ultimate tool for presenting your ideas. Whether in words, numbers, pictures, movies, or sounds; whether printed on a page or experienced online; WordPerfect Suite 8 will bring out the best in what you are trying to say. WordPerfect Suite 8 is centered around three "core" applications: WordPerfect for word processing, Presentations 8 for creating multimedia applications, and Quattro Pro for Data management. In addition to these three are several bonus or helper applications, that contribute greatly to the power of the Suite. For example, Photo House allows you to edit and enrich photographs for use in any application, and Bitstream Font Navigator helps manage fonts on your system.

What is a suite? A suite is a group of applications that are linked by a similar interface and share some of the same components. Suite applications can usually share information; for example, a Corel Presentations slide show can have a link to a document in WordPerfect. Software suites often include complementary programs designed to enhance the main applications. In WordPerfect Suite 8, the main applications are WordPerfect, Quattro Pro, and Corel Presentations; two examples of smaller supporting programs are Corel Quick Tasks and Corel Flow.

The purpose of an office suite such as WordPerfect Suite 8 is to provide everything you need to create, manage, print, post, and distribute any business document. You can create everything from a simple invoice for services rendered to a multimedia presentation for company executives. A good office suite includes a calendar and an organizer, to help you plan events and execute those events on schedule. Another key component of a good office suite is that it provides seamless interaction among its components.

## The Corel Office Suite Environment

A well-designed suite provides a desktop toolbar for easy access to the suite applications. WordPerfect Suite 8 does not create a separate toolbar for Suite applications; instead, it adds icons to the Windows toolbar. (This group of icons is called the Desktop Application Director (DAD), and we'll examine its function shortly.) For now, let's identify the three main applications (see Figure I-1).

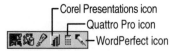

*Figure I-1: The WordPerfect Suite 8 icons. Hold your mouse over each for an identifying ToolTip. The main applications are labeled with callouts.*

To close DAD, right-click on an icon and select Exit DAD from the pop-up menu. You can also start the WordPerfect Suite programs from the Windows Start menu. Select Start | Corel WordPerfect Suite 8 and open your selected program.

## How a Suite's Many Components Can Work for You

Here are some examples of how WordPerfect Suite 8's applications work together to make you more productive:

- A WordPerfect document that shows how well your district branch of the company is doing can include a spreadsheet with all the necessary statistics. As the data in that spreadsheet changes, you can update the embedded spreadsheet data automatically.

- A Corel Presentations slide show can include that same spreadsheet. Both Presentations and WordPerfect can access the same spreadsheet files.

- You can create a business logo and use it in all your WordPerfect Suite applications. You don't have to create a separate logo for your slide show, a separate logo for your printed documents, and so on. In fact, the drawing interface you used to create this logo will look the same in any WordPerfect Suite application. Additionally, all clip art, photographs, and fonts included with WordPerfect Suite are available in all the programs, including Envoy, CorelFlow, and Web page creation tools.

■ The PerfectExpert Project Creator feature on your toolbar lets you create all kinds of documents with components from the different WordPerfect Suite applications.

■ You can schedule mailings, by merging documents from any Suite application with lists created and customized with WordPerfect, Quattro Pro, or Corel Address Book.

## Who Uses WordPerfect Suite 8?

WordPerfect Suite 8 is designed for anybody who writes. It offers tools to enhance creativity in speech and document design. Other tools help you design a business letter for a client mailing list and have it ready to go—envelopes included—in record time. You can convert any document you create in WordPerfect, Presentations, or Quattro Pro to a Web page in a very short time. Even if you are looking primarily for a multimedia tool rather than a word processor, WordPerfect Suite 8 has plenty to offer.

For graduate students, WordPerfect Suite 8 provides templates for theses and term papers. To back up your ideas, you can create graphs and tables. In addition to its advanced data management Quattro Pro delivers some down to earth features as well, with templates that quickly calculate the true cost of a college loan or a student roster that calculates quarterly grades.

For journalists, WordPerfect offers a tool that calculates your document's use of jargon, sentence length, and general readability. A thesaurus on the toolbar delivers suggested synonyms instantly. If you need to create scientific documents, you can create and calculate complex equations right inside your word processor, instead of having to import data from another program.

Grant writers can transfer ideas from the word processor directly into Presentations, in case you get asked to "put together a slide show" stating your case. This updated version of Presentations 8 comes with dozens of ready-to-go templates for business presentations. It's easy to create handouts and speaker notes to complement your presentation, and Presentations provides tips for how to highlight and emphasize the data you think is important. If your company needs to manage huge databases, and requires the flexibility to access only small portions of the data using custom-designed fields and criteria, Quattro Pro has the power you need for these tasks.

If you work with colleagues around the country or the world, you can edit documents created with WordPerfect Suite 8 online, which allows you to save multiple versions of a single document and keep track of *who* made *which* changes. WordPerfect Suite 8 also provides tools for creating links between different locations in a single document, links to another document on the same computer, or links to a World Wide Web site.

And finally, if you are busy writing the Great American Novel or a computer book such as this one, WordPerfect Suite 8 lets you store related documents within a master document. This makes keeping track of multiple chapters very easy, eliminating the cumbersome chore of editing a huge 500-page file every time you want to make a change while avoiding the disorganization of having dozens of little chapters scattered all over your hard drive. WordPerfect's subdocument system allows you to organize all chapters and volumes within one easy-to-manage master document. From the bird's-eye view of this master document, you can choose which chapter to edit or print, without wading through a sea of pages. And when the book finally does get published, you can use Quattro Pro's automatic mortgage calculator to figure out how much you'll *really* pay for that big house on the hill.

## Who Should Read This Book?

If you are interested in exploring WordPerfect Suite 8 more thoroughly, this book is for you. There's a lot beneath the surface within the Suite's programs, and this book provides an in-depth examination of the Suite's features. If you want to tackle these applications with a reference at your fingertips and without having to 'fish for answers,' this book will save you hours of trial and error.

## An Overview of the Main Programs

This section skims over the three WordPerfect Suite core applications: Word Perfect 8, Quattro Pro 8, and Presentations 8. Then we'll take a quick look at the bonus applications. These are small programs that 'round out' the Suite's usefulness, supplementing the main applications.

### WordPerfect 8

WordPerfect 8 is WordPerfect Suite 8's word processing program. It has enjoyed a leading position in the field for many years, continually adding new features based on customer input and as new technology becomes available. WordPerfect lets you change page size and orientation; lettering (font) size, color, and type; and once you create a document you like, you can save its "look" as a style, which makes it easy to create a similar document later. You can quickly add pictures, charts, graphs, and tables to your WordPerfect document, and create bordered boxes for text, which is nice for creating brochures, newsletters, and advertising layouts. With WordPerfect 8, you are never on your own, since help is only a click away. Every dialog box contains a question mark in the upper right corner. Click this, then click any feature you need help with, and you'll get an explanation. For more in-depth help, click the light bulb on the right side of the WordPerfect toolbar.

## Presentations 8

Corel Presentations 8 turns your computer into a slide projector. Each slide can contain text, pictures, sound files, movies, animations, charts, or graphs. You can record your voice as a narration over each slide or over the entire presentation. You have total control over how long each slide and each slide element (such as an animated text headline, for example) is onscreen.

Corel Presentations comes with a marvelous library of predesigned elements you can add to your slide show, as well as templates to get you started creating shows quickly. Some templates are suitable for business presentations, some for the classroom, and some for stand-alone demonstrations—the type of exhibit you might see in a display booth at a conference. You can work with various views of your slides: you can see them all at once, like a storyboard, or one by one, just as they will appear in the presentation. You can also work in an "Outline" view, which helps organize the content of each slide and the presentation as a whole.

## Quattro Pro 8

Quattro Pro 8 is a spreadsheet—a program that lets you organize data. Visually, a spreadsheet is a grid of rectangles called cells. These cells organize data for you; mostly (but not always) numeric data. The cells are organized into columns, which run from left to right and have a letter identifier, and rows, which run top to bottom and have a number identifier. So, a letter-number combination identifies each cell. For example, the cell in the fourth column in the third row is called D:3.

You use each cell in your spreadsheet for data. For example, the first six columns could contain numbers that represent sales totals. You could then report the sum of those sales totals in the seventh column. You can assign complex formulas and functions to any cell, and use data in one cell as input in another. You can also type text into a spreadsheet cell. In fact, this is essential, because it lets you label your various calculations.

Quattro Pro is a powerful spreadsheet that lets you work with your data as it will really appear when it's presented. You can think about design elements even as you organize the number-crunching. Quattro Pro's Cell-Reference checker can check and fix errors in formulas as you input numbers into cells. This is especially important when you move cells that are linked to other cells. The Property bars change according to the type of task you are performing, which means that the tools you need are always handy. Quattro Pro also lets you convert text in any cell into an active **link**. This link can take you to another location in the same spreadsheet, to another document on the same computer, or even to a site on the World Wide Web.

## The Bonus Applications

The bonus applications included with WordPerfect Suite 8 are not simply thrown in to make you feel like you are getting more for your money. They were carefully selected to round out the Suite and make it more powerful and flexible, to better suit your needs.

### Envoy 7

Envoy 7 allows you to share documents with people who don't have WordPerfect. Envoy 7 is a multiplatform viewing and editing application. Your colleagues can edit documents in Envoy and return them to you. Graphics, advanced formatting, tables, and OLE objects will all look the same in your Envoy document as they did in the original application. Envoy documents can be created in most WordPerfect Suite applications. To open an Envoy document, just open the Envoy Viewer. To publish an Envoy, you select File | Publish to Envoy.

### Corel Address Book

Corel Address Book allows you to input and save addresses, including e-mail addresses. By default, the Address Book uses your mail or fax system. You can select Control Panel | Mail and Fax | Add to set up Corel Address Book as your mail/fax system. You can create several address books for different mailing needs. Address books can be imported, exported, and merged for use with other applications. You can add fields, perform custom searches, and modify address books any way you like.

## Bitstream Font Navigator

Bitstream Font Navigator helps manage the fonts on your computer, allowing you to selectively load fonts you need for a particular project, rather than have hundreds or even thousands of fonts clutter your system at all times. After viewing font examples in Bitstream Font Navigator, you can quickly load and unload them, and even store fonts in groups. You can then load, remove, and restore font groups with a single mouse click. WordPerfect Suite 8 includes over a thousand fonts, so Bitstream Font Navigator is a truly useful utility.

## Corel Photo House

Corel Photo House provides some of the same tools for editing photographs that you would find in a professional photoediting program such as PhotoPaint or Adobe Photoshop. If you have a scanned photograph that appears too dark, needs a color touch-up, or is in need of special effects, this is the program for you. Use Corel Photo House to create cards, posters, banners, certificates, and other projects that require small amounts of decorative text mixed with pictures. Creating such projects with a full-fledged word processing program could become a bit cumbersome. Corel Photo House excels at projects with irregular paper sizes, such as coupons, menus, recipe cards, and invitations. If you need to create such items and you don't want to start from scratch, come to Corel Photo House first.

One of the nicest features of this program is the window that opens on the left side of the main workspace. As you work on different tasks, the contents of this window change to offer relevant instructions and further options to get that particular task done. You can import photographs, or use the program's extensive clip-art selections. When you select Import, you see an album with all your choices on the left. This program uses lots of drag-and-drop features. For example, to use one of the decorative text presets, you would simply drag it on to your selected text.

## Perfect Script

Corel Perfect Script allows you to record your actions, save them, and play them back, which means you can automate mundane tasks. The program appears as a small console on top of your current application. Corel Perfect Script allows you to record any keyboard, mouse, or text creation action in WordPerfect, Quattro Pro, and Presentations. After recording, you open the script or macro and press Play to repeat the action. If you know a bit of Visual Basic you can quickly learn Corel's robust scripting language, and create complicated scripts that function in many other applications as well.

### Corel WordPerfect Suite Setup

To add or remove WordPerfect Suite applications, select Start | Corel WordPerfect Suite 8 | Accessories | Corel WordPerfect Suite Setup. Having setup handy is helpful, because many interesting extras (such as Corel Flow 3) are not included in the standard installation.

Other bonus applications WordPerfect Suite 8 provides include Corel Data Modeling Desktop, Quick Finder, and Quick View Plus. Please see Chapter 14 for a more thorough discussion of all the bonus applications.

## What You Need to Run WordPerfect Suite 8

WordPerfect Suite 8 requires Windows 95. It will run on a 486 processor, but if you intend to do a lot of number crunching or create complex multimedia presentations, a Pentium processor is preferable. WordPerfect Suite 8 requires eight megabytes of RAM, but some applications will run slowly unless you have 16MB or more. An SVGA video card is required. To fully enjoy WordPerfect Suite 8, a Pentium 100 computer with 32MB of RAM (or better) will optimize your experience, and greatly reduce delay time in loading large graphics, spreadsheets, and multimedia components (such as narration and video).

For multimedia features such as video playback, sounds, music, and animations, properly configured sound cards and video cards are required. Recording narration for Presentations 8 requires a microphone.

To install WordPerfect Suite 8, you'll need a minimum of 50 megabytes of free hard drive space. You can, of course, simply install one or two of the core programs—for example, only install Presentations 8 and WordPerfect 8, and not Quattro Pro. Still, the program does not install well unless there are 50MB of hard drive space available. The average installation requires between 120 and 200MB of free space.

## What's in This Book?

First, we'll visit the Suite interface, taking a look at the Suite as a whole and learning how to start each Suite application, providing enough information so that you can find your way around the programs. Then we'll examine the Desktop Application Director, which places control of all the Suite's applications right on your desktop, and walk through the PerfectExpert Project Creator, which helps you create unique documents. Then, we'll look at the PerfectExpert Help System, which provides tutorials for any WordPerfect Suite task. The help system is found in each of the core applications.

Next, we'll tackle WordPerfect itself, working through basic and then more advanced tasks. There's a chapter on working with graphics, tables, and charts, and a chapter with special tips for speeding up your productivity in WordPerfect. Presentations 8 and Quattro Pro 8 are explored with a basic, introductory chapter for each, followed by a chapter with more advanced information.

Then we'll thoroughly explore the bonus applications, such as Photo House and Bitstream Font Navigator, and see how each of them can enhance your productivity while working with the core applications.

Finally, we'll examine how each of the Suite programs interact, learning how to create links between each of them and how to link a document to a Web page. Then we'll examine how to create Web pages with WordPerfect Suite 8 core applications. The appendix includes instructions and options for installing WordPerfect Suite 8.

I enjoy working with WordPerfect, and have found many pleasant surprises lurking just beneath the surface. There's much more to WordPerfect Suite 8 than immediately meets the eye. The applications it contains are worth 'growing into' over time. I can well understand why WordPerfect has been a top-selling word processing package for such a long time, and I've found the improvements in each iteration of WordPerfect Suite to be genuinely useful. If you would like to contact me with your comments, I can be reached at Wish4Time@aol.com.

## Part I

# The Suite Environment

# 1

# Getting to Know WordPerfect Suite 8

In this chapter, we'll cover the basics you need to know to get started with any program in the Suite. This includes how to open and close programs, and how to work with dialog boxes, which are windows that pop up and provide choices for the document you are creating. At times, WordPerfect Suite 8 turns your mouse into a tool for performing a particular task. We'll explore how that works as well. Finally, you'll get acquainted with toolbars, which bring the Suite's full power to your fingertips. You'll never have to go far to find what you need to work on your document.

## Opening & Closing WordPerfect Suite Programs

You may open any WordPerfect Suite application by clicking its icon on the Desktop Application Director, found at the bottom right of the Windows 95 workspace (see Figure 1-1). Please note that if you have moved your Windows toolbar to some other part of the screen, that's where the Desktop Application Director will be. To identify any icon, hold your mouse over it and a ToolTip will be displayed.

*Figure 1-1: Click any program on the Desktop Application Director to open it.*

You can also open any WordPerfect Suite application by selecting Start | Corel WordPerfect Suite 8, and then choosing the application name from the submenu. Open any program from the submenu by selecting it. To open one of the bonus applications, click Accessories, and a submenu displays them.

Close any application by clicking the X button (the Close button) in the top right corner of its window. You may notice there are two Close buttons in the corner (see Figure 1-2). The lower X button closes an open document. The one at the upper right closes the application itself.

*Figure 1-2: To close any application, click the uppermost Close button in the upper right hand corner of its window.*

You can open more than one application at once. To open another application, just click its icon on the Desktop Application Director. Please note that the Desktop Application Director is also referred to paternally as the DAD.

## Working With the Mouse

We're used to the standard Windows behavior of the mouse, where clicking or double-clicking with the left mouse button selects an object or makes a choice, and right-clicking on an object displays a shortcut menu of other choices. In certain instances in WordPerfect, the mouse can perform additional tasks.

### Dragging & Dropping

You can open a WordPerfect document by simply dragging its icon and dropping it onto the WordPerfect program icon. You can also insert a picture, music file, or other object into a WordPerfect document, by dragging and dropping the object onto the blank WordPerfect page. Locate the WordPerfect file or graphic object using Windows Explorer or the Windows Find command. Then click the file icon, hold down the mouse button, and move the cursor (and the file icon) onto the WordPerfect page. When you reach the page, release the mouse button. The icon is dropped onto the page. If you dragged and dropped a WordPerfect file, the file is opened. If you dragged and dropped a picture or music file, the file is inserted into the WordPerfect document. The effect is the same as if you had selected Insert | Graphics | Clipart or Insert | Object. The only caveat is that since WordPerfect's window opens full screen, you may need to click the Resize button to be able to see the desktop.

## Creating by Dragging

In WordPerfect, you can create a box for a graphic, right on the page. This is done by dragging to create the box you want. Position the cursor over the blank portion of a page, well away from any text. Then press and hold down the left mouse button. Now, drag in the direction you'd like to create your box. You see an outline form. When the box is the size you want, release the left mouse button. Your box is created.

## Position & Hold

Sometimes when you click the downward arrow to the right of a menu item, you'll see another menu reveal itself. For example, the Highlight, Bullet, and Numbering icons on the WordPerfect toolbar all have their own menus, offering expanded choices. Remember, if you position your mouse and hold it over any button on any WordPerfect toolbar, you'll see a ToolTip. This is a brief label that explains what the tool or button does.

## Right-Clicking for Shortcut Menus

Right-clicking on just about any WordPerfect object, such as a graphic, misspelled word, table, or even a blank page, displays a menu of choices. For example, right-clicking outside the margins of a blank WordPerfect page lets you create a header and/or footer or a watermark. Right-clicking on a table allows you to quickly add or join cells, create a background for the table, or perform other related tasks.

# Understanding Dialogs

Often, when you click an option a dialog box is displayed which contains a number of tabs, extra buttons, and choices. Sometimes you are required to type words or numbers into the dialog box. In other cases you need only toggle a choice on or off. Or you might need to use an arrow to scroll up or down for a number selection. Figure 1-3 shows the Quattro Pro Cell Properties dialog box.

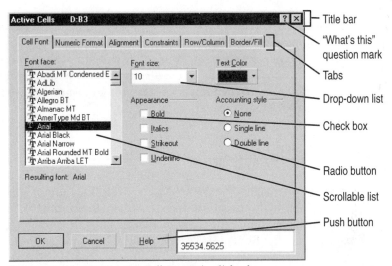

*Figure 1-3: The Quattro Pro Cell Properties dialog box.*

Let's take a look at some of its features:

- **Title bar**. This appears at the top of each dialog box. Here you'll find the name of the dialog box and some indication of its purpose.

- **Tabs**. Notice the six phrases arrayed along the top of the dialog box. These are tabs. Clicking on one reveals another section of the dialog box beneath the one you are looking at right now. Tabs function like card catalogs. The tabs are raised above the card itself, making the cards in the back visible and accessible. In WordPerfect, clicking a tab behind the dialog box in the front brings that hidden tab to the front, so you can access the options.

- **Scrollable lists**. Look at the phrase "Font face." Below it is a list of fonts. All the fonts on your computer can't possibly fit into the preview area provided. So you must use the scroll buttons on the right side of the Font face list to view all the available fonts.

- **Drop-down list**. You can recognize a drop-down list on a dialog box because a downward-facing arrow appears to the right of it. In Figure 1-3, look at "Font size" and "Text Color." Click the arrow to reveal a list of options to apply to the item you selected. Another example of a drop-down list is the Style list, positioned in the middle of the Property bar. The Property bar is the toolbar right under the standard toolbar. Click the downward-facing arrow on the Styles list (you can hold your mouse over it to make sure you are choosing the right tool). The ToolTip will read "Select Style." After you click the arrow, you'll see a number of options appear. These are the various styles you can apply to the selected text.

- **Check boxes** and **radio buttons**. Notice the options under Appearance and Accounting style. Clicking a check box places a check inside it, showing that the option indicated is "toggled on." Radio buttons are similar, but use a small round dot inside a circle instead to indicate that an option has been selected. So, what's the difference? Check boxes are used when you can select more than one option. For example, in the figure you can choose to format your text as Bold, Italic, Strikeout, *and* Underline all at once, if you like. On the other hand, radio buttons indicate that you may select just one option—your Accounting Style may be set *only* to Single Line, Double Line, *or* None.

- **Push buttons**. The buttons at the bottom of the Cell Properties dialog box are push buttons—or just "buttons." Holding your mouse over them changes their appearance slightly. This lets you know that they are active choices. Clicking them causes the specified action to take place.

- **"What's This?" question mark** (Help button). Notice the question mark in the upper right corner of the dialog box. Click it, and your cursor turns into a question mark. Now, click any feature in the dialog box and you'll get a brief explanation of its purpose.

Figure 1-4 shows the Master Gallery dialog box from Presentations.

*Figure 1-4: The Master Gallery dialog box from Presentations.*

Let's look at how its options are arranged:

- **Preview window**. Notice the Category drop-down list at the top. Clicking it changes the eight mini-slides. You can then double-click on one of the mini-slides to make it the active slide style for your presentation.

- **Browse button**. A Browse button is helpful when you need to look for a file to place into your document. This could be a graphic file, a WordPerfect document, or even a sound or video file. Clicking the Browse button displays a Browse dialog box, which lets you search for the file you want.

Figure 1-5 shows the Repeat dialog box. With it, you designate how many times you want to repeat an action you just performed, such as creating a text box, for example. In the example shown, the action just performed would be repeated eight times. The box containing the number '8' is an example of a **data box**. You can type in or use the arrows to scroll up or down to the desired number.

*Figure 1-5: The Repeat dialog box.*

The Merge dialog box, shown in Figure 1-6, displays a button that leads to a related feature. In this example, you can access the Address Book by clicking the icon, as shown. In some dialog boxes, you'll see a handy calculator icon, or a file folder icon for searching a particular folder for a related file.

*Figure 1-6: The Merge dialog box provides a button for accessing a related feature, in this case, the Address Book.*

## The Default Choice

When you select a dialog box, you will see that some of the choices are already filled in. You can use these predetermined options without having to click any extra buttons. WordPerfect strives to make the default menu choices applicable in most cases. For example, the default font choice when you first open WordPerfect is the highly readable Times New Roman. Black text is another example of a default choice—to work in black text, just begin typing. You don't have to go out of your way to choose black text each time you work. Another example of a default choice is what happens when you select File | Save As. By default, your work is saved into the My Files folder. That means that if you make no further adjustments, WordPerfect will always save your work in that default folder. Some menus offer no default choices; you are required to make a selection to continue. For example, selecting Insert | Graphic doesn't insert a default picture. You have to choose a picture from the list.

## Dialog Boxes With Grayed-Out Options

Sometimes, dialog box options are "grayed out." This means a certain choice is not available. If a choice is not available, it could mean that you need to click another option first for such a choice to become accessible. For example, in the Print dialog box, the color adjustment options are not available if you selected Black and White as your print choice. Sometimes an option is unavailable if your computer lacks the necessary hardware. For example, the Print dialog box's PostScript option is grayed out if you don't have a PostScript-capable printer installed. Finally, an option may be grayed out simply because it doesn't apply to the item or situation with which you are working.

# Using Browse Dialog Boxes

A Browse dialog box is helpful when you need to search for a file to place into your document. This might be a graphic file, a WordPerfect document, or even a sound or video file. As you work on different projects, it's hard to keep track of where everything is. The Browse dialog box makes it easy for you to search every folder on your computer for the file you want to include. Figure 1-7 shows the Insert Sound Clip into Document dialog box. The mouse cursor is shown clicking a small icon of a Folder. This will open a Browse dialog box.

*Figure 1-7: Clicking the File icon will open a Browse dialog box.*

### Searching Outside the Current Folder

Sometimes, when searching for a file (whether a document, graphic, or multi-media file), WordPerfect might not open up to the folder where your file is located. You may have developed your own folder system for saving graphics or documents of various types.

WordPerfect facilitates such a search with the Look in box. Click File | Open, or Insert | Graphics | From File, and click the arrow next to the Look in box (see Figure 1-8). Currently, it shows you are searching the ClipArt folder. Click the arrow to display paths to other drives and folders. In this example, the mouse cursor is to the left of a folder with an upward facing arrow on it. Click it, and the Browse dialog begins searching the next folder up, closer to the root directory of the hard drive. The Name text box is where you'll see the name of your graphic appear. If you remember the exact name of the graphic you are looking for, you can type it into this text box. Otherwise, you can click on the icon in the preview area, which is much easier. This Browse dialog box also offers other selections to help narrow your search. For example, the For type box is currently set to search through All Files. Click the arrow to narrow the search to a particular type of file.

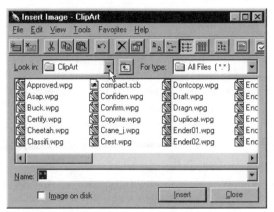

*Figure 1-8: The Look In box is selected by the mouse.*

## Toggle Switches

These are simple on/off buttons that you treat like light switches. Click once and the feature takes effect. Click again, and it's gone. The best examples of these are the Bold, Italic, and Underline buttons, on the standard toolbar. If you select text and then click the Bold button, the text is made bold. Click the Bold button again, and the text returns to normal. These are called toggles because they toggle the feature on and off, just as if you had opened the Font dialog and put a check in the check box next to the feature.

## Using Toolbars

Toolbars are the arrays of buttons and fields found at the top of your window. Clicking any button activates a feature of the application, perhaps underlining text or creating a box for a graphic. Much thought goes into designing toolbars, trying to predict the features users will use most often. For example, placing a button on the standard toolbar that checks complex table formulas will not be helpful to the majority of WordPerfect users. However, a button that makes it easy to select a new font for your lettering will be appreciated by everyone.

In Presentations, you'll find that the main tools you need for working with slide views (Slide Editor, Slide Outliner, and Quick Play) are readily available right on the window. You won't have to dig far to get started.

Toolbars contain more than just buttons. You'll also find drop-down lists there. These are arrows that you click on, that reveal lists of choices for you to select.

## How Toolbars Work

Some toolbar buttons open dialog boxes. These dialog boxes help you identify the specific options available under each feature. For example, clicking the Quick Format button on the standard toolbar opens a dialog box where you can decide what type of formatting to apply. After you make your choices in the dialog box, you can apply the formatting. Here are some other examples:

 Clicking this icon opens the Slide Properties dialog box, giving you control over many aspects of your slide's appearance.

 This icon turns your mouse cursor into a square that creates a chart as you drag it across the page.

 Clicking and holding your mouse over this arrow causes a list of drawing tools to be displayed.

Some toolbar buttons change your mouse cursor into a tool. For example, clicking the Highlight button on the main toolbar turns the mouse cursor into a highlighting pen. Drag it over any text and it is outlined in yellow, making it stand out from the rest of the text. Click and hold the mouse for a second or two for different behavior. This displays a color palette that lets you choose your highlight color, rather than just accepting the default yellow. If additional choices are available, a small down arrow is displayed.

These are buttons that work on text you've selected. That means you've highlighted a portion of text for editing, and clicking a button affects only that selection. For example, clicking the Bold button on a toolbar will only change the formatting of the selected text.

## Toolbars that Change with Your Task

Toolbars change depending on your task. For example, clicking the Change View button on the standard toolbar changes it to include tools necessary for designing Web pages. Clicking it again returns the toolbar to its original state. The Property bar, which is the second toolbar from the top, displays different choices depending on the job you are trying to accomplish.

Figure 1-9 shows the Quattro Pro Property bar that is displayed when you first open the application. It lets you change the horizontal alignment of text, background color, and text color. Figure 1-10 shows the Property bar's appearance after you double-click on a cell. It now allows you to quickly add characters to your cell, or add superscript and subscript text, which is important for creating cells with formulas.

*Figure 1-9: The Quattro Pro Property bar as you first turn on the program.*

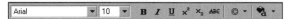

*Figure 1-10: After double-clicking on a cell, the Property bar changes to provide different options.*

## Finding the Button You Need

WordPerfect comes with 15 toolbars, each relevant to a different task. In addition there is the Property bar, a special toolbar that is normally positioned under the standard toolbar; it changes to suit your most immediate needs. But how are you going to tell hundreds of buttons apart? If you hold your mouse over any button for a moment, a ToolTip that describes its purpose is displayed. This feature is available for every button on every toolbar. If you hold your mouse over a button and nothing happens, click once inside the text area of your document and try again. Please note that if you turn off the standard toolbar (by right-clicking on it and clicking WordPerfect 8), then the Property bar will be the uppermost toolbar you see on the screen.

## Using "What's This?"

As mentioned above, you can click on the question mark found in the upper right corner of most dialog boxes. This turns your cursor into a question mark. Then, click on any item in the dialog box to display a brief description of the item. Also, when you right-click on any WordPerfect Suite object—a table or chart for example—a pop-up menu is displayed. About halfway down the menu is a "What's This?" choice. Select it, and you'll see a description of each option in the menu.

## Working With ToolTips

In the Toolbars section of this chapter, we mentioned ToolTips. Holding your mouse momentarily over a toolbar button displays a quick description of the button. This feature has some additional behaviors.

Sometimes, right-clicking on an object (such as the margins) displays a ToolTip, which is a brief description of what you've just clicked on. Most often, holding your mouse momentarily over any object in any program included in WordPerfect Suite 8 will cause a ToolTip to appear.

You can turn off ToolTips in most applications by selecting Edit | Preferences | Display | Turn Off ToolTips.

## Moving On

Now that you know how to open and close a program, work with dialog boxes, toolbars, and extra mouse functions, you won't be mystified when a toolbar changes when you type certain keys, choose a button, or when your mouse changes into a rectangle for creating a chart. In Chapter 2, we'll see that by using the PerfectExpert, you can create a sophisticated document in less than 10 minutes. This is accomplished by clicking the PerfectExpert icon on the Desktop Application Director, which we will also learn about. The PerfectExpert is a multifeatured help system that can guide you through any task.

# 2

# The Desktop Application Director & PerfectExpert

As you get started with WordPerfect Suite 8, two features are key to getting acquainted quickly: the Desktop Application Director and the PerfectExpert. The Desktop Application Director gives you single-click access to any WordPerfect Suite 8 application (or any application on your computer, if you set it up that way). The PerfectExpert gives you the tools to instantly create hundreds of types of documents, while guiding you step-by-step through the process.

## The Desktop Application Director

When you install WordPerfect Suite 8, it automatically places icons for the main WordPerfect Suite applications in the Windows toolbar notification area (see Figure 2-1). This is the far right area of the main Windows 95 toolbar, and the icons can be seen next to the Windows clock, sound, modem, dial-up controls, and other system behaviors. The unobtrusive toolbar that joins the other buttons in this area is called the Desktop Application Director, or the DAD. It provides single-click access to any WordPerfect Suite 8 application you find there.

*Figure 2-1: The Desktop Application Director.*

Besides single-click access to the three main WordPerfect Suite applications, you'll see icons for Photo House, the Quick Finder Manager, Corel PerfectExpert, Quick View Plus (if you installed it), and controls for the Desktop Application Director itself. Hold your mouse momentarily over any icon on the DAD for a ToolTip that describes its actions.

WordPerfect Suite 8 programs which may not be included in the DAD (depending on your installation setup) are Envoy 7, the Address Book, Quick Finder, and Quick View Plus. You may want to add them to the DAD. You can also put other useful utilities there that are not related to WordPerfect. For example, you might set up single-click access to your online service provider or a graphics editing application.

## Adding Applications to the DAD

You can add any application or executable file to the DAD. To add a shortcut to any application on the DAD, thus making it available with a just a single click, do the following:

1. Click the DAD Properties button on the DAD, or right-click anywhere on the DAD itself, and select Properties to display the DAD Properties dialog box (see Figure 2-2).

2. Click the Add button, and use the Browse dialog to search for an executable file. You can also drag and drop an application from Windows Explorer or the Windows Desktop, as shown in Figure 2-3. In that example, Applet Ace is being dragged to the Add dialog box of the DAD.

3. After selecting the file from the Browse dialog box by clicking on it, click the OK button, which closes the DAD Properties dialog box.

4. The new application is displayed at the far right of the DAD.

You may add as many applications as you want. The DAD doesn't use much memory; it merely places Windows shortcuts in an accessible location. New applications you add to the DAD always appear on the far right, pushing everything else to the left.

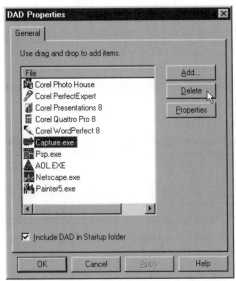

Figure 2-2: The Properties dialog box of the Desktop Application Director.

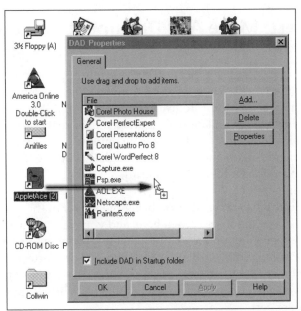

Figure 2-3: Dragging a shortcut from the Windows Desktop to the DAD. You can also add applications from Windows Explorer using this method.

## Deleting a DAD Shortcut

You can delete any shortcut from the DAD by opening the DAD Properties dialog box and clicking once on the name of the application you want to delete. Click the Delete button, and the application is removed from the DAD when you close the dialog box.

## Preventing the DAD From Loading Automatically

If you'd like to prevent the DAD from loading every time you start your computer, right-click on the Windows Start button, and select Programs. Click on the folder labeled StartUp. Now, drag the DAD shortcut to the Windows Desktop. From now on, you have only to click the DAD shortcut on the Windows Desktop to access it. The DAD will no longer load when Windows starts.

To once again make the DAD load as Windows starts up, repeat the above, but this time drag the DAD shortcut *from* the desktop *to* the StartUp Folder. The next time Windows starts, the DAD will load.

# The PerfectExpert: Make Any Document You Like

People often purchase a suite application because one application appears more familiar and practical, while the other suite features are a bit of a mystery. In spite of the best intentions to learn to use the rest of this thing, the suite's other applications often languish as wasted hard drive space. Many software companies create incredibly powerful applications, but apply no creative energy in guiding the novice user through the highlights of the application. Those applications might be wonderful, but the developers expend little effort introducing them to new users.

WordPerfect Suite 8 has taken steps to bring the power of the entire suite to your fingertips. Follow the steps shown here, and you can start using Quattro Pro in five minutes, even if you aren't sure what it is (or how to pronounce it!). Likewise, Corel Presentations is not out of reach to a WordPerfect user who until now has only written basic term papers. WordPerfect Suite 8 helps you get work done even with unfamiliar suite components, without requiring you to first become an expert.

There are two systems in WordPerfect Suite 8 that are referred to as the PerfectExpert. To eliminate confusion, we will call one the PerfectExpert Project Creator. You access the Project Creator by clicking the left-facing pen on the DAD. The Project Creator gets you working quickly without requiring you to be a WordPerfect expert.

After discussing the Project Creator, we'll discuss the PerfectExpert Help System. This is a group of buttons that sits inside your application, offering step-by-step help through any task. The buttons change based on whatever it is you are doing at the moment. The PerfectExpert Help System is available in all three main Suite applications.

## The PerfectExpert Project Creator

WordPerfect installs a set of icons in the lower right side of the Windows 95 toolbar. Click the icon that looks like a small, squarish yellow light bulb leaning to the right (Figure 2-4). It opens the Corel PerfectExpert Project Creator. Its purpose is to walk you through creating various types of documents, regardless of which Suite application they originate in.

*Figure 2-4: Opening the PerfectExpert Project Creator.*

When you first open the Corel PerfectExpert Project Creator, you'll notice two tabs (see Figure 2-5). One is the Create New tab, which lets you create new documents of various types. This Create New tab provides access to hundreds of preformatted documents (templates) included with the suite.

The Create New tab has two sections:

■ The drop-down list at the top lets you select categories of templates to choose from; for example Taxes, Sports and Fitness, Retirement Planning, or Education.

■ The list below explores the templates themselves. Click on one to open it.

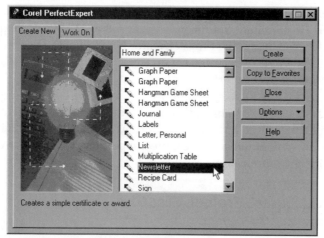

*Figure 2-5: Use the Create New tab to select a category and a template.*

This system shows you ready-made templates for many documents that would otherwise be quite complicated and tedious to create from scratch. For example, templates are provided for a life insurance checklist, year-end tax planning and analysis, job estimates and invoices, or a slide show for teaching and reinforcing a particular concept.

There are hundreds of helpful documents with outlines already created for you. All you need to do is supply the data or type in the necessary text, to replace the placeholder text which shows you how the final product will look. Suite has already done all the hard work for you—the formatting. Everything is lined up nicely; the numbers are lined up in neat rows, the headings are the right size, and name, address, and contact information is already positioned on the page. All you have to do is fill in the gaps.

The second tab (behind the Create New tab) is the Work On tab. It keeps track of the most recent WordPerfect Suite documents you've been working with. Clicking on one shows a small preview of it to the left of the name. This is a very fast way to return to a document you've recently created, regardless of its originating application in WordPerfect Suite 8. Also note that the Create New tab will remember clip art you pulled from the Scrapbook. So, if you recently found the perfect picture for a project and you aren't sure where it came from, check here. You'll be able to open it up again.

## Creating a New Project

Click the Create New tab for a view of all the types of templates to get you started.

Access any of the templates in the Create New tab by first choosing a category from the drop-down list. Some categories only have a few document choices beneath, while others have more than a dozen.

Chapter 6, "Tips for Speeding Up Your Work and Special Projects," discusses how to use templates in greater detail, but for now, click any of the top four categories to see a list of each template, organized by application. For example, click the drop-down list, scroll up using the scroll bar, and then click the Corel Presentations 8 category. You'll then see a list of all the templates (also called projects) created using Presentations (see Figure 2-6).

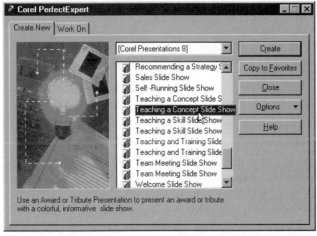

*Figure 2-6: The category is set to Corel Presentations 8 templates. The user is about to open the "Teaching a Concept Slide Show" template.*

However, the real point of this feature is not to think about which application a project came from. The PerfectExpert Project Creator would rather you simply choose a task and get a particular job done. You need not spend hours and hours learning the software before doing something genuinely productive, even with an application you have yet to master.

## Using the Buy vs. Lease a Car Template

Lets take a brief look at a template to help you evaluate the costs of buying or leasing an automobile. If you'd like additional explanation, you can always click one of the buttons on the PerfectExpert Help System, which appears to the left of your document.

1. From the Project Creator, select the category drop-down list (see Figure 2-5), scroll near the top, and click Auto.

2. In the template section, double-click Buy vs. Lease a Car. (Note that there are two other useful documents in this same category, a monthly and weekly auto expense report, ready for you to fill in the data.) The document will open in the Quattro Pro application.

3. Click the orange rectangle to the right of the phrase Make and Model. Notice that a box forms around it. That means the cell (spreadsheet-speak for "rectangle" or "box") is now selected for you to type data into (see Figure 2-7).

To see a portion of the document closer up, click the magnifying glass icon near the upper right of the toolbar at the top of the window. There's a very small arrow to the right of it. Clicking here allows you to adjust the zoom amount. Select 100%, and you'll see the words on your page a bit more clearly. Note that if you simply opened Quattro Pro and began working, the workspace would look nothing like this. The PerfectExpert Project Creator is only showing what you need to see to accomplish the task at hand.

4. Type in the make or model of the car.

5. Click the next orange square in the Lease column, the rectangle across from the phrase "Suggested Retail Price." Type in the amount, and don't worry about commas or dollar symbols. After you type in numbers, and click outside the rectangle, the numbers are formatted for you.

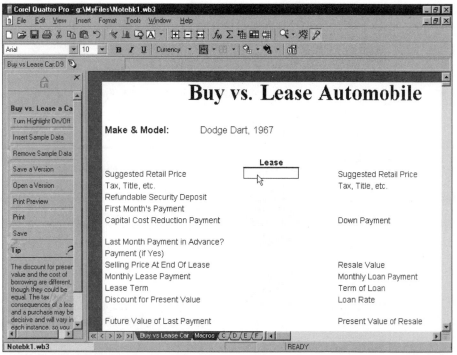

*Figure 2-7: Click on each cell and specify the requested information.*

Any orange area on the document is ready for you to type in some sort of data, such as an interest rate amount or length of payment.

After you've typed in all the relevant data, you'll see sums at the bottom of the page. But what do the sums mean? What value do they have to you? There's a note, "Positive Value Favors Lease" (see Figure 2-8), that explains to you what to make of the results. This user-friendly spreadsheet adds and multiplies numbers for you, and highlights the final value, along with explanatory remarks. This is a big improvement over just having a page full of intimidating squares.

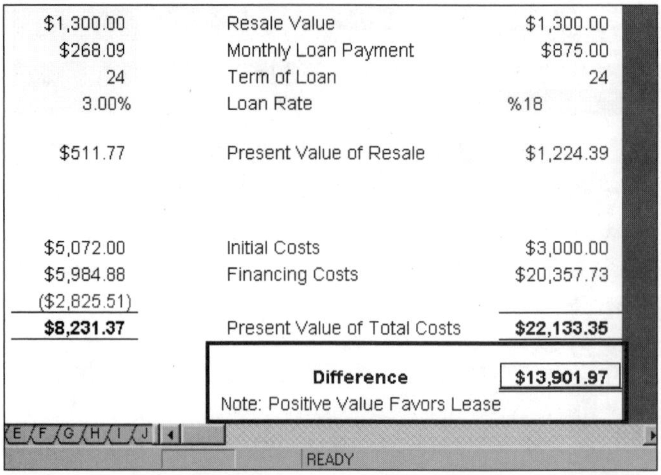

| | | |
|---|---|---|
| $1,300.00 | Resale Value | $1,300.00 |
| $268.09 | Monthly Loan Payment | $875.00 |
| 24 | Term of Loan | 24 |
| 3.00% | Loan Rate | %18 |
| $511.77 | Present Value of Resale | $1,224.39 |
| $5,072.00 | Initial Costs | $3,000.00 |
| $5,984.88 | Financing Costs | $20,357.73 |
| ($2,825.51) | | |
| **$8,231.37** | Present Value of Total Costs | **$22,133.35** |
| | **Difference** | **$13,901.97** |
| | Note: Positive Value Favors Lease | |

E F G H I J ◄ ►  READY

*Figure 2-8: The meaning of the calculation is explained.*

This Buy vs. Lease template is an example of a user-friendly spreadsheet that takes the time to guide, direct, and clarify the data, not simply generate sums and compute formulas. WordPerfect Suite 8 has many of them.

## Managing the PerfectExpert Templates

Click the PerfectExpert Project Creator icon on the DAD, and look at the buttons on the right side of the PerfectExpert dialog box. You can create a template folder called "Favorites," and place any templates you like within it. That way, any templates you use on a regular basis can be handy. Here's how to do this:

1. Click the Options button on the Project Creator.

2. Select Create Category from the pop-up menu.

3. The Add a Project dialog box appears. Type in a name for your category. It should be something brief but descriptive, so that you can recognize its significance at a glance.

4. The next time you click the Category drop-down list, your new category will appear with the rest.

5. You can add any existing project to this new category by selecting any project that appears in the list, and clicking the Copy to Favorites button. This does not remove the project from its original location.

The Options button also allows you to move projects to other categories, erase them entirely, and even create your own template (this is discussed in Chapter 6). The Options button also gives you access to the Address Book. Click Personal Information (see Figure 2-9) to format a return address for yourself. Once you set up your return address in the Personal Information section, templates with return addresses will automatically get your return address from this section. This is handy for letter writing or for any document in which you'd like to provide your return address. Setting up the Personal Information section also lets you include a return address anywhere in your document with just a mouse click.

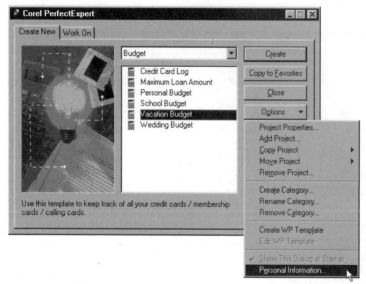

*Figure 2-9: Click Options to record your own return address information, so you only have to type it in once.*

For an example of an Address record with information filled in, see Chapter 11, "The Bonus Applications," which explores the Address Book in detail.

Click the Options button again, and click Project Properties to change the description of any project. Clicking any project once displays a brief description in the area right below the list of templates.

## Using the PerfectExpert Help System

When you open or begin a WordPerfect Suite document, notice the left-facing pen icon at the right side of the toolbar (the icon is identical to the pen you used to initiate the PerfectExpert from the DAD). This icon turns on the PerfectExpert Help System, which will appear at the left side of the screen. Each button provides hands-on help for tasks related to the type of document you are working on and the type of editing you are doing at the moment. The buttons help you navigate this advanced help system. The PerfectExpert Help System is available in WordPerfect, Quattro Pro, and Presentations (see Figure 2-10).

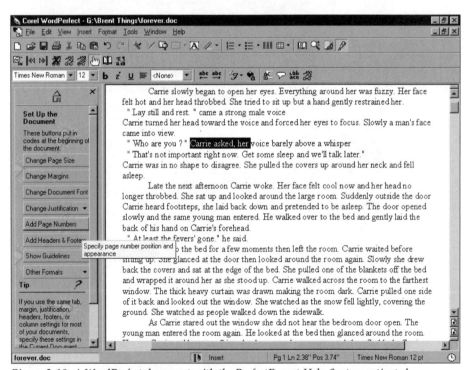

*Figure 2-10: A WordPerfect document with the PerfectExpert Help System activated.*

The PerfectExpert Help System is turned off by clicking the left-facing pen icon in the upper right side of the standard toolbar.

Let's try an example to demonstrate how easy it is to navigate through this system. Create a new, blank WordPerfect document by clicking the Corel WordPerfect 8 icon at the bottom right of the Windows 95 toolbar. (Unless you've moved the Windows 95 taskbar elsewhere.) A blank document is displayed. If the Perfect Expert Help System isn't displayed, click the pen icon at the far right of the toolbar, as mentioned above. It will then appear.

1. Click the button Adding Visual Elements.

2. Now click Add Charts, followed by Add Organizational Chart.

3. The center of your document now has a tree-like structure. This type of chart is used for showing "who's who" in an organization, from the big boss down to the most junior employees.

4. Double-click on the top word (<Name>) inside any box.

5. The box you clicked becomes larger in your view. Type in a name (see Figure 2-11).

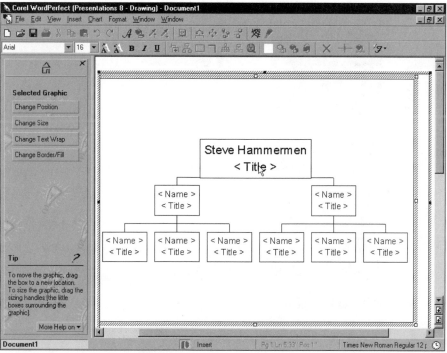

*Figure 2-11: The user typed a name. Click on Title to type in your designation in the company.*

6. Double-click on the <Title> entry below the name.

7. The box you click becomes larger in your view. Type in a title.

If you are ambitious, perhaps you clicked on the very top box, typed in your own name, and made yourself the CEO! You are well on your way to creating an organizational chart. You can add new names and titles by clicking on the <Name> and <Title> placeholders in any square.

## Navigating the PerfectExpert Help System

The PerfectExpert Help System is found in all of the three main Suite applications. It provides a step-by-step guide to help you accomplish just about any task. After opening an application, notice the panel to the left of your main workspace (see Figure 2-12). It has several buttons. Each button leads into a sequential pathway through a particular task.

*Figure 2-12: The PerfectExpert Help System.*

The PerfectExpert Help System tries to anticipate what you will need to do next. To see an example of this in any application, click a button to quickly create a chart and then add a caption to that chart. Then, change the thickness and color of the box around the chart. The PerfectExpert Help system updates its palette of buttons based on what you appear to be doing at the moment.

The PerfectExpert Help System helps you do the following:

- Learn the application while you work on a project. That's because each time you perform a task, the "How To" buttons on the PerfectExpert change to reflect what you might want to do next. Keep an eye on these buttons. You can get quick lessons on just about anything.

- Keep track of what you've been doing. The PerfectExpert can, for example, help you bring back the controls used to color a picture or make an outline, should you forget how you got there in the first place. In other words, the PerfectExpert also helps you retrace your steps.

Lets examine the array of controls at the top and bottom of the PerfectExpert Help System (see Figure 2-12):

- **The Home icon**. The small house icon at the top center of the PerfectExpert is the Home icon. Click it to return to the first Help screen that appeared when you began this task.

- **The PerfectExpert Topic Searcher.** Clicking the question mark on the lower right opens the "normal language" WordPerfect help system. This allows you to type in questions like "How can I make text flow over a graphic?". In most help systems, you'd simply have to type "graphic" and wade through the possible choices until you found a help article involving text and graphics. The PerfectExpert lets you type a question as if it were spoken.

- **The Tip panel.** At the bottom of the PerfectExpert is a description. It tells you something about the button option you've just selected, and provides a More Help On button for further exploration based on your most recent actions. In this way, the PerfectExpert tries to anticipate the WordPerfect features that may be of interest to you, and reveals some of the hidden power of the application that might otherwise remain obscure. The Tip panel and More Help On button help you explore and expand your abilities.

- **The Exit button.** To close the PerfectExpert, click the X at the upper right, next to the arrow, or click the light bulb at the right of the standard WordPerfect toolbar. To bring the PerfectExpert back, click the light bulb again.

# Using the Help Menu

Sometimes it's more helpful to simply look up a word or topic in the Help menu, found at the upper right of the menu bar. Let's take a look at how to use it:

Selecting Help | Help Topics from any application displays a multilevel list of topics. The first level of topics is displayed as a book of general topics for the subject at hand. Click any of the books to display another list, with more specific topics. Click one of these topics to display details about it. Lots of information not available in manuals is found in the Help Topics.

For example, Quattro Pro has very detailed example files to get you going with spreadsheets. These example files can be accessed by selecting Help | Help Topics, and double-clicking on Showcase Corel Quattro Pro. WordPerfect has included detailed examples with callout boxes demonstrating how features work.

## Keeping Track of Help Articles

It's easy to get lost in the Help files, but bookmarks can help. If you find something of interest in the Help menu, select Options | Define a Bookmark. This saves your current location. Later, you can select Display a Bookmark, and choose from a list displaying all your saved bookmarks. This is helpful, because Windows Help files do not save your place when you close Help. If you've searched through several branches of topics to find something you need, bookmarking it will save you from having to repeat your search the next time you open Help.

## Other Help Features

You can also annotate Help files, leaving notes for yourself right inside the Help document. The Help | Options choice allows you to print out an entire topic rather than having to scroll down page by page. Selecting Open a File in the Help | Options selection lets you open an entirely different Help file. For example, while in Presentations you can select Help | Help Topics, click on a topic, choose Options | Open a File, and select the Help file for the Address Book. To do this, use the Browse option to change the current directory to C:\Corel\Office8\Shared\Help 8. (Please note that if you installed WordPerfect Suite into another folder, these directions will not be the same.)

## The Reference Center

You may be wondering where the complete WordPerfect manual is, the one that describes all WordPerfect 8 Suite features point by point. It's called the Reference Center, and is found on the CD-ROM. Select Start | Corel WordPerfect Suite 8 | Accessories | Reference Center to display it.

## Moving On

In this chapter, we've learned about the Desktop Application Director, which provides quick access to all WordPerfect Suite 8 applications. You can add other applications to the DAD, giving you single-click access to any executable file on your computer. We explored the PerfectExpert Project Creator, and learned how to create many types of Suite 8 documents, even if you are unfamiliar with the source application. Finally, we got acquainted with the PerfectExpert Help System, which is a window that provides step-by-step assistance with any WordPerfect Suite task. The PerfectExpert Help System is found in all three of the main WordPerfect Suite applications. We also looked at how to make productive use of the standard WordPerfect Help menu, by keeping track of and annotating Help articles. In the next chapter, we'll begin exploring WordPerfect, and get started creating documents.

## Part II

# Corel WordPerfect 8

# 3

# Getting Started with WordPerfect 8

In this chapter we'll cover WordPerfect 8 basics such as creating a WordPerfect document, adding and editing text, and changing font size and color. We'll look at how to change your view of the document by zooming in for a closer look or zooming out to view two pages at a time. We'll discuss adding bullets and lists, navigating tools and bookmarks, and finally, how to print out your work.

## Creating a New WordPerfect Document

In the previous chapter, we discussed how to create a new document using the PerfectExpert Project Creator. Now we'll learn how to create a new document from scratch, using the Property bar to quickly and conveniently add elements and styles.

## Starting a New Document From Scratch

When beginning a WordPerfect document, you can either use a template (a predesigned layout in which all design issues have already been taken care of), or start from scratch. Let's see how we'd build a document from a blank page.

Open WordPerfect by clicking its icon on the DAD, or from the Windows Start menu (Start | Corel WordPerfect Suite 8 | Corel WordPerfect). WordPerfect opens a blank document, ready for you to begin typing right away. You'll notice a blinking cursor at the upper left corner of the page. The text you begin typing will appear there. The gray lines that intersect near the top, bottom, left, and right sides of your page are your margin guidelines. These govern where text, as well as headers and footers, appear in your document. Later in this chapter, we'll learn how to reposition the margins.

Before you begin typing text, you can turn on the PerfectExpert Help System by clicking the left-facing pen on the right side of the toolbar. You'll see seven buttons on the left. With just one click on any of these buttons, you can learn how to develop an outline, change page size and indentation, or even add tables and pictures to your document. Each button provides access to an in-depth tutorial for each task. Hold your mouse over any of the seven buttons to display a ToolTip that explains what sort of help each tutorial offers. Click the Help buttons to display other lessons related to each primary tutorial.

Besides exploring WordPerfect options using the PerfectExpert Help System, you can build your document step by step using the Property bar.

## Using the Property Bar

The Property bar—the second toolbar from the top—offers the most relevant set of tools for the task you are performing. When you first create a document and begin typing, the Property bar helps you to immediately make changes to the position, size, font, and style of your text.

Figure 3-1 shows the Property bar with the Font drop-down list. As mentioned previously, the Property bar changes any time you select a different type of object. For example, it will display tools for editing pictures when a graphic is selected. If a table is selected, the Property bar changes to a series of table-editing buttons.

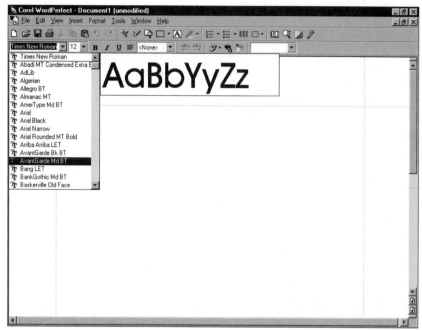

*Figure 3-1: The Property bar with the Font drop-down list open.*

To get familiar with the tools on the Property bar, let's use it to create various styles of headings:

1. After opening WordPerfect, type a heading for your document; for example, "The Story of Cats."

2. You can change the size and position of what you typed so it looks like a heading. Place your cursor anywhere on the line you just typed.

3. On the Property bar, click the Select Styles button (see Figure 3-2). (If you're having trouble finding the Select Styles button, place your cursor over each button in turn to see a ToolTip.) Open the menu and select Heading 1, and the text changes immediately. The Property bar tells you what format has been applied to the area where the blinking cursor is. In this case, you have applied Heading 1 (see Figure 3-2).

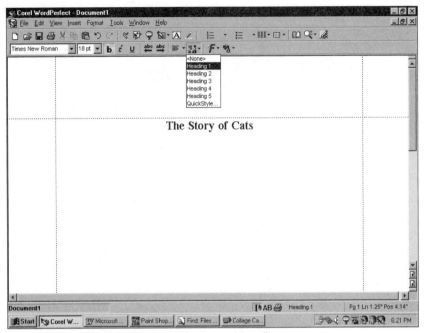

*Figure 3-2: Applying Heading 1 to "The Story of Cats."*

4. Move the cursor to the end of the heading and press return. Type "Calico Cats" on this new line. This will become a subheading under "The Story of Cats."

5. Make sure the cursor is still on the line you just typed. Choose the Select Styles button again, select Heading 2, and click.

The words you typed are now positioned and sized appropriately for a level 2 heading of a document. We'll explore more features of the Property bar later, when we use it to create tables, graphics, and other document elements.

## Editing Text

To enter text, simply begin typing. Your text will appear wherever the blinking cursor (or insertion point) is located. Type something like, "The cat sat on the table," and the text appears at the insertion point.

## Selecting Text

If you change your mind about the appearance of your text after typing it, remember that you can quickly change the font, font size, color, justification, and text style. (There are many font types to work with; businesslike fonts like Times New Roman or more decorative fonts like Lucida Calligraphy.) You can also format text by making it bold, underlined, italicized, superscripted, or subscripted. To perform most of these procedures, you must first *select* the text you want to edit. To select text, place the cursor at the beginning of the text segment, press and hold down the left mouse button while dragging the cursor across the entire segment you want to select, and then release the mouse button (see Figure 3-3). In Figure 3-3, the cursor is opening the drop-down Font list. You can select only a portion of a word for editing if you wish, or even a single letter. Any changes you make will affect the selected portion only.

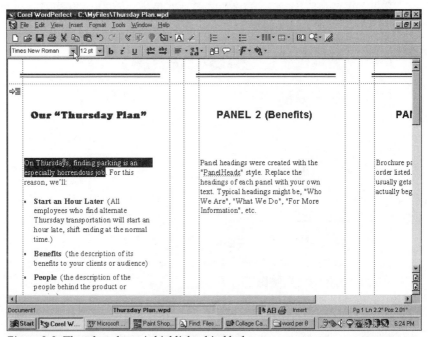

*Figure 3-3: The selected text is highlighted in black.*

Here are some other pointers to remember about selecting text:

- Select a word by double-clicking on it with the mouse. Select an entire sentence by triple-clicking on any word in the sentence.

- To select large amounts of text, place the insertion point at the beginning of the text you want to select. Then press the Shift key and click at the end of the text you want to select. The text between the insertion point and where you clicked with your mouse will be selected.

- To select a paragraph or sentence, place your cursor at any place touching the segment you wish to select, and then choose Edit|Select|Paragraph, or Edit|Select|Sentence.

- To select all the text in your document, choose Edit|Select|All.

## The Shadow Cursor

The gray cursor that follows your mouse around wherever you move it on a page is your **shadow cursor**. It tells you where your blinking cursor (or insertion point) would be located *if* you clicked the mouse. Remember, moving the mouse to a new part of your page does not relocate the cursor until you've clicked there. Figure 3-4 shows the blinking cursor (insertion point) and the shadow cursor. The shadow cursor shows the current position of the mouse. The darker blinking cursor shows you where typing will begin if you start typing.

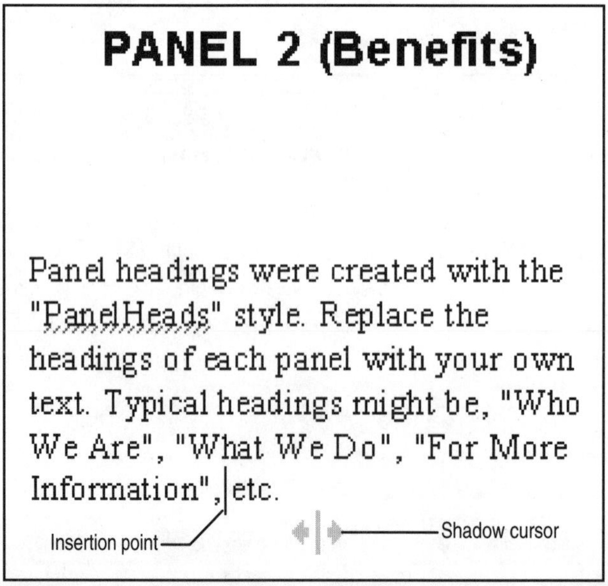

**PANEL 2 (Benefits)**

Panel headings were created with the "PanelHeads" style. Replace the headings of each panel with your own text. Typical headings might be, "Who We Are", "What We Do", "For More Information", etc.

Insertion point——                          ——Shadow cursor

*Figure 3-4: The shadow cursor and blinking cursor (insertion point).*

## Inserting & Overwriting Text

You can add text anywhere in your document, not just at the end. Place the blinking cursor anywhere in your document, by moving your mouse over the text (it will look like a capital letter "I"), and clicking where you'd like to put the new text. Now, begin typing. The text to the right of your new words will be pushed farther to the right as you type. This method *does not* erase text already typed.

If you want to erase text as you type, there are two ways of doing this. One method is to select all the text you want to erase, using the methods outlined above. Then begin typing onto the selected text. Your new words will replace the old. You may notice that your document shrinks abruptly as the old section of text quickly disappears. You can select a word, a sentence, or any amount of text to be replaced by your new typing.

The other method is to position the blinking cursor where you'd like new text to appear, and then move your mouse to the Status bar (located at the bottom of the window). Locate the word Insert, near the middle of that bar. Click it, and it changes to Typeover. From now on, the characters you type will overwrite everything positioned to the right of where you are typing. Most users find it a bit disconcerting when words disappear letter by letter as they type new text. Using the mouse to select all the text you want to eliminate gives you much more control over your writing.

## Cutting, Copying & Pasting Text

To cut, copy, and paste text, do the following:

1. Select the text you want to move.

2. To copy the text, select Edit|Copy. This copies the text to the Clipboard and leaves the original text intact.

    To cut the text, select Edit|Cut. This moves the text to the Clipboard and removes it from the original text.

    Use the keyboard to copy or cut text by selecting Ctrl+C or Ctrl+T, respectively. The text remains in a temporary storage area (until you cut or copy something else), and can be pasted any place you specify.

3. To paste text, place your blinking cursor where you'd like the text to appear, and select Edit ∣ Paste or press Ctrl+V. The text will appear where the blinking cursor is located.

To paste text into another document, first cut or copy text from your current document to the Clipboard, and then open the other document you want to copy the text into. Position your cursor where you want the cut or copied text to appear. Select Edit ∣ Paste, or press Ctrl+V.

### Pasting Text to Another Windows Application

To paste text to a document created in another application (such as Microsoft Word or AmiPro) simply open the document and position the blinking cursor where you want the cut or copied text to appear, and select Edit∣Paste. Depending on the new application, you may notice that some of your text *formatting* is missing. If the text you cut or copied was italicized or the text color was red, for example, those features may not have transferred over to the new document.

## Changing the Font

You can change the font size by clicking on the Font Size drop-down menu just to the right of the Font drop-down list on the Property bar. The default font size is 12 point. Click the Font Size drop-down list to display a list of font sizes from four through 72. Click on any number to change the selected text to any new font size. You can have more than one font size in a word, if you wish. Such an option might prove interesting for some documents, such as for a newsletter or Web page. Although the Property bar Font Size list stops at 72 points, WordPerfect can accommodate even larger font sizes. To apply a font size larger than 72, select the text, choose Format ∣ Font, and type a number into the Font Size data box (see Figure 3-5). I have used font sizes as large as 300 point for artistic purposes.

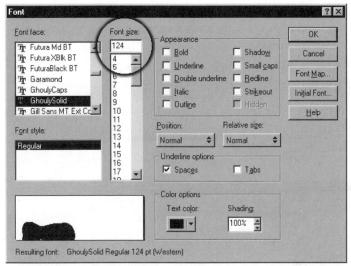

*Figure 3-5: For a font size not listed in the Font drop-down list, simply type one in using the Font Size data box.*

## Applying Bold, Italic & Underlining

In the middle of the toolbar, you'll see a B, an I, and a U button. You can make your text bold, italic, or underlined by selecting the text and clicking the appropriate button on the Property bar. Clicking any of these buttons affects only the selected text. To remove bold, italics, or underlining from text, simply click the button again. You'll find other font style options in the Font dialog box. Select Format | Font, and move your mouse to the Font Appearance pane. Place a check in the box next to the text attribute you want to apply. These are the text Appearance features unique to the Font dialog box (see Figure 3-6):

- **Bold**—makes text bold.
- **Underline**—underlines text with one line.
- **Double underline**—places two lines under the text.
- **Italic**—italicizes text.
- **Outline**—makes the text appear hollow.
- **Shadow**—applies a drop shadow effect to the text, giving it a 3D appearance.

- **Small caps**—text appears in all capital letters, with each initial letter capitalized at full-height, and the remaining letters appearing as smaller, capitalized letters.

- **Redline**—changes the selected text to red.

- **Strikeout**—places a line through the middle of the text.

- **Hidden**—makes the text invisible. It does not erase the text. Select the area where the text used to appear and deselect Hidden to make the text reappear.

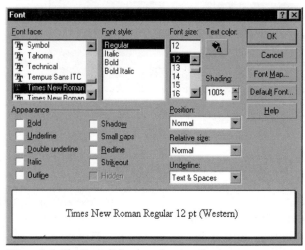

*Figure 3-6: The Font dialog box showing the Appearance pane.*

## Changing the Font Color

Select some text, then choose Format | Font. Click the Text Color button to display small squares representing 42 color choices. Click on any square to select its color. Click OK to close the Font dialog box, and the color is applied to the selected text. The top eight squares represent the most recent colors you've used. Using these top eight squares helps keep your text colors consistent.

## The Select Color Dialog

If none of the 42 colors suits you, click the More button at the bottom of the palette. This displays the Select Color dialog box, which allows you to make further adjustments to your color choices via a color picker and assorted numeric adjustments (see Figure 3-7).

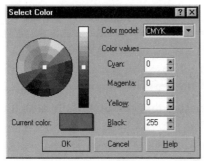

*Figure 3-7: The Select Color dialog box provides tools for creating new colors. The CMYK color model is selected.*

In the Select Color dialog box, you can move your cursor anywhere within the color wheel to select very precise shades of color. Move your mouse up and down the brightness selector (the thin vertical rectangle) to change the brightness of your chosen color.

To the left of the color wheel and brightness selector are three data boxes. These are used to create a specific color by typing in exact numerical values, combining exact amounts of the primary colors: red, green, and blue (or the primaries of the CMYK model: cyan, magenta, yellow, and black).

Notice the Color Model drop-down list. This menu allows you to choose from additional color models. Here are the highlights of each:

- **RGB Color Model**. This is WordPerfect's default color model. It creates colors by combining the three main primary colors, red, green, and blue. The RGB model is capable of creating up to 16 million unique colors.

- **CMYK Color Model**. This color model works best if you are working with a color printer and want the color of the printed work to precisely match what you see on your computer screen. Most printer service bureaus create their color work by combining exact amounts of cyan, magenta, yellow, and black inks (hence, the CMYK label). Creating text with this color model means that your professionally printed work will most closely resemble its appearance on your monitor.

■ **HSB Color Model**. HSB stands for Hue, Saturation, and Brightness. You can create a color with this model by selecting a color (Hue), and modifying its intensity (Saturation) and amount of black blended with the color (Brightness). To create unique colors using the HSB color model, use the data boxes to adjust each of the three parameters.

## Justifying Text

Move your mouse to the Property bar, and select the Justification button (to the left of the Select Style button). Choose one of the five text justification options, and your selected text is aligned. The five options are:

■ **Left**—the left edge of the selected text lines up evenly with the left margin.

■ **Right**—the right edge of the selected text lines up evenly with the right margin.

■ **Centered**—the text moves to the horizontal center of the page, equidistant from the margins.

■ **Full**—both the left and right edges of the text line up evenly with their respective margins, except the final line of each paragraph, which may end anywhere. To accomplish this, extra space is added between words.

■ **All**—both the left and right edges of the text line up evenly with their respective margins. To accomplish this, extra space is added between words and letters.

## Using QuickFormat

After you've gone to all the work of making a heading or paragraph look just the way you want it, use QuickFormat to transfer text and paragraph attributes to another part of your document. Figure 3-8 shows the QuickFormat tool highlighted with a ToolTip.

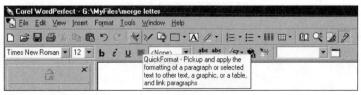

*Figure 3-8: The QuickFormat tool.*

Here are the steps to using QuickFormat:

1. After creating a text phrase that looks the way you want (perhaps you've created a heading with new colors, justification, and font styling), make sure your cursor is positioned inside the text phrase you want to copy *from*. You don't need to select the entire portion of text to use this tool, just having the cursor positioned within the text is sufficient.

2. Select the QuickFormat tool. (Hold your mouse over the tool momentarily for a ToolTip, to make sure you've got the right item selected.) After you click the QuickFormat tool, your cursor will resemble a roller paintbrush.

3. 'Wipe' the text you want to format with the QuickFormat tool. It will take on the characteristics of the *source* text (the text you originally copied *from*). You can sweep across as many text segments as you want, applying the formatting to all of them.

Using QuickFormatting is very helpful for short text segments that have multiple formats applied, such as the following sentence:

*Santa Clara* <u>Romompe</u>, A product of Mexico, **Alcohol 10 % by Volume.**

In this example, you could apply the italics, bold, and underlining all with just one sweep of the QuickFormat tool. This is helpful if you want to apply identical formatting to similar text entries.

## Adding Special Characters & Symbols

You can apply international markings to text, including markings that won't even appear on your computer keyboard. These can be important if you want to include words like *olé*, or *voilá*. They can be quickly inserted into your WordPerfect document, as can the copyright (©) and trademark (®) symbols, as well as special math symbols like infinity (∞) and delta (Δ).

To insert a special character or symbol, select Insert|Symbol (or press Ctrl+W). The Symbols dialog box appears. Choose a character set to work with (see Figure 3-9). The examples listed above are found in the Multinational set. The characters from your chosen character set will fill the preview area. Click on the character you want to add to your document, and select Insert (or Insert and Close). The character appears where the blinking cursor is, just like normal text. Move on to select another character, or close the dialog box when you are finished.

Special characters can be deleted and copied to the clipboard just like ordinary text. There are many sets of characters to work with, including multinational, typographic, icons, math/scientific, Greek, Hebrew, Cyrillic, Japanese, and Arabic.

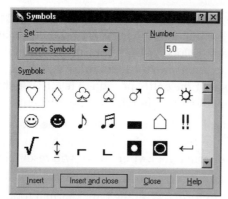

*Figure 3-9: The Symbols dialog box.*

## Changing Typesetting Options

Clicking Format | Typesetting reveals five typesetting options: Advance, Overstrike, Printer, Word/Letter Spacing, and Manual Kerning. All of these involve moving individual letters slightly left or right, or up or down. In the case of Overstrike, one letter is typed directly on top of another.

- **Advance**—opens a dialog box that allows you to determine exactly where the next letters you type will appear on the page. This command affects the position of the insertion point; that is, where text is going to appear when you type it. Use this command to move the blinking cursor to a new location on the page.

- **Overstrike**—provides a data box where you can type in two or more characters. When you close this data box, the characters you typed will appear on top of each other. In Figure 3-10, the Overstrike command has combined two characters in one space.

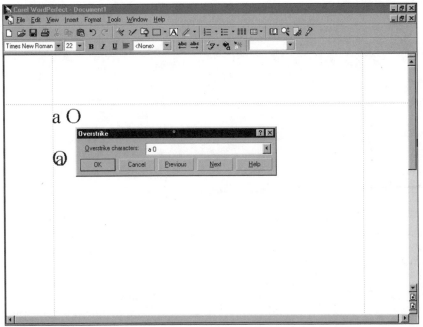

*Figure 3-10: The Overstrike dialog box.*

- **Printer**—lets you send printer-specific messages to your printer by embedding them in your document. If you are one of the few brave souls who actually reads your printer manual, you may have discovered that there are special commands to direct your printer to use certain fonts, resize text, or change the printable area on your document. Use the field provided here to send such commands to your printer.

- **Word/Letter Spacing**—this dialog box (shown in Figure 3-11) provides commands to increase or decrease the space between letters or words, and between lines of text. This dialog box also allows you to adjust the amount of compression and expansion WordPerfect uses to make text fit into a line when you use full justification. You can also control the space between lines of text by selecting Format I Line I Spacing.

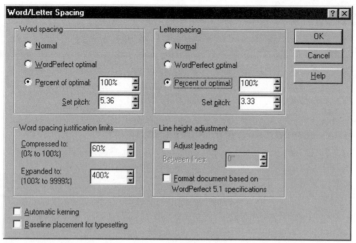

*Figure 3-11: The Word/Letter Spacing dialog box.*

- **Manual Kerning**—this allows individual words to be compressed or expanded. The command consists of a simple data box for typing in a negative number to compress or a positive number to expand the space between letters. Normal spacing is shown by default, with a value of zero.

# Formatting Lists

To highlight key points in a document or show a sequential list, you might want to know how to create bulleted and numbered lists. WordPerfect provides automatically indented bullets and numbering. They come in various styles, preformatted for academic, legal, or business documents, for example. Let's take a look at how to create a bulleted or numbered list. Then we'll learn how to choose a new format, and even create your own.

## Adding Bullets or Numbers to a List

To begin a section of your document in which each point will be bulleted or introduced by a number (or letter), do the following:

1. Place your blinking cursor on the line where your first listed item will appear.

2. Click the Bullet icon on the standard toolbar (at the top of the window).

3. The first bullet or list marker will appear on your page. Type in the text for this point.

4. Press Enter. A new list marker (bullet, letter, or number—whatever you selected) will appear on the next new line. Type in the text for that point.

5. Continue adding points until your list is complete.

6. To stop the bullet or numbering sequence, end your last line by pressing Shift+Enter.

To choose a specific type of bullet and numbering system, select Insert | Outline/Bullets and Numbering. This displays several panes with various numeric outline styles. Click the Bullets tab to display 10 panes that show various bullet options, including circles, arrows, and Wingdings. The Numbers tab also allows you to select from various numbering styles. The Text tab changes the way WordPerfect formats headings, quotations, and definitions (see Figure 3-12).

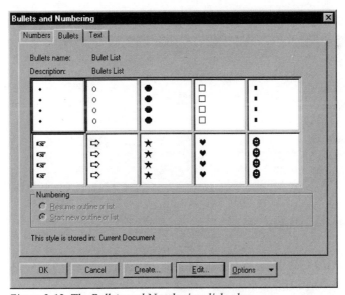

*Figure 3-12: The Bullets and Numbering dialog box.*

### Editing Bullets & Numbered Lists

You can use the Bullets and Numbering dialog box to change the starting value of a numbered or alphabetized list. For example, if you begin a numerical list and stop the list after the fourth item to take time out for a different topic and then return to the list, the default is for the new list to begin at 'one' again. To resume your list from where you left off, put a check by the Starting Value data box, and add the appropriate number.

The Bullets and Numbering dialog box has extensive editing capabilities. You can specify any character to apply to a particular heading. For example, an arrow can be designated as a bullet for the first heading, while another symbol can appear for the second layer of headings.

### Creating a New Bullet or Numbering Style

To create a new bullet or numbering style, do the following:

1. Select Insert | Outline/Bullets and Numbering.

2. Click the Edit button. The Create Format dialog box appears (see Figure 3-13).

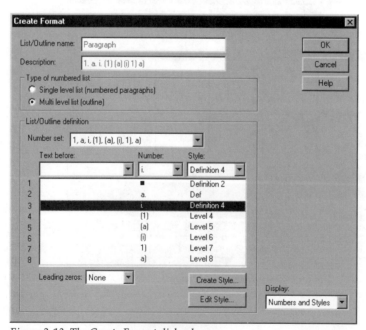

*Figure 3-13: The Create Format dialog box.*

3. The Style drop-down list in the List/Outline definition pane lets you apply a particular bullet to any heading you select.

4. The Number drop-down list lets you select any character or number for the heading you have chosen in the Style drop-down list.

5. Type something in the Text before area if you want a phrase to appear before your number or bullet; a chapter name, for example.

The next time you create a bulleted or numbered list, the symbols you selected here will be applied to it.

## Saving Documents

In this section, we'll discuss saving a document for the first time, and how to save a document under a new name or to a new location. WordPerfect automatically makes a back-up of your document every 10 minutes—we'll look at how to change that time interval.

### Saving a Document for the First Time

When you first save a document, WordPerfect prompts you to name it. Subsequently, WordPerfect assumes you want to save the document using the same name. Therefore, the process of saving a document the first time is unique.

After working on a new document, save it by selecting File | Save As. When you first create a WordPerfect file, it doesn't have a name until you save it the first time. You must save it *as* something. The Save As dialog box displays the folder where your document will be saved. By default, WordPerfect files are saved in the My Files folder. To change the folder where you save, use the Save In drop-down list and other standard directory navigation tools to select a new directory. Type a name for your document in the Name text box. You can use up to 256 characters, including spaces. You do not need to type an extension; WordPerfect automatically adds the .WPD file extension at the end of the filename.

If you choose File | Save when saving a new document, WordPerfect displays the Save As dialog box by default.

## Saving a Document After the First Time

If you simply want to save your document (after you've made some changes) without changing its name or folder location, just select File | Save or press Ctrl+S. If your computer is particularly fast, the saving process may take less than a second. To verify that the document is indeed being saved, notice that your cursor momentarily turns into an hourglass, indicating that your computer is busy saving.

If you want to save the same document under a different name, you must choose File | Save As. To save a file to a new location, you must also choose File | Save As, and specify a new location in the Save In text box.

### Using the Timed Backup Feature

Sometimes, it seems impossible to save often enough. If your computer crashes and you have to restart it, all the work you've done since you saved last will be lost. WordPerfect has a timed backup feature that regularly saves your work in between your own saves. By default, WordPerfect will perform a timed backup every 10 minutes. To change this time interval, select Tools | Settings, double-click on Files, and select the Document tab. Select or type a new number in the Timed Document Backup Every field. If WordPerfect closes (without saving) because of a computer error, WordPerfect will restore this timed backup file for you when you return to the program.

### Making Your Own Backup of a Document

Accidents happen. Folders accidentally get erased by careless coworkers or family members; power outages destroy work in progress. It's a good idea to create a backup copy of your document both in another folder on the same computer, and on a floppy disk. In both instances, when saving, use the Save As option, then save a copy of the file to a different location from the original.

## Copying a Document in WordPerfect

To make a duplicate of a document, simply save it with a slightly different name using File | Save As. For example, if you have a file called notation.wpd, you could save a duplicate as notation2.wpd. You can avoid renaming the file by saving a copy in a different folder. For example, you could create your own folder called Copies. Every so often, simply save your work in this folder, using the File | Save As option. For multiple versions of one document, use WordPerfect's Versioning feature, which is discussed in Chapter 5 of this book.

# Closing a Document

Opening a new document does not close any other open documents. To close a document, you must select File | Close, or click the Close box in the top right corner of the document window. When you close WordPerfect, you'll be prompted to save any work you have not yet saved, and then the document is closed. If you try to close WordPerfect before saving a document that has not yet been named, you'll be prompted to save it, and the Save As dialog box is displayed. Type in a name, and the document is saved. WordPerfect will then close.

# Opening Documents

WordPerfect will open documents from other word processing programs just as easily as from WordPerfect's own format. This section explains how to open a WordPerfect 8 document, an older WordPerfect project, or a file from another word processing program altogether.

## Opening a WordPerfect Document

There are five ways to open a WordPerfect document.

- Open WordPerfect, then select File | Open, use the Open File dialog to locate your document, and then double-click on the document's icon. A WordPerfect document can be identified by its characteristic "quill pen" icon.

- Use Windows Explorer or click on My Computer on the Windows desktop. Locate your document, and double-click on it.

- If you've worked on your document recently, select Start | Documents and locate your file in the list. Click it to open it.

- Open WordPerfect, select the File menu, and scroll down to the numbered list near the bottom. The last four documents you worked on are displayed here. Click your document to open it.

- If you're not sure where your document is located, use the Windows Find function. This will search for files on your entire hard drive. Select Start | Files or Folders | Find, and type any helpful data into the search area. For example, if you know the document you need begins with "Mo," then you should type "mo*.wpd" in the Named text box of the Find dialog box. Windows will list every file that matches the criteria you provide.

## Opening a Document From an Earlier Version of WordPerfect

WordPerfect 8 will automatically open any earlier WordPerfect document and attempt to match the formatting of the original. This may or may not be possible, depending on how old the version of WordPerfect is that was used to create the document. When you save the document, you can either save it in its original format or save it as a WordPerfect 8 file. If you intend to open this same document again in the earlier version, make sure you use the older format, because the older version of WordPerfect cannot open WordPerfect 8 format files. You can, of course, save one new file as a WordPerfect 8 document, and save another version in its earlier format.

## Opening Documents From Other Word Processors

You can open any document created by another word processor. The Convert File Format dialog box with a drop-down list is displayed, where you specify the type of document being converted to WordPerfect (see Figure 3-14). WordPerfect provides its best guess about the format of the document. If this is correct, click OK, and WordPerfect converts the file. If WordPerfect's guess is incorrect, select the correct format from the drop-down list.

If you're having difficulty converting and opening a file, try selecting Rich Text Format (.RTF). When saving the converted file, think about whether you will want to open the file in its original format again. If you do, be careful not to save over the original file with the new WordPerfect 8 format file. Choose a new filename to preserve both files.

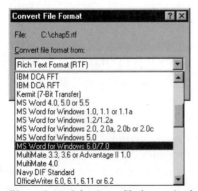

*Figure 3-14: Selecting a file format in the Convert File Format dialog box.*

## Working With Multiple Documents

There are times that you need to keep two or more files open, either to move text back and forth or to verify the contents of each. With WordPerfect, opening a second document does not close the first. The new one you opened will now fill the whole screen, and give the impression that the first document is gone, but it's not. To jump between two or more open documents, click the button with the document's name at the lower left corner of the window (see Figure 3-15). Or select the Window menu, and look at the numbered list below the divider line. This list shows all the WordPerfect documents currently open.

*Figure 3-15: Each time you open another document, a new button is placed at the lower left corner. Click on each to make that document active.*

# Controlling WordPerfect's Display

WordPerfect provides many different ways of looking at your document. Sometimes you'll want to see how an entire page looks, while at other times you'll want to get a close look at a particular phrase or sentence. WordPerfect lets you zoom in and out effortlessly.

First, we'll look at the different ways you can view a WordPerfect document. If you have many charts or pictures on your page, draft mode can save time for casual reading. If you want to see how text looks flowing from one page to another, then two-page mode is more appropriate. If you are building a Web page, you can view your page with a browser gray background and the WordPerfect SGML toolbar at the top of the window.

## Page View or Draft View?

When you first start WordPerfect, you are working in page view. This means all the fonts you use, as well as margins, tables, and pictures, will appear on your screen just as they will when printed. If you have elements on your page that slow down your work, such as headers, watermarks, and high-quality graphics, you might need to switch to draft view (choose View | Draft). If you find that scrolling through your document takes longer than is convenient, or that there is a lag between when you type text and when it appears onscreen, consider switching to draft view.

## Two-Page View

Two-Page view allows you to view two pages of your document side by side. The visible features are the same as in page view. You will see all text and graphics formatting. However, there are no zoom controls available in two-page view. Although you can type while in two-page view, its main purpose is to view your layout. Select View | Two Pages to switch to a two-page view.

## Web Page View

In Web page view, WordPerfect adds a Web-related SGML toolbar that provides quick access to Web features like launching your browser, hypertext creation, and graphic insertion. This mode also changes the WordPerfect menu to include Java applet insertion, adding HTML tags, and special text options that are useful for Web page design. For more information on Web page design, see Chapter 4.

## Fine-Tuning WordPerfect's Display

WordPerfect's various zoom controls let you control how large text appears onscreen. Adjusting the zoom settings is a constant trade-off between viewing the look of your page and the individual characters you are typing. If you zoom in close for typing and never view your whole page, you might miss some problem with your document's overall appearance. Conversely, if you can't see the characters well enough, typos might escape your notice.

### Accessing the Zoom Controls

There are two ways to access zoom controls in your document; you can either select View | Zoom (see Figure 3-16) or click the Zoom button on the standard toolbar.

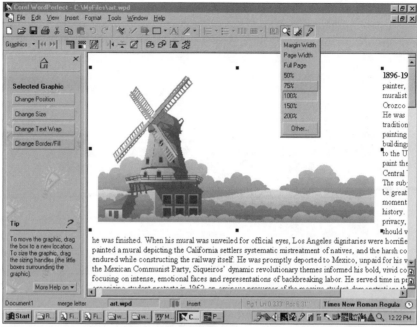

*Figure 3-16: The Zoom menu that appears by selecting the Zoom tool from the standard toolbar.*

The top five percentage numbers correspond to how close 'the camera' is to the document. A zoom level of 100% means that the characters and graphics on the screen are the exact size to your eye as they would be if you printed them out. A zoom level of 50% means that the figures and text are half as big, while 200% zoom renders them twice as big.

## Adjusting the Margin, Page Width, & Full Page Zoom

Margin Width zooms the document close enough so that you can see everything between the margins, but leaves out the page edges. Margin Width is a comfortable zoom level for most people. Page Width allows you to see the left and right edges of the page as well. Click Full Page to zoom back to see the entire page, including the top, bottom, left, and right edges. This zoom setting is good for viewing the overall look of a letter on a page.

## Customizing Zoom Settings

Setting up your own custom zoom setting is a zoom feature that is often overlooked. Click Other, and type in your own number. The number you specify is saved after you click OK and close the Zoom dialog box. Clicking Other from the Zoom tool on the toolbar accesses this, too.

Select Tools | Settings | Display | View/Zoom to specify the default page view and zoom amount that you want WordPerfect to use when it first opens. WordPerfect opens a new, blank document with 100% zoom in Page View by default, but you can change that. Figure 3-17 shows the Display Settings dialog box with the View/Zoom tab on top. Click a radio button to specify the default page view, and either click a radio button or type a number in the Other box for the default zoom level.

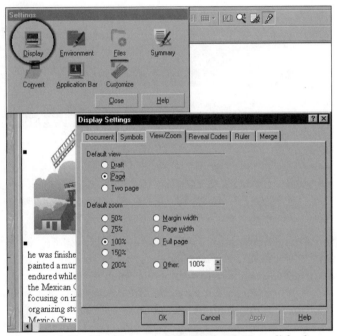

*Figure 3-17: The View/Zoom tab of the Display Settings dialog box.*

## Jumping From Page to Page

There are many ways to move to another page on your document:

- You can select Edit | Go To, choose Page Number box, and type in the page number you want to move to (see Figure 3-18).

- You can also scroll to another page, using the scroll bar on the far right of the WordPerfect window. This method allows you to 'cruise' your document, viewing each page as you move along. Keep an eye on the Application bar at the bottom of the window to verify your page location.

*Figure 3-18: The Go To dialog box, which allows you to move to a new page, QuickMark, Bookmark, or table cell.*

■ Clicking either of the two page icons at the bottom right of the WordPerfect window moves your location up or down one page, respectively (see Figure 3-19).

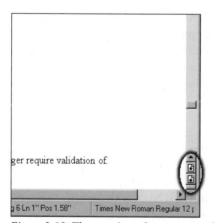

*Figure 3-19: The page icons let you move through each page of your document, one by one.*

■ You can also right-click on the page icon at the bottom right of the workspace, bringing up the same Go To dialog box shown above.

## Using Bookmarks to Move Through Your Document

As you move through your document, you may want to mark a location to return to, perhaps for future editing or just to remember where you left off. For such tasks, WordPerfect provides QuickMarks and Bookmarks. We'll take a more thorough look at these features later in the book, but for now, let's see how to quickly mark a location, and use the Go To controls to return to it.

### Marking a Location in Your Document

Using QuickMark to mark a location means that only the phrase QuickMark appears in the Bookmark list to identify this location. If this nondescript phrase is enough, place your cursor where you'd like to place the mark, and right-click on the page icon at the bottom right of the window. Select Bookmarks, and then click Set QuickMark. If you want to provide a description of the location, then click Create and either accept the bookmark description provided or type in your own.

### Navigating Your Document With QuickMarks & Bookmarks

Later, when you return to this document, you can move through your document using QuickMarks or Bookmarks by right-clicking on the page icon, selecting Go To, and choosing a location from the list. You may also click on each QuickMark reference sequentially, retracing your steps.

## Printing Your Document

WordPerfect provides many options for printing out your work. It can accommodate a draft print job, if you just want to quickly see how everything looks on paper, or you can set up precise parameters for professional, high-quality printing. WordPerfect can collate multiple-page documents, and lets you designate any group of pages for printing, even pages out of sequence. You can also specify reverse-order printing so that the first page comes out on top, set up two-sided print jobs, and instruct WordPerfect to leave enough room in the margin for book-binding. Let's see how all this is done.

## Setting Up to Print a Document

To print a document, select File | Print, which displays the Print dialog box (see Figure 3-20). Most of the options depend upon your particular printer, such as quality controls, for example. For now, let's look at some options that pertain to most standard WordPerfect documents.

- If you are printing multiple copies of a document, you can collate your print job (meaning that the pages will be printed in sequential order). Often this is more convenient than first printing all the 'page ones,' then all the 'page twos,' and so forth.

- You can also print your document in reverse order, which means you can begin reading immediately after printing. If you choose Reverse Order, you'll see page one at the top of your print job when it finishes.

- You can print your entire document or select any number or sequence of pages; for example, you can print pages 1, 3, and 9, and leave out the pages in between.

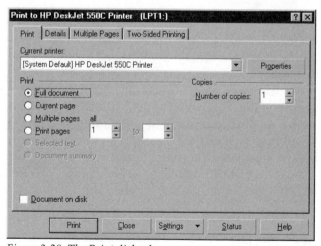

*Figure 3-20: The Print dialog box.*

## Printing a Document

To print a document, click File | Print. WordPerfect does not have a Print Setup option. All printing parameters are adjusted in the four tabs of the Print dialog box. If you are working on a large document with sections and chapters that may need some refining before final printing, WordPerfect has special print options just for you.

When you first select Print, you're asked to choose a printer. WordPerfect automatically installs its own Envoy Print Driver, which has nothing at all to do with printing to paper. We'll discuss Envoy in Chapter 10 of this book, but for now, just make sure Envoy is not selected as the printer. Make sure your own printer is selected in the Current Printer field of the Print dialog box.

To set your printer as the default printer, go to the Windows desktop and choose Start | Settings | Printers. Right-click on the printer you want to use as the default printer, and place a check by Set As Default.

## Setting Printer Options

The Details tab of the Print dialog box contains check boxes for options such as printing in color, or printing with or without graphics. These can be real ink and time savers if you are doing rough draft prints. If you are printing the final copy, make sure there are checks in both check boxes.

From the Print tab of this dialog box you can determine the number of copies and set printing in reverse order. If your printer prints the last page first, then you can read the document in the right order as soon as it's done printing. You don't have to shuffle all the pages around just to get started.

The Properties button opens the setup information for your particular printer. The Details tab of the Print dialog box (see Figure 3-21) lets you change printers, set up paper orientation options, or print quality, and so on.

### When Printing Text is a Problem

The Print text as graphics check box, found at the bottom right of the Details tab, directs WordPerfect to print the fonts used in your document as graphics, rather than by downloading them to your printer. If you use colored text or reversed text (white text on black shading) in a document and run into problems, try using the Print text as graphics option.

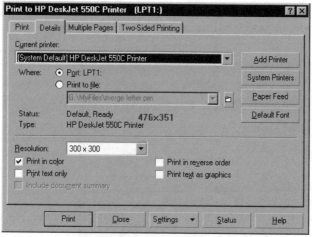

*Figure 3-21: The Details tab of the Print dialog box.*

## Printing Multiple Pages From Your Document

The Print dialog box allows you to print your entire document, the current page that appears onscreen at the moment, or select from a range of pages. If you want to print pages 1, 7, and 9 through 12, for example, WordPerfect can accommodate this.

For complex numbering schemes, click the Multiple Pages tab and select a numbering scheme from the Page(s)/label(s) drop-down list. These numbering schemes are merely examples, to clarify how to set up alternate numbering for printing an odd sequence of pages. You can type in any pages you wish, simply by following the formatting shown in the examples.

Here are some tips for selecting a range of pages to print:

- 7, 9, 15-18: print pages 7, 9, and 15 through 18.

- 2: print from page 2 to the end of the document.

- -6: print from the beginning of the document to page 6. (The beginning of the document is not necessarily page one. It could be envelopes, labels, or a title page.)

- 2, 4, 6, 19: print pages 2, 4, 6, and 19.

You can set up your own sequence, and type it in the appropriate fields in the Page(s)/label(s) field (see Figure 3-22).

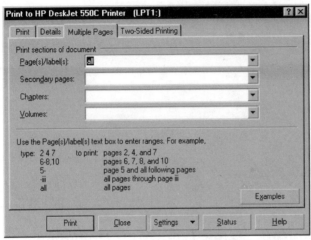

*Figure 3-22: The Multiple Pages tab of the Print dialog box.*

*Note:* In the dialog box pictured above, you can select chapters or volumes for printing. We'll discuss this feature in greater detail in Chapter 4.

## Printing Duplexed Pages (Two-Sided Printing)

In chapter 6, we go into detail about printing long documents, setting up two-sided printing options, and creating booklets. For now, we'll briefly look at two-sided printing, since it is a very convenient paper-saver that most people like to use from time to time.

To set up two-sided printing, select File | Print, and click the Two-Sided Printing tab (see Figure 3-23). Unless you are making a booklet or are using a special printer capable of single-pass two-sided printing, the only parameters you need to set are found under the Manual area of the Two-Sided Printing tab.

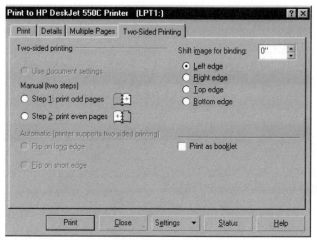

*Figure 3-23: The Two-Sided Printing tab of the Print dialog box.*

You'll be printing out your document in two steps. WordPerfect first prints all the odd pages (side one of each page), then prints the even pages (side two of each page). Here's how it's done:

1. Put blank paper in your printer and click "Step 1: print odd pages." WordPerfect will now print all the odd pages of your document onto the first side of each sheet of paper.

2. When the printing job is finished, turn the paper over *horizontally* (don't turn the stack of printing sheets upside down when re-feeding it in the printer, or all the even pages will be printed upside down). Click "Step 2: print even pages."

## Printing to a File

The Details tab also has a Print to file option. The Print to file feature is ideal for printing your work on somebody else's fancy printer, even if they don't have WordPerfect. To Print to file, do the following:

1. Load the software for the printer that you will print on, using the installation disks that come with that printer.

2. In the Print dialog box (File | Print), this other printer now appears as one of your printer choices. Select it as your current printer.

3. Specify the print options you want in the Print dialog box.

4. In the Details tab, click Print to file. You'll see a text box where you specify a path for your print job. It will be saved as a file for later use, not sent directly to your printer. Instead of printing immediately to the printer itself, it will send the print job to your hard disk.

This file, by the way, will always be in the form of a .PRN file. When you begin a Print to file session, you'll notice that you'll be asked to name your file (see Figure 3-24). If you are creating a resume, for example, and you want to print it out on someone else's really fancy laser printer, you could call the print file RESUME.PRN. If you are preparing a file for a PostScript printer, then your file should be saved as a .PS file.

5. Click the Print button at the bottom of the Print dialog box. The print job is sent to your hard dive. Wait for the disk activity to finish.

6. You can then copy the file to a floppy disk and take the floppy disk to a computer that is connected to the actual printer you want to print out on.

7. Copy the file to that other computer.

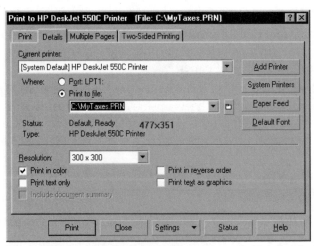

*Figure 3-24: Selecting the Print to File option on the Details tab of the Print dialog box.*

8. Open a DOS window by choosing Start | Programs | MS-DOS Prompt.

9. Type **copy resume.prn lpt1 /b**. In this example, the file we are printing out is called RESUME.PRN. You will type in whatever you named your file.

You are merely copying the printer data to the printer itself. Your computer has already printed the document; the data is waiting for you to send it to the printer itself. When you type **copy resume.prn lpt1 /b**, you are telling the computer to copy the printer data to **lpt1** (which is the port almost every printer uses) and to copy it as binary code (that's what the **/b** means). The data is immediately sent to the printer, and your document is printed out, just as if it came off of your computer. That's because the printing was actually done 'back at your house.' You are merely copying the .PRN data to the printer now.

## Moving On

In this chapter, we got acquainted with the WordPerfect basics: how to create, open, and save documents; type and format text; and add lists. We also discussed changing your view of the page, and annotating your document with bookmarks. We then looked at printing out your work.

In the next chapter, we'll examine more advanced features, such as changing margins, adding footnotes, setting up page numbering, as well as adding columns and headers and changing tab settings.

# 4

# Designing Pages

In this chapter, we'll learn how to change margins, guidelines, and page size, and how to work with the ruler. We'll review how to create columns, and how to change their appearance by adding borders and fills to them. We'll discuss tabs and various typesetting options, such as changing the spacing between words and lines of text. Then we'll go over footnotes and endnotes, how to add numbering, and other automatically updated features such as placing the date and time in documents.

## Setting Up the Page

To begin designing the pages in your document, you'll want to use the Page Setup options. To access them, select File | Page Setup to display the Page Setup dialog box (see Figure 4-1). This is where you can change margins, alter page size and orientation, and add columns quickly.

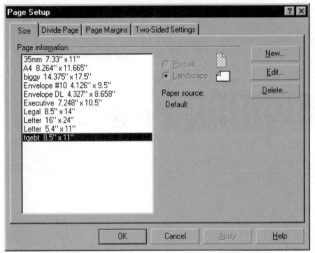

*Figure 4-1: The Page Setup dialog box with the Size tab displayed.*

## Setting Margins

To set the margins for your pages, select Format I Margins, and a dialog box that allows you to specify each of the four margins in inches appears. You can also access this dialog box by choosing File I Page Setup and clicking the Page Margins tab. Type in a new number (decimals are fine), or use the up and down arrows on the right of each field. If you check the Make All Margins Equal check box, any change you make to one number will affect all four margin measurements.

You'll notice your new margin settings reflected in the preview area on the right side of the dialog box. The position of the text on this mini-page shows the results of the values you selected.

### Using the Margin Guidelines

Margins are represented on your pages by four gray guidelines. These form a rectangle around your page. You can change the margins for your entire document by moving these lines. Position the mouse over any guideline and the cursor becomes a two-sided arrow. Drag the guideline to increase or decrease the margin width.

### Turning Off the Margin Guidelines

You can turn off the margin guidelines display. Select View Guidelines, and uncheck Margins. The margins will stay the same, but the gray guidelines disappear. You can actually drag margins to a new location without the guidelines being visible. Simply place your cursor over the area where you think the guideline would be. Your cursor turns into an arrow. Drag the invisible line to a new location.

## Paper Size

If your document is going to be printed on non-standard size paper, WordPerfect can accommodate this. The workspace will reflect any changes in page dimensions you specify in altering paper size.

To change paper size, select File | Page Setup, and choose the Size tab. You'll see a menu of assorted standard paper sizes, and a pair of buttons for choosing paper orientation. Landscape orientation is wide and short. Portrait orientation is tall and skinny.

### Creating Custom Paper Sizes

Sometimes, you may create a document that does not fit on a standard piece of paper. You may want to print an oversized document, or perhaps irregular card stock, for example. To create a custom paper size, click New on the Size tab of the Page Setup dialog box to display the New Page Size dialog box (see Figure 4-2).

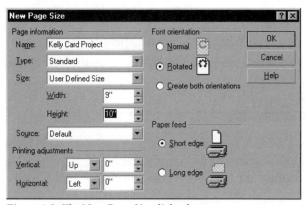

*Figure 4-2: The New Page Size dialog box.*

In the New Page Size dialog box, specify a name for your custom paper size, and set its measurements using the Width and Height fields. You can also specify print options such as font orientation, and which edge of the paper is fed into the printer.

### Editing an Existing Paper Size

You can go back to an existing document and edit paper size, or even edit paper sizes that WordPerfect has provided. You can direct the printer to ignore the top two inches of the page, for example, or change the orientation by which the paper is fed into the printer. To edit page size, select File | Page Setup | Size | Edit and adjust any parameters you like. If you edit one of WordPerfect's preset page sizes, it is saved as a user-defined size; it will not replace the WordPerfect preset.

### Specifying a Paper Source

You can also use the New Page Size dialog box (File | Page Setup | Size | Edit) to select a paper source. This would usually be set to your printer's default, such as Tractor, Paper Tray, or usually just Default. If your printer allows manual feed of certain types of paper, then this dialog box is where you would make those adjustments.

## Working With Columns

When it's necessary to fit lots of text on a page artfully, such as in newsletters or magazines, columns are very helpful. You can arrange text in two or more columns on your WordPerfect page, and change the amount of space between the columns. You can also determine whether the text at the bottom of each column should be aligned; this forces more text onto the next column or page.

## Creating Columns

WordPerfect makes it easy to create columns in various formats; you can specify even columns or set text in a paragraph to stay together at all costs, for example. As you set the number of columns on a page, and how wide each column should be, WordPerfect will do its best to keep related text together on the same line, page, or paragraph.

## Specifying the Number of Columns

To create columns, click the Columns icon on the WordPerfect toolbar. In the drop-down list, select the number of columns (two to five) that you want to add to your document. Begin typing, and your text will automatically flow into the column format you set up.

## Formatting Columns

If you'd like to do more than just specify how many columns you want, select Format from the Column drop-down menu on the WordPerfect toolbar. The Columns dialog box is displayed, which lets you change the space between columns, their width, and their vertical alignment (see Figure 4-3).

Use this dialog box if you want to make each column 3 inches wide, with 0.4 inches between each column, and to make sure the text takes up exactly the same amount of space in each column. You can also balance column widths to accommodate text length; making column 1 slightly wider than column 2, for example, so there is no text overflow at the end of the page.

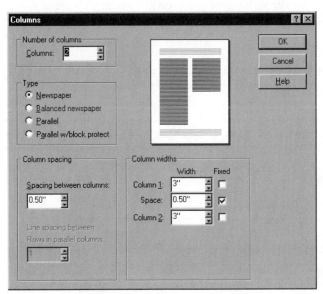

*Figure 4-3: The Columns dialog box.*

# Changing Text Line Spacing

Remember when you were in high school and you wanted to make your paper look longer? How you fiddled with the margins and discovered that you could make your paper double-spaced and really increase the length of the paper? Well, you can also use the line spacing to make text fit into a specified area on your page. To increase or decrease the amount of space between lines of text, select Format | Line | Spacing. A dialog box with the number "1" is displayed. Increasing the number makes the space between each line of text grow. Decreasing it brings the lines of text closer together, which is useful if you need to conserve space. Use the arrows to the right side of the number to change it.

Notice that the preview in this dialog box immediately shows the change in line spacing you select. The procedure we just described changes the spacing between lines of text *for your whole document*. To change space between lines of text for just a part of your document, first select the lines you want to change, and then perform the procedure outlined above. The changes will be applied to the lines of text you selected.

# Breaking Lines, Columns & Pages

When working with regular text or columns, you might want to force the text onto the next page, even though you have room left on the first for typing. You can force WordPerfect to start a new page or a new column with just a few clicks. This section describes some of WordPerfect's page formatting options.

## Controlling Line Breaks

Sometimes the first line of a paragraph will appear by itself at the bottom of a page, because there's not enough room for the following lines. In other cases, the last line of a paragraph will appear alone at the top of a page (see Figures 4-4 and 4-5). These situations are called text widows and orphans, respectively, and are the result of the standard page formatting simply indicating that it's time to start a new page, no matter how awkward it looks. You can make WordPerfect override regular formatting by using the Keep Text Together option. Select Format | Keep Text Together, and check the options you want. You can indicate that the first and last lines of paragraphs not be separated across pages, or select a whole block of text that you do not want split across two pages.

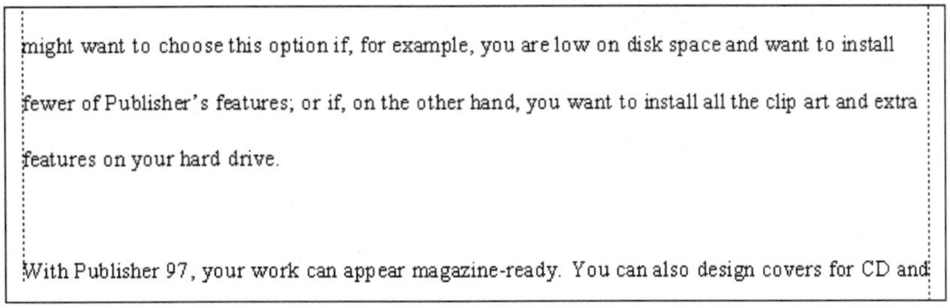

might want to choose this option if, for example, you are low on disk space and want to install fewer of Publisher's features; or if, on the other hand, you want to install all the clip art and extra features on your hard drive.

With Publisher 97, your work can appear magazine-ready. You can also design covers for CD and

*Figure 4-4: A text widow.*

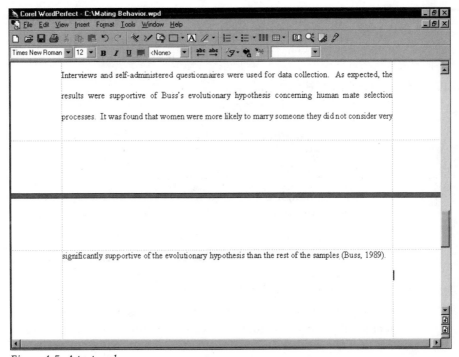

*Figure 4-5: A text orphan.*

## Forcing a Page Break

To force a page break, place your cursor where you want to place the break and press Shift+Ctrl+Enter. All text positioned after the cursor will be forced onto a new page, regardless of how much empty space is left at the bottom of the first page.

## Forcing Column Breaks

WordPerfect's columns have their own formatting rules that dictate when text flows to a new column. If you want to force text into a new column, press Ctrl+Enter. All text positioned after the cursor will be forced onto the next column, regardless of how much space is left at the bottom of the first column.

# Formatting Paragraphs

Let's examine how to format paragraphs and create indent settings that will suit the type of document you want to create. WordPerfect can quickly set up the most popular indent styles, and you can create your own as needed.

## Indenting Paragraphs

After typing a paragraph, place the cursor at the beginning of the first paragraph.

- To add a simple indent, press Tab.
- To add a hanging indent, in which every line *except* the first line is indented, press Ctrl+F7 (or click Format | Paragraph | Hanging Indent).
- To indent every line in the paragraph, press F7.
- To indent both the right and left sides of the paragraph, so that it is moved inward and centered, press Ctrl+Shift+F7 (or click Format | Paragraph | Double Indent).

Note that all indents move forward to the first tab setting. The WordPerfect default tab settings are quite standard, and should meet your needs. Note also that tabs are not the same as the old five forward spaces on a typewriter. Paragraph indents and tabs are special formatting codes saved and remembered by your computer. If you add text later, you won't end up with odd spaces in the middle of a line. If you try to emulate tabs and indents by pressing the space bar several times, the results are unpredictable and usually make extra work later. Working with tabs is covered in more detail later in this chapter.

### Adding Indents & Margins to All the Paragraphs of a Document

If, after composing a document, you decide you want to have the same indent and margins for each paragraph of a document, select Format | Paragraph | Format and provide the numerical values you want. Note that any numbers you specify for the margins are *added* to the existing margins. For example, if your document has a 1-inch margin and you add 0.5 inch to either the Left or Right Margin Adjustment settings, your *total margin* will be 1.5 inches on the affected side.

The Paragraph Format dialog box has a preview area that lets you see how your changes will look (see Figure 4-6).

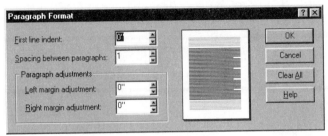

*Figure 4-6: The Paragraph Format dialog box.*

## Working With Tabs

Tabs affect your document's appearance in many ways. They allow you to indent paragraphs and force space between list items. WordPerfect's tabs are flexible and easy to adjust. There are two very quick ways to do so:

- On the PerfectExpert Help System, select Typing | Change Tab Settings.
- Choose Format | Line | Tab Set.

Both methods display the Tab Set dialog box (see Figure 4-7) and the ruler, which reveals the tab settings as a series of black triangles spaced one half inch apart.

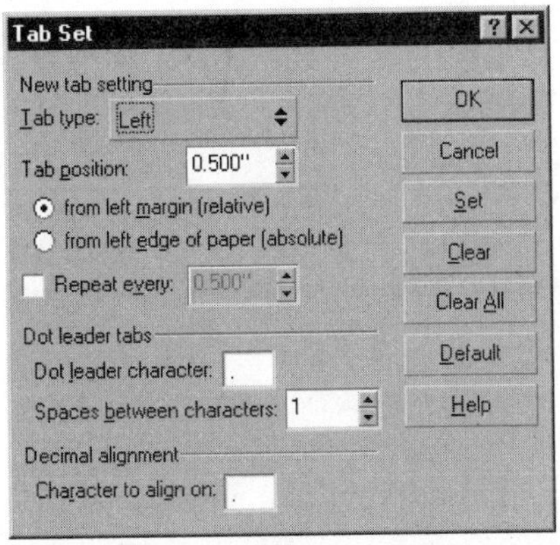

*Figure 4-7: The Tab Set dialog box.*

## Changing Tab Settings

The tab settings default to one half inch to the right of the margin, and repeat every half inch. To see this, close the Tab Set dialog box, and double-click on the tab marker to the right of the numeral one. It falls halfway between one and two, so it marks the 1.5 inch point of your document.

When you double-click on the tab marker, the Tab Set dialog box opens again. Look at the Tab position data box with the value .500 inches in it. Use the arrow keys to the right of the data box to increase or decrease the number, or type in a new value. Remember to retain the decimal point in the field. Your indent will reflect the change you made to the first tab amount. You can double-click on any of the tab markers and change their numeric values. (You'll have to close the Tab Set dialog box before you can double-click on the tabs in the ruler.)

To change all the tab values simultaneously, do the following:

1. Double-click on any tab and click Clear All in the Tab Set dialog box. (Notice that all the triangles disappear.) This allows you to set entirely new tabs, rather than just superimposing new tabs on top of the old ones, which can create a real mess.

2. In the Tab position data box, specify the first indent amount (as you did in the above example).

3. Now you need to select how much space to place between each tab. Click the Repeat every check box. A field that was grayed out is now available. Type in a value (in fractions of an inch) or use the arrow keys to change the existing value. Your tabs are now spaced apart by the amount indicated in the Repeat every field.

Don't be afraid to experiment with tab settings. You can restore the default settings with one click. Simply right-click on the tab bar and select Default Tab Settings.

## Creating a Document With Custom Tab Settings

Figure 4-8 shows a restaurant menu formatted by manipulating WordPerfect's tab settings. You can set tabs to provide all the dot leader points in between these item prices. It would have taken much longer to space the dot leaders evenly and center the product prices and menu items without such formatting. As the menu grows, all items, prices, and dot leaders will be centered correctly.

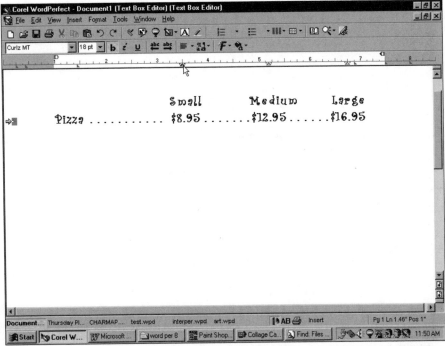

*Figure 4-8: This formatting was easily created using decimal presets on the Tab Set dialog box. The mouse is shown highlighting one of the decimal tab markers.*

To reproduce something similar to the above figure, do the following:

1. Select View | Ruler.

2. Right-click on the tab bar, select Set Tabs, and choose Clear All.

3. Click once where you'd like your first tab (for the word Pizza) to appear. Notice the new triangular tab on the ruler. Type your text.

4. Click where you'd like the first price for the Small Pizza to appear. Again, you'll see a new triangular tab on the ruler. Double-click on it to display a pop-up menu, and click the Tab Type button (see Figure 4-9). Select dot Decimal. Right-clicking on a tab reveals a list of tab types without the text labels.

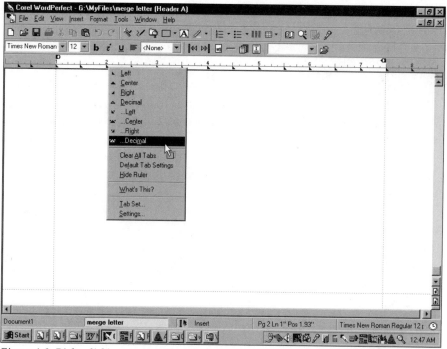

*Figure 4-9: Right-clicking on a tab displays a pop-up menu of various tab types.*

5. Type the price for the small pizza.

6. Repeat this process, creating a tab and typing prices for the medium and large pizzas.

7. Position the cursor directly above each price and type the appropriate size of pizza. The tabs you set will keep text and numbers aligned for all future items added to the pizza menu.

To choose a character for your dot leader other than the default period, double-click on any tab to display the Tab Set dialog box. In the Dot leader character field, type in the character you want to use. Your change is applied immediately when you click OK.

# Working With the Ruler Bar & Guidelines

Guidelines and rulers give you control over the exact spacing of objects on your page, such as the space between tables and charts or between a picture and the bottom of a page. Remember that most objects provide controls for determining how far or close they are placed to other objects. Right-click on any picture, for example, and select Position. You'll see a field and menu controls for setting an exact distance between any picture and anything else on a page. But still, there are many instances where guidelines and rulers are helpful.

## The Ruler Bar

Select View | Ruler, and the Ruler is displayed at the top of the page. It's called the Ruler because it includes tab and margin controls as well as ruler markings. Right-clicking on the ruler provides access to a number of page and paragraph formatting options.

### Checking Indentation

The Ruler cannot be dragged into your document. If you want to make sure one of your margins or indents is exactly where you think it is, click on any tab marker. A blue, vertical, dotted line appears in your document as long as you hold down the mouse button. This lets you check whether text is lined up properly.

When you create a custom tab setting (as discussed earlier), you'll see a right-facing arrow appear in the margin of your document, as shown in Figure 4-10. Clicking this arrow creates a tab bar at that exact spot, as shown. This makes it easy to see where your tabs line up in your document. Right-clicking on the arrow displays a pop-up menu, which includes a command to delete the custom tab settings, and return to the default.

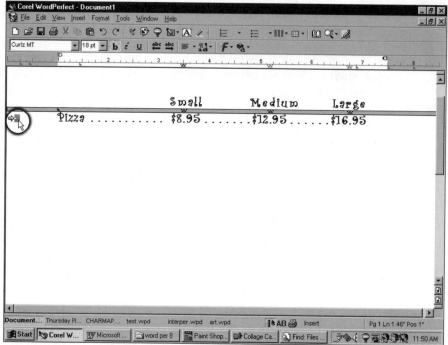

*Figure 4-10: Creating a new tab setting causes this right-facing arrow to appear.*

### Setting Margins & Indentation

There are two sets of margin markers (in the white space above the tab markers) on the Ruler. The set farthest to the left and right, on the outer edges of the document, are the margin markers. Drag these to set new margins. This has the same effect as dragging the dotted line that appears in your document. There are two triangles right next to the margin markers. Dragging these sets up indents for paragraphs. You might not see them until you drag them out from the margin markers. You can double-click on these markers to display the Paragraph Format dialog box, where you can modify the settings.

## Guidelines

WordPerfect provides guidelines for margins, tables, headers and footers, and columns. You can turn any guideline type on or off by selecting View | Guidelines. Figure 4-11 shows a document with three guideline types. The margin guidelines are probably familiar to you by now. The guideline surrounding the word "Title" can be resized just like any other guideline. Notice the column guidelines surrounding the text in the middle of the page. Dragging any guideline inward or outward resizes it, and changes the positioning of the text or graphic inside the guideline. When you move a guideline you'll see measurements onscreen, that report margin width and spacing between columns. This numerical information changes as you reposition the guidelines.

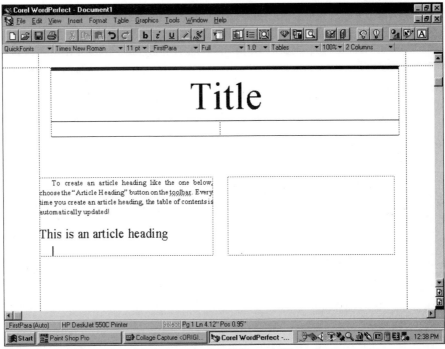

*Figure 4-11: A document with three types of guidelines visible on the page.*

## Creating Footnotes & Endnotes

Footnotes are source references that appear at the bottom of a page. They allow the reader to review the source of information presented by the author of the document. Endnotes are similar but all appear at the end of a document, rather than at the bottom of each page containing a quote or reference.

With conventional tools, footnotes are tedious to create. It's hard to predict where the final portion of text requiring a footnote is going to appear, because after all, you have to allow room for the footnotes. WordPerfect can accurately place footnotes on the same page as the relevant quote or reference, and can even create a clickable link between each footnote and endnote and its related text segment.

## Creating Footnotes

When you add a footnote with WordPerfect, the cursor is automatically moved down the page to where a footnote should be placed. A two-inch line is drawn at the bottom left of the page, and a superscript numeral is inserted (see Figure 4-12). Now that you have indicated you want a footnote, all you have to do is type in the relevant information. To add a footnote, select Insert | Footnote/Endnote, make sure Footnote Number is selected and that the number is appropriate, click Create, and begin typing. A superscript numeral is also placed in the source text as well. To edit that same footnote later, select Insert | Footnote/Endnote, enter the appropriate number in the Footnote Number field, click Edit, and the cursor automatically moves to the beginning of the footnote you selected.

[1]Felix Green, *The Enemy,* **pp 26-28.** Penguin Books, 1958.

*Figure 4-12: A footnote. WordPerfect added the line, the sequential numeral, and placed the footnote at the bottom of the page.*

To add another footnote later in your document, select Insert | Footnote/ Endnote, make sure Footnote Number is selected, click Create, and another superscript number will be positioned underneath the first footnote (if you are still working on the same page) or on a new page, if appropriate. WordPerfect automatically keeps track of how many footnotes you have created. After you've written several footnotes, when you want to edit a footnote, WordPerfect prompts you for which footnote you want to fix, and the blinking cursor automatically appears at the beginning of that note, even if it's on a different page.

If you are working on a footnote and want to switch to a different footnote for further editing, the footnote options are grayed out. Move the cursor to a normal text area, and the footnote options will return. Then, you can indicate which footnote you want to edit.

## Creating Endnotes

Endnotes are placed at the end of a document rather than at the bottom of each page. To start endnotes, insert a hard page break (Ctrl+Enter) after your document is finished, and begin adding endnotes. To add an endnote, select Insert | Footnote/Endnote, select Endnote Number, enter an appropriate number, click Create, and begin typing. The procedure is similar to creating and editing footnotes, with WordPerfect automatically providing the sequencing, numbering, and space formatting for the endnotes.

## Changing the Footnote or Endnote Style

You can change the way footnotes are numbered, and alter the line style used to separate your footnotes from text. These and other options are available by selecting Insert | Footnote/Endnote, and choosing Footnote or Endnote from the options. Click Options. Here you can set the starting footnote or endnote number, and add a horizontal separator between your text and the footnote. Or, click Advanced for more options.

The Advanced Footnote Options (see Figure 4-13) and Advanced Endnote Options dialog boxes let you edit the amount of space between footnotes, and edit the way a footnote is numbered in one particular instance (Edit numbering style in Note). You can change footnote indicators from Arabic to Roman numerals, or to letters. The Amount of footnote (or endnote) to keep together option indicates how much space must be available at the end of your document for WordPerfect to start a footnote on that page. If the minimum space you indicate is not there, WordPerfect will begin the footnote on the following page.

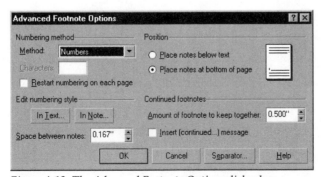

*Figure 4-13: The Advanced Footnote Options dialog box.*

## Working With Headers & Footers

Headers and footers are sections at the top or bottom of your page where you can place automatically updatable information such as dates, times, and page numbers, as well as repetitive information, such as the document title and author name. You may have two headers and footers active in your document at one time; page three might have the document's full name and subtitle, for example, while page four's header might include the chapter and volume number. The first header would be created as Header A, and the second as Header B. To insert a header or footer, do the following:

1. Select Insert | Headers/Footers, and choose Header or Footer A, (unless you've already created the first, and are now making an alternate header or footer). See Figure 4-14.

2. A new Property bar offering special options for creating headers and footers appears at the top of the window. Create the text you'd like to see on the header or footer.

3. Begin editing using any tools found on the Property bar (reviewed in detail below). Standard font options, such as text justification, font size, color, and style are also available from the Property bar.

4. Before you can resume working on your document, you must close the Header and Footer Property bar by clicking the small file icon on the upper right side. Your Header or Footer will be visible onscreen as you work.

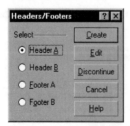

*Figure 4-14: The Headers/Footers dialog box.*

Here are some of the features of the Headers/Footers dialog box, referenced here by their ToolTips:

- **Page Numbering**—you can insert a page, volume, or chapter number, a reference to total pages (Page 33 of 57, for example) or some type of secondary number (perhaps the numbering of an advertising supplement within a magazine or introduction to a book).

- **Horizontal Line**—clicking this button inserts a line separating the header and footer from the rest of the text.

- **Header or Footer Placement**—lets you decide to place your header or footer on odd, even, or every page.

- **Distance**—click here to determine the distance between the header and footer and the rest of the text.

- **Previous**—takes you to the previous header or footer.

- **Next**—takes you to the next header or footer in your document.

## Adding Automatically Updated Features

Some WordPerfect features automatically update themselves to provide truly accurate  information. For example, when you insert "Date and Time" into your document, you are not just putting in the current values. The date and time will continue to be updated within your document. Let's look at some of these automatically updating features.

### Adding Page Numbers

In most word processing programs, page numbers are added to the header or footer. Headers and footers are used to insert repetitive information that you'd rather not have to type on every page, such as the document name, chapter or volume number, or author name. Sequential data that would be tedious to track manually is also inserted on headers and footers, such as dates, times, and page numbers. These are the kinds of chores we'd rather leave to computers. We will explore headers and footers in greater detail later in this chapter, but for now, let's insert a simple page number without using a header or footer.

To insert a page number, select Format | Page | Numbering, and select a numbering style from the Page numbering format list. As soon as you click OK, your number appears at the bottom of each page of the document. Notice the various styles in the Page numbering format list, especially the "Page 1 of xx" option (which can be handy for sending faxes) and the "Chap 1 Pg. xx" option, which provides updated chapter and page numbering (see Figure 4-15).

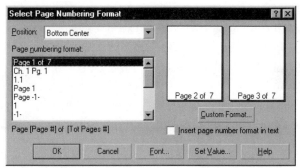

*Figure 4-15: The Select Page Numbering Format dialog box.*

Select Format | Header/Footer, and choose which element to create. Page numbers are most often placed on footers, so for now, select Footer A, as shown in Figure 4-16. (Header and Footer B are provided so that alternate information can be provided every other page.)

*Figure 4-16: The Headers/Footers dialog box.*

After selecting Footer A, select Create, and the Property tools for formatting your footer are displayed. Click the Number button, select Page Number, and you'll notice the appropriate page number is inserted. I say "appropriate page number," because you need not necessarily create a footer while working on page one. Your footer will be inserted on every page, and your page number will be updated, no matter how much text you add or remove as your document changes over time. That's why you spent your money on a computer, so that it can do this kind of tedious stuff for you.

After formatting your footer so that it provides the number, you can use the standard tools to change the number's font, size, justification, and appearance attributes (such as bold or italics). Each page number will retain any formatting you apply to a single page number. The page number and section number will move forward as each page and section progresses. The book reference and description will not be altered. To further edit your page number, or to employ Roman numerals or letters rather than Arabic numerals (as might be done in an appendix, for example), select Format | Page | Numbering | Set Value. You can also turn page numbers off and back on again for particular pages here.

There is another method for inserting a page number with WordPerfect; you can use Formatting | Page | Numbering, and click the Insert Page Number Format in Text command. This method only puts the page number on the current page; page numbers will not appear on any other page in the document.

What if you don't want every page to have the same style of numbering? That's what Header B and Footer B are for, so that you can apply alternate information to every other page.

### Adding Date & Time to Your Document

Date and time are also generally applied to a document's header or footer. They also fall in the category of information that is best updated automatically. However, there are times that you may need to add a "date/time stamp" to a document, such as a legal document that needs to be verified with a particular date or time attached. In this case you would not want date and time to be automatically updated. WordPerfect allows you to choose between several date and time formats for your document.

To place the date in your document and have it update itself, place your cursor where you'd like the date to appear, and select Insert | Date/ Time | Insert and check the Automatic update check box (see Figure 4-17). To place a "time stamp" in your document, which simply inserts the current date and does not automatically update itself, *do not* put a check in the Automatic update box. Scroll through the Date/Time formats list to select a Date or Date and Time style that suits your document.

You can also create a custom date format by clicking the New Format button. This displays four tabs that provide tools for building your own style of date and time format. The four tabs are Year, Month, Day, and Time. Options you choose in these tabs can be combined to create an entire date/time line.

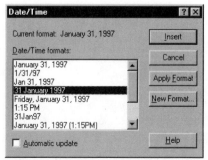

*Figure 4-17: The Date/Time dialog box. In this example, Automatic update is not selected; thus, the date and time that appear in the document will not change after being initially inserted.*

## Moving On

In this chapter, we covered setting up your page, working with columns and formatting text, rulers, and guidelines, as well as adding headers and footers to your document, and automatically updating features such as page numbers, date, and times. In Chapter 5, we'll examine how WordPerfect works with pictures, tables, and charts.

# 5

# Adding Pictures, Borders, Tables & Charts

Wordperfect lets you add various visual elements to your document. It's a cliché, but in many cases a picture really is worth a thousand words. Pictures, tables, and charts can often get your point across much better than trying to describe something in words.

The WordPerfect Suite 8 CD-ROM includes huge quantities of photographs and clip art. You can use the graphics that the Suite provides, or you can insert your own.

In this chapter, we'll explain how to insert clip-art, photographs, and other graphics files into your document, how to add decorative fills and borders to your graphics, and how to create and edit tables and charts.

## Adding Pictures to Documents

Even if you're using WordPerfect for simple documents like memos, you'll need to know how to insert pictures. You might, for example, want to add your company logo at the top of your memo.

Once you've added a picture, you'll want to take advantage of WordPerfect's graphics control features. You can change almost every attribute of a graphic once you've inserted it into your WordPerfect document; you can move it around on the page, change the color, add a border or fill, and make many other changes. In addition, you can save a particular border and fill combination as a *style*, which lets you apply it quickly to any other graphic; instead of redoing all the graphic settings, you just apply the appropriate style. We'll discuss all of this later in this section.

One special use of pictures is as *watermarks.* Traditionally, a watermark is a symbol that is embedded in a piece of paper and is only visible if you hold the paper up to the light. WordPerfect lets you do something similar with your documents. A WordPerfect watermark is a faint image (usually a graphic) that you place in your page. When you print your document, the watermark appears as a faded image behind the text on your page.

## Inserting Clip Art

The WordPerfect CD-ROM includes thousands of clip-art drawings, which could be quite a handful to search through. Fortunately, WordPerfect includes a Scrapbook, which organizes the clip-art into folders by category. This makes it much easier to find the image you want. Here's how to insert a clip-art image:

1. Click and drag with your mouse to create a box anywhere in your document. This box will become the container for your clip-art image.

2. When you release the mouse button, a pop-up menu is displayed. Select Clipart from this menu.

After a few moments, the WordPerfect Scrapbook is displayed (see Figure 5-1).

*Figure 5-1: The WordPerfect Scrapbook.*

The Clipart tab lets you view the images on your hard drive, and the CD Clipart tab lets you view the images on the WordPerfect Suite 8 CD-ROM (you must have the CD in your CD-ROM drive). The choices you made when you installed the software determine how many images are available on your hard drive now. If you did a minimal install, you'll have only a few images available in the Clipart tab, and you'll need to look in the CD Clipart tab for more choices. If you did a full install, you'll have more choices in the Clipart tab, but you'll still have lots of additional images available in the CD Clipart tab.

3. Select an image you like and drag it out onto the page. The clip-art selection is fitted into the box you just created.

4. Place your mouse over the picture, and click and drag it to any place on your page. You can place a picture near or right on top of text. The text is pushed aside to make room for the clip-art.

## Tip

*If you plan to add several images to your work in one session, minimize the Scrapbook after inserting an image, rather than closing it. This will save time the next time you need to use the Scrapbook.*

## Exploring the Scrapbook

The clip-art in the Scrapbook's CD Clipart tab is organized in folders. To find a picture, browse through the folders using the scroll bar. Double-click a folder to display the images inside. When you find an image you want to use, drag it from the Scrapbook to your page.

Some folders contain more folders instead of images. This occurs if there are a lot of clip-art images in a particular category. The second level of folders divides the images into subcategories, which makes it easier for you to find an appropriate image. Double-click a subfolder to display the images it contains.

To leave a folder and return to the next higher level of the Scrapbook, click the Up Folder icon (see Figure 5-2).

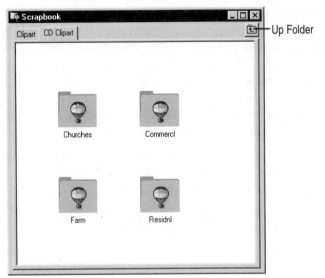

*Figure 5-2: The CD Clipart tab and Up Folder icon.*

## Locating a WordPerfect Photograph

In addition to clip-art images (which are drawings) the Suite also includes thousands of photographs. You use the Insert Image dialog box to browse the photos. Here's how to insert a photo:

1. Make sure the WordPerfect Suite CD-ROM is in your CD-ROM drive.

2. Select Insert | Graphics | From File.

3. The Insert Image dialog box is displayed. Click the down arrow next to the Look in drop-down menu (see Figure 5-3) to display a list of drives attached to your computer.

4. Select your CD-ROM drive. A list of folders on your CD-ROM is displayed.

5. Double-click the Photos folder to display a list of folders with various topics.

6. Double-click on a folder with a topic that interests you. This displays a long list of photos in that category.

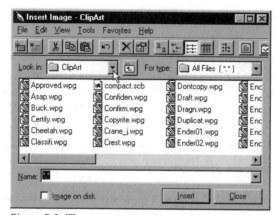

*Figure 5-3: The mouse cursor is over the Look In drop-down menu, where you select which folder to search in for graphics.*

7. If you want to see previews as you're browsing, choose
View | Preview | Use Separate Window. This opens a preview window. As you click on an image, its preview is displayed in the preview window (see Figure 5-4). To view a smaller version of the image, uncheck the Use Separate Window option.

8. To insert an image into your document, double-click it.

*Figure 5-4: Selecting View | Preview | Use Separate Window allows you to preview any image by clicking on it.*

## Working With Other Artwork

In addition to using WordPerfect's clip-art and photographs, you can import other types of artwork. WordPerfect supports most major bitmap formats like BMP, TIFF, and PCX, and vector image formats, such as CorelDraw and Adobe Illustrator. When you import an image, WordPerfect converts it to WordPerfect format, so you can edit the image in WordPerfect.

Here's how to import images:

1. Select Insert | Graphics | From File. This displays the Insert Image dialog box.

2. Use the dialog box to find the image you want to import, and double-click it.

3. WordPerfect imports and converts the image. You see the message, "Conversion in Progress." If you are converting a particularly complex graphic, this process may take up to a minute or so.

4. Once the conversion is completed, the image is displayed in a standard WordPerfect graphics box.

You can now use WordPerfect's graphics and graphics box tools to fine-tune the image's appearance.

## Controlling Image Size

By default, WordPerfect inserts images into one-inch boxes, but you can change the size of the image after inserting it. You can resize precisely by specifying exact numbers for the width and height, or you can resize visually by dragging the edges of the graphics box.

### Resizing an Image Numerically

Here's how to resize an image by specifying exact numbers:

1. Right-click the image and select Size from the pop-up menu to display the Box Size dialog box (see Figure 5-5).

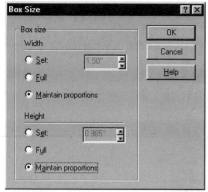

*Figure 5-5: The Box Size dialog box.*

2. You have three identical choices for Width and Height: Set, Full, or Maintain proportions. You make one choice for Width and one for Height:

   ■ Click the Set radio button and type a number in the data box to set the new width or height numerically.

   ■ Click the Full radio button to make the image as wide or high as possible on the page.

   ■ Click the Maintain Proportions radio button if you want WordPerfect to calculate the one proportion for you, based on the setting you specify for the other. This option will keep the image's width-to-height ratio the same as the current image.

All of this sounds confusing, so let's look at an example. You have imported an image that is 1 inch wide and 0.5 inch high. If for the width you select Set and specify 2 inches and for the height click Maintain Proportions, then WordPerfect calculates that your new image will be 2 inches wide and 1 inch high.

### Resizing an Image Manually

Instead of resizing using the Box Size dialog box, you can manually drag the image to resize it. This isn't as exact as the method described above, but it lets you see the effect of your changes as you make them.

Here's how to resize an image manually:

1. Click on your image to select it. Notice that six small black boxes appear around the image. These are called handles. Imagine a line connecting all six points—this is called the bounding box, because it indicates the boundaries of the image.

2. Position the cursor over one of the bounding boxes. The cursor changes to a two-way arrow (see Figure 5-6).

*Figure 5-6: Your mouse becomes a two-way resizing arrow when positioned over an image border.*

3. Drag the bounding box to change the size and shape of your image. If you drag a corner bounding box, your image maintains its proportions as you resize it. If you drag an edge bounding box, only that edge moves, which means that your image's proportions change.

## Moving an Image

Just as you can resize images manually or numerically, you can also move images manually or numerically.

### Positioning an Image Manually

To move an image in your document, put your cursor inside the image and click and hold the left mouse button. The cursor changes to a four-way arrow, which means that you can move the image. Drag the image to the new location, and release the mouse button.

### Positioning an Image Numerically

To position your image by specifying a precise page location, follow these steps:

1. Right-click on the image to display a pop-up menu, and select Position.

2. The Attach box to drop-down list lets you determine what object on the page this graphic "belongs to." Here are the choices:

   - **Page**. The box moves with the page. Use the lower half of the Box Position dialog box to control where on the page the box is positioned. You can specify a location based on the margins, the center point of the page, or other page attributes.

   - **Paragraph**. The box moves with the nearest paragraph. Use the lower half of the Box Position dialog box to adjust the amount of space between the paragraph and the image.

   - **Character**. The box moves with a particular text character. Use the lower half of the Box Position dialog box to adjust the position of the image's upper, lower, or center boundary relative to the associated line of text.

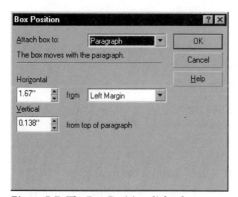

*Figure 5-7: The Box Position dialog box.*

## Editing an Image's Border & Fill

WordPerfect lets you edit the graphics box that surrounds an image. You can add a decorative border around the box or fill the background with color. In this section, we'll explain how to create those borders and fills and explore what colors are available.

### Creating a Border

A border helps to set off your image from the surrounding text. WordPerfect gives you lots of different border choices, everything from thin lines to fancy decorative borders (see Figure 5-8). Here's how to create a border for an image:

1. Right-click on the image and select Border/Fill from the pop-up menu. The Box Border/Fill dialog box is displayed with a selection of 24 border types (see Figure 5-8).

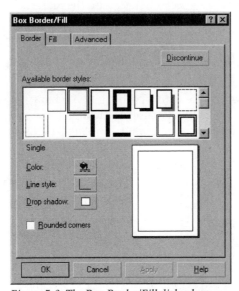

*Figure 5-8: The Box Border/Fill dialog box.*

2. Click on a border style to select it for your image.

3. Click on the Color button to display a palette of color swatches. Click a swatch to select it as your border color.

4. Click on the Line Style button to display a palette of line styles. Click a style to select it for your border.

5. Click on the Drop Shadow button to display the drop shadow choices. Click a choice to set your drop shadow.

6. If you want your border to have rounded corners, check the Rounded Corners check box (which isn't available for every border).

7. Click the Apply button to apply your changes to the current image, or click the OK button to apply your changes to the current image and close the Box Border/Fill dialog box.

Notice that the rectangle in the lower right of the Box Border/Fill dialog box displays a preview of your settings.

### Setting a Fill

If you want your image to have a colored background, you need to set a fill for it. Here's how to set a fill for an image:

1. Right-click the image and select Border/Fill from the pop-up menu. The Box Border/Fill dialog box is displayed.

2. Click the Fill tab to display the fill options (see Figure 5-9).

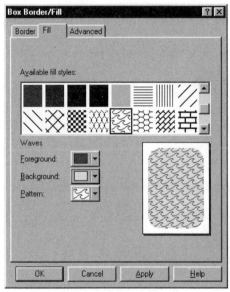

*Figure 5-9: The Box Border/Fill dialog box. A multicolor fill with a pattern is shown.*

3. Click on a fill style to select it for your image.

4. Click on the Foreground button to display a palette of color swatches. Click a swatch to select it as the foreground color for your fill. If you want a solid fill as your background, then you're done.

5. Click on the Background button to display a palette of color swatches. Click a swatch to select it as the background color for your fill.

6. Click on the Pattern button to display the available patterns. Click a pattern to select it for your image.

7. Click the Apply button to apply your changes to the current image, or click the OK button to apply your changes to the current image and close the Box Border/Fill dialog box.

Notice that the rectangle in the lower right of the Box Border/Fill dialog box displays a preview of your settings.

### Advanced Border & Fill Options

The Advanced tab in the Box Border/Fill dialog box lets you set expert settings for your borders and fills. Use this tab to control the space between your border and the image inside it, the color of the border's drop shadow, the gradient color settings, and the radius of your border's rounded edges. Figure 5-10 shows the Advanced tab.

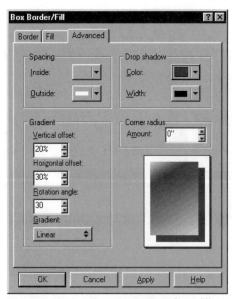

*Figure 5-10: Creating a custom gradient fill using the Advanced tab of the Box Border/Fill dialog box.*

### Working With Colors

WordPerfect provides several color swatches for you to use, but you can also create your own color combinations. Follow these steps to create a new color swatch:

1. Right-click on any image and select Border/Fill to display the Box Border/Fill dialog box.

2. Click the Color button to display the color palette.

3. Click the More button. This displays the Select Color dialog box (see Figure 5-11).

4. Choose a new color. You can do this either by manipulating the color wheel and saturation ramp, or by choosing a color model and typing in the color values.

*Figure 5-11: The Select Color dialog box.*

## Creating a Watermark Image

A watermark image is a faint picture that appears behind text. Often, watermarks are used on the first page of a document for company logos or messages like "confidential" or "draft." WordPerfect lets you quickly create a watermark image. Figure 5-12 shows an example of an image used as a watermark behind a table of contents.

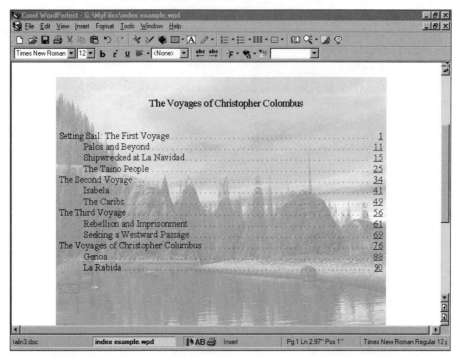

*Figure 5-12: A page with a watermark.*

To create a watermark, follow these steps:

1. Select Insert | Watermark. A dialog box prompts you to create Watermark A or B. Select Watermark A, and click the Create button.

Notice that various graphic tools are now available on your toolbar.

2. Select the Clipart button on the toolbar, which lets you insert clip-art or any compatible image. The Scrapbook appears.

3. Scroll to the "W" area of the Scrapbook (almost at the bottom). Here you'll find a number of ready-made watermark graphics. Select one and drag it onto your document.

A faded version of the image is now displayed on your page. Any text you type will go on top of the image. Normally, the image would displace text, but watermark images do not do this.

To close the Watermark creator, click the small "file" icon in the upper right side of the Property Bar.

## Editing the Watermark's Brightness

If the image is too faint, do the following:

1. Right-click on the image.

2. Select Image Tools, then click the Brightness button.

3. Select a new brightness setting with a bit more color (see Figure 5-13).

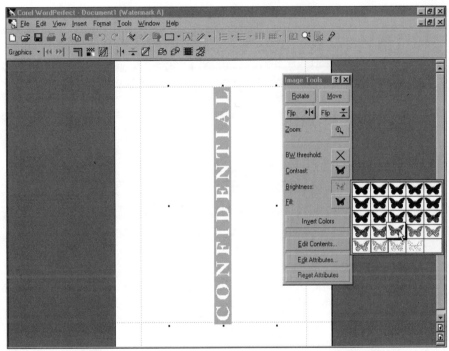

*Figure 5-13: Adjusting the brightness of a watermark image with the image tools.*

## Creating a Watermark Caption

You can add a caption for the watermark, and display the watermark and caption together on every page. To do so, right-click the image and select Caption. Click the Edit button and type the caption text you want at the bottom of your watermark, then close the caption toolbar.

### Suppressing a Watermark

To prevent a watermark from appearing on a particular page, select
Format | Page | Suppress and check Watermark A. The watermark does not
appear on that page. To suppress the watermark for the rest of the document,
right-click on the page, select Watermark from the pop-up menu, and click the
Discontinue button.

### Creating a Secondary Watermark

WordPerfect lets you create two watermarks: Watermark A and Watermark B.
This means that you can set up one watermark for all your even pages and a
second watermark for all your odd pages. Or, you could use Watermark B
only on specific pages for which Watermark A isn't appropriate.

You can edit Watermark B the same way you edit Watermark A; just make
sure that you specify the correct watermark and follow the steps described
earlier.

## Formatting an Image

WordPerfect lets you control how text is wrapped around an image, add a
caption to an image, recolor an image, and flip an image.

### Wrapping Text Around an Image

Your text wrapping settings determine the distance from the image to the text
that surrounds it. You can wrap the text around the image or wrap it around the
graphics box that surrounds the image. Here's how to control text wrapping:

1. Right-click on any image and select Wrap.

2. The Wrap Text dialog box appears, displaying text wrapping options.

3. Each text wrapping option has an icon to its right that shows you how
   the text would be wrapped if you chose that setting. The lines on the icon
   represent the text, and the shapes represent the image. Click an option to
   select it.

4. Click OK to close the dialog box. You'll see your change reflected in the
   text box.

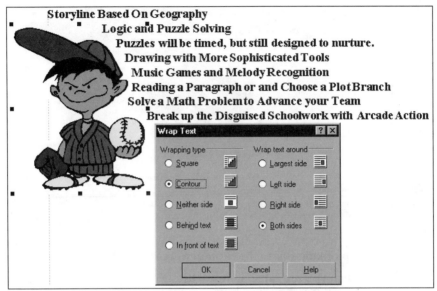

*Figure 5-14: Select a Wrap Text option to make text wrap around an image.*

## Adding a Caption to Your Image

WordPerfect's captions automatically number your images. For example, if the picture for which you create a caption is the third picture in your document, the caption "Figure 3" is displayed when you create a caption. Captions are numbered sequentially throughout your document. In addition to creating a figure number in your caption, you can also provide more descriptive text in your captions.

To add a caption to an image, follow these steps:

1. Right-click on the image and select Caption.

The image now has a numeric caption.

2. To edit the caption's settings, right-click on the image, and select Edit Caption.

The Property bar now provides tools for coloring text, setting justifications, and standard font options such as bold and italics (see Figure 5-15).

3. Use the Property bar to format your caption text. The changes you make now affect only the caption, not the main body text.

*Figure 5-15: The Property bar tools for editing a caption.*

4. Type changes into the caption to get the text you want.

5. When you are finished formatting your caption, click outside the cap-tioned picture to leave caption editing mode and restore your normal Property bar.

### Flipping Your Image

To flip your image on a horizontal or vertical axis, right-click the image and select Image Tools. Click one of the Flip buttons to flip the image.

### Recoloring Your Image

You can recolor your image using the image tools. Right-click on the image, and select Image Tools. The Image Tools dialog box is displayed (see Figure 5-16). To change your color settings, use one of the four button-invoked palettes in the middle of the dialog box or the Invert Colors button.

*Figure 5-16: The Image Tools dialog box. Use the Flip feature to change the direction a picture is facing.*

## Browsing Images in Sequence

If you need to edit several images in your document, you may want to let WordPerfect help you browse the images. If you select an image in your document, WordPerfect provides two browse buttons, Previous Box and Next Box, which take you to the previous and next graphic, respectively.

To browse through your graphics, click an image in your document. The Property bar displays a Previous Box button and a Next Box button (see Figure 5-17). Click the Previous Box button to display the previous image in your document, or click the Next Box button to display the next image in your document.

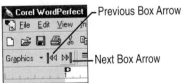

*Figure 5-17: The Previous Box and Next Box buttons let you browse your images.*

## Creating & Saving a Fill

You can create a custom fill and save it in the list of fills that WordPerfect displays when you display the Fill palette (for example, when defining your image's background). Here's how:

1. Make sure nothing is selected on your page, and choose Format | Graphics Styles. The Graphics Styles dialog box is displayed (see Figure 5-18).

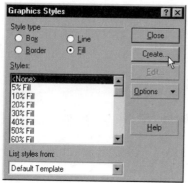

*Figure 5-18: Creating a Fill Style for later use.*

2. Click the Fill radio button.

3. Click the Create button to display the Create Fill Style dialog box (see Figure 5-19). Note that your dialog will not initially display the Gradient Options area—you must select Gradient for that to appear.

Note also that you can choose a Pattern for your fill. A pattern is a preset picture provided by WordPerfect that repeats across the area you want filled. A gradient is a blend between two colors, in which you control the angle and amount of the blending.

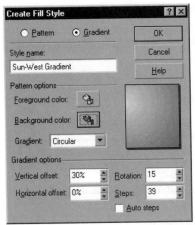

*Figure 5-19: Creating and naming a gradient fill.*

1. In the Style name text box, type in a name for your style.

2. In the Pattern options section of the dialog box, create your fill settings.

3. When you are finished, click OK to return to the Graphics Styles dialog box.

4. In the Graphics Styles dialog box, click Close to return to your document.

Your new style is now available in the list of standard fills. To see it, right-click an image, select Border/Fill, choose the Fill tab, and verify that your fill is now available in the Fill palette. You've successfully created a fill, and saved it for later use in any WordPerfect document.

## Creating & Applying a Graphics Style

If you're creating a lot of graphics, and you want all your graphics boxes to have the same settings, you'll appreciate WordPerfect's graphics styles feature. Without styles, you would have to change the size, content type, border, and fill settings individually for each graphic. But instead, you can save these settings in a graphics style, and then apply the style to each graphic. This will save you time and aggravation.

You can create your own graphics styles for graphics boxes, lines, borders, and fills, and add them to the selection lists. For example, if you create a new border style, that border is displayed in the Available Borders list, along with all the borders that WordPerfect supplies.

To create a graphics box style, follow these steps:

1. Select Insert | Graphics | Custom Box.

2. In the Custom Box dialog box, click the Styles button.

3. In the Box Styles dialog box, click Image in the list of style types.

4. Click Create.

The Create Box Style dialog box is displayed (see Figure 5-20).

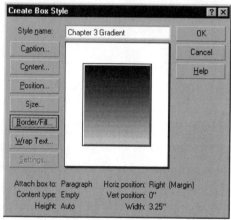

*Figure 5-20: Using the Create Box Style dialog box to create and name a style.*

5. In the Style name text box, type a name for your style.

6. Click the Border/Fill button. The Box Border/Fill dialog box is displayed.

7. Use the tools to create border and fill settings for your new graphics style.

8. When you are finished, click OK to close the Border/Fill dialog box.

Your style is now available in the list of box styles, along with the other preset styles. To apply your new style to an image, follow these steps:

1. Right-click an image and choose Styles from the pop-up menu.

The Box Style dialog box is displayed.

2. Locate your style in the style list, and click it (see Figure 5-21).

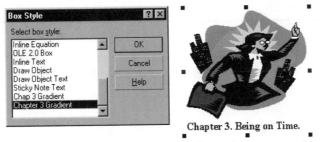

*Figure 5-21: Selecting a style you created to apply to your graphic.*

3. The graphics box settings that you set up in your style are applied to the selected image (see Figure 5-22).

*Figure 5-22: The style you previously created is now applied to the selected graphic.*

To create graphics styles for your lines, fills, and borders, the procedure is similar to the one described here for graphics boxes.

# Adding Shapes to Your Document

Instead of using clip-art that someone has created for you, you can draw your own figures. WordPerfect provides some tools that let you create stars, arrows, building blocks, or any other objects that you can assemble from basic shapes.

## The Basics of Shape Creation

WordPerfect provides tools for creating various basic shapes and lines. They are:

- Polyline
- Polygon
- Rectangle
- Rounded Rectangle
- Circle
- Ellipse
- Arrow

Figure 5-23 shows examples of the less familiar shape types.

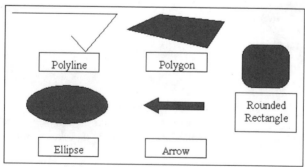

*Figure 5-23: Examples of WordPerfect shape types.*

To insert a shape or line, select Insert | Shape and the type of shape you want to create. Your cursor changes to a drawing tool for that shape. Drag your cursor across the page to create the shape.

If you want to create an ellipse, circle, or rectangle, click where you want the center of your shape and drag your cursor outward from the center. Release the mouse button to finish creating the shape.

If you are creating a polyline or polygon, you create your shape one line at a time. Click to start your line, then click again to create a corner. Create as many corners as you want for your shape, then double-click to finish creating your shape.

**Coloring a Shape**  If you are creating a "closed" object, such as a rectangle, polygon, or an ellipse, your object is filled with the currently selected color. A closed object is any object whose interior is completed enclosed. In Figure 5-23, every object except the polyline is closed.

To change the fill of a closed object after creating it, select a new foreground color from the Property bar (see Figure 5-24).

To change the color of the shape's outline or the color of a line, click the Foreground Color or Line Color tools on the Property bar, and choose a new color from the drop-down list (see Figure 5-24).

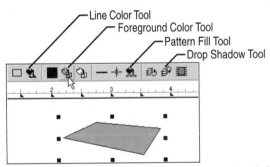

*Figure 5-24: Property Bar tools for changing a shape's fill and outline color.*

To the right of the Line Color and Foreground Color tools are tools to apply a pattern fill and a shadow to your shape. The Pattern Fill tool only works on closed objects.

**Moving, Editing & Grouping Shapes**  Once you've created your shapes, you can move them, reshape them, and group them. This helps you manage your shapes.

- To move a shape, drag it with your mouse.
- To move several shapes together, hold down the Shift key and click on each of the shapes. Notice that the bounding box surrounds all of the shapes. Drag the shapes to move them. When you release the mouse button and click outside the shapes, they are all deselected.

- To group several shapes, hold down the Shift key and select the shapes you want to group. Click the Graphics drop-down menu on the Property bar and choose Group (see Figure 5-25). The shapes are grouped into one unit.

- To separate (or ungroup) the shapes, click the Graphics drop-down menu and choose Separate.

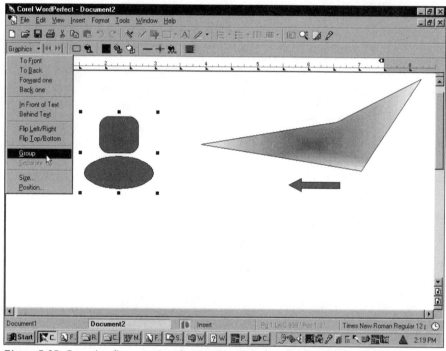

*Figure 5-25: Grouping figures using the Graphics drop-down menu on the Property bar.*

- You can reshape certain shapes, like irregular polygons. To reshape an irregular polygon, double-click on a corner of your shape and drag the corner (or control point) to a new location.

## Other Positioning Tools

The Graphics drop-down menu on the Property bar provides you with several ways to rearrange and reposition graphics on your page. You can, for example, flip a graphic, or specify that text should flow over your graphic.

Click your image, then click the Graphics button on the Property bar to display the Graphics drop-down menu (see Figure 5-26). Select a choice to make changes to your graphic. For example, select Behind Text to position your graphic behind the text, which allows the text to flow right over the image. (Unlike watermarks, the image does not appear faded and is not repeated on every page.)

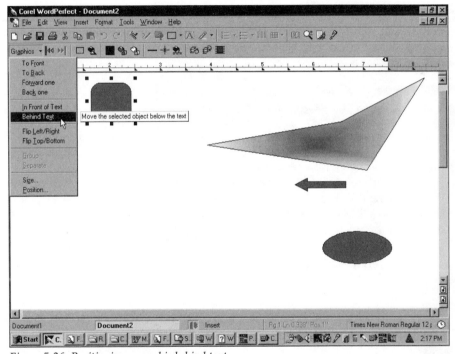

*Figure 5-26: Positioning a graphic behind text.*

## Creating Lines

To create a simple horizontal or vertical line, click Insert | Shape | Horizontal Line or Insert | Shape | Vertical Line, respectively. If you want to create a more complicated line, choose Insert | Shape | Custom Line. This displays the Create Graphics Line dialog box (see Figure 5-27), where you can set the line's width, color, style, direction, length, space above, and space below.

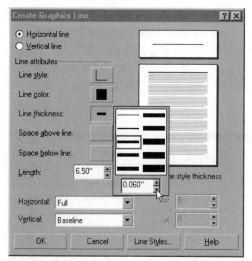

*Figure 5-27: The Create Graphics Line dialog box. The cursor is selecting a line width.*

If you want to create a line style, click the Line Styles button, and then click Create in the Line Styles dialog box. This displays the Create Line Style dialog box. Type a name for your new line style, and then specify the settings for the line. When you are finished, click OK. The new line style is displayed in the list of line styles in the Line Styles dialog box, and you can select it and use it in your document.

## Creating & Editing a Picture in WordPerfect Draw

You can use WordPerfect Draw, a drawing application, to create a new picture. Select Insert | Graphics | Draw Picture to launch Draw and display a 3-inch square blank drawing. You can then use Draw's tools to create a simple drawing.

If you have an existing image, double-click it to open it in Draw. Figure 5-28 shows the WordPerfect Draw work area and the Draw tools on the Property bar.

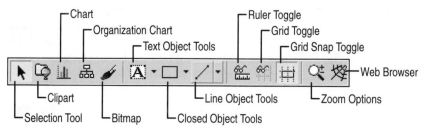

*Figure 5-28: The WordPerfect Draw tools.*

Let's take a look at the tools that Draw provides. The Ruler, Grid, and Grid Snap tools help you line up your drawing objects: the Ruler and the Grid add alignment lines to your drawing space, and the Grid Snap tool causes your objects to stick to those lines.

The Line Object Tools and Closed Object Tools drop-down menus let you select an object to draw in your workspace. The Regular Polygon tool (in the Closed Objects drop-down menu) is especially interesting, because it lets you draw equilateral polygons and triangles. Click the Regular Polygon tool, then specify how many sides you want for your polygon in the dialog box (see Figure 5-29). Close the dialog box and draw your regular polygon.

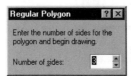

*Figure 5-29: The Regular Polygon dialog box.*

The Text Object Tools drop-down menu (see Figure 5-30) lets you create a text box, create a line of text, or select the TextArt tool, which we'll discuss later in this chapter.

*Figure 5-30: The Text Object Tools drop-down list.*

## Adding Fills & Lines to Your Draw Object

WordPerfect Draw provides line and fill tools that are different from the line and fill tools provided in WordPerfect itself. To display Draw's tools, right-click on the Draw object and select Object Properties. The Object Properties dialog box is displayed. Let's take a look at the three tabs in this dialog box:

- **Line tab** (see Figure 5-31). You can format the line color, width, end shape, corner shape, and line style with a few clicks. You can make normal lines into arrows or convert regular lines into dotted and dashed lines, such as for a tear-off coupon.

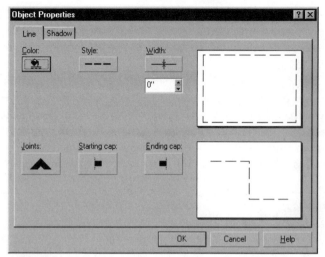

*Figure 5-31: The Line tab of the Object Properties dialog box.*

■ **Fill tab** (see Figure 5-32). You can select picture, pattern, gradient, or texture fills. A texture fill is shown in Figure 5-32. Click OK to fill the selected graphic with the fill selected in the dialog box.

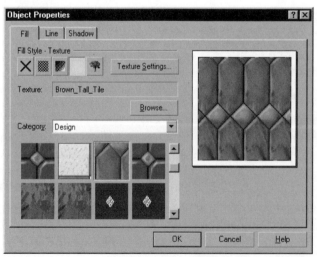

*Figure 5-32: Many more fills are provided here than in the standard WordPerfect Border/Fill dialog.*

If you want to use a picture to fill your object, click the Picture button in the Fill tab. You can select one of the pictures provide by WordPerfect by selecting a category and choosing a picture, or you can click the Browse button and select an image file from your hard drive.

Remember that this expanded menu of fills is only available when you are using WordPerfect Draw.

- **Shadows tab** (see Figure 5-33). The Shadows tab provides several present shadows, or you can set your own shadow options and change the color of the shadow.

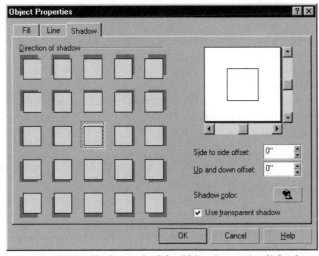

*Figure 5-33: The Shadows tab of the Object Properties dialog box.*

### QuickWarp & Quick3-D

You can warp any Draw object and apply special 3D effects to it. To warp an image, select it, then choose Tools | QuickWarp, and choose a warp effect (see Figure 5-34). Warping an image distorts it in various interesting ways. As you try out warp effects, the preview pane on the right displays the results. When you are satisfied with the effect, click OK to leave the QuickWarp dialog box and apply the warp setting.

## Tip

*QuickWarp or Quick3-D may not be available if you converted clip-art to Draw format by double-clicking on it. To fix this problem, right-click on your image, and select Separate Objects from the pop-up menu. QuickWarp and Quick3-D will now be available.*

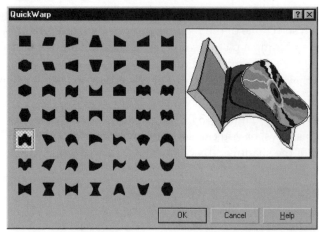

*Figure 5-34: QuickWarp is used here to distort an image of a CD in a jewel case.*

Give your selected drawing a 3D appearance by choosing Tools | Quick3-D. This displays the Quick3-D dialog box (see Figure 5-35), where you can create 3D effects by rotating and extruding your object and by applying perspective to it.

The Rotation tab (see Figure 5-35) lets you apply various predefined 3D effects or specify the exact angles you want to use.

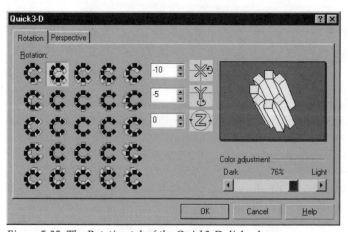

*Figure 5-35: The Rotation tab of the Quick3-D dialog box.*

The Perspective tab determines how "deep" the 3D effect is. Set a perspective type and a depth number. Higher depths make the 3D effect more obvious. Figure 5-36 shows some clip-art before and after applying Quick3-D.

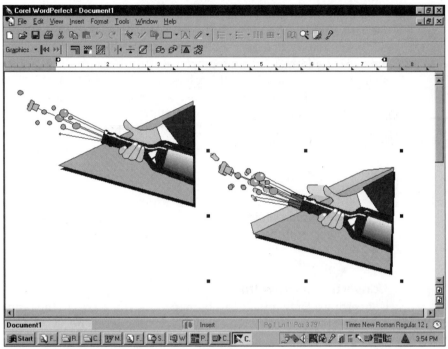

*Figure 5-36: Clip-art before and after being treated with Quick3-D.*

**Tip**

*Because you launched WordPerfect Draw by double-clicking on an image or by selecting Insert | Graphics | Draw Picture, you can use the Draw tools only inside the object's area. If you click outside the Draw object's box, you return to the standard WordPerfect workspace.*

## Creating & Editing Bitmapped Images

It's important that you understand the difference between **vector images** and **bitmap images**. Vector images are composed of various shapes, like lines, circles, and rectangles. If you resize a vector image, the image scales gracefully, without any loss of quality. Bitmap images, on the other hand, are composed of dots. If you try to rescale a bitmap, you usually get the "jaggies." Bitmaps are used as a format for photographs, and the bitmap editing tools let you sharpen, adjust, and distort the colors of your image, as if you were painting.

You can convert a Draw picture to a bitmap to gain access to the photo editing and paint tools in the bitmap editor. Once you convert an image to a bitmap, you will no longer be able to edit the shapes and lines that make up the image.

**Tip**

*To create or edit a bitmapped image, you must be in Draw mode. You can tell you are in Draw mode because the top of the screen reads [Presentations 8 Drawing].*

### Converting a Draw Image to a Bitmap

Converting a Draw image to a bitmap gives you access to the Bitmap Property bar's painting and color tools and to several special effects. To convert an image, follow these steps:

1. Select an image.

2. If the picture is actually a group of drawings, right-click on the image, and select Separate.

3. Select the portion of the image that you want to convert to a bitmap.

4. Select Tools | Convert to Bitmap.

5. Right-click on the image and select Edit Bitmap. The Property bar changes, and now provides various paintbrushes, text creation, and object creation tools (see Figure 5-37).

*Figure 5-37: The Bitmap Property bar. The mouse cursor is shown selecting the Selective Replace tool.*

While using the bitmap tools, you can change the size of the paintbrush you're using. Select Format | Brush to display the Brush Attributes dialog box (see Figure 5-38) and choose new paintbrush options.

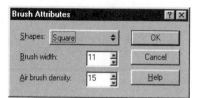

*Figure 5-38: The Brush Attributes dialog box.*

To change the paint color, select Format | Object Properties | Fill, and choose a new color from the Foreground or Background Color drop-down list.

The Select Area tool lets you select a portion of your image. You can then apply a special effect to the selected area only. Select the Effects tool (or select Tools | Special Effects) to display the Special Effects dialog box (see Figure 5-39).

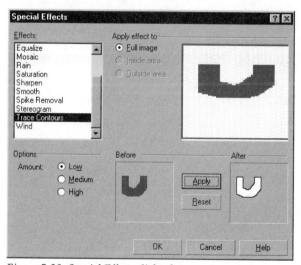

*Figure 5-39: Special Effects dialog box.*

To apply a special effect, select the effect you want in the Effects list. Specify the amount of the effect that you want to apply in the lower section of the dialog box. Click the Apply button to preview the effect. When you are satisfied, click OK to apply it to your image. Figure 5-40 shows the Blur effect applied to a clip-art item. Figure 5-41 shows the Trace Contour effect applied to the same item. Emboss and Rain are two other interesting effects.

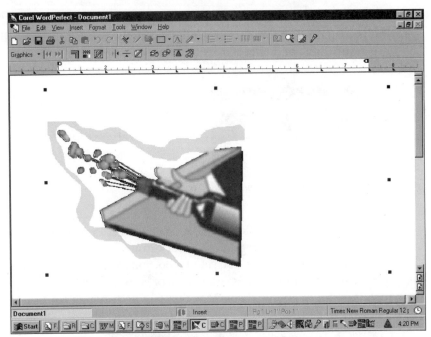

*Figure 5-40: Clip-art treated with the Blur effect.*

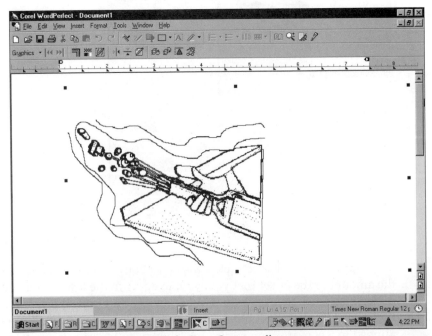

*Figure 5-41: Clip-art treated with the Trace Contour effect.*

Note that you can apply an effect to the entire image, to the selected area of the image, or the unselected area of the image.

### Creating a Bitmap From Scratch

If you want to create a new bitmap, select Insert | Graphics | Draw Picture and then select Insert | Bitmap. Your cursor turns into a hand holding a box. Drag inside your Draw area to create a box for your bitmap. All the bitmap tools are now available on your toolbar.

To leave bitmap editing mode, click outside the graphics box. The picture you've been working on appears in your WordPerfect document.

## Creating a TextArt Object

WordPerfect TextArt lets you turn text into a decorative heading. You can reshape and skew text, and add fills, patterns, and shadows to turn a line of text into a unique image. To create a TextArt object, follow these steps:

1. Select Insert | Graphics | TextArt. The TextArt dialog box is displayed (see Figure 5-42).

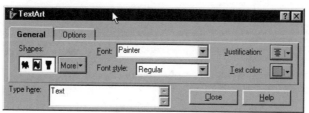

*Figure 5-42: The TextArt dialog box.*

2. Type the text you want into the Type here field.

3. Choose a text color, shape, font, and justification.

4. Click the More button next to the Shapes list to display the available shapes, and select a shape for your text (see Figure 5-43).

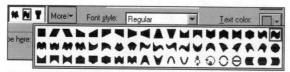

*Figure 5-43: Clicking More reveals 57 more shapes from which you can choose.*

5. Click the 2D Options tab. Use the options to apply a pattern and a shadow (changing the color and thickness of your text), and set the smoothness.

6. Click outside your TextArt object to finish editing the TextArt object.

To edit a TextArt object again, right-click the object and select Corel TextArt 8 Document Object | Open. Selecting Open instead of edit gives you a larger workspace, which allows you to see the changes you make more clearly.

TextArt objects are just like regular WordPerfect objects; you can add custom borders and captions, rotate and resize it and so forth, by right-clicking on the object and selecting styles from the pop-up menu.

## Overlapping Pictures, Text Boxes & Text

As we pointed out earlier, when you insert a graphic the text surrounding it is displaced. To fine-tune the graphic's location, move it around until the text and the graphic look the way you want. If you need to make a fine adjustment, zoom in on the area with the Zoom tool and then move the picture.

Figure 5-44 shows an example of precise positioning of text and graphics. In this figure, the left margin was adjusted to prevent the text from flowing onto the "The Phoenix" graphic at the bottom left.

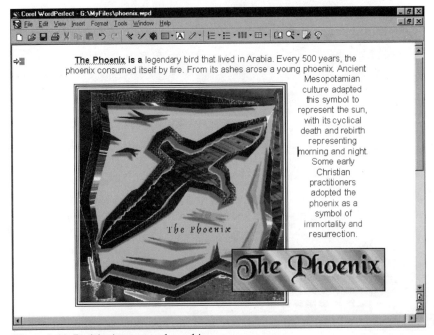

*Figure 5-44: Positioning text and graphics on a page.*

## Order & Placement of Graphics

Notice that the "The Phoenix" TextArt title overlaps the "Phoenix" picture. To move a graphic to the front like this, right-click on the lettered graphic and select Order | To Front. To move a graphic to the back, right-click it and select Order | To Back.

If you have several graphics overlapping each other, you can use the Order | Back One and Order | Forward One commands. These move a graphic back one level or forward one level, respectively, in the stack of graphics.

**Tip**

*Each picture in this figure has its own border design. Using an outline border enhances the effectiveness of overlapping images.*

The main Phoenix graphic had its Text Wrap feature set to Contour and Both Sides. To display the Wrap Text dialog box, right-click the image and choose Wrap from the pop-up menu.

## Creating Text Boxes

A text box is a resizable box that you can type text into. As you type, the text fits itself between the boundaries of the box. Like all WordPerfect boxes, you can resize the box and add borders, fills, and shadows. If you resize the text, the flow of the text changes to fit in the new box size. You can move text boxes around on the page, and use cut, copy, and paste commands on them. Text boxes can also be overlapped with other text boxes or with graphics boxes.

To create a text box, select Insert | Text Box. Click inside the box to type or edit text. You can change the text size, font, font color, and even apply styles to text in a text box (see Figure 5-45) using the Property bar.

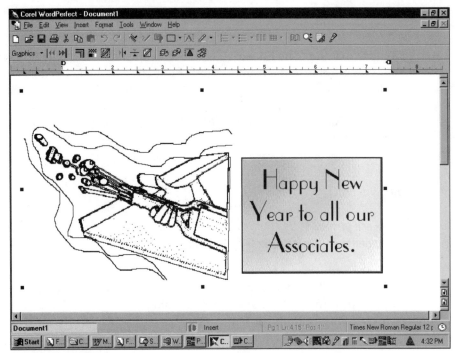

*Figure 5-45: A text box, shown here next to our clip-art creation.*

To change the box's border style or add a shadow or fill, click the box's border. The Property bar now displays the standard line and fill tools for editing boxes. When you are finished with your text box, click anywhere outside the text box on the WordPerfect page.

## Working With Borders, Shading & Color

Earlier in this chapter, we explained how to add a fill or a border to any text or graphics box. In this section, we'll explore some advanced techniques for using borders, shading, and color to make your document more interesting.

### Creating a Custom Fill Behind a Page of Text

You can use a custom fill to create an attractive backdrop for your text. In Figure 5-46, we have used a graphics box to create a backdrop for the text. The box is actually empty.

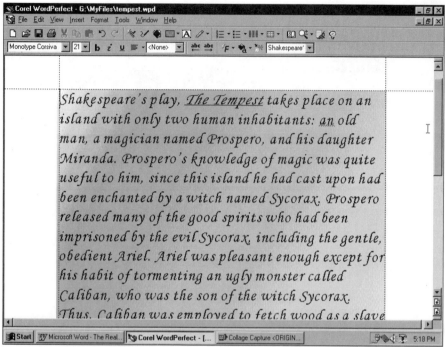

*Figure 5-46: A graphics box used as a simple backdrop for a page of text.*

You can use a watermark to accomplish something similar, but using a graphics box lets you change the coloring, fill angle, and fill offset, and resize the graphics box so that it nearly fits between the margins. Here's how to create a graphics box without inserting a graphic:

1. Select Insert | Graphics | Custom Box to display the Custom Box dialog box.

2. Click the Styles button to display the Box Styles dialog box.

3. Click the Create button to display the Create Box Style dialog box.

4. Type in a style name.

5. Click the Size button. In both the Width and Height section, select the Full radio button. Click OK.

6. Click the Border/Fill button, and select the Fill tab.

7. In the Available fill styles list, select the fill named Gradient1. It should be the fifth fill from the left in the bottom row.

8. Click the Inside Color drop-down list and select a light gray (see Figure 5-47).

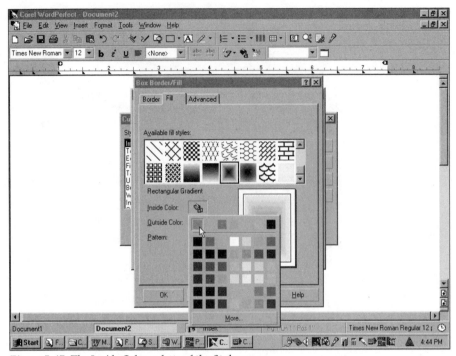

*Figure 5-47: The Inside Color palette of the Styles menu.*

9. Click the Advanced tab, and change the number in the Rotation data box to 135 degrees. This creates a nice slant to the fill, offsetting the text without being obtrusive or too showy.

10. Click OK to close the Border/Fill dialog box.

11. Click the Wrap Text button, and click the Behind Text radio button. This allows you to type text on top of this filled graphics box. If you forget to do this, your graphics box will displace text that you type, and since the graphics box takes up almost the entire page, you don't want this to happen. Click OK to close the Wrap Text dialog.

12. Click OK to close the Create Box Style dialog box. Click OK to close the Box Styles dialog, and OK again to close the Custom Box dialog.

To create another box using these settings, click Insert | Graphics | Custom Box, and select the box style name in the list.

## Placing a Decorative Border or Design on a Page

Instead of using a graphics box behind the page, you can apply a border to the page itself. Select Format | Page | Border/Fill and select a design from the Available border styles list (see Figure 5-48). Click OK to apply the border to your pages.

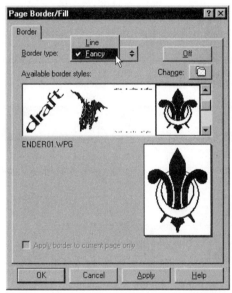

*Figure 5-48: Selecting a border for the entire page.*

Using this method has some limitations. Once you place the border on the page, you cannot make any changes to it—you can't move it, resize it, or change its colors. Often, it's better to use a watermark instead of a page border.

# Working With Tables

In this section, we'll discuss how to create and edit tables, how to use the Speed Format to quickly set up a table design, how to do calculations in a table, and how to change table formatting.

## Creating a Simple Table

To create a table, do the following:

1. Click the TableQuickCreate button on the WordPerfect 8 toolbar. A grid appears under the icon. This is a thumbnail of the rows and columns you're about to create.

2. Drag across the grid to set the number of cells in your table. As you drag, the top of the grid tells you how many rows and columns you are creating (see Figure 5-49). For example, if you see "4x5," you have selected four columns and five rows.

3. Release your mouse button to create the table.

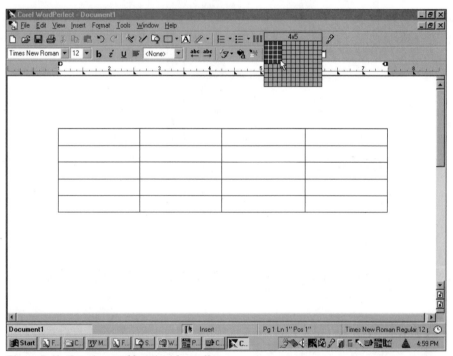

*Figure 5-49: Creating a table using the toolbar.*

You can also create a table by selecting Insert | Table, which displays the Create Table dialog box, shown in Figure 5-50.

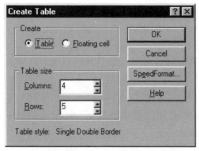

*Figure 5-50: The Create Table dialog box.*

### Creating a Sample Table

Let's create a sample table and apply a table style to it:

1. Create a table with four columns and five rows, using either of the methods described in the previous section.

## Tip

*When working with tables, columns are arranged vertically (up and down) and rows are arranged horizontally (from left to right).*

2. Right-click on the table and select SpeedFormat from the pop-up menu.

3. Choose the Single Double Border table style, as shown in Figure 5-51, and click Apply. If you find a table style here that you'd like to apply to every new table, click the Use as default button. If you select an initial style, each table you create will have that style applied by default.

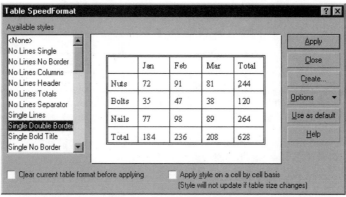

*Figure 5-51: The Table SpeedFormat dialog box with Single Double Border selected.*

## Creating & Formatting a Table's Contents

Now, we need to add information to our table. To type text in a cell, you click inside the cell and begin typing. To select a cell, click on its edge. Selecting a cell lets you change its border width, add a fill, or associate the cell with a formula. Follow these steps to put information in your table's cells:

1. Type in the three months as shown in Figure 5-52. Click in a cell, then type the information. To move to another cell, click in it. Note that the first cell in the first row is blank.

|  | Jan | Feb | Mar |
|---|---|---|---|
| Nails |  |  |  |
| Hammers |  |  |  |
| Pliers |  |  |  |
| Total |  |  |  |

*Figure 5-52: Building a table starting with text fields.*

2. Type in the tool names in the first column of the table, and type in the word Total in the bottom cell.

3. To change the appearance of the text in any cell, right-click on it and select Font. This displays the Font dialog box, where you can change the appearance of your text.

4. Type in the numbers in the table, as shown in Figure 5-53. Leave the bottom row blank; we're going to have WordPerfect calculate the totals for us.

|  | Jan | Feb | Mar |
|---|---|---|---|
| Nails | 13 | 48 | 54 |
| Hammers | 45 | 27 | 103 |
| Pliers | 53 | 53 | 43 |
| Total |  |  |  |

*Figure 5-53: Fill in numbers for all remaining spaces except Total lines.*

## Selecting Tables & Cells

Each cell in your table has a unique identifier: a letter that identifies the column and a number that identifies the row. For example, cell B3 would be located at the intersection of the second column and third row. WordPerfect can display information in the margins of your document to help you identify each row and column. Make sure your cursor is in the table, then select the Table drop-down menu from the toolbar and then select Row/Col Indicators (see Figure 5-54).

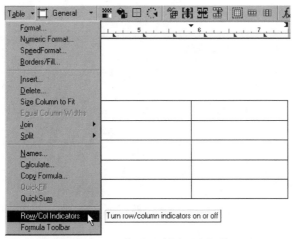

*Figure 5-54: Turning on the Row/Column Indicators.*

WordPerfect now displays the letters and numbers that identify the columns and rows in the margins. Click any letter or number button to select the entire column or row. Click the button in the upper left corner to select the entire table.

Let's take a look at some of the ways that you can edit your table.

## Resizing Cells

You can resize any table cell by positioning your cursor over a cell border and dragging the border. If you drag to increase the cell's size, the neighboring cell gets smaller. If you drag to decrease the cell's size, the neighboring cell gets bigger. You are actually changing the positioning of the cell border that the two cells share.

## Inserting & Deleting Columns & Rows

WordPerfect lets you add or delete columns and rows after you create a table. This lets you adjust the size of the table if your data changes. To add rows or columns, follow these steps:

1. Click in a cell next to where you want to add the cells.

2. Right-click and select Insert from the pop-up menu.

3. Specify how many rows or columns you want to add.

4. Click the mouse in a cell right next to the location where you want to make an addition.

5. Right-click, and select Insert. This displays the Insert Column/Rows dialog box.

6. Select either Columns or Rows, and type in the number that you want in the appropriate field.

7. Specify whether you want the new cells inserted before or after your cursor location.

8. Click OK. Your new rows or columns appear.

To delete columns or rows, do the following:

1. Right-click a cell in the row or column you want to delete.

2. Select Delete from the pop-up menu. This displays the Delete Structure/Contents dialog box.

3. Select either Columns or Rows, and type in the number that you want in the appropriate data box.

4. Click OK to delete the rows or columns.

## Tip

*If you want to empty the cells without removing them, select the Cell Contents Only radio button in step 3.*

## Setting Up Automatic Computation

WordPerfect can calculate totals for a column of numbers. To set this up, follow these steps:

1. Select a column of numbers. You must have a blank cell at the bottom of the column.

2. Right-click, and select QuickSum from the pop-up menu (see Figure 5-55). The sum appears in the cell at the bottom of the column.

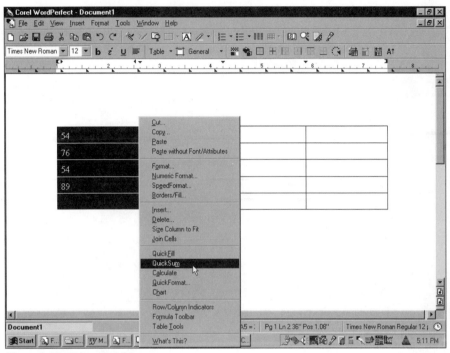

*Figure 5-55: Using QuickSum.*

You can also set up WordPerfect so that it automatically calculates a sum for each column of numbers whenever the numbers change. Again, you'll need a blank cell at the bottom of the column of numbers, where WordPerfect will insert the calculation. To set up automatic calculation, follow these steps:

1. Use the QuickSum feature, described above, to set up the bottom cell in your column as a total.

2. Click the Select Table button in the top left corner of the row/column indicators.

3. Click the Table drop-down menu on the toolbar and select Calculate. (If you have not clicked in a table, the Table menu will not be available.)

4. In the Calculate dialog box, select the Calculate Table radio button.

5. Click OK to close the dialog box.

6. Close the dialog box. From now on, whenever you add new numbers to this column, WordPerfect will immediately update the calculations.

To demonstrate how QuickSum works, let's return to the table we created and use QuickSum to add each column of numbers. Follow these steps:

1. Right-click on the table and select Formula Bar, as shown in Figure 5-56. The Formula bar appears at the top of the window, attached to the bottom of the Property bar.

|         | Jan | Paste                    | Mar |
|---------|-----|--------------------------|-----|
| Nails   | 13  | Format...                | 54  |
|         |     | Numeric Format...        |     |
| Hammers | 45  | SpeedFormat...           | 103 |
|         |     | Lines/Fill...            |     |
| Pliers  | 53  |                          | 43  |
|         |     | Insert...                |     |
| Total   |     | Delete...                | 200 |
|         |     | Size Column to Fit       |     |
|         |     | Split Cell...            |     |
|         |     |                          |     |
|         |     | QuickSum                 |     |
|         |     | Calculate                |     |
|         |     | Row/Column Indicators    |     |
|         |     | Formula Bar              |     |
|         |     | Table Tools              |     |
|         |     |                          |     |
|         |     | What's This?             |     |

*Figure 5-56: Selecting Formula Bar, so we can add formulas to our table.*

2. Select the entire Jan column in the table. (Click at the top of the Jan column, then drag your cursor down to the bottom of the column and release the mouse button.) When the column is selected, all of the cells turn black.

3. Right-click on the selected column, and select QuickSum from the pop-up menu. This creates a formula that adds the numbers in the first three rows of the column and places the sum in the fourth blank row at the bottom of the column. QuickSum works only if the final row you selected in your column is blank.

Even though QuickSum is doing the work for us, it's helpful to understand what's going on. Look at Figure 5-57. The Formula bar tells us that cell B5 is selected. Cell B5 contains the results of our QuickSum, and the formula that WordPerfect used to calculate this sum is displayed on the Formula Bar. The formula is:

```
+SUM(B1:B4)
```

This translates to "sum the values of all of the cells between B1 and B4." So, WordPerfect adds the values of B1, B2, B3, and B4, and displays the result in the current cell, B5.

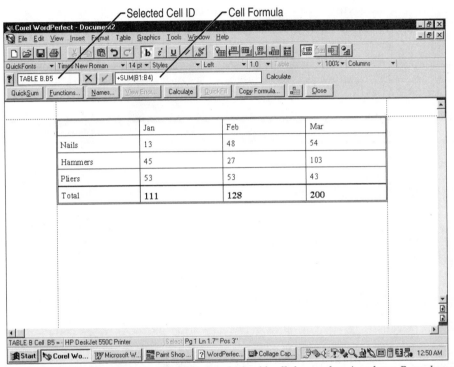

*Figure 5-57: Tracing the work of QuickSum, which adds all the numbers in column B, as shown in the Formula area to the right of the check mark.*

4. Use QuickSum to total the numbers for February and March. Notice that the formula now changes to:

   +SUM(C1:C4)

   for February, and

   +SUM(D1:D4)

   for March.

## Changing the Numeric Format

Instead of displaying plain numbers, WordPerfect can format your numbers to look like currency values. Here's how:

1. Select all the numeric cells in your table, then right-click and select Numeric Format from the pop-up menu (see Figure 5-58).

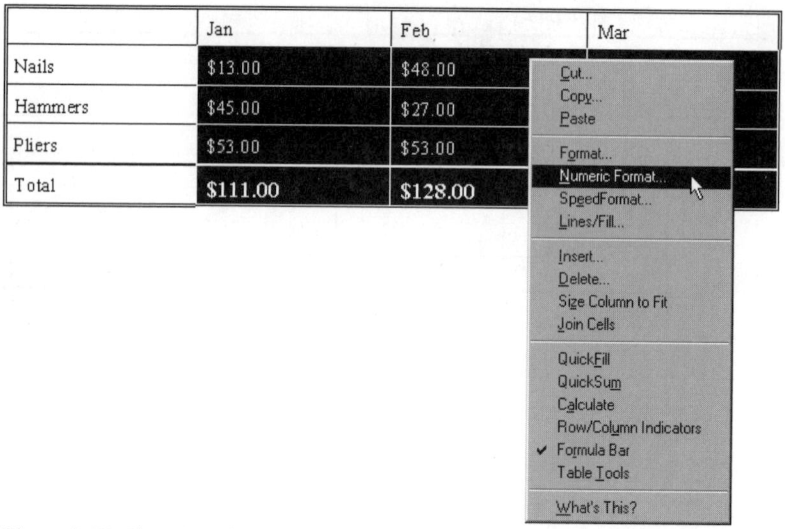

*Figure 5-58: Changing the Numeric Format to Currency.*

2. In the Properties for Table Numeric Format dialog box, select the Currency radio button.

3. Click OK. The numbers in your cell change. The values stay the same, but the numbers are now displayed with dollar signs, commas, decimal points, and zeroes.

If you want to apply a particular numeric format to every number in the table (instead of just to the selected cells), follow these steps:

1. Click in your table.

2. Right-click, and select Numeric Format from the pop-up menu.

3. In the Properties for Table Numeric Format dialog box, click the Table tab.

4. Select the Currency radio button.

5. Click OK to apply your changes and close the dialog box.

## Adding Labels to the Table

Now that we've formatted our numbers, we need a new row of cells at the top of the table so we can provide labels over the columns. Follow these steps:

1. Right-click in the top row of the table, and select Insert from the pop-up menu.

2. Select Row, type 1 in the field, and check the Before radio button for Placement.

3. Click OK to insert your new row at the top of the table.

4. Type "Product Type" in the first new cell on the left.

5. Use the Format toolbar or the Property bar to change the text to a bolder font and then center the phrase using the Justification button.

6. Click the column indicator at the top of the window to select the entire first column.

7. Right-click inside the selected column, and select Border/Fill from the pop-up menu. The Border/Fill dialog box is displayed.

8. Select the Right drop-down list and select an interesting line type. This will become the line that separates this column from the others.

9. Click OK to close the Border/Fill dialog box and see the new cell line pattern applied to the right side of the column (see Figure 5-59).

| Product Type | | | |
|---|---|---|---|
|  | Jan | Feb | Mar |
| Nails | $13.00 | $48.00 | $54.00 |
| Hammers | $45.00 | $27.00 | $103.00 |
| Pliers | $53.00 | $53.00 | $43.00 |
| Total | **$111.00** | **$128.00** | **$200.00** |

*Figure 5-59: Adding borders and labeling our table.*

As evident in the figure above, we need to add a thicker line to separate the row of totals from the rest of the table. Follow these steps:

1. Click the row indicator to select the last row in the table.

2. Click the Change the Top Line button on the toolbar. (Use the ToolTips to locate it.) A drop-down list of line styles is displayed.

3. Select a line style from the list. The new style is applied to the top line of the selected row.

## Joining Cells

Joining cells lets you center a title across several cells. We need a title for our Jan, Feb, and Mar columns, so we're going to join the cells above these columns and make a title. Follow these steps:

1. Select the three cells directly above the Jan, Feb, and Mar column headings.

2. Right-click on the cells, and select Join Cells in the pop-up menu. Notice that the lines that separated the three cells now disappear.

3. Type "Month" in the new joined cell, and format it to make it look like a heading. (For example, center the word, and then increase the character spacing by selecting Format | Typesetting | Word/Letter Spacing, and typing 150% in the Percent of Optimal data box.)

## Creating & Copying a Formula

Let's return to our table. What if we needed to add sales tax to the table? First, add two rows to the bottom of the table; one row for the sales tax and one for the grand total. In the first cell of the first new row, type "Sales Tax." In the first cell of the second new row, type "Grand Total." Then, change the word "Total" to "Subtotal" (see Figure 5-60). To erase text, press the Backspace key.

| Product Type | MONTH | | |
|---|---|---|---|
| | Jan | Feb | Mar |
| Nails | $13.00 | $48.00 | $54.00 |
| Hammers | $45.00 | $27.00 | $103.00 |
| Pliers | $53.00 | $53.00 | $43.00 |
| Subtotal | $111.00 | $128.00 | $200.00 |
| Sales Tax | $9.16| | $10.56 | $16.50 |
| Grand Total | | | |

*Figure 5-60: Applying a Sales Tax formula to our table.*

Here's how to add the formula to include the sales tax in the total:

1. Click on the second cell in the Sales Tax row. We are going to create a formula here to calculate the sales tax.

2. In the formula area of the Formula Bar, type:

   B6*.0825

   This formula multiplies the subtotal by 8.25% to get the sales tax. (The exact sales tax percentage might be different in your area.)

3. Click the check next to the formula you just typed. You have now created a formula.

## Copying the Formula

The other two columns need the same formula. You could, of course, type the formula into the other cells, but it's quicker and easier to copy the formula you just created. Follow these steps:

1. Make sure cell B7 is still selected.

2. Click the Copy Formula button found on the Formula bar. A dialog box asks you which cell to copy the formula to.

3. Type in C7. WordPerfect copies the formula to cell C7, and automatically changes the formula so that it refers to the numbers in column C and not the numbers in column B.

4. Repeat this process for column D.

In each column, you now have a subtotal and a sales tax amount. Now, we need to add those two numbers to get the grand total. Follow these steps:

1. Click in cell B8 (the second cell from the left in the bottom row). Check the Formula bar to make sure you have the correct cell.

2. In the formula area, type:

   B6+B7

   and click the check mark. Notice that B8 now shows the total.

3. Copy this new formula to the grand total cells in columns C and D. The final result should look like Figure 5-61.

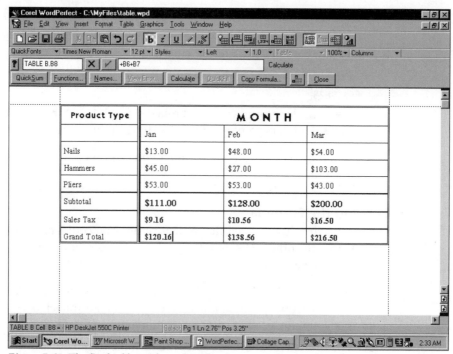

*Figure 5-61: The final table, with a subtotal, sales tax, and a grand total.*

## Importing Data Into a Table

You can import a table or a database into WordPerfect and create a new table from the data. Follow these steps:

1. Select Insert | Spreadsheet/Database | Import. This displays the Import Data dialog box.

2. From the Data Type drop-down list, select the type of data you want to import. WordPerfect supports many types of database programs.

3. From the Import As drop-down list, select Table to indicate that you want to import the data as a table.

4. If necessary, click the Filename button to locate the data you want to import. For example, you can use this sample file:

   `c:\corel\suite8\samples\volume.db`

## Tip

*For ODBC data sources, you only need to specify the data source.*

5. Click OK.

6. WordPerfect displays the message "Conversion in Progress," as the table is converted.

7. You data is displayed as a table in your WordPerfect document (see Figure 5-62). You can edit the table just like any other table.

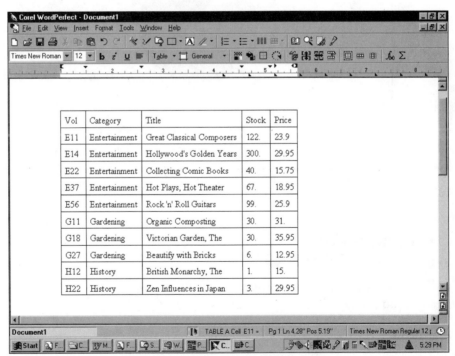

*Figure 5-62: A table imported from a spreadsheet into WordPerfect.*

For a thorough discussion of linking spreadsheets and other data to WordPerfect, please see Chapter 13.

## Creating a Chart From a Table

You can create a chart that shows the data in your table visually. To do so, click inside the table and select Insert | Graphics | Chart. A chart is displayed on your page with data from the table. By default, the chart is a vertical bar style chart, but you can change this. Figure 5-63 shows a pie chart of the data in the table that we've been working on. When you change the table data, the changes are reflected in the chart.

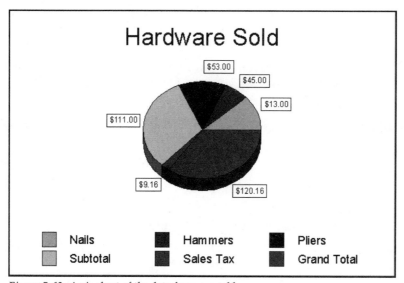

*Figure 5-63: A pie chart of the data from our table.*

# Adding a Chart

WordPerfect lets you create charts (like the one shown in the previous section) to display numeric data visually.

**Tip**

*You must have Presentations installed to create WordPerfect charts, because WordPerfect is actually using the chart feature from Presentations.*

## A First Look Around

Select Insert | Graphics | Chart to create a chart (see Figure 5-64). WordPerfect creates a new chart and fills the datasheet with sample data to give you an idea of how data looks in the chart. The datasheet is where you specify the data you want represented in the chart.

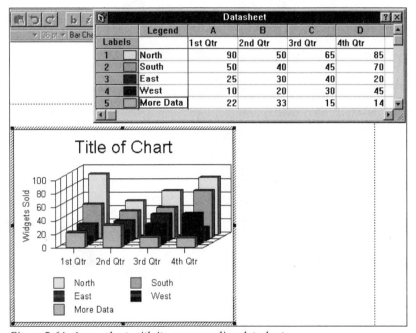

Figure 5-64: A new chart with its corresponding datasheet.

## Working With the Datasheet

When you first create a chart, you are in Chart Edit mode. You can see the datasheet which is the source for your chart data, and the chart itself. In normal viewing mode you cannot see the datasheet, and it is not printed.

As you type numbers into the datasheet, your chart changes to reflect the new numbers. Here's how it works:

1. Click on a datasheet cell that contains a number. Note that your cursor changes to a wide cross when it's over a data area, as shown in Figure 5-65.

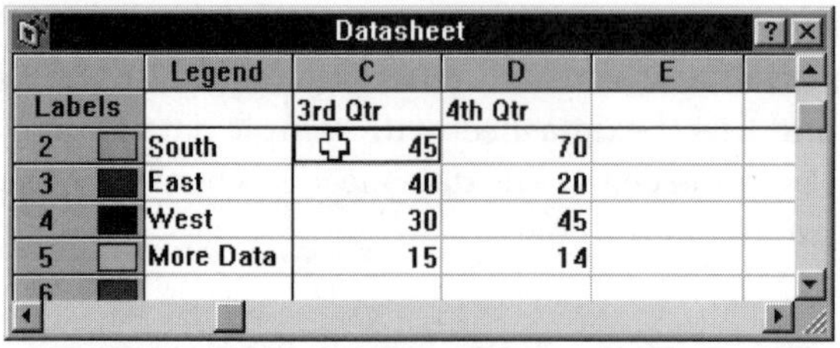

*Figure 5-65: The cursor changes into a wide cross when placed over a datasheet cell.*

2. Type a new number into the cell.

3. The new value that you've supplied is now reflected on the chart.

To create your own chart, replace the placeholder values that are in the datasheet by default with your own numbers.

## Adding a New Data Series

If you want to add additional data to your chart, type the new data in the next available row or column in the datasheet window. Each row in the datasheet is called a data series.

In Figure 5-65 above, someone has added a data series labeled More Data. When you first create a chart, it has four default data series (North, South, East, and West).

To add another series, follow these steps:

1. Click the first blank cell in the Legend column. Type a legend for this new data series.

2. Provide data in each column for this new data series. Click on each blank data cell area and type in a number.

After you add numbers to each cell, look at the chart and notice that the data series appears there. The legend area of the chart is also updated and now includes your new data series heading and its corresponding color square.

You can also add columns or rows to your chart by right-clicking on the datasheet and selecting Insert. This lets you insert a new row or column before the currently selected one.

To change the format of your numbers, right-click on the datasheet and select Format. You can add dollar signs and decimal points to your currency values, for example.

## Labeling & Titling the Chart

To truly make a chart your own, you'll have to add new labels and give the chart a title. Figures 5-66 and 5-67 show charts that have been customized.

Figure 5-66 shows a chart completely revamped with labels, titles, data, and perspective applied by the user. Figure 5-67 shows the same chart with new object styles and pattern fills applied.

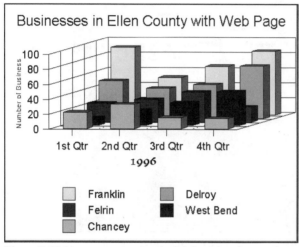

*Figure 5-66: You can customize the labels, titles, data, and perspective of the chart.*

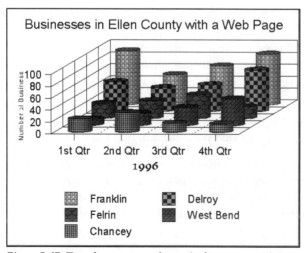

*Figure 5-67: To make even more dramatic changes, try using new object styles and patterned fills.*

Let's see how some of these changes were made:

1. We'll start by changing the title of the chart. Right-click on the title of the chart and select Title Properties from the pop-up menu. The Title Properties dialog box is displayed (see Figure 5-68).

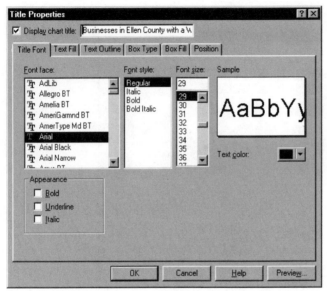

*Figure 5-68: The Title Font tab of the Title Properties dialog box.*

2. Check the Display chart title check box and type a title in the text box. If you type in a title that is much longer than the "Title of Chart" placeholder, you'll need to use a smaller font size. Use the Font face and other font options to achieve the appearance you want.

3. The other tabs let you add a box around your title, fill it with a pattern fill, and outline the text with various types of lines. Figure 5-69 shows a gradient fill selection.

4. Click OK to close the Title Properties dialog box.

5. Now, right-click on the numbers on the left side of the chart (0 through 100, arranged vertically), and click Primary Y Axis Properties in the pop-up menu. This displays the Primary Y Axis Properties dialog box. You can manipulate the Y-axis labels, title, and numbering type here.

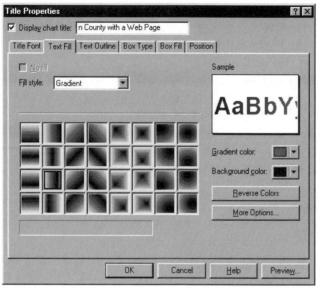

*Figure 5-69: Creating a title with a gradient fill using the Title Properties dialog box.*

6. Click on the Title Font tab. Make sure that Display title is checked. In Figure 5-70, the phrase Number of Businesses is the new title. Change the font type and size to suit you.

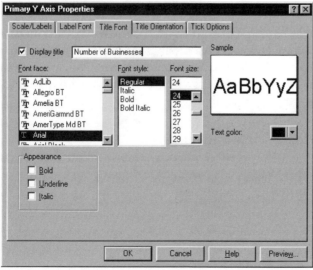

*Figure 5-70: The Title Font tab of the Primary Y Axis Properties dialog box.*

7. Click the Scale/Labels tab. This tab lets you change the numeric distance between each label on your Y-axis (in this case 20) and set a starting and ending value (in this case, the starting value is zero and ending value is 100).

8. Click the Tick Option tab. This tab lets you determines the number and type of little lines that connect the vertical numbers themselves with the grid. These are called ticks. You can choose to have a tick only at zero and 100, or have a tick connecting *each number* to the grid itself. In this case, a tick is connecting each number to the grid. Figure 5-71 shows ticks connecting each number along the Y-axis.

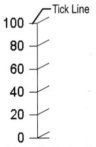

*Figure 5-71: Small tick lines connect each number to the grid.*

## Customizing the Appearance of Charts

As you edit the properties of your chart's components, you can customize your chart's appearance and data capabilities. The series, axis, frame, and legend of your chart all have properties, which we will discuss in this section. In addition, we'll look at how to switch between data groups and chart types, and investigate the Chart toolbar.

### Changing How Each Series Looks

Instead of using the same old rectangles to represent the data on your chart, you can use other shapes, like pyramids, cylinders, or octagons. Follow these steps to customize your shapes:

1. Right-click on any of the rectangular bars that represent data, and select Series Properties from the pop-up menu. The Series Properties dialog box is displayed (see Figure 5-72).

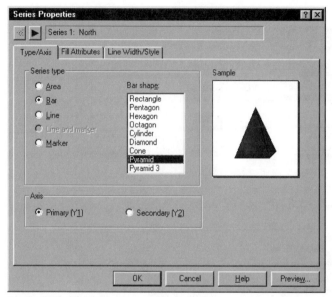

*Figure 5-72: The Series Properties dialog box.*

Each group of rectangles is a series. You must make changes to each group individually. At the top left of the Series Properties dialog box, you see two arrows. These let you switch from one series to another.

2. Click a shape in the Bar shape list to select a new shape for your current series. If you want to, change the fill and line attributes for the shape using the two other tabs.

3. When you are happy with the first series, click the left arrow at the top left of the dialog box to move on to the next series.

Once you have defined shapes for each series, click OK to close the dialog box.

## Changing the Appearance of Data Labels

Right-click on one of the data markers along the bottom of the chart, and select X-Axis Properties. This displays the X-Axis Properties dialog box (see Figure 5-73).

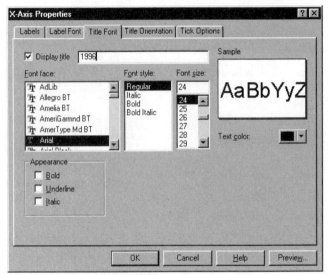

*Figure 5-73: The X-Axis Properties dialog box.*

In the X-Axis Properties dialog box, you can add a title for the X-axis labels. You can also change the font type, size, tick options, data label placement, and title orientation.

Note that you cannot use the X-Axis Properties dialog box to change the data labels themselves. To change the data labels, you must use the datasheet.

## Changing the Frame Properties

You can change the background of the chart as well. Figure 5-74 shows a graph with a patterned background and thickened frame borders. To make changes to your frame properties, right-click in between the grids of the graph and select Frame Properties. This displays the Frame Properties dialog box, which has two tabs (see Figure 5-75).

The Display Options tab lets you make changes to the lines around the frame of the chart.

The Fill tab lets you add patterns, colors, and fill to the background of the chart. In the example in Figure 5-74, light and dark brown were selected as the colors, along with a cross-hatch pattern.

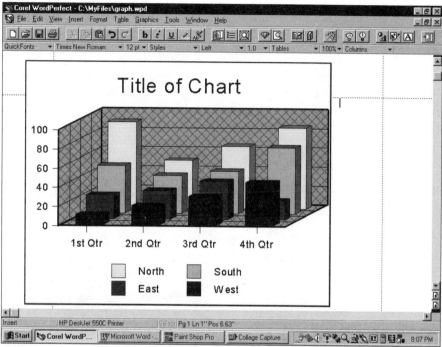

*Figure 5-74: A graph with a pattern and thickened frame lines applied.*

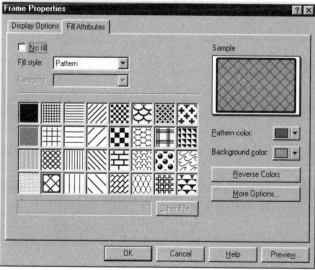

*Figure 5-75: The Frame Properties dialog box for adjusting frame colors and fills.*

## Legend Properties

The graph legend shows what each color rectangle means. It provides a key for the data series by identifying which color represents which subject. When you first create a chart, the legend reads North, South, East, and West. You can alter the legend properties to convey information appropriate to your chart—in Figure 5-66, for example, the legend lists cities in Ellen County.

Figure 5-76 shows the legend with a border around it. You can easily edit any aspect of how the legend appears by creating a label for it or changing the font, font size, and color.

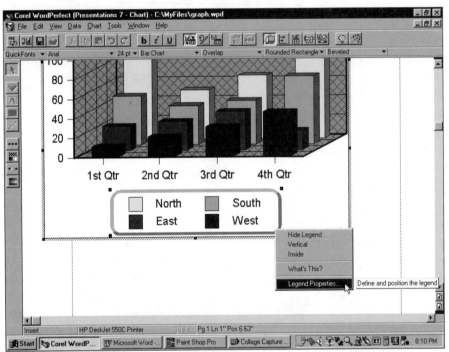

*Figure 5-76: A legend with a border around it. Right-clicking reveals the path to the Legend Properties dialog box.*

Right-click anywhere in the legend and select Legend Properties to display the Legend Properties dialog box (see Figure 5-77).

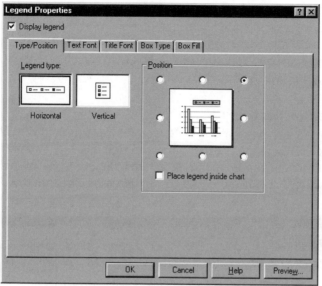

*Figure 5-77: The Legend Properties dialog box with the Type/Position tab showing.*

- The Type/Position tab of the Legend Properties dialog box lets you reposition the legend relative to the chart.

- Legends use two different kinds of text: the title text and the label text. You can set the font settings for the title text and the label text separately.

- The Box Type tab lets you choose from various types of boxes to surround the legend. Using a box around the legend can help you make your chart look clean.

- If you add a box using the Box Type tab, then several options become available in the Box Fill tab. The Box Fill tab lets you choose a pattern, gradient, texture, or picture fill for your box. Be careful about what kind of a box fill you select; you don't want to obscure your data with a loud fill.

**Tip**

*Don't click outside the chart until you are done editing! To perform the chart editing procedures we've discussed, you need to be in Chart Edit mode. If you click outside the chart, you immediately return to the WordPerfect window and normal mode. In normal mode, you can edit the box surrounding the chart, and the chart's position on the WordPerfect page. But to edit the chart again, you have to right-click on the chart and select Chart Object | Edit.*

## Changing Your Chart's Grid Properties

Right-click on any of the thin horizontal or vertical grid lines in your chart, and select Grid Properties from the pop-up menu to edit the chart's grid properties. In the Grid Properties dialog box, you can change the width and color of the grid lines in your chart.

## Creating a Box for Your Chart

You can create a box for your chart after you return to normal WordPerfect mode. Click anywhere outside the chart, then right-click on the chart, and select Border/Fill from the pop-up menu, as shown in Figure 5-78. This displays the standard Border/Fill dialog box, which we discussed earlier in this chapter.

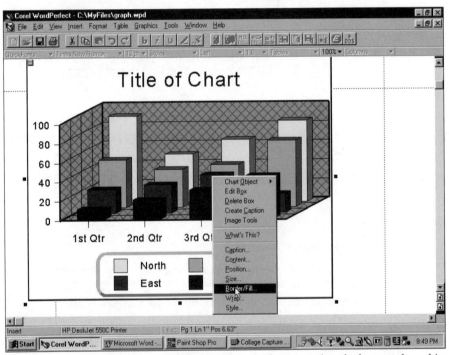

*Figure 5-78: After leaving Chart Edit mode, the standard menu options for boxes and graphics become available.*

## Changing the Chart Type

While in Chart Edit mode, right-click on any blank space inside the chart, and select Gallery from the pop-up menu. The Data Chart Gallery dialog box is displayed (see Figure 5-79). In this dialog box, you can select from 66 different kinds of charts—everything from pie charts to radar charts. The type of data you are displaying will determine which type of chart is most appropriate.

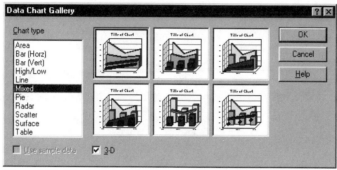

*Figure 5-79: The Data Chart Gallery dialog box.*

# Moving On

In this chapter, we discussed adding graphics of all sorts to your document. These include selections from WordPerfect's clip-art collection, photographs, WordPerfect Draw objects, and bitmaps. We also explored creating tables and graphs. We discovered that it's easy to add borders and fills to any WordPerfect graphic, including tables and graphs. What follows is our final chapter on WordPerfect. We'll be exploring ways to work faster and more efficiently in WordPerfect.

# 6

# Working Faster in WordPerfect 8

In this chapter, we'll discuss how you can customize the WordPerfect environment to help you work more efficiently. For example, you can add tools or menu choices to the toolbars or place a button on the toolbar that "plays back" a typed sequence (like a return address).

We'll also explain how to work with templates and save formatting as a style, explore the spell checker and grammar checker, and look at the find and replace feature. To round out WordPerfect's productivity tools, we'll discuss the outline and list creation tools, how to insert and review comments, and how to use macros.

## Enhancing the Property Bars

Until now, we've focused on the tools that are available on the Property bar by default, such as font selection, justification, and table creation. You know that the Property bar tools change depending on what you're currently doing in your document. You might not know, however, that the Property bar is customizable; you can change its appearance and add more features to it.

## Modifying the Property Bars

To add a new feature to the Property bar, right-click on it to display a pop-up menu. Click Settings to display the Customize Settings dialog box. Determine which Property bar to add features to, and click Edit to add the features. If you don't like the results, click the Reset button to return to the default settings for that particular Property bar.

To add a feature to the currently displayed Property bar, follow these steps:

1. Right-click on the Property bar and select Edit from the pop-up menu. This displays the Property Bar Editor (see Figure 6-1).

*Figure 6-1: The Property Bar Editor.*

2. In the Feature Categories drop-down list, select the name of the menu on which the feature that you want to add is located.

3. The Features list now displays each menu choice available on the menu you selected. In addition to those menu choices, you'll find many more features than are currently available from the menus, because including all of them on menus would make the menus too long. Select the item you want to add to the Property bar.

4. Click on Add Button (see Figure 6-2). The item you chose is now displayed as a new button on the right of the Property bar. You can also drag the item from the Features list to the Property bar.

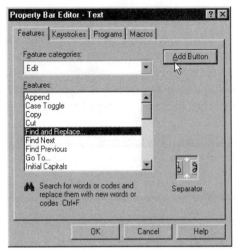

*Figure 6-2: Adding Find and Replace to the Property Bar.*

From now on, the item you selected is available as an icon on the Property bar. By the way, adding a feature to the Property bar *does not* remove it from its menu.

To specify which Property bar you want to add features to, right-click on the Property bar and select Settings from the pop-up menu (see Figure 6-3). In the Available property bars list, select the toolbar that you want to change. Click the Edit button to proceed and follow the steps described above.

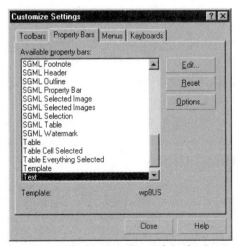

*Figure 6-3: The Property Bars tab in the Customize Settings dialog box.*

## Changing the Appearance of Property Bar Items

Instead of showing picture icons, you can display text labels or text labels and pictures for each tool on the Property bar. You can also enable scrolling for the toolbar, which is useful if you have so many items on your Property bar that they don't fit on one row. To change these settings, right-click on the Property bar, and select Settings from the pop-up menu. This displays the Customize Settings dialog box. Click the Options button to display the Property Bar Options dialog box (see Figure 6-4).

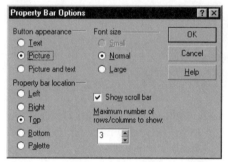

Figure 6-4: The Property Bar Options dialog box.

## Removing a Button

To remove a button from the Property bar, do the following:

1. Right-click on the Property bar, and select Edit from the pop-up menu. This displays the Property Bar Editor (see Figure 6-1).

2. Drag the button you want to delete from the Property bar to the Property Bar Editor. The button turns into a trash can.

3. Release the mouse button, and the icon disappears from the Property bar.

## Saving Keystroke Combinations

You can put a button on the Property bar that types text when you click on it. If you start many documents with the same opening paragraph, you could create a button that types that text for you when you click on it. To create a button that types saved text, follow these steps:

1. Right-click on the Property bar, and select Edit from the pop-up menu. The Property Bar Editor is displayed.

2. Click the Keystrokes tab.

3. In the appropriate field, type the text you want.

4. Click the Add Keystrokes button.

A new button appears on the Property bar. Click this button to insert the type you specified into your document.

In Figure 6-5, the Keystrokes feature recorded a name and address, which can be inserted into the document by clicking the button on the toolbar. You cannot edit the font size or style in this data box. To apply formatting, first insert the text, then format it as usual.

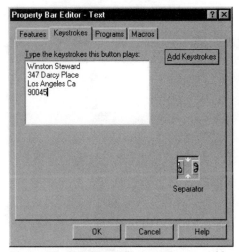

*Figure 6-5: Creating an "Instant Return Address" button and adding it to the Property bar.*

## Adding Programs to the Property Bar

So far, we've focused on buttons that are shortcuts for WordPerfect features or that type text for you. But WordPerfect provides another exciting feature—it lets you add programs to your Property bar. You can, for example, add a button to your Property bar that launches the Windows Calculator. To add a program button to your Property bar, follow these steps:

1. Right-click on the Property bar, and select Edit from the pop-up menu.

2. Click the Programs tab.

3. Click the Add Program button to display a Browse dialog box.

4. Locate the executable file that you want to make available on the Property bar and select it.

5. Click Open. A button for your program is added to the Property bar.

This feature is handy for attaching utility programs like PKZIP, screen capture tools, the Windows Calculator, or even PaintShop Pro.

Figure 6-6 shows the process of adding the Windows Calculator to the Property bar. The Calculator icon on the Property bar is circled.

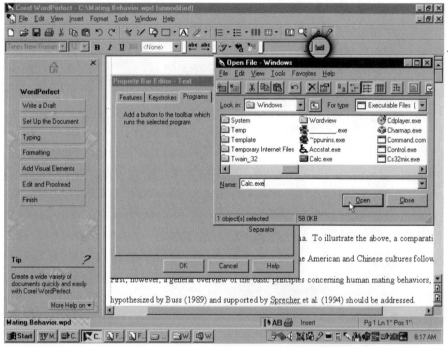

*Figure 6-6: Locate the Calculator program's executable file "calc.exe" and select it to add a calculator icon to your Property bar.*

## Putting a Macro on the Property Bar

A macro file contains a sequence of commands (which can be keystrokes or mouse-clicks). When you run the macro, it executes the saved commands. A macro could, for example, automatically open the last two saved documents or fill a table with a gradient pattern and thicken the outline. WordPerfect provides many useful macros. See the section later in this chapter for details on how to create and edit macros.

You can create buttons for your macros on your Property bar. Follow these steps:

1. Right-click on the Property bar, and select Edit from the pop-up menu. This displays the Property Bar Editor.

2. Click the Macros tab.

3. Click the Add Macro button to display the Select Macro dialog box (see Figure 6-7).

4. Click on the macro you want to add, and click the Select button.

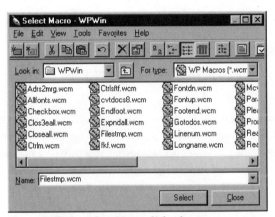

*Figure 6-7: The Select Macro dialog box.*

Often, it's hard to figure out from the filename what each macro does. To find out, right-click on a macro, select Properties from the pop-up menu, and click the Summary tab to display a short description of the macro.

Here are some particularly useful macros:

- **Expndall.wcm**—expands all the abbreviations in your document to the unabbreviated forms.

- **GotoDos.wcm**—opens a DOS window.

- **Saveall.wcm**—saves all open documents.

# Using a Template to Create a New Document

When you create a new document in WordPerfect, you don't have to select New and then stare fearfully at a blank page; WordPerfect provides lots of help to get you started. Before you begin typing on that blank page, consider using a template—a predesigned document that is much less work to use than building a page from scratch.

## Tip

*For an introduction to templates, see Chapter 2 "The Desktop Application Director & PerfectExpert," where we introduced templates using the PerfectExpert Project Creator.*

To access a template, do one of the following:

- On the Desktop Application Director (DAD), click the Project Creator icon.
- In WordPerfect, select File | New.

Either action displays the New Document dialog box. Click on the Create New tab, then double-click a template to open it.

Each template is designed to meet your needs for a particular document type. You can use them to avoid having to start over from scratch every time you need a document. Later in this chapter we'll discuss how to modify the templates.

## Transforming a Template Into Your Own Document

Let's start with the Personal Letter template and create our own letter from it. Follow these steps:

1. Access the list of templates by clicking File | New. This displays the New Document dialog box.

2. Click the Create New tab.

3. Double-click on Letter, Personal (see Figure 6-8).

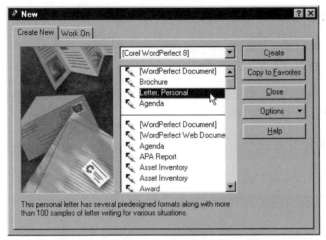

*Figure 6-8: Starting a letter using the Create New tab.*

4. A dialog box prompts you to provide return address information. If you have not yet personalized WordPerfect with your return address information, click OK to open the Address Book. Select Person, and input your address information.

5. Click OK to close the Address Book Add tab, and then OK again to close the Address Book itself.

6. A blank WordPerfect document appears with the Letter PerfectExpert (see Figure 6-9).

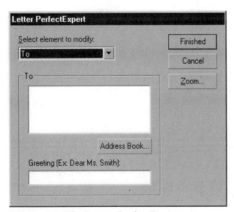

*Figure 6-9: The Letter PerfectExpert.*

The Letter PerfectExpert helps you standardize the appearance of your letters. The Letter PerfectExpert prompts you to fill in information for each letter element. When your letter appears on the page, WordPerfect arranges the elements on the page according to the type of letter you want to create. While using the Letter PerfectExpert, you won't see anything occur on the page of the letter itself. The Letter PerfectExpert does not create letter content. You will type in body text for your letter later.

7. Select a letter element that you want to modify in the Select Element to Modify drop-down list. Fill in the required information for the various elements.

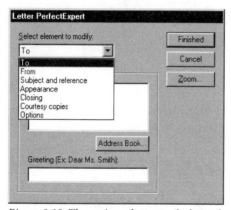

*Figure 6-10: The various elements of a letter from the template.*

WordPerfect will make a guess at the appropriate greeting. You can modify this field if necessary.

8. In the Appearance section, select a style for the letter.

9. Choose a closing style that's appropriate and decide whether to send courtesy copies of the letter to other recipients.

10. Click Finished to return to the normal WordPerfect view of the letter. You can now type in the actual body text of the letter.

Alas, you still are required to think of something to say in the body of your letter. Just select the placeholder Latin text and type your own text instead.

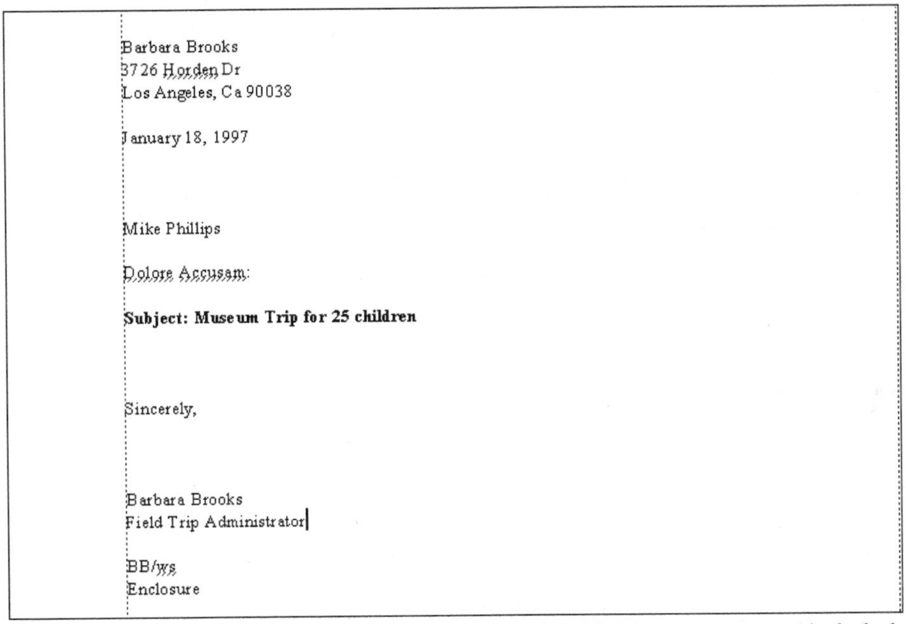

```
Barbara Brooks
3726 Horden Dr
Los Angeles, Ca 90038

January 18, 1997



Mike Phillips

Dolore Accusam:

Subject: Museum Trip for 25 children



Sincerely,



Barbara Brooks
Field Trip Administrator

BB/ws
Enclosure
```

*Figure 6-11: A letter with all the elements from the template filled in. You must provide the body of text.*

## Editing Templates to Suit Your Project

Instead of using the templates that WordPerfect provides "as is," you can customize them to suit your needs. Here's how to customize the Brochure template:

1. Select File | New again.

2. Select the Brochure template. The Template Information dialog box is displayed.

3. In the Template Information dialog box, type the brochure title and a descriptive subtitle or slogan in the appropriate fields.

4. Click OK, and your new brochure is displayed with the information you supplied positioned on the page.

But where did the information go? In the Brochure template, WordPerfect places the title and subtitle at the far right edge of the paper. (This is because when you print the page and fold it into thirds, this panel will end up being the front of the brochure.) But we can't see the information on our page.

5. In the Zoom drop-down list on the toolbar, select 50%. This makes the page smaller onscreen, so that you can see more of the page (see Figure 6-12).

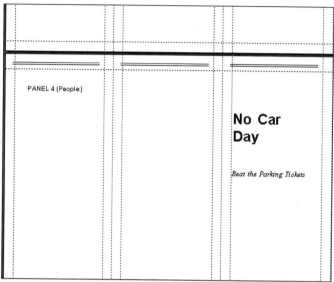

PANEL 4 (People)

**No Car Day**

*Beat the Parking Tickets*

*Figure 6-12: "Zooming back" to 50% shows the title of the brochure in the far right edge of the paper.*

6. If necessary, use the scroll bars to reposition the brochure so that you can see the rest of the page.

## Moving the Subtitle to a Better Location

At the bottom of the page, you'll see the phrase "Beat the Parking Tickets" (or whatever you used as a subtitle). Let's move this phrase to somewhere more suitable:

1. Select the entire subtitle phrase.

2. Right-click on the phrase, and select Cut from the pop-up menu. This moves the text to the Windows clipboard.

3. Click the mouse one space beneath the QuickArt object (kind of a "plume-in-ring" decoration). This is where we'll place the new text.

4. Right-click, and select Paste from the pop-up menu (see Figure 6-13). The subtitle phrase reappears.

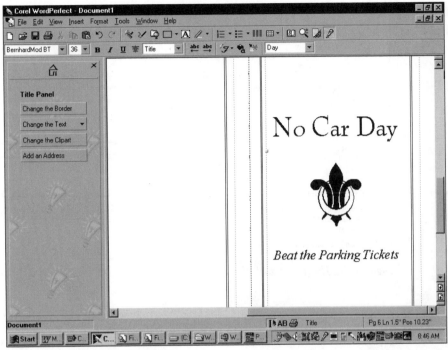

*Figure 6-13: Positioning the subtitle.*

5. Select the subtitle text again.

Now we are going to change the font size and justification of this phrase:

6. Click the Justification button on the Property bar and select Center from the drop-down list. Then click outside the Justification list to close it.

7. Make sure that your text is still selected, then click the Font Size drop-down list. Select 16 point. Then click outside the Font Size list to close it.

You've now typed in a title and subtitle for your brochure, repositioned the subtitle in a more desirable location, and resized the subtitle. Let's perform one more exercise with this brochure:

1. Use your scroll bars to move to the top left of the page. You'll notice a title that says "Panel1." This is placeholder text.

2. Select the phrase "Panel 1" and type "Our Thursday Plan" in its place.

3. Replace the placeholder text under "Our Thursday Plan" with a brief topic sentence introducing your main text (see Figure 6-14).

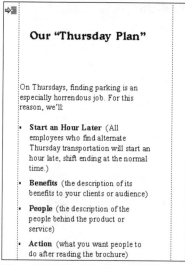

*Figure 6-14: The title "Panel 1" is replaced with relevant text.*

4. Now, keep erasing the placeholder text and replacing it with your own text. The template provides lots of convenient formatting for you.

This walk-through has given you an introduction to WordPerfect's templates, and has given me a chance to blow off steam about my second parking ticket in a month.

## Working With Styles

In WordPerfect, you can save any combination of text and paragraph formatting, including various menu selections, as a style. Styles can include line spacing options, margins, an inserted date, or a header. After saving the style, you can apply it to another section of your document. You can also create a watermark graphic (a faint background picture that appears on every page in your document) and save it as a style.

## Creating a Style

To create a style, follow these steps:

1. Select Format | Styles to display the Style List dialog.

2. Click the Create button to display the Styles Editor dialog box (see Figure 6-15).

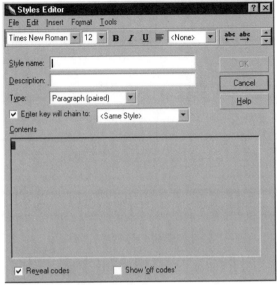

*Figure 6-15: Creating a style.*

3. In the Style name text box, type a name for your new style.

4. In the Description text box, type a brief description of the new style.

The Contents field will list all the selections you make for this style in the form of codes. Fortunately, you can ignore all these codes. Notice that the Styles Editor contains menus that correspond to the menus in WordPerfect.

5. Select items from the menus in the Styles Editor or from the Styles Editor toolbar to begin formatting your style. For example, select Format | Font to display the Font dialog box. You can set the font face, style, size, color, appearance, and position here, just to get started.

As you select items, you'll see corresponding codes in the Contents field.

6. Select an option from the Type drop-down list:

- **Paragraph (paired)**. When you apply the style, it is applied to the current paragraph.

- **Character (paired)**. When you apply the style, it is applied only to the currently selected text.

- **Paragraph (auto)**. When you apply the style, it is applied to every paragraph in your document.

- **Document (open)**. When you apply the style, it is applied to every paragraph in the document from your cursor forward.

7. Select an option in the Enter key will chain to drop-down list. Selecting None means that pressing Enter ends this style. Selecting Same Style means that pressing Enter creates another paragraph with this same style. Selecting a paragraph style means that pressing Enter creates a new paragraph with the specified style.

8. Click OK to leave the Styles Editor.

9. In the Style List dialog box, make sure your new style is selected in the Available Styles list.

10. Click the Options button, and choose Setup. Click the Current Document radio button to save this style only in the current document; click the Default Template radio button to save this style in the default template.

The default template is applied whenever you create a new, blank document.

11. Click OK to leave the Styles Setup dialog box.

12. Click Apply to close the Style List dialog box and apply the selected style, or click Close to close the dialog box without applying the selected style.

## Warning

*Be careful about creating text in your style. Creating a paragraph of text and saving it as a style might seem like a nice shortcut, because you can apply it quickly, but you can't really erase a style from a page. If you save actual text as a style, you could get stuck with text that's impossible to remove. It's safer to use formatting options only.*

## Applying a Style

Once you've saved your style, click the Style drop-down list on the Property bar, and select your style to apply it. For character styles, make sure that you've selected the text you want to apply the style to first. For paragraph styles, just click in the paragraph to which you want to apply the style.

## Working With QuickStyle

QuickStyle lets you save the formatting in effect for a section of text as a style. This can be quicker and easier than using the Styles Editor. You can then apply this new style to other paragraphs.

## Creating a QuickStyle

In Figure 6-16, the word "Duotone" is formatted with the font DellaRobia BT, at a size of 14 points, with bold and underlining.

To create a QuickStyle, follow these steps:

1. Select the formatted text.

2. Format the text exactly as you want it.

3. Select QuickStyle from the Style drop-down list in the Property bar (see Figure 6-16). This displays the QuickStyle dialog box (see Figure 6-17).

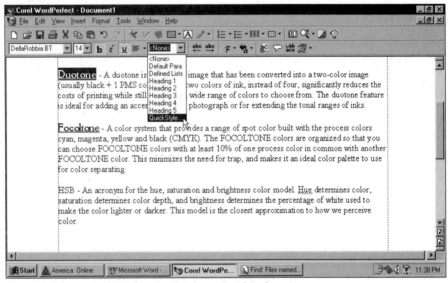

*Figure 6-16: Creating a style to be saved as a QuickStyle.*

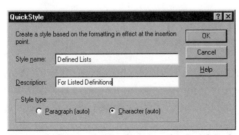

*Figure 6-17: Naming and saving the QuickStyle.*

4. Type in a name and description for your style.

5. Select a style type.

6. Click OK to save your style. It now appears in the Style drop-down list.

## Applying a QuickStyle

To apply your QuickStyle, select some text, then locate your style in the Style drop-down list on the Property bar and select it. In Figure 6-18, the term "HSB" will have the same formatting as the word "Duotone." Remember, you created the Defined Lists style based on the formatting of the word "Duotone" in the previous section.

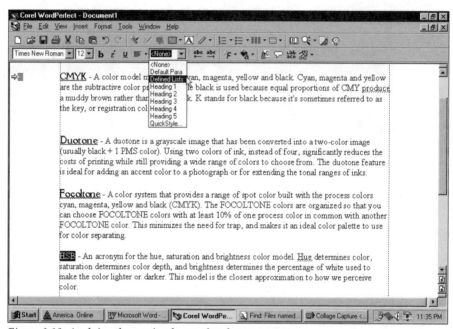

*Figure 6-18: Applying the previously saved style to new text.*

# WordPerfect's Outline Creator

If you think that creating outlines is a tedious chore, you'll love WordPerfect's Outline Creator. It automatically provides indenting and the number/letter system for various levels of the outline. The Outline Creator keeps track of which level is which, so you can click a button to view only the first level of headings, and hide everything else for the moment. You can type text under an outline heading, and then hide the text so that you can focus on the headings in your outline. If you decide that an entire section of your document belongs in a different place, you can easily move the headings and their subordinate text to a new location.

## Creating an Outline

To display the WordPerfect Outline bar at the top of the window, right-click on the standard toolbar (not the Property bar) and select Outline Tools. Begin typing your outline, using the Bullet or Numbering icons on the toolbar to create your outline's levels. Figure 6-19 shows an outline created with the Outline bar.

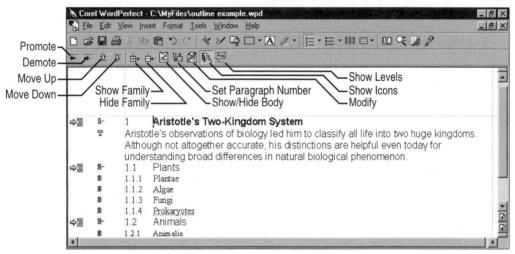

*Figure 6-19: An outline with the Outline bar visible onscreen.*

The various outline tools make it easy to create a comprehensive outline:

- **Promote**—changes the current outline item to one level higher.

- **Demote**—changes the current outline item to one level lower.

- **Move Up**—moves the current outline item (including any subordinate items) up in the outline.

- **Move Down**—moves the current outline item (including any subordinate items) down in the outline.

- **Show Family**—shows all the subordinate items of the current outline item.

- **Hide Family**—hides all the subordinate items of the current outline item.

- **Show/Hide Body**—toggles the display of the body text.

- **Set Paragraph Number**—lets you specify a paragraph number for the current item.

- **Modify**—lets you change the appearance of the outline.
- **Show Icons**—toggles the display of the outline icons in the margin.
- **Show Levels**—lets you control how many levels of the outline are displayed.

Figure 6-20 shows the same outline as above, but Outline controls were used to make only the top two levels visible.

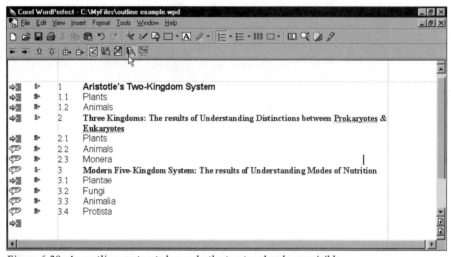

*Figure 6-20: An outline contracted so only the top two levels are visible.*

## Navigating the Outline Controls

Figure 6-21 shows an outline that also contains text. To move a text paragraph, select the T, or text, button on the Outline bar. To make the paragraph text invisible, click the Hide Body Text button on the Outline bar.

Click on a number in the margin of the outline to select that entire line. To promote or demote the outline item, click the appropriate button on the Outline bar. To select an entire outline segment, click a number followed by a hyphen. Then, click an arrow to promote or demote the entire section. To adjust the tab marks, click the fat, right-facing arrow (see Figure 6-22).

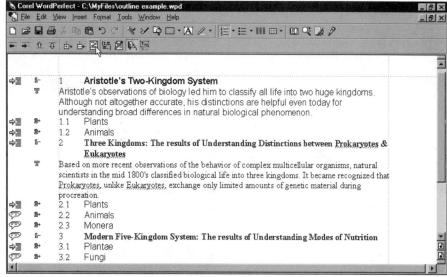

*Figure 6-21: Paragraph text in the outline.*

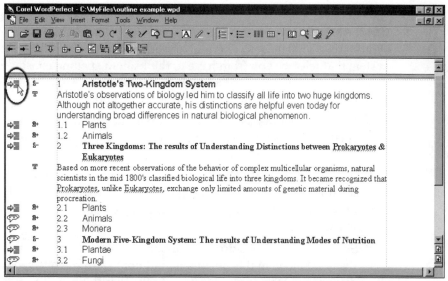

*Figure 6-22: Turning on a tab control to adjust the indent distance of an outline level.*

The Modify button controls the outline style. Changing to a different outline style totally changes the appearance of your outline.

# Improving Your Writing

WordPerfect helps you improve your writing with tools for correcting your spelling, suggesting synonyms, critiquing your grammar, and even analyzing the readability of your document. Let's take a look at some of those writing tools.

## Checking Your Spelling

Spell-as-you-go automatically underlines in red every spelling error it detects. Right-click on a misspelled word to see a list of suggestions at the top of the pop-up menu. Click a suggestion to fix the misspelling. If QuickCorrect recognizes your misspelling, it will correct it automatically. For example, if you type "teh," WordPerfect will automatically correct this to "the."

The Spell Checker searches your document for spelling errors, offers corrections, and lets you identify misspelling for automatic correction. Let's take a closer look at these two features.

### Spell-As-You-Go

WordPerfect's Spell-as-you-go is a very advanced automated spell-checking system that releases you from have to think about spelling constantly. If you misspell a word, it is underlined with a curly red line. Right-click a word that is flagged as misspelled, and you'll have several options. You can:

- Choose a replacement word. The top of the pop-menu offers a number of spelling suggestions. Click one to use the suggestion instead of your misspelled word (see Figure 6-23).

- Add the word to the WordPerfect dictionary. Choose Add. This Add feature allows you to add unique words or proper names to the dictionary. Once you have added a word to the dictionary, the red underlining will disappear.

- Skip the word. The Skip in Document feature tells WordPerfect to leave the word alone in this document, but not to add the selected word to the dictionary. Once a word is added to the WordPerfect dictionary, it will never be flagged as misspelled. Skip in Document lets you remove the red underline without adding the word to your dictionary.

- Choose a replacement word and specify that you always want WordPerfect to make this correction automatically. Click QuickCorrect, as shown in Figure 6-23, and select the correct spelling.

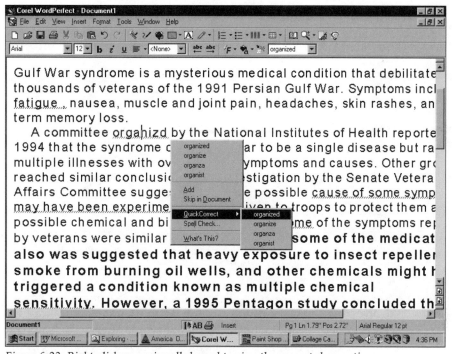

*Figure 6-23: Right-click on a misspelled word to view the suggested corrections.*

**Spelling Shortcuts**   You can use QuickCorrect creatively; for example, to automatically type a long phrase like "Los Angeles County Board of Registrars" using only a few letters, like "lacb." Then, typing "lacb" will create the phrase "Los Angeles County Board of Registrars."

Select Tools | QuickCorrect to display the QuickCorrect dialog box (see Figure 6-24). In the Replace text box, type the short, easy phrase. In the With text box, type in the longer phrase that you want to replace the short phrase with. Click Add Entry to add this item to your list. Click OK to close the dialog box. Now, try typing "lacb" in your document and QuickCorrect replaces it with the official "Los Angeles County Board of Registrars."

*Figure 6-24: The QuickCorrect dialog box. In your document, typing the short phrase on the left results in the long phrase on the right.*

**Correcting Capitalization Errors & Double Spaces**  You can tell WordPerfect to automatically capitalize words after periods, fix unwanted DOuble CAps, change the space after a sentence to your specifications, and remove extra spaces after words. Follow these steps:

1. Select Tools | QuickCorrect to display the QuickCorrect dialog box.

2. Click the Format-As-You-Go tab.

This tab is crammed with various options for sentence correction and format-as-you-go.

By default, this Format-As-You-Go tab defaults to the most standard usage. It makes sure only one space occurs between words and sentences, capitalizes most words that occur after a period, question mark, or exclamation mark, and corrects all DOuble CAps within words.

3. Make any changes to the settings that you want.

4. Click OK to apply your changes.

**Specifying Exceptions to Automatic Capitalization**  The Format-As-You-Go tab contains an Exceptions button. Click it to display the Exception List, where you can tell WordPerfect when to bypass automatic capitalization after a period. For example, you would not want the "o" in "of" in the phrase "Dept. of Motor Vehicles" capitalized just because it comes after a period. You can add exceptions to the list, or delete exceptions that are getting in the way.

## Using the Spell Checker Efficiently

The Spell Checker lets you check every word in your document at one time, instead of using QuickCorrect to fix one word at a time as you notice them. While using QuickCorrect, you may have instructed WordPerfect to skip certain words. You can force the Spell Checker to check all the text. Select Tools | Spell Check and click the Options button. In the pop-up menu, check the Recheck all Text option (see Figure 6-25).

Other choices in the Options pop-up menu let you instruct the Spell Checker to ignore irregular capitalization, which may be helpful for unusual proper nouns, or for a piece of poetry that demands the e.e. cummings treatment.

The Spell Checker's Auto Replace button is similar to QuickCorrect, but more automated. In Figure 6-25, clicking Auto Replace would cause every instance of "referenc" to be replaced with "reference."

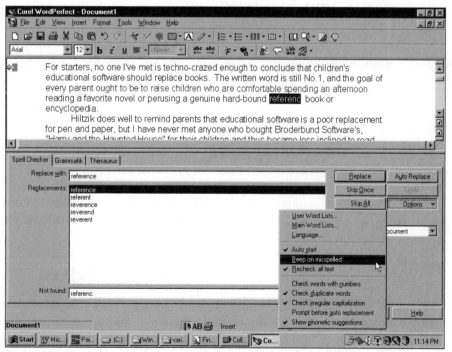

*Figure 6-25: Setting up Auto Replace to automatically fix a particular spelling error.*

### Using QuickWords

The QuickWords feature lets you type in certain characters and have WordPerfect replace them with words or phrases. This is very similar to the example we discussed above in the Spell-As-You-Go section. Here's how to use QuickWords:

1. Select a word or phrase in your text for which you want to create a QuickWord.

2. Select Tools | QuickWords to display the QuickWords tab in the QuickCorrect dialog box.

3. In the Abbreviated Form text area, type in the two or three letters you'd like to type to generate this phrase.

4. Click the Add Entry button.

5. Click OK to close the dialog box.

The next time you type the sequence you defined in the Abbreviated Form text area, your word or phrase is displayed.

## Correcting Your Grammar

Like Spell-As-You-Go, Grammar-As-You-Go underlines errors it finds as you type, but Grammar-As-You-Go uses blue instead of red. Right-click the underlined phrase to reveal a suggested correction for the phrase. Grammatik is a feature you implement after you've typed your document; it provides in-depth analysis of the grammar in your work.

### Using Grammar-As-You-Go

WordPerfect checks your work for grammar errors as you type. Potential errors are underlined with a curvy blue line. Right-click on the word or phrase to display a suggestion to correct the item. For more detailed information, click Grammatik (see Figure 6-26) to display the Grammatik dialog box, shown in Figure 6-27.

Grammatik will look for errors in verb agreement, improper clauses, dangling participles, and basic grammatical errors. If Grammatik finds an error, the error is highlighted in the main text of the document, and suggestions are displayed in the Grammatik dialog box. Click Replace to accept the selected suggestion. At the bottom of the Grammatik dialog box, Grammatik explains the error.

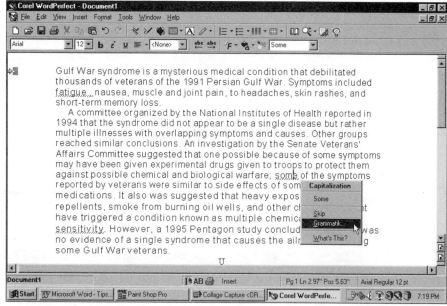

*Figure 6-26: Right-clicking on a word with a grammar error to open Grammatik.*

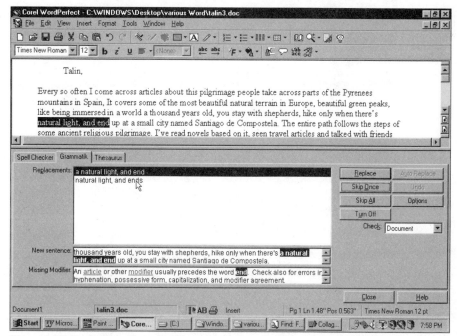

*Figure 6-27: Evaluating Grammatik's suggestions to fix a grammar error.*

## Grammar Checking Your Entire Document

To check your entire document for correct grammar, select Tools | Grammatik. Each questionable phrase is displayed in the Replacements section of the Grammatik dialog box, with a suggested new sentence below it. After you accept or reject the suggestion, Grammatik moves on to the next phrase.

Grammatik offers some unique features, which you can access by clicking the Options button and selecting Analysis from the pop-up menu. For example, if you are not sure how to apply the advice that Grammatik offers, select Options, then Analysis, then Parts of Speech. Your document is display one line at a time; each word's part of speech is identified (see Figure 6-28).

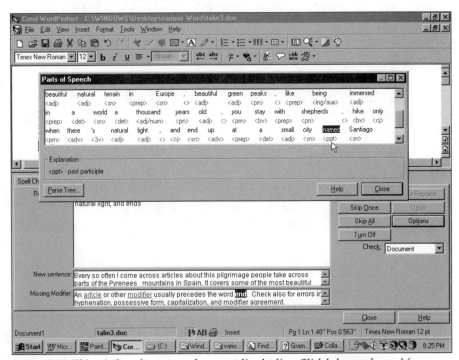

*Figure 6-28: This window shows your document line by line. Click below each word for a definition of its parts of speech.*

**Checking the Readability of Your Work**    Grammatik's Options will analyze the complexity and readability of your work. Select Tools | Grammatik, then Options, then Analysis, then Readability. You can compare your document to other works, such as a Hemingway short story, and determine whether you need shorter sentences or maybe a slightly less flowery vocabulary

The Readability option also analyzes your work according to the Flesch-Kincaid formula, which provides a measure of the complexity of your text. Figure 6-29 shows a short story measured against such parameters. The bar scale indicates that a 12th grade education is necessary for comprehending this story, and that sentence complexity rates a whopping 78 percent. This high-flown prose is definitely not bound for *People* magazine!

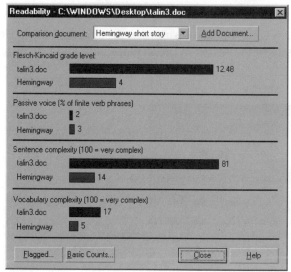

*Figure 6-29: A graph showing the readability of a short story. In this example, the story is compared with a Hemingway short story. Other examples for comparison are the Gettysburg Address and a complex instruction manual.*

## Counting Your Document's Words, Paragraphs & Long Sentences

Another analysis tool is the Basic Counts command. Click it to find out how many sentences in your document are particularly long or short, the average number of syllables per word, the total number of words and paragraphs, and the average number of words per sentence. If you are a journalist with a strict editor or a student who has to write to specific guidelines, quick access to this information can be critical.

# Finding & Replacing Text & Formatting

You can automatically locate any group of letters, words, or a phrase in your document. To do so, select Edit | Find and type in the text string you want to search for (see Figure 6-30).

## Finding & Replacing Text

You can click Find to view the next instance of the specified text string, or you can replace the string with the text in the Replace with text box, as shown in Figure 6-30.

*Figure 6-30: The Find and Replace dialog box. The user is about to replace every instance of RBG& with the words Red Green Blue.*

Click the Replace button to search the document for the next instance of the text string you are looking for and to replace it with the new text. Click Replace All to search the document for every instance of the string and replace every one with the new text.

The Find and Replace feature is invaluable for many tasks; for example, searching a document for double periods and removing them (simply type ".." in the Find text box and type "." in the Replace with text box). You can also use the Find feature to move around a long document; type in a key word or phrase into the Find text box to locate a particular section. If you decide to rename a character in your novel, you can use Find and Replace to locate and change every instance of that name in your document.

You can restrict the Find feature so that it only finds words that match the case of the specified word exactly; for example, replacing every instance of "Bill," but leaving "bill" untouched. Select Match | Case to force WordPerfect to match the case.

To restrict your search even further, you can specify a font for the located text. Select Match | Font and specify the font settings you want.

## Finding & Replacing Formatted Text

To search for particular formatting in your text, choose Match | Codes and specify the codes you want WordPerfect to locate. You can search for tabs, italics, changes in font size, or for hidden text, and replace the formatting with different formatting. Figure 6-31 shows the setting for searching for a change in font size.

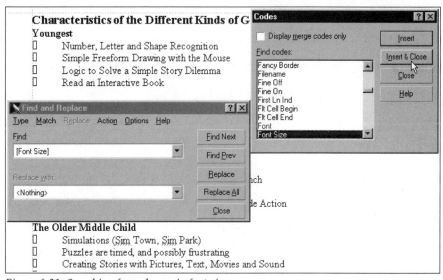

*Figure 6-31: Searching for a change in font size.*

# Working With Comments

Select Insert | Comment | Create to create a new comment. The Comment bar is displayed at the top of the window (see Figure 6-32). Authors or editors can use comments to put notes in the text.

Type in some comment text. You can use the Comment bar to insert your name, initials, the date, or the time. When you are finished, select File | Close to return to your WordPerfect document. The comment appears as a tiny text bubble icon in the left margin of the document.

*Figure 6-32: The Comment bar. You can type your comment, and add your name, the date, and the time. The comment initially appears in the text as a tiny text bubble in the left margin.*

To see the comment, click the icon (see Figure 6-33). Click again to close the comment.

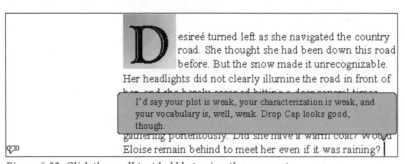

*Figure 6-33: Click the small text bubble to view the comment.*

Double-click the comment icon to edit the comment. If you want to navigate through the comments, use the Next and Previous Comment buttons on the Comment bar. (This feature is available only while you are editing your comments.)

If you want to turn comments off, select Tools | Settings and double-click the Display icon. In the Display Settings dialog box, uncheck the Comments check box and click OK. Click Close to close the Settings dialog box. This does not remove the comments; it only hides them. If you return to the Display Settings dialog box and check the Comments box again, the comment icons reappear.

To change the name or initial of the commentator, or to change the background color for the comment itself, select Tool | Settings and double-click the Environment icon.

## Working With Lists & Sorting a Document

WordPerfect provides tools for locating and sorting repeating phrases in your document, grouping them into lists, indexes, and cross-references. It's also very easy to highlight certain phrases as you read along, and generate a table of contents based on your highlights. We'll learn to do these things in the following sections.

### Creating Cross-References in a Document

Figure 6-34 shows essays on the lives of three artists, each related by work and nationality. Notice the hand hovering over the numeral "1" at the top. A cross-reference was created there. When this number is clicked, the reader jumps to the link that the author created. In this case, the target is on the same page, and the document will scroll to the next paragraph to the phrase "Mexican painter" beside the name "Kahlo Frida." A link can be created to another page, another document, or a World Wide Web site.

Here's how to create a cross-reference:

1. Select a reference point, which the reader sees first. At this reference point you will type some linking text; for example, "See also page 22."

2. Select Tools | Reference | Cross-Reference. The Cross-Reference toolbar is added at the top of the window. Make sure your cursor is located where you want the reference number to appear, and type a short, memorable text phrase in the Target text box.

3. Click the Reference drop-down menu on the toolbar, and select Page.

4. Click Mark Reference. You have now created a reference number; a "jumping-off point" to the target. The target is where the reader goes after clicking this reference number.

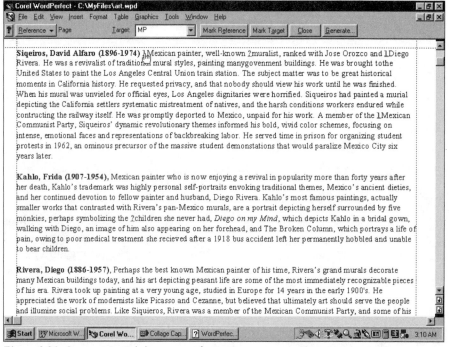

*Figure 6-34: An essay containing cross-references.*

5. Now, position your cursor at the point in your document where you want the reference to take the reader. Make sure that the same text phrase is still present in the Target text box.

6. Click Mark Target. A question mark appears at the reference location.

7. Click the Generate button on the toolbar. A number replaces the cross-reference, which indicates that the cross-reference has been created.

You can now click on the cross-reference number to jump to the target. Repeat this procedure to create as many cross-references as you want. This will highlight the importance of using short, memorable phrases in the Target text box—these phrases are the only way to keep track of and edit your cross-references.

Let's review this process, selecting entire words as reference and target points, rather than just marking the insertion point of the blinking cursor:

1. Select Tools | Reference | Cross-Reference to display the Cross-Reference bar at the top of the window.

2. Select a word or phrase in your document. This will become the link that the reader clicks.

3. In the Cross-Reference bar, click the Reference drop-down menu and select Page.

4. Type text in the Target text box and click Mark Reference. Notice that in Figure 6-34, the author typed MP (short for "Mexican Painter").

5. Select a word in your document as the target link. Click Mark Target.

Repeat this process as often as you want.

The Cross-Reference feature does have some limitations:

- You can only link one target to one reference; you cannot create a chain of links.

- You cannot make the target link back to the reference, which would create a loop. You can work around this limitation by creating one link from "Rivera" early in the document, then creating a link using his first name ("Diego") later in the document and sending that link to another instance where the name appears.

If you create links on other pages in your document, you'll notice that the numbers used to mark the links correspond to the page numbers. That's because we've used the Page settings in the Reference drop-down menu.

When you've created all the links you want, click the Generate button on the Cross-Reference bar. In the Generate dialog box, check Save Subdocuments and Build Hypertext Links. WordPerfect then generates the links. Even for a large number of links, this should take less than a minute.

## Creating & Using Bookmarks

For a long document, you may want to create bookmarks to help you navigate your document. You could, for example, bookmark the major sections of your document. To go to one of those sections, you would then use the bookmarks.

To create a Bookmark, follow these steps:

1. Place the cursor where you want the bookmark to be located, and select Tools | Bookmark. This displays the Bookmark dialog box.

2. Click the Create button to display the Create Bookmark dialog box. WordPerfect provides a default name for your bookmark (see Figure 6-35).

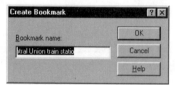

*Figure 6-35: The Create Bookmark dialog box.*

3. Edit the bookmark name to something useful. Remember that in a long document with many bookmarks, a long, descriptive bookmark could be very useful.

4. Click OK. Your new bookmark now appears in the Bookmark list.

If you do not specify a name for the bookmark, WordPerfect inserts a QuickMark (see Figure 6-36). QuickMarks let you set sequential placeholders in your document rapidly, but every QuickMark is labeled "QuickMark," which makes it impossible to figure out which QuickMark is where.

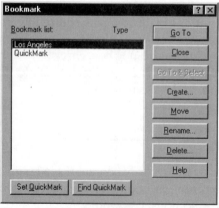

*Figure 6-36: The Bookmark list shows the first bookmark. The second bookmark is a QuickMark.*

To use the bookmarks for navigation, select Tools | Bookmark, select a bookmark, then click the Go To button. This takes you to that bookmark in the document.

You can only set bookmarks in the current document. You cannot create a bookmark to another document or to a World Wide Web site.

## Creating Text-Based Cross-References

You can use bookmarks to create a way for your readers to find each instance of a particular word. In the artist example above, one such word might be "muralists." This word could appear as a footnote in the text and point toward the next instance of the word in your document.

To create such text-based references, first use the bookmark feature to bookmark each instance of the word. Then, move through your bookmarks and for each one create a footnote in the text; for example, "see also page xx, 'Muralists'."

This method lets you link as many references as you like. The Footnote Options dialog box (shown in Figure 6-37) lets you insert a footnote right in the text itself, not just at the bottom of the page. To display this dialog box, click Insert | Footnote/Endnote, then select the Options button, then select Advanced.

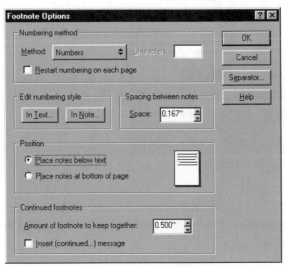

*Figure 6-37: The Footnote Options dialog box.*

# Creating & Using Macros

A **macro** is a set of recorded commands, such as keystrokes and mouse-clicks. WordPerfect comes with many ready-to-use macros. This means that someone at Corel Corporation actually performed a task in WordPerfect and recorded these actions using the Macro feature. They saved the macro and made the macro file available to you. Click on the macro, and the recorded commands "play back" in your document.

## Using Existing Macros

You can use any macro by selecting Tools | Macro | Play. This displays the Select Macro dialog box (see Figure 6-38), where you can choose a macro. Double-click the macro to play it back.

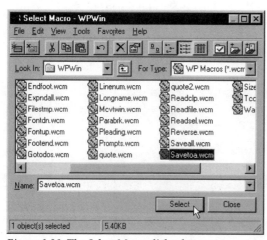

*Figure 6-38: The Select Macro dialog box.*

The savetoa.wcm macro saves the current document on your hard drive and saves a copy to a disk in your floppy drive. (All WordPerfect macros have a .wcm file extension.)

If you have a macro that you use frequently, you can add a button for the macro to your toolbar. This was discussed earlier in this chapter.

## Creating & Using Your Own Macros

The controls you use to create a macro are very intuitive; they function just like controls on a tape recorder. The Macro toolbar's Record, Pause, Stop, and Play buttons provide all you need to create simple, useful macros (see Figure 6-39).

As an example, we are going to create a macro that turns ordinary text into decoratively formatted text, as shown in Figure 6-40.

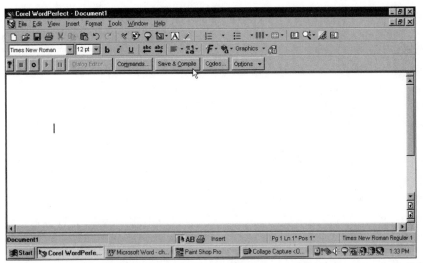

*Figure 6-39: In this figure the cursor is shown saving a macro. The button towards the left, with the small round symbol on it, is the Record Macro button.*

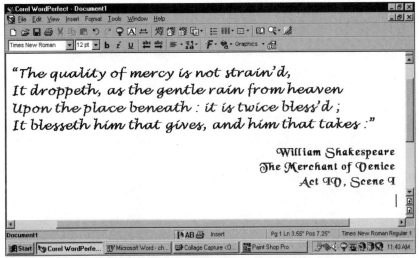

*Figure 6-40: Text automatically formatted by a user-created macro.*

The macro will apply the Lucida Handwriting font to the selected text, change the font size to 14, bold it, and apply increased letterspacing. Using the macro, you'll be able to do all of this with a single click. Here's how to create the macro:

1. Rehearse your macro so that you can run through it smoothly without mistakes. If many steps are involved, consider writing them down. It doesn't matter if you have to pause for a second to remember what to do next, or to view your notes. The macro will not record any time lags in between your keystrokes or mouse-clicks. It is, however, very important that you record only the steps in the macro.

2. Click Tools | Macros | Record to display the Record Macros dialog box.

3. Provide a name for your macro.

4. Click Record to save the name and begin recording. You are now in Record mode. As they say, "it's show time, folks."

5. Perform all your keystrokes and mouse-clicks. WordPerfect records any text you type in addition to the commands. For example, you can create a macro that places a fully formatted return address at the upper right of your document.

For our macro, perform these steps:

   5a. Click the Font drop-down list on the toolbar. Type the letter L to jump to the fonts that begin with the letter L.

   5b. Select Lucida Handwriting and click.

   5c. Click the Font Size drop-down list and select 14 points.

   5d. Click the Bold button.

   5e. Select Format | Typesetting | Word/Letter Spacing.

   5f. In the Letterspacing pane, click the Percent of Optimal check box, and change the number to 118%.

   5g. Click OK to close the Typesetting dialog box.

Now, to finish recording the Macro:

6. Click the Stop Record button on the Macro toolbar.

7. Select Save & Compile on the Macro toolbar. Since you already named your macro, you are not prompted again for additional information.

Now you need to create a summary for your macro, so you can identify it easily later:

1. Click Tools I Macro I Edit, and double-click on the macro you just created. The macro's commands are displayed in your window.

2. Select File I Properties, and type in a descriptive name (see Figure 6-41).

3. Save the macro. Now you can right-click on the new macro in the Browse menu, select Properties from the pop-up menu, and view the description text you added in the Summary tab.

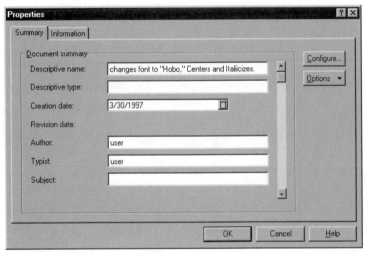

*Figure 6-41: Typing in a descriptive name for a macro on the Summary tab of the Properties dialog box.*

# Moving On

In this chapter, we covered how to edit the Property bar, adding your own features and convenient tools. We looked at how to work with templates and create styles and outlines. We then explored tools to improve your writing, such as WordPerfect's Spelling and Grammar checkers, and finding and replacing text. We discussed working with comments, lists, cross-references, and indexing tools. Finally, we learned about WordPerfect's macro feature. In the next chapter, we'll begin exploring WordPerfect's multimedia program, Presentations 8.

## Part III

# Presentations

# 7

# Corel Presentations 8: Learning the Basics

Corel Presentations is an application that lets you create professional-looking slide shows, overhead transparencies, and other presentation materials including audience handouts and speaker notes. You can create presentations to be displayed on your computer, print out your presentations, or create presentations that can be viewed on other computers, even if the other computer doesn't have Corel Presentations installed. Finally, you can add animation, sound, and other special effects to create the image you want. Your presentation is limited only by your imagination!

## Creating a New Slide Show

Open Presentations by clicking on its icon in the Desktop Application Director on your Windows desktop. When Presentations first opens, you have a choice: either open an existing presentation or create a new presentation. Click on the Create New tab (see Figure 7-1), then choose Presentations Slide Show to start creating your own slide show.

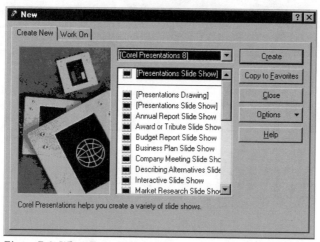

*Figure 7-1: When Presentations starts, you are asked to open an existing presentation or create a new one.*

## Working With the Gallery Masters

Your first assignment is to choose a "master" slide from the Startup Master Gallery. A master provides the framework for your presentation. When you select a master, the background color, design, and type style are chosen, and those features are then applied to each slide in your presentation. Worried about picking the right one? Make a choice now and you can change your mind later. If you decide you want to change the master design of your presentation, right-click on any slide. Select Master Gallery from the pop-up menu and choose a new master for your entire presentation.

From the masters displayed onscreen, click on one, or click on Category to view masters from different categories. Click the master design you like, then click OK. Your first slide appears onscreen, with the background you chose. You'll see a designated place for a title and a subtitle (see Figure 7-2).

Double-click on the title area and your cursor appears as a vertical blinking line in the title area. Type your title. Press Enter if you need a second line. Double-click on the subtitle area to enter a subtitle. If you don't need the subtitle, single-click on the area so the area is selected (black handles appear on the outside edges), then press the Delete key (see Figure 7-3).

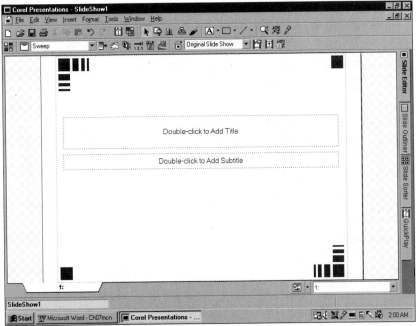

*Figure 7-2: Your first slide sports the background you selected, and there are designated spaces for a title and subtitle.*

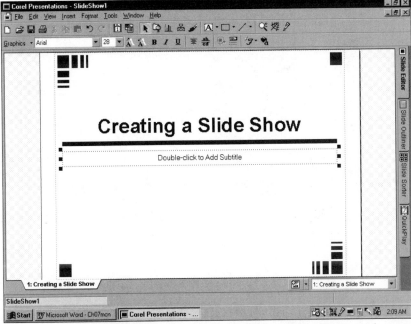

*Figure 7-3: Enter text in the title areas of your slide by first double-clicking on the area, then typing your text.*

## Adding Slides to Your Presentation

To add a new slide to your presentation, select Insert | New Slide. The New Slide dialog box appears (see Figure 7-4). Enter the number of slides you want to add, click on a Layout selection, then click OK.

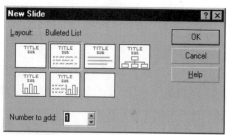

*Figure 7-4: The New Slide dialog box appears when you click on Insert | New Slide.*

When you click OK, the first of your new slides appears onscreen, ready for you to add titles or other information.

### Slide Layout Choices

Presentations offers six choices of predefined layouts, and a blank layout choice as well. The layouts provide placeholders for headings, body text, and certain graphic images. Predefined layouts include:

- **Title.** The slide has a placeholder for title and subtitle.

- **Bulleted List.** The slide has placeholders for title, subtitle, and a bulleted list.

- **Text.** The slide has placeholders for title, subtitle, and a text box.

- **Org Chart.** The slide has placeholders for title, subtitle, and an organization chart.

- **Data Chart.** The slide has placeholders for title, subtitle, and a data chart.

- **Combination.** The slide has placeholders for title, subtitle, a data chart, and a bulleted list.

## Playing Your Slide Show

Whether your show is still in pretty raw form or a finished product, you can play the show at any time to see how it looks in a presentation format.

To view your slide show, click on the Play Show button (shown in left margin) on your toolbar. The slide show begins with slide one, filling your screen. Click the left mouse button, or press the spacebar, each time you want to advance a slide. When your last slide has played, you will be returned to the screen on which you created your slides.

# The Presentation Toolbar

The standard toolbar in Presentations has a number of similarities with the other Corel programs as well as some features that are unique.

## Toolbar Features in Common With Corel Programs

The left and right sides of the Presentations toolbar features tools familiar to users of other Corel programs.

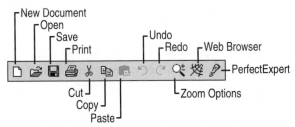

*Figure 7-5: The tools Presentations shares with other Corel programs.*

## Toolbar Features Unique to Presentations

Presentations has its own group of toolbar icons that you can use in your slide shows.

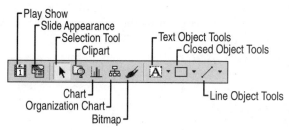

*Figure 7-6: Tools unique to Presentations.*

## Editing Presentation Toolbar Preferences

Not content with the buttons on your toolbar? Okay, have it your own way:

1. Right-click on the toolbar and choose Edit.

2. You will be asked if you want to make a copy of the toolbar that you can edit. Click on Yes.

3. In the Copy Toolbar box that appears, enter a name (such as My Toolbar) for you new toolbar. Click on OK.

4. When the Toolbar Editor dialog box appears you can click on a feature in the dialog box, then click on the Add Button button to add a button for that feature to your toolbar. You can drag unwanted buttons right off the toolbar and deposit them in the wide open space of your desktop screen. Drag buttons around on the toolbar if you want to change the order of the buttons. Click on OK when you're happy with your new toolbar.

The next time you open Presentations you will see your toolbar in place of the original slide show toolbar.

## Welcome to the Property Bar

As with the other Corel Suite programs, Presentations comes equipped with an intelligent toolbar, the Property bar. The Property bar responds to the action onscreen, changing its tools depending on what type of object is presently selected or what action is being performed. You cannot edit or change the Property bar; it has a life of its own.

For example, if you are entering text on your slide, the Property bar includes buttons for features such as font, type size, justification, line spacing, and so on.

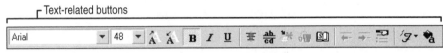

*Figure 7-7: The Property bar responds to your current needs.*

# Working With the Slide Views

Presentations provides you with three ways in which to look at and work with your slides: the Slide Editor view, the Slide Outliner view, and the Slide Sorter view. Use the one that fits your needs at the moment, then easily flip over to another view when required.

## The Slide Editor View

Use the Slide Editor view to change the appearance of individual slides. Edit the text, add graphics, cut, paste, drag, change color, resize, move, play to your heart's content. Choose Slide Editor view by clicking on the Slide Editor tab at the right side of your Presentations window (see Figure 7-8).

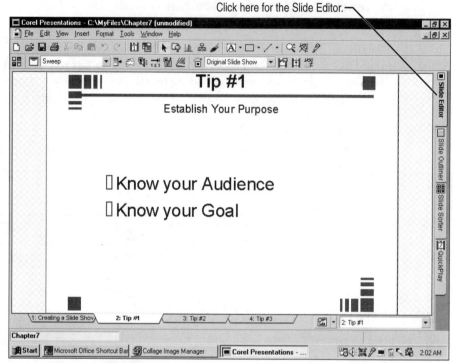

*Figure 7-8: You can change the information on your slide in the Slide Editor view.*

## Adding Text to Your Slide

Many slide layouts come equipped with centered boxes for titles, subtitles, and other text. You can add to the text boxes already there, you can delete the ones that are there and replace them with your own, or you can even start from a blank layout and add everything from scratch.

To add text to your slide, follow these steps:

1. Click on the down arrow next to the Text Object Tools button on the toolbar. A submenu appears (see Figure 7-9).

2. Choose among a regular text box, a single line of text, a bulleted list, or a TextArt object.

3. Drag in your slide to create a rectangular shape for your text, or click once to indicate where you want the text to begin—the text will continue to the right margin of the slide if you don't give the text the confines of a rectangle.

4. Begin entering your text. The text will wrap within the text box and the text box will increase in height to accommodate your text.

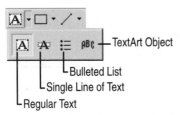

*Figure 7-9: Choose from several types of text boxes.*

### Editing Text in Your Slide

Double-click on text to place your cursor inside the text area. Then your editing features from WordPerfect take over:

■ Use the Backspace and Delete keys to remove characters.

■ Begin typing to insert characters.

■ Drag over characters or words to select text.

Double-click on a text area to make a cursor available. Then drag over text to select it before formatting. Once selected, choose items from the Property bar for formatting.

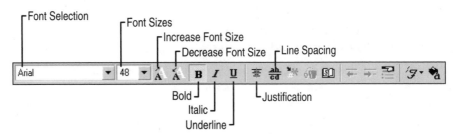

*Figure 7-10: You can drag over text to select it, then use the buttons on the Property bar to format the selected text.*

## Placing Clip Art in Your Slide

Reinforce your text with illustrations from the vast Corel clip-art gallery, or from your own sources. Add clip art to your image by following these steps:

1. Click on the Clipart button (shown in left margin) on the toolbar. The Scrapbook will open.

2. Click on the CD Clipart tab (see Figure 7-11) to access the full array of Corel clip art.

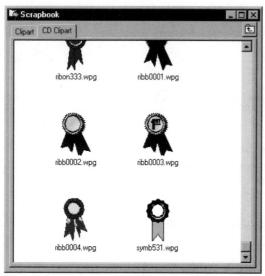

*Figure 7-11: Click on CD Clipart to view Corel's clip-art library. Double-click on the category of clip art you wish to use and double-click again on a subcategory. A collection of images will appear. You can preview the images by scrolling through the selections.*

3. When you find an image you want to use, drag it over from the Scrapbook to your slide.

4. Click on the Scrapbook's Close button to close the Scrapbook.

## Resizing & Moving Objects

You can resize any of the objects that appear on your slides. Objects include a clip-art image, a chart, a heading, a subheading, a text box, or a free-form object that you draw. Click once on an object to select it. Black handles appear around the outside edge of the object (see Figure 7-12).

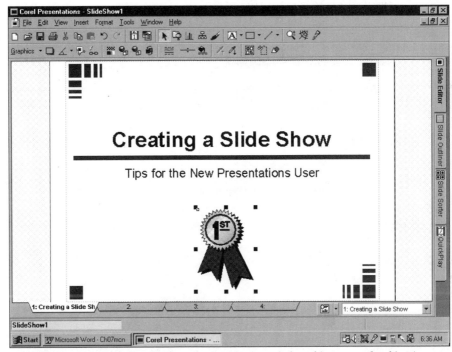

*Figure 7-12: Little black "handles" on the outside corners of an object mean the object is selected.*

To resize a selected object, place your mouse pointer over one of the corners and drag. Dragging away from the object makes it larger; dragging toward the center makes the object smaller. When you resize a text box, the text in the box wraps wherever you place the edges of the box.

To move a selected object, place your mouse pointer inside the object. Your mouse pointer appears as a black, four-sided arrow. Drag the object across the screen to a new location.

To rotate an object, right-click on a selected object and choose Rotate. Small, curved arrows appear at the corners of your object. Drag one of the corners to rotate the object in place. You can even rotate text boxes to display your text at a new angle (see Figure 7-13)!

*Figure 7-13: Rotate text to give a new angle to your statement.*

## Using the Draft Mode to Decrease Redraw Time

If you feel as though your slide creation time is dragging along, maybe you should switch to Draft mode. Select View | Draft. Your slides go from color to black and white, art images appear as outlines only—kind of an X-ray view of the slide (see Figure 7-14). This is a work-only view; when you run or print your actual slide show the real colors shine through.

*Figure 7-14: Choose View | Draft to switch to draft mode.*

## Tip

*Try switching to Draft mode if you do a lot of overlapping of objects. Sometimes you can find lost objects in Draft mode when all you see is the transparent out-line—pictures that are hiding behind other objects will suddenly reappear.*

### Placing Sound Objects on Your Slide

Recorded music, WAV and MIDI files you download from the Internet, or your own recorded voice—any sound you can get into your computer—can be added to slides. Play background music while the slide show is running, or record important dialog that describes the contents of the slides.

To add sound to a slide, right-click on any slide (it doesn't have to be the one that will receive the sound clip), then click on Sound. Choose a slide number at the bottom of the Sound tab of the Slide Properties dialog box, then specify a filename in the Wave or MIDI box (see Figure 7-15), or click the CD button to choose a track from a CD.

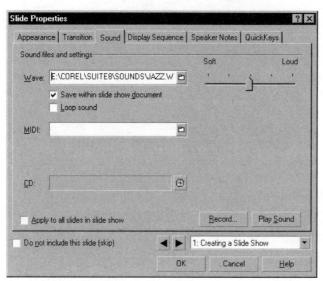

*Figure 7-15: Right-click and choose Sound, then pick a sound filename to accompany your slide.*

The Sound Properties dialog box appears after a sound has been selected. You can specify loudness for the sound by dragging the volume slider higher or lower. If you enable Loop sound, your sound will automatically begin playing again each time it reaches its end, continuing for the rest of the presentation or until another sound is encountered.

By default, your sound will automatically be saved with your presentation. (You can choose not to save the sound with the slide show file by unchecking the Save Within Slide Show Document box in the Sound Properties dialog box. This will save disk space. However, if you plan to make a portable presentation to play on another machine or send via e-mail, you will want to save the sound with your presentation.)

When choosing a sound to accompany your presentation you will want to consider copyright issues. You don't have to get permission to use the sounds that accompany your Corel software. If, however, you are using a recorded sound track from a CD or sound that you have downloaded from another source, you may have to get permission from the recording company or the owner of the sound.

### Recording a Narration for Your Slide Show

Record your own narration for the slides by following these steps:

1. Right-click on a slide.

2. Click on Sound on the pop-up menu.

3. Select the slide number to which your recording will apply.

4. Click the Record button.

5. Click Record, then make your recording.

6. Click Stop when you have finished recording.

7. Choose File | Save As to save the recording. Indicate a filename, then click on Save.

8. Click on File | Exit in the Sound/Sound Recorder dialog box.

9. In the Wave text box, insert the filename of the sound you just recorded.

## The Slide Outliner View

Choose Slide Outliner view by clicking on the Outliner tab at the right side of your Presentations window. Slide Outliner presents the text contents of your slides in an outline format, complete with indented rows (see Figure 7-16). Titles are first, then subtitles are at the second level. Bulleted lists and text boxes appear, too.

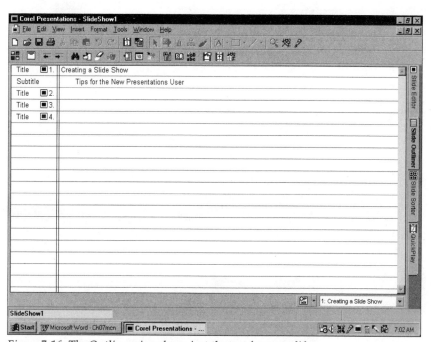

*Figure 7-16: The Outliner view shows just the text for your slides.*

## Creating New Slides & Entering Text in Slide Outliner

You can create slides directly in the Slide Outliner. Select Insert | New Slide to add a slide. When you insert a new slide, the title line appears first. Type a title (or not, your choice), then press Enter. The subtitle line appears. Type a subtitle (or not, your choice), then press Enter. You are ready to enter text in the slide (see Figure 7-17).

You can type in the Slide Outliner to add text. Press Enter at the end of any line to add a new line of text. By default, titles and subtitles appear first at the top of the slide. Enter a title, press Enter, and you're ready to enter a subtitle. Press Enter to add bullet points to the slide. Press the down arrow to continue with the next slide.

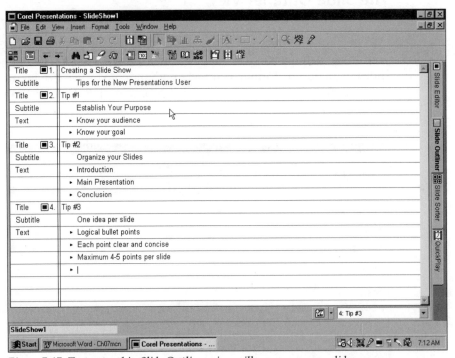

*Figure 7-17: Text entered in Slide Outliner view will appear on your slide.*

## Rearranging Slides in Slide Outliner

You can rearrange slides in the Outliner by dragging the slide icon, which appears with the slide number in the left margin of the Outliner. A red horizontal bar shows you exactly where the slide is being dragged (see Figure 7-18). Release your mouse button when the slide is where you want it.

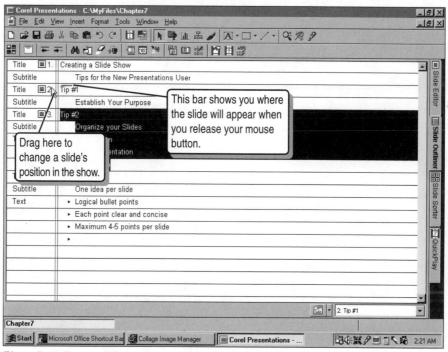

*Figure 7-18: Drag a slide icon to a new location in the Outliner view.*

# The Slide Sorter View

Click on the Slide Sorter tab at the right side of your window and see all of your slides in thumbnail, on the same, scrollable window (see Figure 7-19).

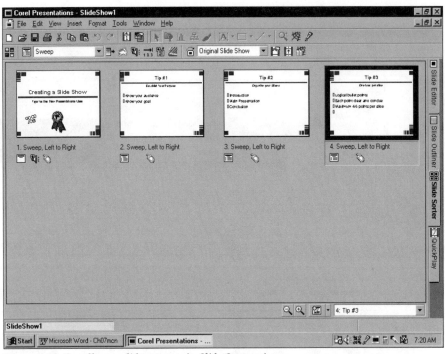

*Figure 7-19: See all your slides at once in Slide Sorter view.*

## Rearranging & Adding Slides in the Slide Sorter

Drag any slide on this window to a new location. A red vertical bar appears when you are dragging so you can see just where the slide is going to land when you release your mouse button (see Figure 7-20).

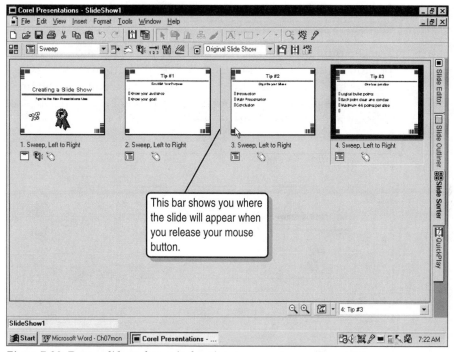

*Figure 7-20: Drag a slide to change its location.*

Add a slide in this view by choosing Insert I New Slide. Choose a layout and the slide is added to your slide show.

## Creating Speaker Notes

Use Speaker Notes to write notes to yourself that will remind you of important topics during your slide show. Maybe your speaker notes will include a list of props to show with the slide, a joke you want to tell, or a special comment you want to make. The notes are for you and can contain any information that will be helpful while you make your presentation.

Right-click in Slide Sorter view or Slide Editor view and choose Speaker Notes. You can create speaker notes for any or all of the slides from this window. Choose the slide to which the notes apply, then type specific notes for that slide. Click to import text from the slide to the speaker notes.

Print speaker notes by clicking on File I Print, then choosing Speaker Notes. By default, these appear four slides to a page, but you can change that number in the Print dialog box.

## Making Printed Handouts of Your Slides

You can print handouts of your slides so your slide show audience can have a printout of the presentation. Choose File | Print, then click on Handouts. You can designate from one to four slides per printed page (see Figure 7-21). The fewer slides per page, the more room participants have to make notes. Click on Print and your handouts are sent to the printer.

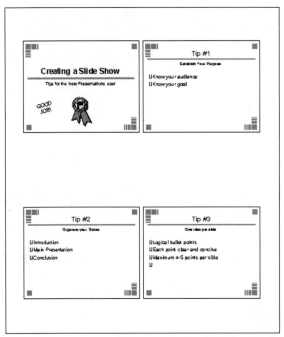

*Figure 7-21: You can print a copy of your slide show in the form of audience handouts.*

# Moving On

In this chapter, you covered the basics of creating a presentation, adding graphics and sound to your slides, rearranging your slides, playing your slide show, and creating printed handouts and speaker notes. In Chapter 8 you will be introduced to the worlds of animation and transition, and you'll learn how to gain more control over the appearance of your slides by working with grids, guidelines, and rulers. Chapter 8 also shows you how to make your presentation portable so it can be shown on other computers or sent via e-mail.

# 8

# Corel Presentations 8: Advanced Techniques

Once you've created a basic presentation—slides that present your topic in clear, concise points on a nice background with some clip art and appropriate typefaces—you're ready to add pizzazz to your slide show. In this chapter you'll learn about adding animation, customizing how the slides appear onscreen, and controlling the placement of objects on the slides. You'll also learn how to make a portable copy of your presentation for viewing on other computers.

## Working With Layers

When you are working in the Slide Editor, your slide objects appear to be all on the same plane. You get a sense, however, of the multiple layers in your slide, if you switch from Normal to Draft view, where you can see outlines of all the objects on the slide, even those overlaying others.

No matter in which way you view your slide, your slide is actually a compilation of three layers: the background layer, the layout layer, and the slide layer. You can control on which layers you place your objects, and, as a result, have control over how those objects are treated.

## The Background Layer

The Background layer includes your background color and the size of your page. You can place objects like text and clip art (such as a company logo, or some other design that you want to see on each slide) directly on the background layer. Items on other layers will overlap these objects. When you are working in the other layers you cannot access items on the background layer.

We think of our master slide as a background master, with features that can't be changed when you are working in the Slide or Layout layers. You can access the background layer of your slide show by clicking on Edit | Background Layer (see Figure 8-1).

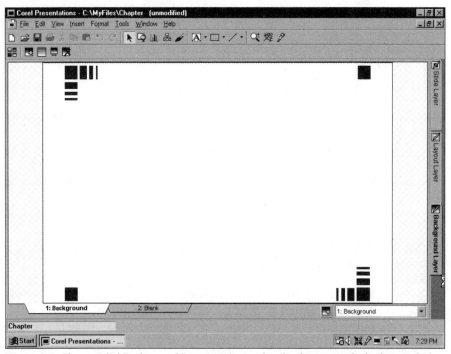

*Figure 8-1: Choose Edit | Background Layer to view and make changes to the background of your slides.*

## The Layout Layer

On top of the Background layer lies the Layout layer. Predefined objects such as titles, subtitles, bulleted lists, and charts—the items you choose when you select a slide layout—are all part of the Layout layer. The Layout layer defines areas for your titles, lists, and so on. Typical areas include a title box, a subtitle box, and a text box. The actual content of these objects doesn't appear in the Layout layer. For example, a title box in the Layout layer appears as a box bordered with a dashed line and the legend *Title of Show*. The actual title you type appears only on the slide layer.

The Background layer provides a backdrop for the entire slide show. The Layout layer is unique to each individual slide in the slide show. When you insert a new slide, you are asked to choose a layout for that slide. Later, you can view or change the layout by selecting Edit I Layout Layer (see Figure 8-2).

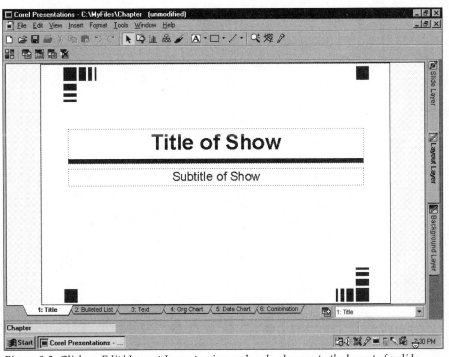

*Figure 8-2: Click on Edit I Layout Layer to view and make changes to the layout of a slide.*

## The Slide Layer

The Slide layer is where you actually place the content of your slide—your text, lists, pictures, and charts. Double-click on items that were inserted on the Layout layer and enter the actual text, images, or other data. The Slide layer shows the Background layer, the Layout layer, and the Slide layer all put together to make up the actual slide (see Figure 8-3).

*Figure 8-3: The Slide layer shows all the layers of the slide combined.*

# Working With Grids, Guides & Rulers

You can drag items around your slides complacently and hope that they are spaced in a way that will look neat and orderly in the slide show, or you can let Presentations guide you with its grids, guides, and ruler features. Hidden grids are lurking underneath your slides, waiting for you to let them pop into life. Placing grids on your slides doesn't mean your slide show turns into a series of checkered flags (sorry, I'm writing this the weekend of the Indy 500…). Grid and guide lines do not print. The lines are there for your guidance and assistance as you place items on your slides.

Use the grid to line things up yourself. You'll find that when you present a slide show, there is a great benefit in having graphic items placed at exactly the same location on different slides, on the same horizontal or vertical plane. It provides a sense of continuity and professionalism in your presentation.

## Using the Ruler

One of the nicest features of Presentations is the ruler. Turn on the ruler by clicking View | Ruler. Both a vertical and a horizontal ruler appear onscreen (see Figure 8-4).

*Figure 8-4: Small red lines on the rulers show you the exact placement of your cursor.*

You will see an indicator on each ruler shows you the location of your cursor on the slide.

Use the ruler to create guides for your use on slides. Place your mouse over one of the rulers, then drag onto your slide. A magic red guide comes right off the ruler and onto your slide (see Figure 8-5). Use the opposing ruler to determine exactly where the guide should be placed. Pull as many guides off a ruler as you like. It's just like a magician pulling rabbits out of his hat.

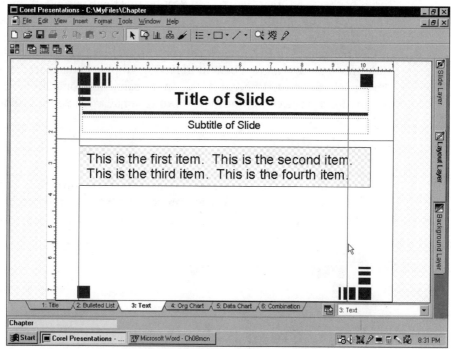

*Figure 8-5: Use guides to help line up objects on your slide.*

If you no longer need the guides, or if you just got carried away and placed a few too many guides on your slide, throw a guide away by dragging it right back to the ruler where it came from (see Figure 8-6).

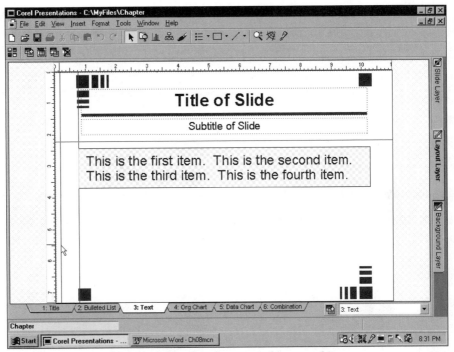

*Figure 8-6: Drag a guide back to the ruler when you no longer need it.*

## Using the Grid or Guides

Grid lines exist as a background checkerboard on your slides, providing points at various intervals to guide your objects. Every fourth grid appears by default. Grid lines are stationary and cannot be moved.

Guides may be vertical or horizontal. You can move guides, or you can use them as an anchor; a point from which other items are measured. Guides are the red lines that come from your rulers. You can change the position of guides by dragging them.

Make the grids or guides visible (or not) by clicking on View | Grid/ Guides/Snap. Click on Display Grid to show the grid lines, or click on Display Guides to show the guides. If the items are checked, they are currently being displayed (see Figure 8-7).

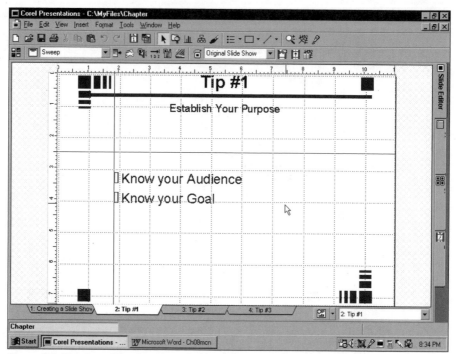

*Figure 8-7: Use the grid and guides to help you line up objects on your slides.*

Turning on the Snap to Grid/Guides feature tells Presentations that you want your movable items to adhere to the nearest gridline or guide when you drag them onscreen. This ensures continuity among your slides and enables you to place items precisely without guessing.

For example:

1. Select an object (a text box or a clip-art object).

2. Select View | Grid/Guides/Snap. If Snap to Grid is not checked, click on Snap to Grid. If Snap to Grid is already selected, just click outside the menu.

3. Drag the object. You may notice that the object seems to move a bit clumsily, as if moving from point to point rather than smoothly gliding across the screen. (You may not notice this clumsiness until, in step 5, you try moving the object without the Snap to Grid feature turned on.)

4. Select View I Grid/Guides/Snap, and click on Snap to Grid to turn off the feature.

5. Drag the object. You should notice that now it moves smoothly and you can place it wherever you want.

## Customizing the Grids

Customize the grid feature by clicking on View I Grid/Guides/Snap I Grid/Guides/Snap Options. In the Grid/Guide/Snap Options dialog box that appears (see Figure 8-8), you can designate whether or not you want the grids to display, specify how much space to leave between the grid lines, indicate the frequency with which the grid lines appear on the screen, and indicate how close an object can get to a grid line before it is grabbed and pulled over to the line. Selecting Snap to Grid forces objects to adhere to the nearest grid line or guide when they are close to the line.

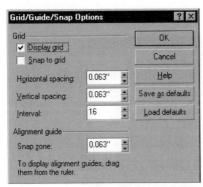

*Figure 8-8: Set grid line options by clicking on View I Grid/Guide/Snap I Grid/Guide/Snap Options.*

To save the settings of the grids or guides for future slide slows, click on Save as Defaults in the Grid/Guide/Snap Options dialog box.

# Adding Transitions to Your Slides

Frequently, we create slides that are printed or made into overhead transparencies (see the "Printing & Publishing Your Slide Show" section later in this chapter). But the real power of a slide show presentation is to view it directly on the computer screen.

You don't have to settle for your slides just blinking onto the screen one after another, when you can use simple tools to have your slides make a dramatic entrance.

Choose among dozens of transition effects for your slides. From the Slide Editor, right-click on a slide, then choose Transition. The Transition tab of the Slide Properties dialog box is displayed (see Figure 8-9). Select from the Effects list (try them all at least once, to see what they do). Choose a direction for your transition (some transitions have more directions to choose from than others), and choose a speed for your transition. Each time you make a choice you will see a little preview of how the slide will behave when the transition is applied to it.

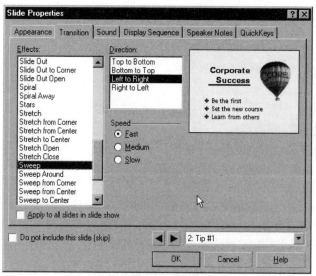

Figure 8-9: Choose a transition for your slide by right-clicking, then clicking on Transition.

Apply transitions to other slides while you're in the Transition dialog box by selecting another slide number at the bottom of the box.

# Adding Animation to Your Slides

Things start to really get fun when you add animation effects to your slides. Charts shoot in from outer space, bullet points fade in one by one, clip art explodes onscreen in a starburst. These are effects that look stunning and are remarkably easy to create.

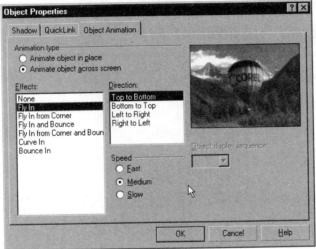

Figure 8-10: Select an object, then right-click and click on Object Animation.

Click on an object on your slide to select it. Right-click on the object and choose Object Animation. In the Object Animation tab of the Object Properties dialog box that appears, choose from the following options:

- Choose to animate the object in place or have it move across the screen.
- Choose from the list of animation techniques.
- Choose a direction for the animation.
- Choose a speed.
- If you are animating more than one object on a slide, indicate the order of appearance for this object.

If the object you choose to animate is a bulleted list, you will see the Bullet List Properties dialog box. In this box, you can choose how to animate the objects and you can choose to have your bullet items displayed one at a time during your slide show.

# Setting Up the Presentation Page

There are several considerations to keep in mind when creating your Presentation page. Click on File | Page Setup to make changes in your page definition (see Figure 8-11).

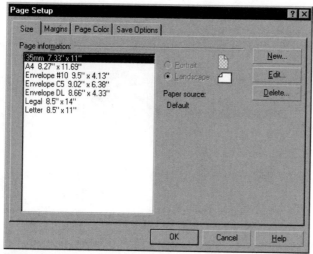

*Figure 8-11: Choose File | Page Setup and click Size to select a paper size and an orientation for printing your slide show.*

On the Size tab of the Page Setup dialog box, indicate the paper size and orientation (either portrait or landscape). If the paper size you want to use is not listed, click on New to add a paper size to the list. The choice of paper size only affects a printed version of your slide show. The display of the show on your computer screen is not affected by this choice.

In the Margins tab, enter the precise margins you want to have on your printed page (see Figure 8-12). The little preview picture will give you an idea of how your choices will appear on a real page.

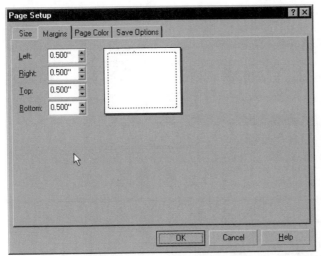

*Figure 8-12: Choose File | Page Setup, then click Margins to indicate margins for the printed copy of your slide show.*

On the Page Color tab, click on a style, then choose from a spectrum of patterns and colors (see Figure 8-13). Click on the X to use the same color scheme as that of the master (this is the default choice), or choose another color to override the master. If your master has dark colors, you may want to use this option to change to a lighter color scheme for printing purposes.

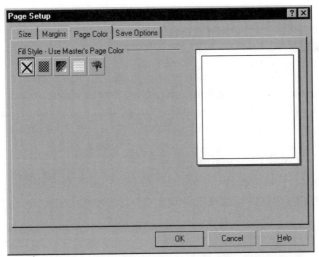

*Figure 8-13: Choose File | Page Setup, then click a Fill Style to override the color scheme of your master when printing your slide show.*

Use the Save Options tab of the Page Setup dialog box to indicate how much white space you want to save with graphic images you create in Presentations (see Figure 8-14). In other words, if you draw a graphic image, then want to save the image for use in another program, such as WordPerfect, you can use this option to indicate the amount of space saved around the image.

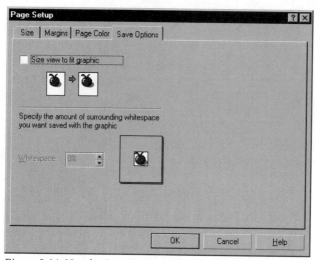

*Figure 8-14: Use the Save Options tab to indicate the amount of white space to save with a graphic image.*

## Making a Portable Presentation

You can take your show on the road with a portable presentation. You can save the presentation to a disk and you can play your slide show on a computer that doesn't even have Presentations installed. Or, you can e-mail your presentation, sending it to someone who may not even have Presentations software.

To make a portable presentation, follow these steps:

1. With your presentation open, click on File | Show on the Go (see Figure 8-15).

2. Specify the drive location (or e-mail address) to which you want to send your portable show.

3. Examine the specifications for Windows designations of the receiving computer. If there are changes to be made, click the Change button and make your changes.

4. Click on the Create button. Presentations creates a portable show in the designated location.

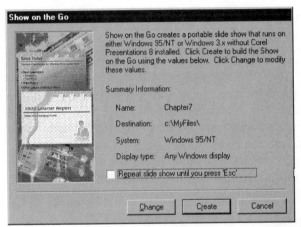

*Figure 8-15: Select File | Show on the Go to create a portable slide show that you can display on other computers.*

The portable show, or presentation *runtime*, is ready to be played on any machine, whether or not Presentations is installed.

Keep in mind that the file created may be too large to hold on a single floppy disk. Files that are several megabytes in size are not uncommon. It is best to save your runtime presentation on your hard drive first, then consider copying the file onto several disks, or compressing the file (with a program such as PKZIP) so that it fits on a single disk. If you plan to e-mail the file, consider compression. E-mail takes a long time to send and receive if the file is several megabytes in size.

# Printing & Publishing Your Slide Show

You can print out your slide show either by printing the slides on paper or transparency film, or printing speaker notes that contain the slides and notations that you made to help you with your presentation. Alternatively, you can publish your slide show by sending it via e-mail or by making it available for viewing on the Internet.

## Printing Slides

You can print out your slides either on paper or on transparency film. Use the transparencies on an overhead projector. With a color printer you have the option of printing your screen objects in the colors selected. On a black and white printer, your colors print as various shades of gray. Be creative—you can always resort to colored markers on your overheads to brighten them up.

Print your presentation by selecting File | Print (see Figure 8-16). The default print setting prints every slide in the presentation and all other items created with the presentation: speaker notes, handouts, and audience notes.

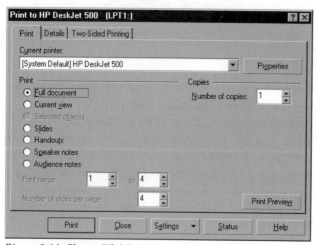

Figure 8-16: Choose File | Print to send your slides to your printer.

Print just the slides by selecting Slides. Choose selected slides to print by indicating the specific slide numbers in the Print range area of the Print dialog box. Print Speaker notes, Handouts, or Audience notes by clicking on any one of those items. Click Print after making your selection.

To print out the speaker notes you created while you made your slide show, click on Speaker notes, then click Print (see Figure 8-17). A small version of each slide prints with the speaker notes underneath. By default, four slide images with speaker notes print per page. Change the number of notes per page by changing the Number of slides per page data box in the Print dialog box.

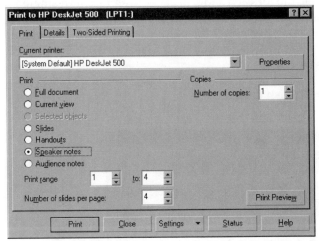

*Figure 8-17: Click on Speaker notes in the Print dialog box to print your slides with speaker notes.*

Click on Print Preview to view your slides/notes before printing. When you've finished with Print Preview, press the Esc key or click once on the preview window to return to the Print dialog box. Click Print when you're ready to print.

## Publishing to the Internet

If you have a Web site, you can publish Presentations slide shows right to the Web. Publish the slides alone or add all the bells and whistles, publishing the slides with full sound and animation just as they appear in your onscreen slide show.

### Publishing in HTML Format

When you publish to HTML format, your slide show is saved as separate HTML files, one file for each slide. Each slide represents a single Web page that other Web users can see with their Web browsers. To publish to HTML, first make sure you have saved the latest version of your presentation. Then, with the presentation open, follow these steps:

1. Click on File | Internet Publisher.

2. Click on Publish to HTML.

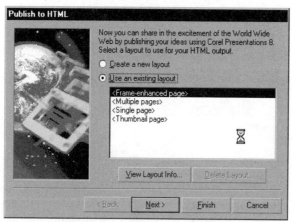

*Figure 8-18: Click on File | Internet Publisher, then click on Publish to HTML to display this dialog box.*

3. Click on Use an existing layout to use the presentation you already created, then click on Next.

4. Give your slide show a title. This is the title that will appear in the title bar of the browser of anyone looking at your presentation.

5. Select the directory and folder on your hard drive for the HTML files that will be created, then click on Next.

6. Select from several information options that you can use, then click Next.

7. Enter any footer information you may want to include.

8. Choose how the slides should be displayed—thumbnails, framed, and so on.

9. Choose from color and background options, then click Next.

10. When all choices have been made, click on Finish.

Your files will be saved in HTML format. You can open your own browser to view the files.

### Publish to Show It!

If you want your presentation to come alive on the Internet, complete with all sound, animation, and transitions so that Internet users can view the slide show just as you see it on your computer, select File | Internet Publisher, then click Publish to Show It! The Show It! dialog box appears (see Figure 8-19).

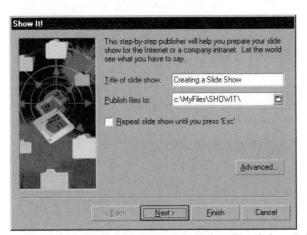

*Figure 8-19: Click on File | Internet Publisher, then click on Publish to Show It! to produce a portable slide show that you can take on the road.*

Indicate the name of your slide show, your home page, and display options. Indicate color settings, then click on Finish to complete your Show It! file. Presentations will create the files necessary to publish your show to the Internet.

## Printing 35mm Slides From Your Presentation

There are a couple of housekeeping steps to perform before creating a 35mm slide presentation. First, set all page margins to 0 by clicking on File | Page Setup, then clicking on the Margins tab and making the appropriate changes. Then, click on the Size tab and select 35mm in the Page Information list.

If you plan to print to a film recorder, you should choose one of the 35mm masters from the master gallery when you design your slide show.

In addition, you need to select your film recorder as the current printer (see Figure 8-20). If the film recorder you plan to use is not listed on the printer list, you must add it to your system. Click on the Start button on your taskbar, then click on Settings | Printers. Double click on the Add Printer icon and the Add a Printer wizard will walk you through the steps of entering information about your recorder.

### Tip

*Check your film recorder manual for the specific printer specifications that you will need. If you don't own a film recorder but plan to use one that belongs to someone else (or rent one), you'll need to contact the owner of the recorder and ask for specific information for printing from a computer to the recorder. The recorder manual will include specifications for your printer setup.*

Select File | Print. Click on the Print tab, then select your film recorder from the Current printer drop-down menu.

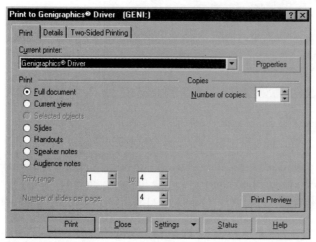

*Figure 8-20: Choose the name of the film recorder as the Current printer in the Print dialog box.*

Select Slides so that just the slides print to the recorder. Click on Print in the Print dialog box and your slide show will be printed to your film recorder.

## Using the Standard Corel Editing Tools

You really have to try hard to type something incorrectly, with all the editing tools that Corel provides. Corel offers QuickCorrect, which magically erases your misspelled words as you type them and replaces them with the correctly spelled words; a thesaurus, in which you can search for synonyms and antonyms; a spell check, which lets you search your entire document for misspelled words and offers helpful suggestions for getting them right; and Grammatik, which tells you when your English ain't so good. All of these tools are available in Presentations. See the detailed description of the tools in Chapter 6.

## Creating Macros for Corel Presentations 8

A macro is a little robot that automatically performs tasks that you taught it. A macro is a wonderful tool for performing repetitive tasks, and for making sure they are done exactly the same way each time they are performed.

For example, let's say you want to place a text message on several of your slides and you want it to appear in the same place on every slide. But you don't want to put it on your background master, because not every slide will display the message. You can make a macro to insert this message, size it, and place it in a precise location, then whenever you open a slide that should display this message, simply order your macro to place the message in the exact place where it belongs.

To create a macro, you first perform the actual steps, recording them as you go. Then your macro mimics what you did.

## Recording a Macro

Begin recording a macro by selecting Tools | Macro | Record (see Figure 8-21). Type a name for the macro, then click the Record button. Step by step, perform each task you want the macro to learn, and your steps are recorded as you perform them. Click on Tools | Macro | Stop when you have finished recording your steps.

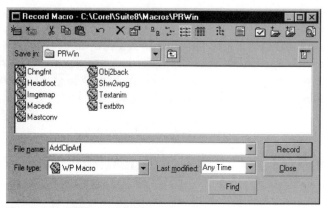

*Figure 8-21: Click on Tools | Macro | Record and give your macro a name, then you're ready to begin recording.*

## Playing a Macro

To use your macro, click on the slide on which you want to use the macro, then click on Tools | Macro | Play. Double-click on the name of the macro you wish to play.

The macro will perform the tasks you taught it, in the same order in which you recorded them. If the macro isn't doing what you want it to do, you can record the macro again using the same name. The new macro will replace the original macro.

# Getting Help

Have a question about how something works in Presentations? Getting help is painless and the help you can get is top-notch. You can ask questions in plain English, search through an alphabetical list of topics, perform a word search through the various help windows, or turn to the Corel Reference Center.

## Don't Forget the PerfectExpert

Click on Help | Ask the PerfectExpert. You can word your questions in complete sentences (such as, How do I right-justify my heading?), then click on the Search button. Several topics will be listed in the Search Results (see Figure 8-22). Click on a topic, then click on Display to read about the chosen topic.

*Figure 8-22: Click on Help | Ask the PerfectExpert, then pose your question.*

You can use the PerfectExpert to help you create your slide show. Click on the PerfectExpert button on your Presentations toolbar to place the PerfectExpert panel onscreen (see Figure 8-23). Use the buttons on the PerfectExpert panel in place of the menu and right-click options to perform the tasks you have learned in this chapter and Chapter 7.

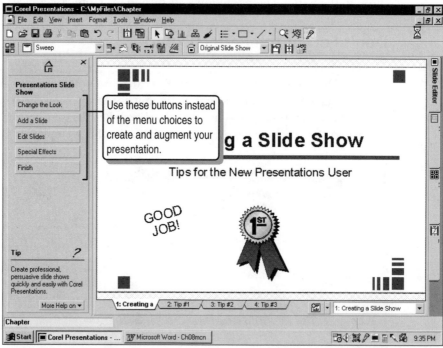

*Figure 8-23: Click on the PerfectExpert button to display the PerfectExpert pane.*

## Clever Tricks You can Play With Templates

The **template** in your slide show presentation is the layout layer of your presentation. It is on this layer that the outlines for titles, charts, clip-art images, and so on appear. Even though you can't change the layout of your slide when you are normally editing the slide, remember that you can get to the layout layer at any time by clicking on Edit | Layout Layer.

You can rearrange, add, delete, and resize any of the items on the layout layer. Change the background behind layout items by clicking on Format | Assign Background while working on the layout layer. When you are finished changing the layouts, click on Edit | Slide Layer to return to your normal editing window.

From this point forward, your changed layout will appear as a layout option when you display the layout drop-down list, so this edited layout can be used on any other slides in your slide show. Note, however, that your edited layout is available in this slide show only, not on the master list that is available to all slide shows.

## Moving On

This concludes the sections on Presentations. You have learned how to create a slide show, make it dance with animation and transition techniques, print out the show, and display the show either on your computer or on someone else's computer.

The next chapter introduces you to Quattro Pro, Corel's spreadsheet program. In Chapter 9 you will learn the basics of creating a spreadsheet, entering data into the spreadsheet, setting up titles, and entering formulas.

# Quattro Pro 8

# 9

# Introduction to Corel Quattro Pro 8

Use Quattro Pro to organize your financial information, sort lists of data, calculate formulas from the very easy to the extremely complex, and generate professional-looking reports. If you are a new Quattro Pro user, you will find the program easy to use and capable of performing all of your numerical tasks. If you have used earlier versions of Quattro Pro you will find not only the same comfortable interface with which you are familiar, but a host of new features as well. For a complete update on features new to the Corel WordPerfect Suite 8 including Quattro Pro, visit Corel's Web site at www.corel.com.

## What is a Spreadsheet?

Simply put, a spreadsheet is a two-dimensional collection of intersecting rows and columns. We use spreadsheets for gathering and analyzing numerical data.

A Quattro Pro spreadsheet features 256 columns and 8,192 rows for a total of 2,097,152 cells or unique row and column intersections (see Figure 9-1).

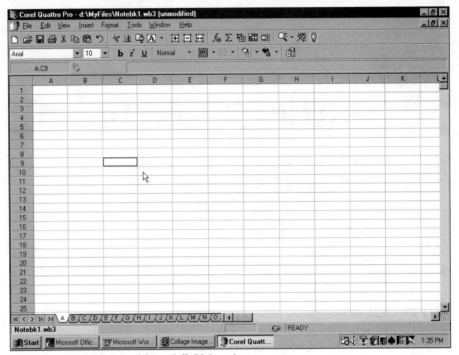

*Figure 9-1: The basic spreadsheet. Cell C9 is active.*

You identify locations on a spreadsheet by referring to the column and row reference. Thus, as illustrated in Figure 9-1, cell C9 is the intersection of Column C and Row 9. The active cell, the one in which your data is entered when you start to type, is emphasized by a dark border.

## Necessary Terminology

If you've been around spreadsheets for a while, most (or all) of these terms may already be part of your vocabulary. For new users, here's a quick introduction to spreadsheet lingo:

- **Row**. A spreadsheet row is horizontal. Each row has a unique number, from 1 to 8,192.

- **Column**. A spreadsheet column is vertical and has a unique letter or letter combination beginning with A. Since there are only 26 letters, the 27th column is AB, then AC, AD, and so on to AZ, then BA, BB, BC, and so on. The last column is the 256th column and is called IV.

- **Cell**. A cell is an intersection of a row and a column. Refer to cells by their column and row references, such as H57, R66, or CY6492.

- **Heading**. A heading is a title that usually appears at the top of a column or the left side of a row. The heading appears in the same location on each page of the spreadsheet.

- **Label**. A text entry in a cell is a label. A text entry is an entry that begins with a letter or a punctuation mark. The label has no value in numerical computations.

- **Formula**. A formula is a mathematical computation made up of numbers and/or cell references, and mathematical operators. We use formulas to perform the calculations in our spreadsheet.

- **Function**. Quattro Pro has created several formulas for your use; these are called functions. Usually you fill in missing information to make the function work. For example, the @AVG function adds a group of numbers that you specify, then divides by the quantity of numbers in order to calculate the average. All Quattro Pro functions begin with the @ symbol.

- **Block**. A group of cells in a spreadsheet is a block. A block can contain one cell, the entire spreadsheet, or a rectangular chunk of the spreadsheet. We generally use blocks to refer to more than one cell at a time and perform some activity or apply a spreadsheet feature all at once to the specified block.

- **Notebook**. A notebook is a collection of spreadsheet pages, all of which belong to the same file. Quattro Pro provides you with 256 spreadsheet pages in a single notebook as well as one final page, called the Objects page, which summarizes special features you have created in your notebook. You are not required to use all the pages of a notebook.

## What Does Quattro Pro Do?

It's true, Quattro Pro won't do your laundry or rake your leaves, but you won't mind doing those things yourself when you see all the other neat tasks that Quattro Pro can perform:

- **Create spreadsheets.** No matter what kind of information you want to gather, you can assemble the numbers in Quattro Pro. And because Quattro Pro creates electronic spreadsheets, you can depend on your calculations to be right every time. Whenever you change a number in your spreadsheet, Quattro Pro updates every formula in the entire notebook, every column, every row, and every notebook sheet.

■ **Graphing capabilities.** You choose the numbers from your spread-sheet—Quattro Pro does the rest by creating full-color two-dimensional or three-dimensional graphs, giving visual meaning to your data. Make your presentations look professional and let the Quattro Pro graphs tell the story behind your numbers.

■ **Manage data and lists.** Keep track of your inventory, your employees, your investments—anything that lends itself to a list. Use Quattro Pro's data analysis features to sort and organize your lists, search for items meeting particular criteria, keep track of shipments and inventory in stock, or even organize your personal address book.

■ **Perform calculations with variables.** No mathematical calculation is too complex for Quattro Pro. You can indicate which numbers or cells you want to include in a calculation, or even show Quattro Pro how to figure out for itself which items to include by creating logical arguments that Quattro Pro can solve.

■ **Automate spreadsheets with macros.** Using simple macro programming techniques explained in this book, you can turn your spreadsheets into little robots, going about their business while you sit back and watch. Macros save you time by taking over the job of performing repetitive tasks. Macros are also useful when you want to prepare a spreadsheet for use by someone not as skilled as you are with the program.

■ **Make spreadsheets work together.** Using Quattro Pro's linking and embedding techniques, you can make your spreadsheets "talk" to one another, draw on each other's resources, and trade information.

I think it's safe to say we've come a long way from handwritten paper spreadsheets!

## Creating a Quattro Pro 8 Document

There are several ways in which you can create or add to a document in Quattro Pro.

■ You can create a document using Quattro Pro's built-in templates, which have predesigned spreadsheets already started for you. Templates are fill-in-the-blank spreadsheets that give you guidance as you enter your information. Choose from a selection of templates by clicking on File | New (see Figure 9-2).

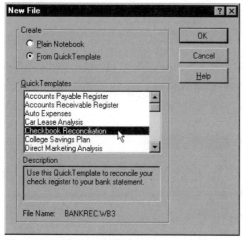

*Figure 9-2: The New File dialog box offers a selection of templates.*

■ You can create your spreadsheet from scratch, entering all your own titles and headings and creating formulas based on the information you enter onscreen.

■ Once your spreadsheet is underway, you can use an Expert to assist you with specific areas of your spreadsheet, entering calculations or creating graphs based on the information you provided.

■ You can add a template to an existing document, enhancing the data you began entering from scratch.

■ You can create or import graphic images right on your spreadsheet.

All of these techniques are covered in the following sections.

## Working the Spreadsheet

It's time to get your feet wet in spreadsheet land! Creating a spreadsheet is easy—the trick is knowing what you want to create before you begin, so you will have some goals in mind as you work. In this section we'll create a sample spreadsheet that incorporates basic spreadsheet features that will carry over to much of the work you do. You will learn how to enter text and numbers into a spreadsheet, create some computations using those numbers, and save your work.

## Moving Around the Spreadsheet

You can use your mouse to move around the spreadsheet, or you can let your fingers do the walking by working with the cursor keys on your keyboard. Either way, make sure the cell you want to use is highlighted with a dark border before you begin typing (see Figure 9-3).

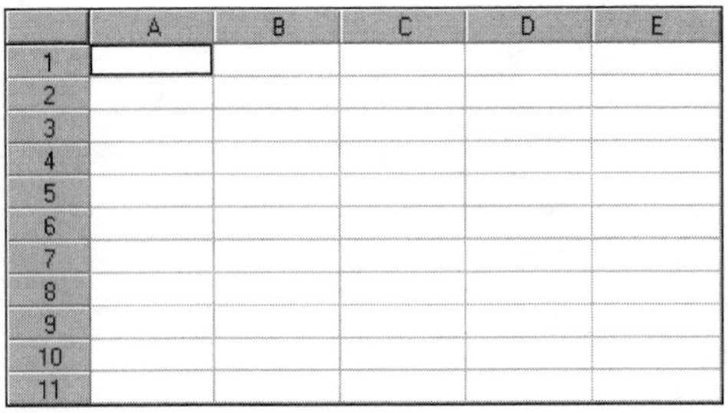

*Figure 9-3: The active cell is the cell into which you type.*

### Using Your Mouse to Move the Cellpointer

Slide your mouse around your mouse pad and you will see the white arrow move over the spreadsheet onscreen. But the highlighted (active) cell remains the same until you click your mouse at a new cell location.

**Tip**

*Even if you can't see which cell is the active cell, Quattro Pro constantly provides you with this information. Look at the left side of your Input line (see Figure 9-4) and you will see the column and row reference of the active cell. Click on a new cell with your mouse and this reference is immediately updated.*

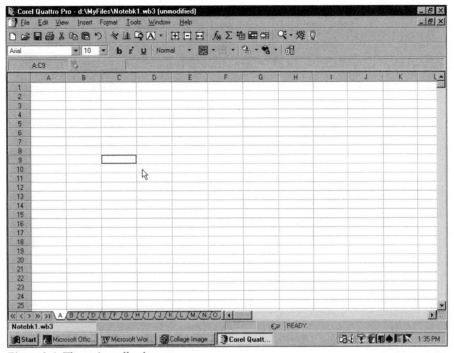

*Figure 9-4: The active cell reference.*

If the cell you want to make active is out of sight, you need to slide your spreadsheet around until you can see the area that contains the cell of your choice. Do this by clicking on the scroll bars at the bottom and right side of your spreadsheet. Note that when you use the scroll bars for viewing different parts of the spreadsheet, the cellpointer doesn't move with you. It stays right where you left it.

### Using Your Keyboard to Move the Cellpointer

Having a bad mouse day? You can avoid the mouse altogether and use your keyboard to get around on your spreadsheet. The arrow keys move your cellpointer one cell at a time in any direction you choose.

Lean a little on the arrow keys and your cellpointer will zip around your spreadsheet faster than you can say, "Look at that cellpointer go!"

## Putting Numbers in Cells

As you type a number, the digits appear both on the spreadsheet in the active cell, and above the spreadsheet in the Input line (see Figure 9-5). If you make an error while typing a number you can press Backspace to eliminate characters you have already typed. Notice that while you are typing the number, the indicator on the status line reads VALUE (if you were typing text rather than a number, this indicator would read LABEL).

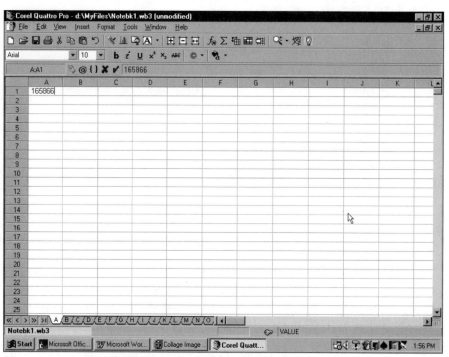

*Figure 9-5: Entering information on the spreadsheet and in the Input Line.*

When you finish typing the number, press Enter to place the number in the cell. The indicator on the status line returns to READY, the standard indication that the spreadsheet is ready for you to enter additional information.

If you change your mind and don't want to place the number in the cell, or realize that your cellpointer is pointing to the wrong cell, you can press Esc. The information you were typing will be removed and the cell returned to its original contents.

## Tip

*If you attempt to move your cellpointer into a new cell and the spreadsheet doesn't seem to want to let you move, check the status indicator at the bottom of the window. If it reads VALUE, LABEL, or EDIT, then Quattro Pro thinks you are still changing or entering information in the current cell. Until you press Enter or Esc, Quattro Pro will keep your cellpointer on the current cell.*

By default, when you press Enter, Quattro Pro moves your cellpointer to the cell beneath your current cell. This saves you the step of moving your cellpointer down a row.

Quattro Pro moves your cellpointer down a row each time you press Enter. If you prefer to have your cellpointer remain on the current row, select Tools | Settings | General, and uncheck the Move Cell Selector on Enter Key option (see Figure 9-6). This change will remain in effect until you return to this choice and change it back.

*Figure 9-6: Uncheck the Move Cell Selector on Enter Key box to have your cellpointer stay in the same cell when you press the Enter key.*

Notice that a number cannot stretch beyond the boundaries of a cell. If the number is too wide to fit within the cell boundaries, Quattro Pro will take certain measures to make sure it doesn't spill into the next adjacent cell. See "Formatting Your Numbers" below for a discussion on what Quattro Pro does and what you can do with numbers that don't fit within the normal cell boundaries.

## Entering Text in Cells

Click on a cell and begin typing text. The text will appear left justified in the cell by default, meaning the letters will start at the left side of the cell. If the letters are wider than the cell, they will spill over into the next cell to the right, if that cell is unoccupied. If the cell to the right is occupied with even a single digit or letter and your text fills more than the width of the current cell, the text that goes beyond the border of your current cell is displayed. The text still exists (and you can see it displayed in full when you click on that cell and look at the input line at the top of the window) but you won't be able to see it in the spreadsheet.

## Selecting Cells & Blocks of Cells

You will find yourself needing to select cells for many reasons:

- To change the appearance of cells, by changing the font, changing the size of the typeface, or changing the way in which the numbers appear (dollar signs, extra decimal places, and so on).
- To change the justification of cells.
- To apply an enhancement, such as bold face or underlining, to cells.
- To copy the content of cells.
- To move cells to a new location in the spreadsheet.
- To refer to particular cells in a formula.

These are only some of the reasons for selecting cells. You'll probably find many more reasons once you see how easy it is to make a selection.

### Selecting Cells With Your Mouse

Select cells on your spreadsheet using your mouse in the following ways:

- Click on a single cell to select that cell.
- Drag your mouse over a rectangular series of cells to select all the adjacent cells. The first cell with which you come in contact remains white; the rest of the selection is highlighted with black.

■ Select one area of the spreadsheet, then hold down the Ctrl key on the keyboard while you select additional, noncontiguous areas of the spreadsheet. This is particularly useful when you want to apply a format to several areas of a spreadsheet at once.

■ Click on a single cell of the spreadsheet. Move your mouse to the opposite corner of a rectangular area you wish to select (you can scroll to a new area of the spreadsheet if you can't see the end of the area you wish to select). Hold down the Shift key on your keyboard, then click on the cell in the opposite corner of the selection area. The entire rectangle is selected.

■ Click once in the Select All box in the top left cell in the spreadsheet (see Figure 9-7) to select the entire spreadsheet. This is handy when you want to apply a universal change to the spreadsheet.

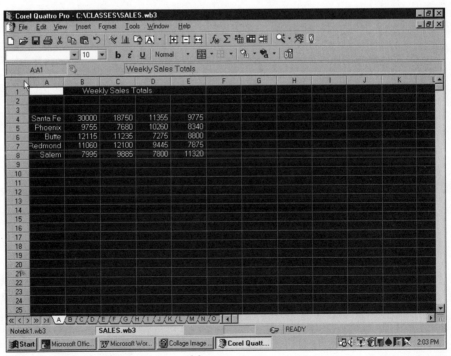

*Figure 9-7: Selecting your entire spreadsheet.*

■ Click the letter of a column or the number of a row to select that column or row (drag over several columns or rows to select more than one, or hold down Ctrl and select nonadjacent columns and/or rows).

To turn off any selection, simply click once on any cell.

### Selecting Cells From the Keyboard

If your mouse is giving you headaches, you can select cells from your keyboard instead of using the mouse by holding down the Shift key and moving your cellpointer with the arrow keys on your keyboard.

## Formatting Your Numbers

When typing numbers in a Quattro Pro spreadsheet, you are expected to type the number plainly—just the digits of the number with no dollar signs and no commas separating every three digits. Quattro Pro assumes nothing about decimal places. If you want to include decimal places, you need to type the period and the extra digits yourself. The following numbers would appear just as they are typed:

```
12.3
1.23
123
12345
123456
1234567
```

If you want the numbers to appear with a fixed format of two decimal places, first select the cells to which you want to apply the format, then click the Format Style button (see Figure 9-8), which reads Normal by default, and click on Fixed. Quattro Pro chooses two decimal places by default, and applies this format to all selected cells, even if you haven't yet entered numbers in the cells.

When you begin typing numbers in a new spreadsheet, Quattro Pro assigns what it calls a general format to the numbers in the cells. A general number format means a number appears plain, just as you type it: no commas, no dollar signs, and no decimal places.

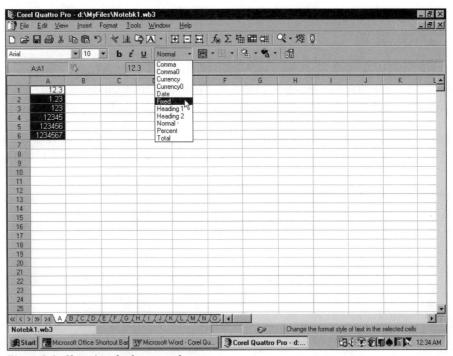

*Figure 9-8: Changing the format style.*

## Fit-As-You-Go

Sometimes, your numbers are just too wide to fit in your cell. This can happen when you are typing large numbers, when you are typing numbers that include decimal places or dollar signs or commas, or when you are using a very large type size.

Whatever the cause, if your numbers don't fit in the cell, one of two things will happen:

- Asterisks will appear in place of your numbers

- The column width will automatically adjust to fit the number

To turn on or off the automatic column width adjustment feature, choose Tools | Settings. Click on the General tab, then either check (to turn on) or uncheck the Fit-As-You-Go option.

# Changing the Width of Columns Manually

You can easily control the width of your columns onscreen. Place your cursor on the line that separates two column letters at the top of your spreadsheet. Your cursor becomes a black bar with an arrow on either side.

Drag the column separator line right or left. The column will expand or contract as you drag your mouse. To adjust the column width to particular specifications, notice the indicator at the bottom right corner of the screen while you drag the column separator. This indicator gives you the column width in characters, inches, and centimeters, and constantly adjusts itself as you drag the column separator. These techniques work for adjusting the height of rows as well.

If dragging doesn't get you to the precise size you want, try this technique instead:

1. Select the columns or rows you want to adjust.

2. Click the Display Properties button at the far right edge of your property bar (see Figure 9-9).

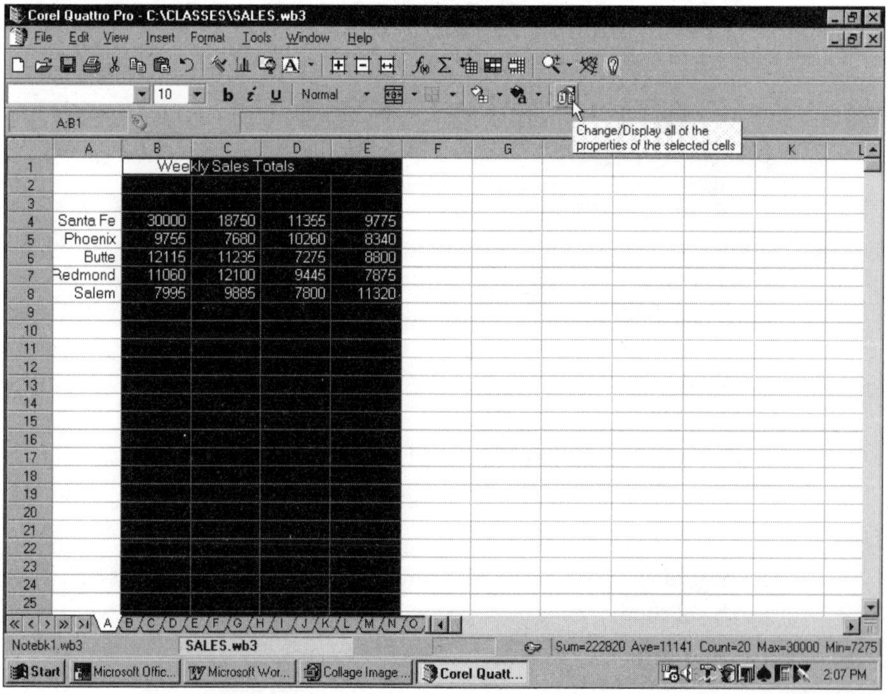

*Figure 9-9: Changing properties for the selected area.*

3. In the dialog box that appears (see Figure 9-10), choose the Row/Column tab. In this window you can make precise adjustments to the width of your selected column(s) or row(s).

4. Click OK when you have finished making changes.

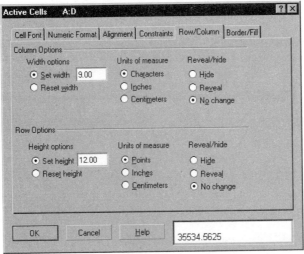

*Figure 9-10: Adjust the width of selected columns.*

## Putting Results in Cells

Entering numbers is fine, but eventually you're going to want to perform some calculations on those numbers. Say, for example, you want to add a column of numbers. Follow these easy steps:

1. Place your cursor in the cell of your spreadsheet where you wish the sum to appear.

2. Click the SpeedSum button on your upper toolbar (see Figure 9-11).

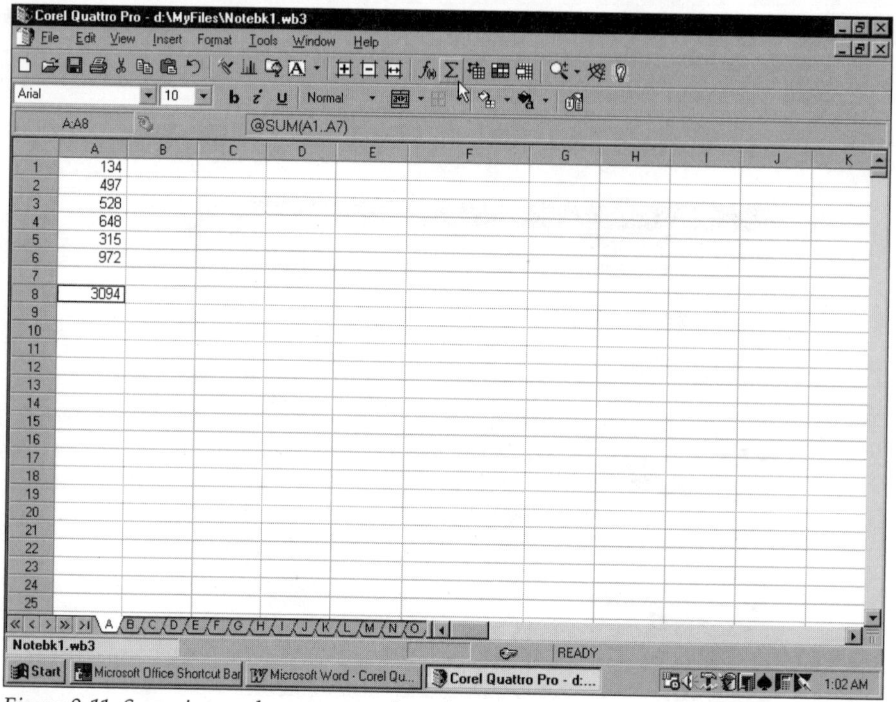

*Figure 9-11: Summing a column or row of numbers.*

The sum appears in the cell you selected. This is a nice shortcut and you'll use it frequently, but if the cell you choose for the sum is far away from the numbers you wish to add, Quattro Pro may not be able to figure out which cells to add. SpeedSum is for putting totals right at the bottom of a column of numbers, or at the right side of a row of numbers. See the next section, "Working With Operators," for basic information on creating your own formulas.

## Working With Operators

To begin a mathematical formula, type in a math operator such as +, -, =, or /. This tells Quattro Pro you plan to enter a mathematical formula instead of just typing letters and/or numbers.

When you think of entering formulas in Quattro Pro, think in terms of using cell references in the formulas as much as possible, instead of actual numbers. If you are multiplying the contents of cells A1 and A2, for example, it makes much more sense to create a formula that reads:

=A1*A2

than it does to create the formula:

=3*6

The reason we use cell references in formulas is the foundation of working in the electronic spreadsheet environment: if your formulas are based on cell references and the contents of those cells change, the formulas are automatically updated, whereas formulas based on actual numbers must be changed along with the numbers in the cells if you want them to update.

You enter the formula in the cell in which you want the answer to appear. The formula doesn't appear in the spreadsheet, but you can view it on the Input line whenever you select the cell containing the computation.

The math operators you will use to create formulas are as follows:

- ( )        parentheses

- ^        exponentiation

- * and /    multiplication and division

- + and -    addition and subtraction

When you enter a mathematical calculation, Quattro Pro reads the formula from left to right; however, the math operators are given priority in the order listed above. (My daughter informs me that you can remember this order with the following phrase: Please Excuse My Dear Aunt Sally—Parentheses Exponentiation Multiplication Division Addition Subtraction.) Thus the formula:

3 + 3 * 8 /( 4 + 2) – 3 = ?

will result in an answer of 4. The calculation in parentheses is performed first, then multiplication and division are performed from left to right (3*8=24, 24/6=4), then addition and subtraction are performed from left to right (3+4=7, 7–3=4).

If you want to force a calculation to occur in an order different than the above order, you must override the natural order by strategically placing parentheses in the formula. Thus:

(3 + 3) * 8/4 + 2 – 3 = ?

will result in an answer of 11.

The more complicated the formulas you create, the more important these simple rules will become.

## Entering Formulas in Cells

Okay, now that you know how Quattro Pro is going to read your math operators, how do you put these operators to use? Enter a formula in a cell by starting with an equal sign or a plus sign. This tells Quattro Pro that the numbers
you are about to enter will form something that needs to be calculated. Then
type in your formula and press Enter.

If you want to add the contents of cells A1 and A2 and put the result in cell
A3, your cellpointer would appear in cell A3, and your formula would read:

=A1+A2

### Tip

*Try to use cell references in your formulas instead of actual numbers (=35+74)
whenever possible. When the contents of cells referenced in a formula change, the
formula will automatically change too.*

## Working With Functions

Quattro Pro has saved you the trouble of creating many standard mathematical formulas with its built-in functions. Hundreds of functions exist to make
your life easier, from basic summing and counting functions to complicated
financial planning and higher math functions.

Some functions are provided automatically for you by Quattro Pro. Select a
group of cells containing numerical information, then observe the bottom right
corner of your window (see Figure 9-12). Quattro Pro automatically gives you
the sum of the range of cells, the average, the count, the maximum value, and
the minimum value.

Explore the functions that accompany the program by clicking on the Function button on your Notebook toolbar. The Formula Composer appears
onscreen (see Figure 9-13).

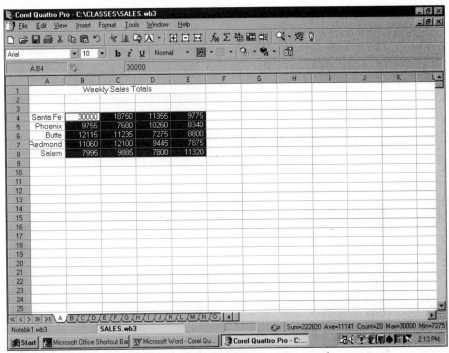

Figure 9-12: Select a range of numbers and Quattro Pro goes to work.

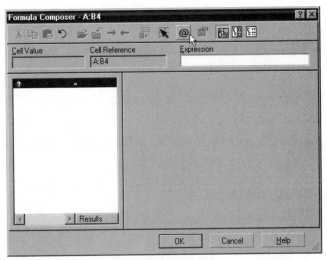

Figure 9-13: The Formula Composer.

Click on the Insert a Function button to see a scrollable list of all the functions available in Quattro Pro (Figure 9-14). Click an individual function to read a description of what the function can do. Clicking on OK sends you back to the Formula Composer and you're ready to fill in the information necessary for the operation of the function. (*Note:* Different functions look for different information. In fact, some functions don't require any information to operate.)

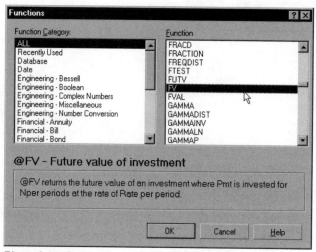

*Figure 9-14: Quattro Pro's many built-in functions.*

For example, say you want to determine the future value of an annuity. You plan to deposit $2,000 per year in an annuity for 25 years, starting this year, and you expect to earn 9% interest. What will the annuity be worth in 25 years?

1. First, enter the information you know in your spreadsheet (see Figure 9-15).

2. Place your cursor at the location where you want to see the future value calculation.

3. Choose the Future Value function (@fv)—you'll find it in the Financial category.

4. Enter cell references for the data in your spreadsheet (see Figure 9-16).

5. Click OK to calculate the future value. The future value will be displayed in the cell containing your cellpointer.

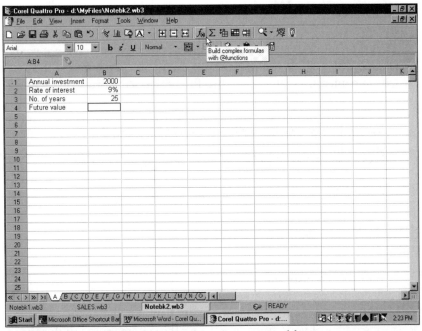

*Figure 9-15: Enter the information you know in your spreadsheet.*

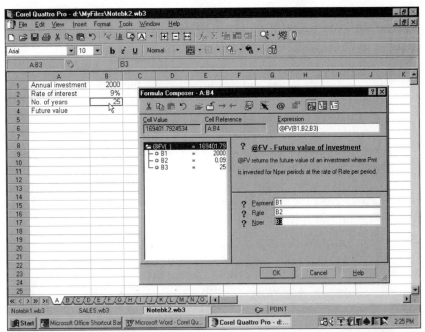

*Figure 9-16: Enter the pertinent information for calculating future value in the Formula Composer.*

## Saving Your Workspace

Click on File | Save to save your spreadsheet. If you have not yet named the spreadsheet, Quattro Pro prompts you to give it a name. If the spreadsheet has been named previously, Quattro Pro replaces the original version of the spreadsheet with the current, updated version.

Click on File | Save As to save the current spreadsheet with a new name, preserving the previously saved version of the spreadsheet with its own name. After using File | Save As, two versions of the spreadsheet exist on your disk.

You can also click on the File Save button on the toolbar to quickly save your work.

# Editing Your Spreadsheet

You may be one of the lucky few who creates perfection right from the start. If you're like most of us, however, you may find you need to make changes in your spreadsheet from time to time. Changing, enhancing, and improving the appearance of your spreadsheet—all these items come under the umbrella of Editing.

## Creating Labels & Headings

Often we think our numbers speak for themselves. This, however, isn't always the case. Create labels and headings to give meaning to the numerical contents of your cells.

Plain text can be boring, so use the enhancement tools at hand to add some power to your text. Quattro Pro comes with a full complement of fonts, type sizes, quality enhancements such as boldface, underline, and italics, as well as shading, patterning, and borders. Let your creative juices flow, keeping in mind that you are, in the end, trying to make a numerical statement.

First, select the text which you want to enhance, then choose the attributes you want to apply to that text (Figure 9-17).

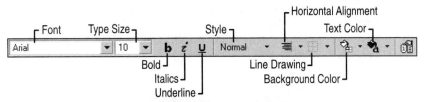

*Figure 9-17: Choose from the following enhancements, all available on your Property bar.*

## Aligning & Centering

By default, Quattro Pro aligns your text to the left as you type it. Override this by first selecting the text you wish to change. Then click the Alignment button on the toolbar. A drop-down list presents you with the following options:

- **Left alignment**—the default for text, begins text at the left side of a cell.
- **Centered**—text is centered in the cell.
- **Right alignment**—text is placed in the right side of a cell.
- **Centered over columns**—first, enter the text in the leftmost column over which you want to center the text. Then select all the columns over which you want the text centered. Finally, click the Centered over columns button. Your text will be centered over all the selected columns.

## Entering Dates & Times

Enter a date as you would when typing text, and Quattro Pro realizes that you mean for the date to read as a date, not as a division problem:

5/12/97

(In fact, if you *want* 5/12/97 to read like a division problem, you must precede the entry with an "=" sign).

You can enter a time without any special technique; simply type the time as you wish it to appear (*4:23 p.m.*, for example).

If you want a different appearance for your date or time, click on the cell, then click the Cell Properties button on the property bar. The Active Cells dialog box opens and you can choose from among several date formats by first clicking on the Numeric Format tab (see Figure 9-18).

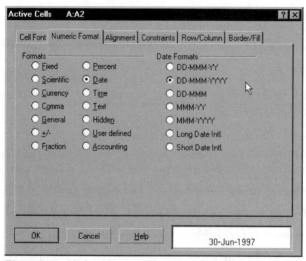

*Figure 9-18: Click on Date or Time, then click the style you wish to apply.*

## Finding & Replacing

Use the Find and Replace features on the Edit menu to search for and replace information in your spreadsheet. Use Find to search the contents of cells for specified information. Enter text, numbers, or cell references in the Find box.

If you merely want to search for the information, click the Find button. To replace items you search for, fill in the replacement information in the Replace box. Click Find to find the next occurrence of an item; click Replace to replace that individual occurrence of the item. Click Replace All to have Quattro Pro search the entire spreadsheet for your Find item, replacing each occurrence with the Replace item.

## Cell Borders & Grids

Select the cells to which you would like to apply cell borders. Borders can be applied to the outside edge of the selected group and to the inside grid as well (Figure 9-19).

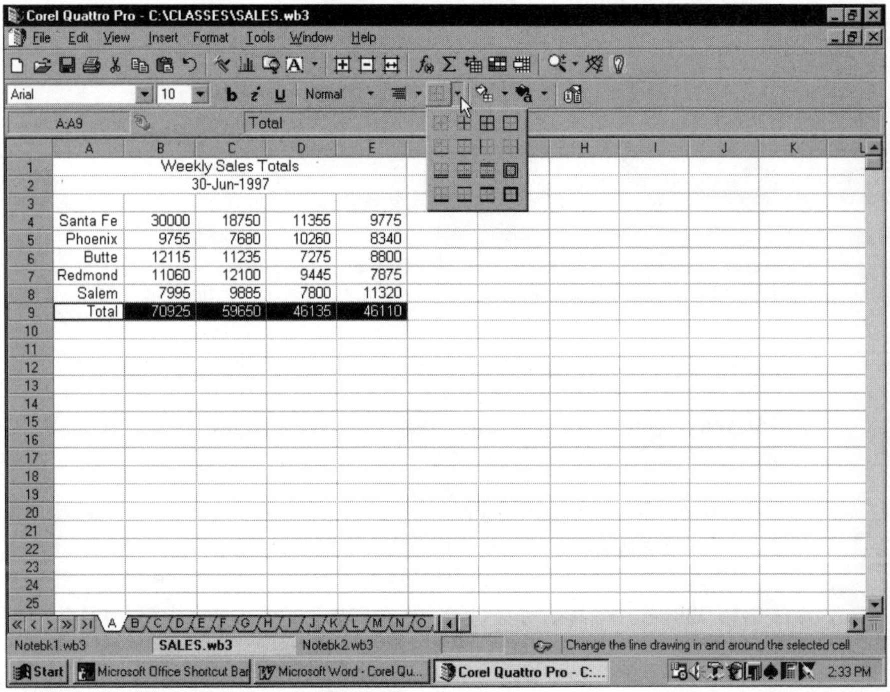

*Figure 9-19: Applying borders and grids.*

Click the Borders button on the Property bar. Several choices appear for both outside and grid borders. Click on the option you want to apply to the selected area. You can apply more than one border to a selected area.

Alternatively, click on the Cell Properties button on the Property bar. Click on the Border/Fill tab (see Figure 9-20) of the Active Cells dialog box. Choose the borders you wish to affect by clicking on them individually (hold down Shift while you click to select more than one), or clicking on the buttons which select outside or inside borders. Then click on a border type to apply to the selected borders. You can also apply color in this dialog box.

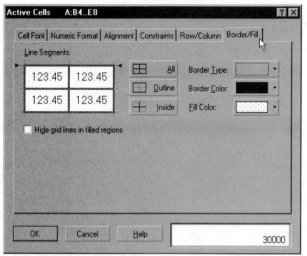

*Figure 9-20: Click on the Border/Fill tab of the Active Cells dialog box to dress up your cells.*

## Working With More Than One Page

The sheet tabs at the bottom of your spreadsheet lead you to additional spreadsheet pages in your file. Click on any sheet tab to bring it to the top.

When you work with multiple sheets it makes sense to use the same layout on all sheets in a file. That way you can insert formatting and formulas in one sheet and order it to flow through to the same location in all the other sheets.

You can rename the sheet tabs (instead of A, B, C, etc.) so that there is some indication on the tab of what the sheet holds. Rename a sheet by double-clicking on the tab itself. Then type in the new name and press Enter.

Apply headings or formatting or formulas to several sheets at once by grouping them together. To group pages together:

1. Select the pages in your group. Select pages by clicking on the first page, holding down the Shift key, and clicking on the last page. A black bar appears under the tabs of the selected sheets.

2. Select Insert | Name | Group of Sheets. The Define/Modify Group dialog box is displayed.

3. The sheets in your group will already be entered in the dialog box, because you selected them before you opened this dialog box. Enter a name for your group. Click OK.

Once you've named your group you can apply changes to the group as a whole. Select View | Group Mode. A blue bar appears under the sheets in your group. You can now make formatting changes to one page in your group, and they will be applied to the entire group. To enter text (such as headings) in the entire group at once, enter your text on one sheet in the group, then instead of pressing Enter, press Ctrl+Enter. The text is "drilled" through all the sheets of the group.

To turn off group mode, select View | Group Mode again. Now changes you make in one sheet will apply only to that sheet.

## Creating a Floating Chart

You can create a chart based on numbers in your spreadsheet, then have the chart appear right on your spreadsheet as a graphic image you can resize and move to fit your needs.

First, select the numbers in your spreadsheet that you want to plot in your chart. Include column and row headings in your selection if you want these headings to appear on your chart. Then, click the QuickChart button on the toolbar. Drag over to a place in the spreadsheet where you want the chart to appear. This does not have to be a permanent spot—one advantage of a floating chart is that you can easily move it to another location in the spreadsheet. If the numbers in your spreadsheet change, your chart is automatically updated to reflect the change.

You can place as many charts as you like in your spreadsheet, selecting different collections of data from your spreadsheet numbers, and using different charting types to display the data in different ways.

### Editing a Chart

You can edit the chart by clicking on it to select it, then right-clicking on the chart and choosing an item that you want to change.

- **Type/Layout**—changes to a different type of chart.
- **Series**—changes the data series (the range of data used to create the chart). For example, if you only selected two columns of data to include in your chart and now you want to include a third column, choosing Series lets you expand the selected data range.
- **Titles**—adds titles to the chart (including axis titles).
- **Properties**—changes the appearance of individual aspects of the chart, such as borders, background, gridlines, colors, and so on.

### Moving & Resizing a Chart

To move a chart on your spreadsheet, place your cursor along the outside edge of the chart. The cursor turns into a four-sided arrow. Move the chart in any direction you choose. The chart displays handles at the corners and the sides. You can drag any of these handles to change the size of the chart.

### Changing Chart Axis Properties

Click once on the chart. Notice that the Property bar now contains chart tools, and a Chart menu has appeared. Choose Chart | Axes. Choose from X-axis (usually the horizontal axis along the bottom edge of your chart), Y-axis (usually the vertical axis along the left edge of your chart), and Secondary Y-axis (the vertical axis along the edge opposite the main Y-axis, usually the right edge of your chart). Depending on which axis you choose, you can adjust the scale, the format of numbers, the type face, tick marks, and the style of grid.

### Labeling Your Chart

If you select row and column headings as part of your data series, you'll already have some labels in your chart. In addition, you can add a chart title and axis titles to help in describing what it is that your chart is depicting.

Add labels to your chart by selecting Chart | Titles. Then enter titles for the chart itself as well as the axes. Click OK to place your titles in the chart.

### Drawing & Annotating Charts

You can add your own features to your chart, for example arrows, callout boxes, and graphic illustrations (depending on your artistic prowess with a mouse). To do so, right-click on the standard toolbar and click on Chart and Drawing Tools. The Drawing tools let you drag arrowhead pointers, circles, and rectangles onto your chart. Enter additional text on your chart by clicking the Text Box tool, dragging a rectangle on your chart, then typing text into the rectangle.

Not the creative type? Click on the Template button at the right end of the Chart and Drawing Tools toolbar to choose from standard chart types and a template of color schemes. Preview your selections before actually applying them to your chart, then click OK when you are satisfied with a selection, or Cancel to return to the chart as you had drawn it.

### Creating a Slide Show From Your Charts

You can create a slide show right in Quattro Pro using your charts as the slides. When you save your Quattro Pro file the slide show is saved too, so you can use it in the future.

1. Click on Tools | New Slide Show. You are prompted to give your slide show a name, then click OK. The slide display window that appears has room for a display of many slides, but you don't need to fill the entire screen—use only the charts you want (even just two or three) to make slides.

2. To add a slide to your slide show, click on Slides | New Slide. Choose From Existing Chart. A list of your charts associated with the current worksheet appears; the charts are numbered in order of when you created them. Click on the first chart you want to include in your slide show, then click OK.

3. Add additional charts in the same way until you have completed the slides for your show.

4. Play your slide show right from this window by clicking on Slides | Play Slide Show. Click once to change slides.

The slide show is saved with your spreadsheet file, so you can access it whenever you need to. To play a slide show from your regular spreadsheet window, click on Tools | Slide Show | Play. Choose the slide show you wish to view (there may only be one), then click OK. Click once to advance a slide.

## Using QuickFills

Quattro Pro can fill a group of cells with any of the following items, with only a small amount of prompting on your part:

- Days of the week
- Abbreviated days of the week (three-letter abbreviation)
- Months of the year
- Abbreviated months of the year (three-letter abbreviation)
- Quarters (1st Quarter, 2nd Quarter, etc., or Quarter 1, Quarter 2, etc.)
- Abbreviated Quarters (1st Qtr, 2nd Qtr, etc., or Qtr 1, Qtr 2, etc.)
- Any combination of text and numbers (the numbers will increment)
- Any series of names that you define (such as cities in a region, states, employee names, etc.)

Using QuickFill is as easy as dragging your mouse. Enter one item from the QuickFill options (such as *Tuesday*). Place your cursor in the lower right corner of the cell containing the QuickFill item. Your cursor becomes a thin black cross. Drag the cursor across the cells to which you want to apply the QuickFill. Quattro Pro fills the remaining cells with the next items from the QuickFill series (in this case, *Wednesday, Thursday, Friday,* and so on).

To define your own QuickFill list:

1. Click on a blank cell in your spreadsheet.

2. Click on the QuickFill button on the toolbar.

3. Click on Create in the QuickFill dialog box.

4. Type a name for your list in the Series Name box.

5. Type each item from your list in the Series Elements box, clicking on Add after each item.

6. Click on OK when your list is finished.

7. Click on OK again to close the QuickFill dialog box.

From this point on, whenever you want to use your QuickFill series, type one name from your list, place the cursor over the lower right corner of the cell, drag over the number of cells you wish to fill, and presto! Your personal QuickFill list appears!

## Moving Data Around Your Spreadsheet

Once you've entered information in your spreadsheet, you'll no doubt start thinking about where you'd like to move it. Pick up information and move it effortlessly with these techniques.

### Copying, Cutting & Pasting

When you **copy** information, you leave the original intact and make a copy in a new location. When you **cut** information, you remove it from the original location and place it in a new location. No matter which procedure you use, the information is placed in the new location in the same way.

Copy information by first selecting the cell or cells you wish to copy, then clicking on the Copy button on your toolbar. The information you are copying remains in its original location.

Move your cursor to a new location, either on the same spreadsheet, on a different sheet of the same spreadsheet file, to a completely different spreadsheet, or even to a completely different program. When your cursor has arrived at its designated location, click the Clipboard button on your toolbar. The information you copied is pasted to the new location.

The clipboard is a holding area, accessible by any Windows program. Only one item can reside in the clipboard area at a time.

To move information from one location to another, select the cell or cells containing the information you wish to move. Click on the Cut button on your toolbar. The original information disappears from sight and is being held in the clipboard area (replacing any information previously being held in the clipboard).

Move your cursor to the location where you wish to move the information. Click the Clipboard button on your toolbar. (Even if you move the information to a new program entirely, all Windows programs have a clipboard (or a paste button) on their toolbars.) The information you cut from the original location reappears in the new location. Note that if you copy spreadsheet information from Quattro Pro into a WordPerfect window, your information will appear with a dashed border surrounding it, indicating the spreadsheet columns and rows.

## Setting Up Your Quattro Pro Page

You're almost ready to print your spreadsheet. But first, you may want to change the size of the paper and add a header or footer, or perhaps you need to change the margins. There are many items to consider before finishing the job.

### Page Orientation & Size

By default, Quattro Pro wants you to print your spreadsheet in a portrait orientation on regular letter paper that is 8.5" wide by 11" tall. You can change both the orientation and the size of the paper.

Click on File | Page Setup. The Spreadsheet Page Setup dialog box is displayed. Select a paper size from the scrollable list. Click Landscape if you prefer the wide appearance of a spreadsheet to the upright, Portrait appearance. Click OK to record your selections.

### Headers & Footers

By default, Quattro Pro does not place any header or footer on your page. You can change this by selecting File | Page Setup, then clicking the Header/Footer tab. Click the Create box next to either the header or the footer area to create a header or footer. The header or footer you create will appear on each printed page of your document.

Quattro Pro has special codes you can use in your headers and footers that can make your life easier. Here is a list of the header and footer codes:

■ | (vertical bar) Determines the position of the text: left-aligned, right-aligned, or centered. So if you want to type centered text in your header you would begin by typing one vertical bar, then the text. No vertical bars gives you left-aligned text. A second vertical bar right-aligns the text.

■ #d Enters the current date in a short format.

■ #D Enters the current date in a long format.

■ #t Enters the current time in a short format.

■ #T Enters the current time in a long format.

■ #p Enters the current page number.

■ #p+n Enters the current page number plus the number n (you fill in an amount for n)—this is used for advancing the page number past the actual number as calculated by Quattro Pro.

■ #P Enters the total number of pages in the document.

■ #P+n Enters the total number of pages in the document plus the number n (you fill in an amount for n).

■ #f Enters the filename.

■ #F Enters the filename with a full path.

■ #n Allows the header or footer to wrap to a second line.

*Note:* If you want a # character to appear in your header or footer, precede the character with a backslash (\).

## Margins & Page Breaks

By default, top and bottom page margins are set at .33", and left and right page margins are set at .40". You can change these measurements by selecting File | Page Setup, and then clicking the Print Margins tab. Enter the amounts you want for margins.

In addition, Quattro Pro sports a full WYSIWYG onscreen display. Select View | Page. All margins are visible as dashed lines. You can drag any margin to a new location.

Alternatively, you can select File | Print Preview. You see your full page as it is prepared for printing. Margins should be visible as dashed lines. If margins are not visible, click the Margins button on the toolbar to display them. You can drag any of the margins on this window to a new location.

## Using Print to Fit & Scaling

Some of the nicest features about Quattro Pro are the Print to Fit and the Scaling options. Is your spreadsheet a little too small for the margins of your paper? Or is it just a little too wide to fit on one page?

Select File | Page Setup, then click the Print Scaling tab. Your options include setting scaling to a particular percentage (indicating you want your document enlarged to 125%, for example, or reduced to 80%), or selecting Print to Desired Width (x number of pages) or Print to Desired Height (x number of pages).

If your document is a column or two wider than one page, you would request a desired width of one page to fit the spreadsheet all on one piece of paper. If there are a few too many rows for the length of the paper, you would request a desired height of one page to fit the spreadsheet on one piece of paper. Quattro Pro then reduces the entire spreadsheet in order to make it fit.

## Printing Row & Column Headings

Spreadsheets that extend beyond one page generally require a repetition of the row or column headings that began on the first page. You can make these headings appear on every page by clicking on File | Page Setup, then clicking on the Options tab (Figure 9-21).

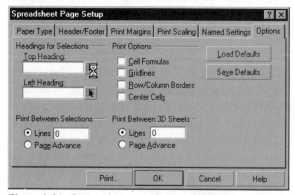

*Figure 9-21: Generating repeating row headings.*

Click on the pointer arrow to move your mouse pointer back to the spreadsheet, then click on the row numbers of the rows containing your headings. Click the Restore button of the Page Setup window to bring Page Setup back onscreen (see Figure 9-22).

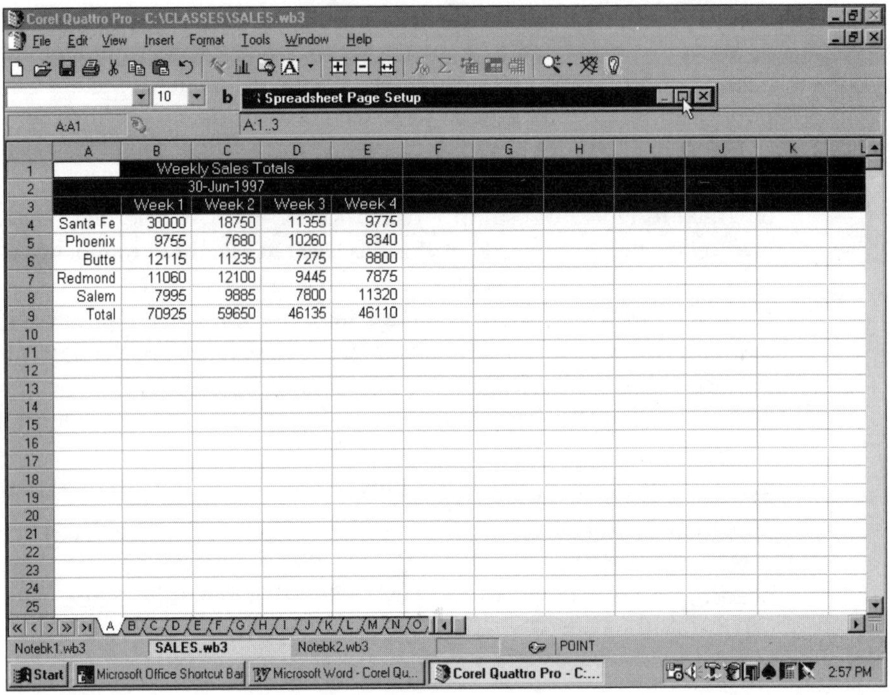

*Figure 9-22: Restore Page Setup to the screen.*

For top headings to repeat, you need to specify the row numbers that contain your headings. Click on the arrow to the right of the Top Heading box. Your cellpointer is returned to your spreadsheet. Click right on the row number(s) of the row(s) that contain(s) your headings. Click back on the Restore button of the Page Setup title bar to restore the dialog box.

For left headings, click on the arrow to the right of the Left Heading box. Then click on the column numbers for the columns containing your headings that appear on the left side of your spreadsheet. Restore the Page Setup dialog box. Click on OK after designating all of your repeating headings.

## Splitting the Screen

A small spreadsheet that fits all in one window is easy to work with because you can see the entire work area. But what if you are working in a spreadsheet with hundreds of rows and dozens of columns, and numbers in one part of the spreadsheet affect formulas that are out of sight?

To see more of your spreadsheet you can split the screen and view distant parts of the spreadsheet at the same time. When you split the screen you are presented with two scrollable windows, each capable of displaying any part of your spreadsheet.

To split your spreadsheet screen, place your mouse pointer over the Split View button in the lower right corner of your spreadsheet. Notice the direction of the mouse arrow changes depending on where in this little box you place your mouse.

Drag this box to the left to split your screen vertically. The box relocates to the place in the screen where the split occurs. Drag the box back to the original location to remove the split.

Drag the Split View box up to split the screen horizontally. Return the box to its original location to remove the split.

When you split your screen, you are looking at two views of the same spreadsheet. Changes in one pane may well be reflected in parts of the other pane.

By default, the split windows are synchronized with each other. This means that scrolling in one window automatically causes scrolling in the other window.

You can turn off this synchronization (or turn it back on), by clicking on View | Split Window. In the Split Window dialog box that appears, there is a Synchronize check box. When the box is checked, the windows appear in synch; uncheck it and you can scroll one window without causing a similar scroll in the other window.

## Moving On

This chapter's introduction to Quattro Pro gave you the basic skills you need for creating spreadsheets, formatting your titles, entering information in the spreadsheet, creating formulas, printing your spreadsheet, and saving your work. In Chapter 10, you'll be introduced to Quattro Pro's advanced topics including customizing toolbars, working with databases, linking information across spreadsheets, using Quattro Pro's numeric tools, and working with macros.

# 10

# Corel Quattro Pro 8: Advanced Topics

Quattro Pro is a magnificently powerful program than can perform calculations with lightning speed. Now that you know the basics of how to set up your spreadsheets, it's time to delve into some of the special features that Quattro Pro has to offer so that you can put this program to work for you.

In this chapter you'll learn how to customize your toolbars so they feature buttons that you use frequently. You'll also learn how to work with databases, sorting and extracting data that fits certain criteria. Get a taste of the mathematical tools that accompany your program, and learn how to create a macro.

## Working With the Toolbars

Take a look at all the tools available for your use in Quattro Pro. Toolbars are interchangeable in your Quattro Pro window, or you can create your own toolbars using the buttons on the toolbars provided.

Quattro Pro provides several toolbars that work with different types of projects:

- **The Notebook Toolbar** provides shortcuts for most of your everyday tasks. This toolbar is typically present on your window, no matter what you are doing on your spreadsheet.

- **The Property bar** is an intelligent, constantly changing toolbar that provides tools that are appropriate to the activity performed on the spreadsheet. For example, if you are typing text, text tools, such as font selection and justification options, are available on the Property bar. If you create a graph, buttons for graphing tools, such as chart type and axis titles, appear on the Property bar. This innovative Property bar is available in all the Corel Suite 8 programs.

- **The Charting and Drawing Toolbar** provides drawing tools that give you the power to add pizzazz to your chart.

- **The Selection Formatting Toolbar** appears when you select an area of the spreadsheet (even a single cell). It gives you shortcuts for tasks such as copying, pasting, sorting, and aligning.

- **The Outlining Toolbar** gives you the tools to group data into collapsible and expandable sets.

- **The Data Manipulation Toolbar** provides tools for working with your database.

- **The Auditing Toolbar** has tools that let you trace the components of any formula or determine which formulas make use of the contents of a particular cell.

- **The Chart Color Schemes Toolbar** is a whole toolbar full of colors! Use this toolbar to select and change colors in your graphs by selecting a colored area of the graph, then clicking on the color you want to apply from the palette on the toolbar.

## Editing Toolbars

You can change the components of a toolbar—put the buttons you want to use on the bar and get rid of the ones you never bother with.

### Changing Toolbars

You can edit all of the toolbars except the Property bar. The Property bar is an intelligent toolbar that changes itself to fit the needs of the user at a particular time. Because the buttons on the Property bar aren't stable, you can't add buttons to this bar or remove buttons from it.

To edit a toolbar, follow these steps:

1. Open the toolbar you wish to change.

2. Right-click in the toolbar area. Choose Edit from the pop-up menu.

3. Drag a button off a toolbar into the work area of your spreadsheet, then release your mouse button. The button is no longer on the toolbar.

4. Drag a button from the Edit Toolbar dialog box (see Figure 10-1) up to a toolbar. The button you choose becomes part of the toolbar.

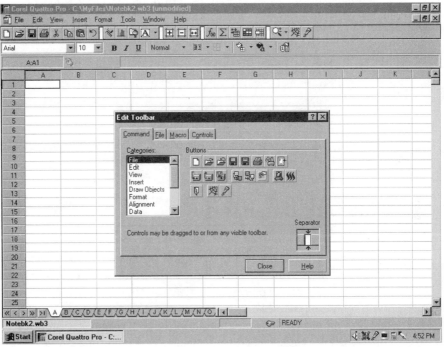

*Figure 10-1: You can drag buttons off of and onto a toolbar while the Edit Toolbar dialog box is open.*

5. Drag a separator up to the toolbar from the Edit Toolbar dialog box if you want to space out your toolbar buttons.

6. Click on Categories in the Edit Toolbar dialog box to display other buttons.

7. Click on Close when you've finished making changes in your toolbar. The changes will be saved with the toolbars.

## Designing Your Own Toolbar

A toolbar of your very own! You can create your own toolbar in much the same way as you edit toolbars.

To create your own toolbar, follow these steps:

1. Right-click in the Toolbar area. Choose Settings from the pop-up menu.

2. Click on Create in the Toolbar Settings dialog box. You are prompted to name your toolbar (something personal, like My Toolbar, or perhaps Favorite Tools) and provide an optional filename (Quattro Pro will provide a filename if you leave this blank).

3. Click on OK to add your toolbar to the list.

4. Click on Edit and the Toolbar Editor dialog box opens.

5. Add buttons to your toolbar by dragging the buttons you want up to the new, blank toolbar that has appeared at the top of the window.

6. Click on Close when you are finished.

From this point forward your toolbar will appear on the pop-up list with the others and you can display it whenever you like.

# Working With Databases

A database is a collection of information. Typically, the data is stored in spreadsheet-like tables with each row representing an individual record of data and each cell in the row representing a field within the record. For example, a database containing names and addresses of employees would include a single row for each employee. In separate cells of the row would appear items that make up the whole employee's record, such as first name, last name, street address, city, state, and zip code. Each employee's record would contain these items in the same order. That is, column one would always contain the last name, column two would always contain the first name, and so on.

Generally, you need a database software program (such as Paradox) if you are creating a large database. A spreadsheet program works well if the database you are using is relatively small (perhaps only a few thousand records) and you don't need extensive reporting capability from the database.

You can create a database in Quattro Pro by putting titles in the first row (First name, Last name, Street Address, and so on, one title at the head of each column), then filling in the records beneath the titles.

**Tip**

*You can import a database from another application (such as Paradox) and then use the information within Quattro Pro. To import from another database, choose Insert | External Data | Import. Indicate the type of data you plan to import and the location of the data on your computer. Click on Filter if you want to import only a portion of the database that meets particular requirements (such as only people who live within a certain zip code), indicate the field which you want to narrow (zip code, in this example), then enter the criteria (such as =46208). Then click on Finish to perform the import.*

## Searching for Records & Sorting Data

Sort items alphabetically, chronologically, or by whatever criteria you choose. To sort your database, first select the items you want to sort, including the headings, then choose Tools | QuickFilter. A down arrow appears at the top of each column, next to the headings.

Click on the down arrow at the top of the column containing the information by which you want to sort (see Figure 10-2). For example, if you want to sort your employee list by last name, click on the arrow at the top of the last name column.

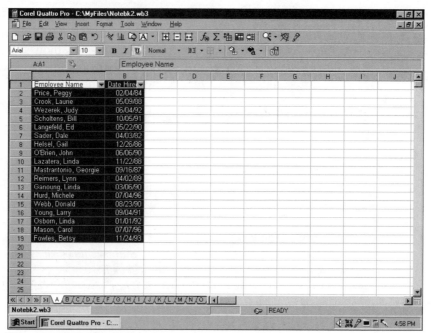

*Figure 10-2: Click on the down arrow at the top of a column to sort your database by the type of information in that column.*

From the drop-down list that appears, select the sort or selection method. For an alphabetical sort, click on Sort A-Z. The database is sorted alphabetically by last name.

Alternatively, if you click on a person's name that appears in the drop-down list, only records containing that name will appear in your results.

*Note:* If you filter a list so that only records containing a particular name or other piece of information show in your results, you can return to the full list by clicking the down arrow at the top of the column again and selecting Show All.

## Sorting by Multiple Criteria

What if you sort your data list by city and there are 42 records in the list for Indianapolis alone? You may want to sort further, perhaps to alphabetize your list by last name within each city. Follow these steps to sort by more than one criterion.

1. Select the database records you wish to sort, including titles.

2. Press Ctrl+Shift. While holding down these keys, click on columns in the order in which you want to sort items. You might, for example, click on the city column first, then last name, then first name. You can sort by as many as five columns.

3. Right-click on the toolbar, then click Selection Formatting to open the Selection Formatting toolbar.

4. Click the A...Z button to sort in ascending order, or click Z...A to sort in descending order.

### Custom Sorts

To customize the sort rather than simply sorting alphabetically or chronologically, you can select your data, choose Tools | QuickFilter, then click the down arrow at the top of a column. Choose Custom from the drop-down list.

Once you choose Custom, you can enter the exact search you want to perform. You can use operators such as +, >, <, as well as AND and OR to customize your sort. For example, if you want to search a database for records containing zip codes beginning with "46," your customized search in the zip code column would read ">45999 AND <47000" (see Figure 10-3).

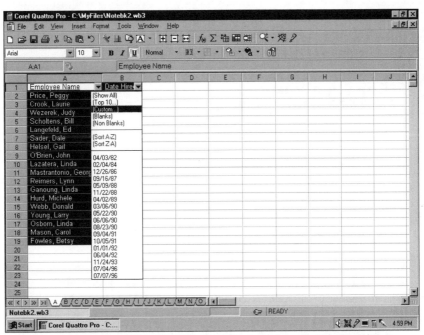

*Figure 10-3: Customize your sort by choosing "Custom" from the list of sortable items.*

# Using Links

You can create live links between your spreadsheets. When information in one spreadsheet changes, it is automatically updated in the other sheet.

To create a link, follow these steps:

1. Select the cell or range of cells you wish to link.

2. Click on the Copy button on the toolbar.

3. Open the spreadsheet to which you want to copy the cells.

4. Click on the upper left cell of the range in which you want to paste the linked cells.

5. Right-click, and choose Paste Special from the pop-up menu.

6. Click on Link.

From now on, whenever you open the file containing the linked cells, Quattro Pro will examine the original file and update the linked cells with current information. *Note:* If you delete the original file, ERR (error) appears in the cells of the linked file.

## Changing Links

If you change the name of your original file, Quattro Pro can no longer find the links in the linked spreadsheet. You can easily work around this problem by changing the links in the linked spreadsheet.

Choose Edit | Links | Change Link, and enter the name of the spreadsheet than now contains the linked information.

## Refreshing Links

If the file containing your linked information changes, your linked file is automatically updated whenever you reopen the linked file. But what if both files are open at the same time and changes are being made to the original file (perhaps the files are being used on a network and another user is making changes to the original file)?

As soon as a file to which you are linked is saved or closed, you can update the information in your linked file. Choose Edit | Links | Refresh Links. Quattro Pro examines the status of the original file—even if it is still open and in use—and updates the information in your linked file.

## Deleting Links

Finished with the links in your spreadsheet? You can remove links by selecting Edit | Links | Delete Links to remove all links in your spreadsheet.

The linked cells in your spreadsheet change to ERR when you remove the links. Unlike other spreadsheet operations, deleting links is an operation that cannot be restored by clicking on the Undo button.

If you want to keep the linked data in your spreadsheet before you destroy the link, select the linked cells. Then choose Edit | Convert to Values. Click OK, and the cells that contained links will now contain only the values that were represented by those links. Now you can remove the links without removing the data.

# Numeric Tools

Several special tools in Quattro Pro help you analyze the information in your spreadsheets and even make predictions based on the information that you have.

When you use a numerical tool, you click an arrow in the dialog box for the particular tool. The arrow returns you to your spreadsheet and leaves just the title bar of the Numerical Tool dialog box floating onscreen. You restore the dialog box by clicking on the Restore button on the floating title bar.

## The Optimizer

Although it sounds like a good name for a television show, you can use the Optimizer to solve for variables in problems. Set up a problem with a group of variables, then indicate whether you are looking for a maximum value, a minimum value, or a specific target value.

For example, say you want to borrow some money. You know you can afford to pay no more than $250 per month. So how much can you borrow? Follow these steps to get help from the Optimizer:

1. Enter labels for all the pieces of information in the problem, those you know and those you don't know: loan amount, term, interest rate, and monthly payment.

2. Fill in the information you know (in this example, the term and the interest rate).

*Note:* Since the payments you have designated (the *term*) are to be monthly, the interest rate should also be stated in a monthly form. Interest rates generally appear in annual form (9% per year, for example). Divide the annual interest rate by 12 (9/12 would yield .75%) to get the monthly rate.

3. In one cell, set up the formula that would solve this problem, without regard for the Optimizer (in this example, the formula would be @PMT(cell1, cell2, cell3), where cell1 is the unknown loan amount, cell2 is the interest rate, and cell3 is the term). This cell is referred to as the Solution Cell (see Figure 10-4).

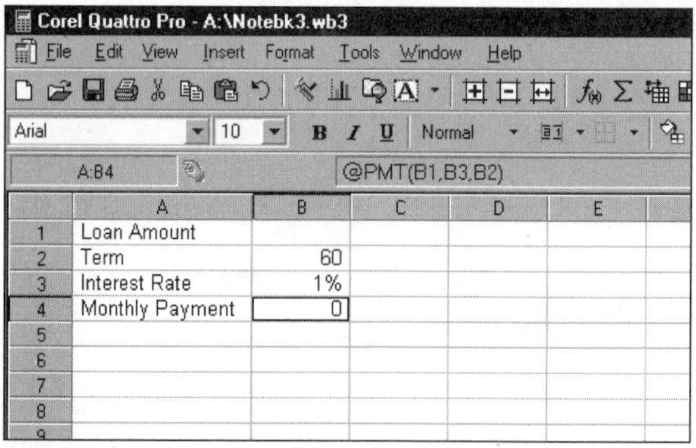

*Figure 10-4: Set up your spreadsheet so that you can use the Optimizer to find the optimum solution.*

4. Choose Tools | Numeric Tools | Optimizer.

5. Click on the arrow to the right of the Solution cell in the Optimizer dialog box. This returns you to your spreadsheet, where you will indicate the cell containing your formula (see Figure 10-5).

6. Click on the cell containing your formula in the spreadsheet. Restore the Optimizer dialog.

7. Click on Target, then enter the amount you can afford to pay on a monthly basis (in this example, 250).

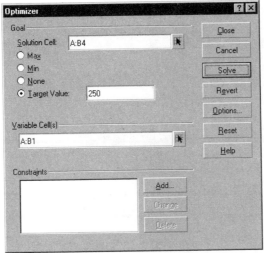

*Figure 10-5: The Optimizer dialog box.*

8. Click on the arrow to the right of the Variable Cells box, then click on the cell where the loan amount should appear in your spreadsheet. Restore the Optimizer dialog.

9. Click on Solve. The Optimizer will fill in the information in your spreadsheet, showing how much you can afford to borrow based on the target payment you have indicated.

## Using What-If

You can use a What-If table to see a range of possible answers for a particular problem. There are many ways to set up a What-If table. Below is a basic format that can be adjusted to fit your needs.

1. Create a mathematical formula that contains a variable (such as A1/.05), in a cell in your spreadsheet, leaving the variable cell (A1, in this case) blank.

2. On a clear area of your spreadsheet, enter a range of possible candidates for the variable.

3. Choose Tools | Numeric Tools | What If (see Figure 10-6).

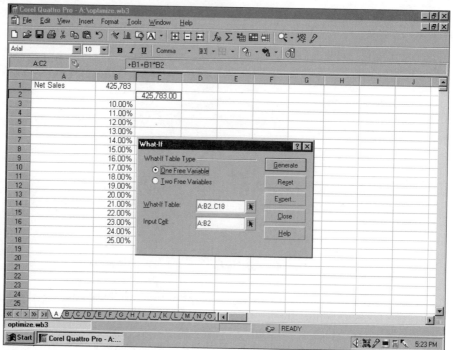

*Figure 10-6: Use the What-If numerical tool to find a range of possible answers for your problem.*

4. Select One Free Variable.

5. Click the arrow to the right of the What-If table, and highlight the area of your spreadsheet that contains the formula, the blank cell, the candidates for the variable, and the cells in which a solution can be generated. Then restore the What-If dialog box.

6. Click the arrow to the right of Input Cell and click on the blank, variable cell in your spreadsheet (A1, in this case). Restore the What-If dialog box.

7. Click on Generate. Values are inserted into the solution cells based on all the possible candidates you listed.

If you change information (change the formula, add an additional formula referencing the same variable, change or add to the variable candidates), you must regenerate the What-If scenario.

## Using Solve For

Solve For is a tool that lets you calculate a formula in reverse! You indicate the result you want and tell Quattro Pro which variable it can adjust to achieve that result, and Solve For finds the amount necessary to reach the result you want.

To use Solve For, follow these steps:

1. Enter a formula that contains a cell reference.

2. Click on Tools | Numeric Tools | Solve For (see Figure 10-7).

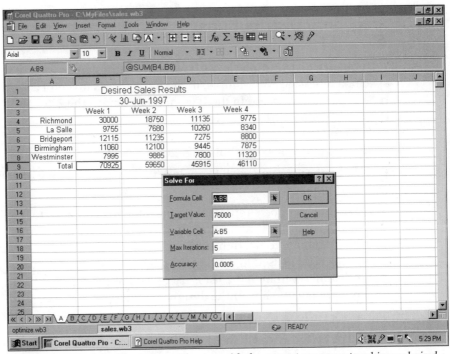

*Figure 10-7: The Solve For tool provides you with the amount necessary to achieve a desired result.*

3. Click the arrow to the right of Formula Cell. Click on the cell containing the formula, then restore the Solve For dialog box.

4. Click on Target Value, and enter the amount you want the formula to generate.

5. Click on the arrow to the right of Variable Cell. Click on the cell in the spreadsheet that can contain the resulting amount. Restore the Solve For dialog box.

6. Max Iterations means how many times you want to let Solve For make a stab at finding an answer. The higher this number, the longer the calculation may take, depending on the complexity of the formula.

7. Accuracy specifies how precise you want the answer to be.

8. Click on OK. Solve For will place the result in the variable cell on your spreadsheet.

## Frequency Distributions

A **frequency distribution** shows how many entries are in each of several specified intervals. For example, if you have a parts inventory listing and one type of part is numbered in the 100s, another type in the 200s, and so on, you can use a frequency distribution to find out how many part items there are in each interval of numbers.

To use a frequency distribution, follow these steps:

1. Enter the data you wish to analyze (in this case, a listing of your parts by part number).

2. Enter the numbers representing the intervals you wish to track (in this case, 100, 200, 300, and so on), in ascending order in a column that has a blank column to the right and one blank row beneath. The blank column to the right is used to display the frequency of each interval. The blank cell at the bottom of the list is used to display a count of the items that did not fall into any of the designated intervals (see Figure 10-8).

3. Click on Tools | Numeric Tools | Frequency.

4. Click on the arrow to the right of the Value Cells box. Select the cells in your spreadsheet that contain your data. Restore the Frequency Tables dialog box.

5. Click on the arrow to the right of the Bin Cells box. Select the cells in your spreadsheet that contain the frequency intervals. Restore the Frequency Tables dialog box.

6. Click on OK. Quattro Pro will enter the frequency numbers in the column to the right of your intervals.

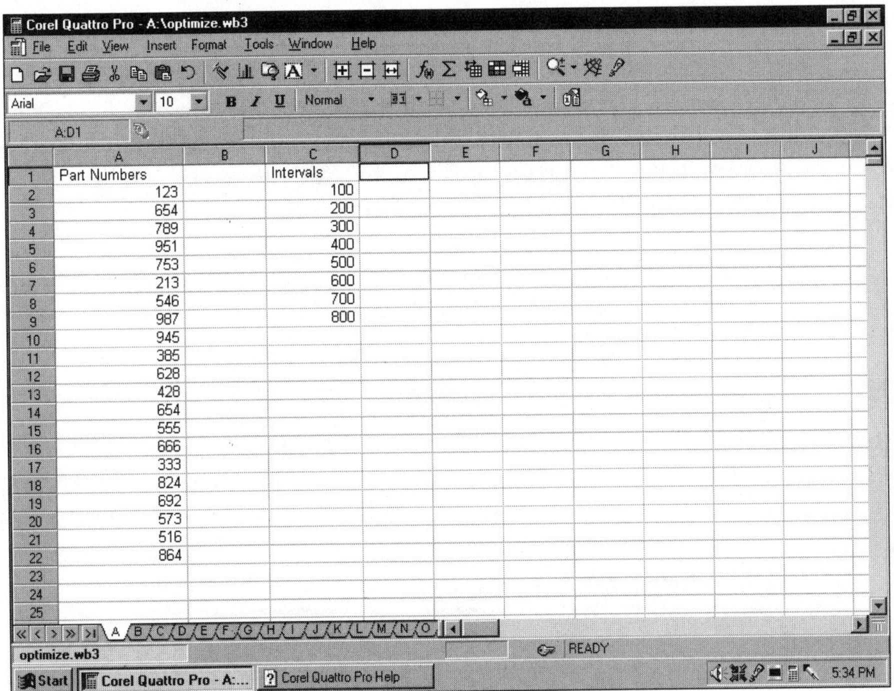

*Figure 10-8: Set up a list of intervals to determine the frequency with which items fall in each interval.*

In the blank cell beneath the frequency numbers Quattro Pro will compute the number of data items that exceed the highest interval. Once you've generated the frequencies, you can select the intervals and the results and use the information for creating a graph (the intervals would be the X-axis titles and the quantity in each interval would be graphed along the Y-axis). The graph would then provide you with a visual analysis of how many inventory items exist in each category.

## Working With Macros

A macro is like a little robot, automatically performing steps over and over again, working all by itself with little or no human contact. Create a macro by recording the steps you want the macro to perform. When you record steps, you are, in effect, teaching the macro what to do. Then when you play the macro, it plays back the steps you taught it.

## Recording & Playing Macros

Record a macro by clicking on Tools | Macro | Record. Click on Quattro Pro Macro, then select an area of your spreadsheet in which to store the macro commands. Click on OK and you are ready to record.

Perform the steps of the task you wish to automate. Click on Tools | Macro | Record to stop recording.

To play your macro, click on Tools | Macro | Play. Select the location of your macro, then click on OK. Your macro will play, performing the job you taught it to do.

You can create a shortcut for playing your macro after you record the macro. Click on Insert | Name | Cells. In the Cell(s) field, indicate the upper left cell of the macro. In the Names field, type a backslash (\) followed by a letter of the alphabet. Click on Add. From this point forward, to play the macro, press Ctrl+Shift, then type the letter you assigned to the macro name.

## Debugging Macros

Believe it or not, sometimes your macro may not run the way you intended. You can play your macro step-by-step in order to see just where it is going awry, then make changes in it. To debug a macro, click on Tools | Macro | Debugger. Then click Tools | Macro | Play, and select the macro you wish to debug. Press the spacebar to advance the macro one step at a time. When you have found a problem you can either rerecord the macro, or go to a macro cell to make a change.

# Moving On

The advanced Quattro Pro techniques you learned in this chapter, such as customizing toolbars, working with databases, linking to other spreadsheets, and using numeric tools and macros, are skills that you will polish with time. The more you work with these techniques, the more you will find practical uses for them. From here you will receive an overview of the bonus applications that accompany Corel WordPerfect Suite 8, including Bitstream Font Navigator, QuickFinder, QuickView Plus, Envoy 7, and the Address Book. Learn about how each bonus application helps round out the Suite to make it more useful.

# Bonus Applications

# 11

# The Bonus Applications

In this chapter, we'll look at the helper or "bonus" applications that are included with WordPerfect. These helper applications perform specific chores, and add convenient features to the three main Suite components. Let's start with the Address Book.

## The Address Book

The Address Book gives you quick access to any address. You can insert an address into a document, select several addresses to send the same letter to, or send a large mailing to an entire address list. You can use multiple Address Books to group your addresses. You can also retrieve addresses that meet specific criteria; for example, you can specify that everyone in a particular state should receive a particular mailing.

In this section, we'll use the Address Book as a source for the addressees of a particular mailing. We'll create letters and envelopes for every name in your Address Book, investigate how to choose which fields from your Address Book you want to include in your letter, and learn how to control where each field appears in your letter.

## Working With the Address Book

Launch the Address Book by choosing Start | Corel WordPerfect Suite 8 | Accessories | Corel Address Book 8. (In WordPerfect, you can also choose Tools | Address Book.)

**Tip**

*If you use the Address Book frequently, consider placing it on the Desktop Application Director. See Chapter 2 for more information on the DAD.*

The Address Book opens with the most recent Address Book file you used. By default, this file is named My Addresses. If you have not yet created an Address Book file, a blank one is opened.

### Adding Addresses to the Address Book

Figure 11-1 shows an Address Book. Each section of an address is called a field. You can control which fields are included in your Address Book, and which ones appear onscreen as you scroll through your addresses. Position your cursor over the bar between the fields, and drag it to increase or decrease the field's size.

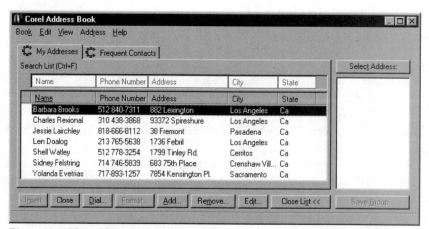

*Figure 11-1: The Address Book with five fields: Name, Phone Number, Address, City, and State.*

Click the Add button to add a new address to the Address book. Choose Person or Organization. This displays a dialog box where you can type in information about the new address (see Figure 11-2).

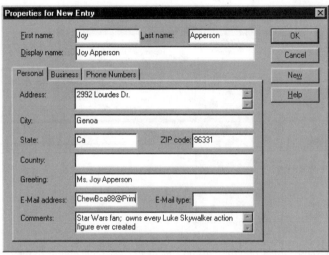

*Figure 11-2: Clicking the Add button opens this dialog box for adding a new address to your Address book.*

## Changing the Fields That Appear in the Address Book

Return to the main Address Book window by clicking OK. You'll notice that, by default, the WordPerfect Address Book displays the E-mail address and E-mail type fields. You might prefer to have other fields instead. To change which information appears in the Address Book select Edit | Columns, which displays a submenu where you can select which fields to include (see Figure 11-3). Check a particular field to include it in the main Address Book window. Note that this does not change the data in your Address Book, only what is displayed in the main window.

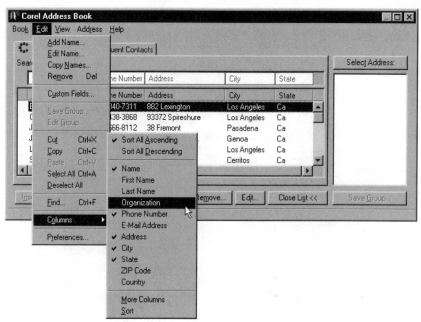

*Figure 11-3: Choose Edit | Columns and check fields to make them appear in the Address Book's main window.*

## Changing the Name Format

You can change the name format so that, for example, the first name appears last, which is useful for creating an alphabetical list of addressees. Select View | Name Format, and choose the name format you want.

## Editing Data in the Address Book

To change information for an address entry, select any name in the list and click the Edit button. Note that when you add information, it may not be displayed in the main window, but it is saved as part of your record. You can also use this data in a merge.

## Creating a Mailing List

By default, the Address Book uses every entry when you perform a merge or print envelopes. You can, however, restrict which entries you use. Follow these steps:

1. Click the Address List button at the bottom right of the main window.

2. The Select Address list is displayed in the right of the window.

3. To add an address to your selected list, click it, then click the Select Address button.

Repeat this process for every address you want to add to your list (see Figure 11-4).

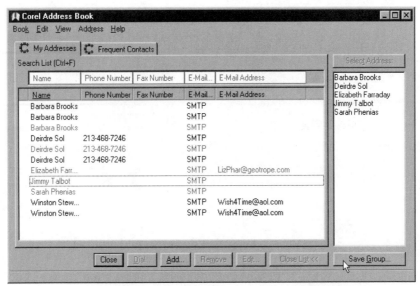

Figure 11-4: A selected group of addresses. Click Save Group to save the list.

4. Click Save Group. This creates a group for your selected addresses.

You can then display this group and use it for a select mailing by merging it with a document.

## Formatting How an Address Appears in a Letter

If you are working in WordPerfect, you may want to change the format of the address for your letter. Launch the Address Book through your WordPerfect menus (Tools | Address Book). Click the Format button on the main window. (Before selecting the Format button, you must select some addresses and transfer them to the Selection list, as described above.) If you've launched the Address Book from the Start Menu or Explorer, the Format button will not appear.

Unless you have added Country, Business, and Title fields to your addresses, you may not see any difference when you select a new address format.

## Creating Filters

The Define Filter feature (View I Define Filter) lets you display only certain addresses in your list. For example, you can select Jones in the Name field, and Los Angeles for the City field and view only those addressees whose entries meet those criteria. The Building a Filter dialog box, shown in Figure 11-5, displays all your choices in sentence form, which makes it clear what the filter will do.

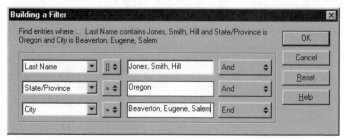

*Figure 11-5: The upper part of the Building a Filter dialog box provides a "natural speech" interpretation of your filter.*

Figure 11-6 shows how to include names and add fields to your filter. The Qualifier Selector is open. It lets you specify a filter "James, AND Hill but NOT Mike Hill." Or, "Smith, AND Jones, in Beaverton Oregon, but NOT in Eugene Oregon." If your Address Book grows to several hundred entries, the ability to limit the names you are searching through is helpful.

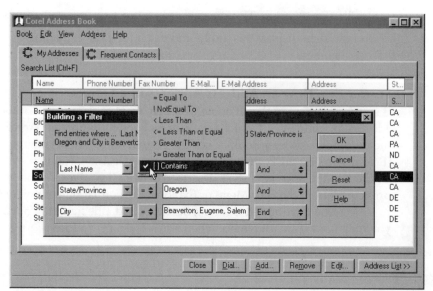

*Figure 11-6: Filter qualifiers separate each field you want to add to your filter. Selecting And causes a new field to appear.*

## Importing & Exporting Address Book Data

You can import addresses from various databases and export them back using the File | Import and File | Export commands. If you have address data in a FoxPro or Paradox file, it's easy to import it. After selecting File | Import, you are prompted to specify a database type (for example, any file with a .DB file extension), then the Import Expert is displayed, which lets you identify how fields in the database correspond to fields in your Address Book (see Figure 11-7). The data on the left is data that you are importing from the database. The field names on the right are existing fields in your Address Book.

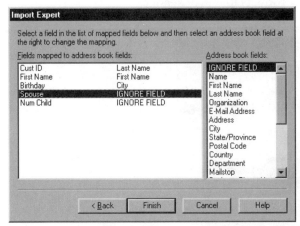

*Figure 11-7: To import a database into your Address Book, select File | Import. You can then map the data to the existing Address Book fields.*

## Creating Custom Address Book Fields

You can create custom fields for your Address Book; for example, to identify all those people who donated more than 500 dollars per year to a particular cause, or people you met at a professional conference. Select Edit | Custom Field and provide a name for your new field. This field is then available for all your existing addresses and any new ones you add.

## Inserting an Address in Your Document

To insert an address from an Address Book into your document, click in your document where you want the address to appear, then select Tools | Address Book. Double-click on the address you want, and it is displayed in your document.

Letter templates, and any other WordPerfect templates that involve correspondence, provide a direct link to the Address Book. Figure 11-8 shows the Letter PerfectExpert. Click the Address Book button to select any address as a recipient, courtesy copy recipient, or sender.

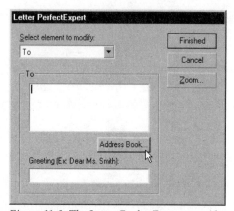

*Figure 11-8: The Letter PerfectExpert provides access to the Address Book.*

## Merging Address Book Data With a Document

In this section, we'll create an unaddressed letter, then use data from the Address Book to create a letter for as many addressees as you want, and create envelopes for them as well.

### The Merge Dialog Box

After creating the letter you want to send, do the following:

1. Position the cursor where you want the address to appear on each letter.

2. Select Tools | Merge to display the Merge dialog box. Note that it provides a button to display the Address Book, which lets you do any last-minute editing before you merge your data.

3. Click the Perform Merge button to display the Perform Merge dialog box.

4. In the Form Document drop-down list, you must specify what document to use as the container for your merge. Make sure that Current Document is selected.

5. In the Data Source drop-down list, choose Address Book. If you have more than one Address Book file, specify the one you want using the Select Records button.

6. In the Output drop-down list, select Current Document.

7. Click Merge.

The Merge toolbar is displayed at the top of the window (see Figure 11-9). Make sure there is room at the top of the page for the address. We are going to be adding field "placeholders" to specify where each field should appear.

8. Click Insert Field on the Merge toolbar, and the Insert Field Name or Number dialog box is displayed (see Figure 11-9).

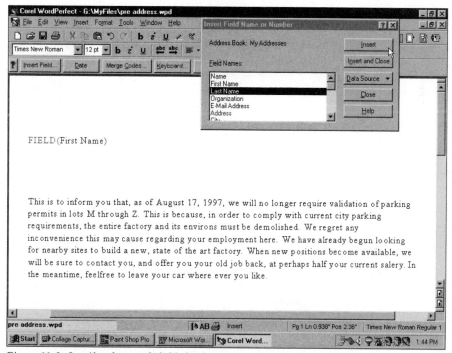

*Figure 11-9: Specify where each field should appear using the Merge toolbar. The cursor is about to add a Last Name field marker. When the data is merged, this marker will be where the last name appears in each letter.*

9. Position your cursor where you want a field to appear after you merge the data, select the appropriate field name, and click Insert.

Continue adding placeholders until you have defined locations for all the fields you want. Don't forget to add spaces! If you forget to put a space between the first and last name, for example, then every letter you print will have the first and last name running together like one word. (And that's just the type of thing that goes unnoticed until *after* you print.)

10. Use the Enter key and the spacebar to position the fields as you want them to appear. Figure 11-10 shows the fields for the entire address in place in the letter, the Greeting being added last.

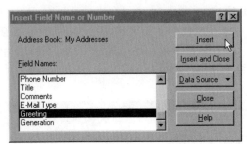

*Figure 11-10: The address portion of the letter filled in with placeholder fields. When the letter is printed, each copy of the letter will contain information from a record in your Address Book in each field.*

## Creating Automatically Addressed Envelopes

WordPerfect provides an automated envelope generation feature, which is much more efficient than trying to format another merge for your envelopes. Here's how to use it:

1. In the Perform Merge dialog box, click the Envelopes button to display the Envelope dialog box.

2. In the Return Address pane, type in your return address or click the Address Book button to select the return address there. Your return address appears on the envelope preview.

3. Click in the Mailing Address data area, and click the Field button at the bottom.

4. Add the field placeholders you want to your envelope (see Figure 11-11).

5. Close the Insert Field or Number and the Envelope dialog boxes. We're ready to merge the data.

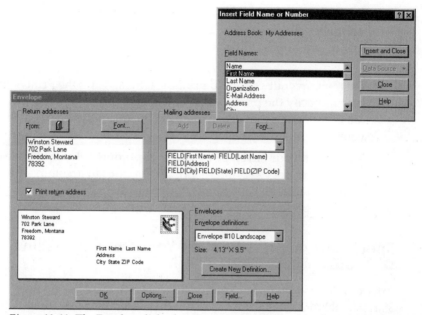

*Figure 11-11: The Envelope dialog box. Insert Field Name or Number is available to place field markers in the Mailing addresses area.*

## Merging the Data

Now that we've set up your letter and your envelopes, we're ready to merge the data. Follow these steps to create a separate letter for every addressee you've selected:

1. In the Perform Merge dialog box, make sure that Current Document is selected as the output. You can also create a new document that contains the result of the merge, or, if you're *really* brave, send the result straight to the printer.

2. Finally, you get to click the Merge button. WordPerfect creates a new page for every addressee.

These new pages will consist of the letter you wrote with an address from your Address Book. The pages—individual letters, really—will appear in the same order as the addresses appear in your Address Book.

After the letters, you'll find your envelope pages. Notice that all the envelopes have return addresses and that there is an envelope corresponding to each letter.

## Printing Your Merged File

Your document now consists of a number of normal-sized pages, followed by just as many envelopes. To print them successfully, you'll have to work in two stages:

1. First, set up your printer to print the letters, using the Print Setup dialog box to specify the print quality and collating parameters that you want. Make sure you set the Page Range to include only the pages that contain your letter, not the envelopes.

2. Then, print your envelopes. Place the appropriately sized envelopes in your printer, set the printer's printing options to accommodate envelopes, and use the Page Range options to include only your document's envelope pages.

# Specifying Address Book as Your Default Mailing System

After installing WordPerfect Suite 8, you can open the Address Book by clicking Start | Corel WordPerfect Suite 8 | Accessories | Corel Address Book 8. If you are using the Address Book for a project, you might need to choose between it and Microsoft Mail, which is probably installed on your system. Microsoft Mail or Microsoft Exchange is installed with your Windows 95 operating system to handle e-mail and address data on your computer. If you want to use Address Book instead, you'll need to tell Microsoft to move over. Here's how to do it:

1. From the desktop, select Start | Corel WordPerfect Suite 8 | Accessories | Corel Address Book 8. If Corel Address Book opens just fine, with the Address dialog box ready for input, then your system configuration is fine, and you're done.

2. If you see a message from Microsoft Mail about configuring Microsoft Mail to receive e-mail configured exactly *their way*, here are your options:

   ■ If your computer is online and you plan to use Microsoft Mail as your main e-mail program, follow the on-screen instructions. Eventually, you'll be returned to Corel Address Book. You'll notice, though, that all you'll have for address fields is various e-mail options.

   ■ If you want to make Corel Address Book available to your whole system as a source of addresses for all your word processing and publishing documents, go to the Control Panel and select Mail and Fax, then Add, and choose Corel Address Book (if it's not already there). See Figure 11-12 for a picture of this process. Click Properties to confirm that Corel Address Book 8 is indeed the database source for mail.

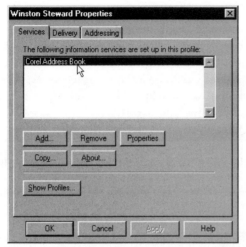

*Figure 11-12: Adding the Corel Address Book to your Mail and Fax settings.*

# QuickFinder

QuickFinder is similar to Microsoft Explorer, but it offers an additional feature: you can search almost any kind of text document to find a string of text.

## Using QuickFinder

QuickFinder is set up by specifying a folder that will be searched, not only for particular text files, but for text strings within the files themselves. Subfolders within the specified folder will also be searched.

To set up QuickFinder, select Start | Corel WordPerfect Suite 8 | Tools | QuickFinder Manager 8 from the Windows desktop. Figure 11-13 shows the QuickFinder window set to search *all* documents for the string "It was the best of times."

Once you've opened QuickFinder Manager 8, click Create. Specify a folder to search through. This process creates a search file that WordPerfect updates regularly. In the future, simply click the specified folder and type in the text string. Since you've set up a QuickFinder file for that folder, you'll be able to search for any text string you like.

After clicking Create and specifying a folder, QuickFinder works to create a Search file. This is the working file setup that facilitates quick searching for text strings for that selected folder and its subfolders.

This process may take a few minutes, depending on how extensive the folder is (subfolders are searched as well, remember). For example, if you've created a QuickFinder Search file for C:\, then you've designated that your entire hard drive be searched for text strings from now on. In such a case, you might have a two-hour wait after clicking Create. If you specify, perhaps, that only the folder "My Documents" or "My Files" be searched, then creating the QuickFinder Search file is almost instantaneous.

You can create several QuickFinder Search files, meaning that you can specify that several folders be searched. For example, you can create a QuickFinder Search for "My Files," and also one for "My Documents." When searching for a text string, you'd have to search each of these folders (and their subfolders) individually.

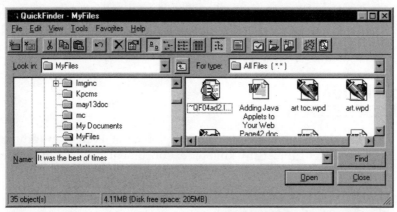

*Figure 11-13: The QuickFinder window, ready to search all documents on the computer.*

Later, QuickFinder can be accessed from the Start menu (Start | Find | Using Quick Finder). When you select Using QuickFinder, you'll see a Find dialog box that looks suspiciously like the standard 'find-the-file' dialog box we've grown used to by now. But to use QuickFinder's ability to search for a string of text, use the extended Look in Panel and open the folder you've specified to be searched with QuickFinder. (Remember, you can create more than one Quick Search, but only one folder and group of subfolders will be searched at a time.)

If you know the name of the document you're looking for, type it in the File Name field. But if you don't, just type a phrase that occurs in the document in the Content data box, and select Find.

QuickFinder searches the specified folder and its subfolders for the document name or the text phrase you've specified. Try to make your search text as specific as possible. If you type in a phrase that occurs frequently, you'll end up having to open dozens of files to find the one you're looking for.

## Updating QuickFinder Manager

QuickFinder keeps a record of the files on your hard drive. By default, it updates this record every two hours, whether WordPerfect is open or not. These updates can slow down your computer quite a bit. If you prefer to have QuickFinder update its information less frequently, select Start I Corel WordPerfect Suite 8 I Tools I QuickFinder Manager 8 I Edit, and change the Automatic update time (see Figure 11-14).

Click the Options button to specify that QuickFinder should search only the heading of your document, or just the document summary. You can also specify that QuickFinder ignore numbers in your search, as well as set aside a secondary location for QuickFinder Search files. If you find yourself creating Search files for many folders, setting up a secondary storage area for them is a good idea. That's because as you update your search files, they grow in size as you add to the numbers of documents stored in those folders.

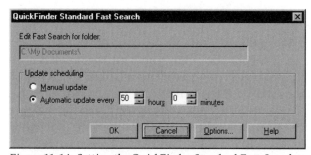

*Figure 11-14: Setting the QuickFinder Standard Fast Search to update files less frequently.*

# Bitstream Font Navigator

WordPerfect Suite 8 comes with thousands of fonts, and loading all of them could slow your system down considerably. But lots of the fonts that WordPerfect Suite provides are quite nice, and you might want to use them. Instead of loading all the fonts, which means that they take up memory and system resources, you can use **font management** to keep them available, but not loaded into your system until you need them.

The Bitstream Font Navigator is a bonus application that appears in your Windows Program menu, not in the WordPerfect Suite 8 group. It allows you to see examples of each font on the WordPerfect CD-ROM, load the ones you want for your current project, and uninstall the ones you don't need.

## Starting Font Navigator

When you first start Font Navigator (Start | Programs | Bitstream Font Navigator | Font Navigator 2.0), you'll see the Wizard for making a catalog. As explained later, a Font Navigator Catalog is a record of fonts used to select which fonts to use at the moment, or which to erase from your hard drive during times of non-use. So, when you first start Font Navigator, allow the Wizard to make a catalog of the fonts found on the WordPerfect Suite 8 CD-ROM, as well as on your hard drive. As we'll see shortly, these steps will allow you to take full advantage of Font Navigator later, as you work with your fonts.

To make a Font Catalog, simply select the drive(s) to search for fonts and click Finish. Font Navigator Wizard will take care of the rest.

Later when you start Font Navigator, you'll see that the left pane (labeled Contents of Font Catalog) lists fonts (see Figure 11-15). Once you create a font catalog with all the fonts on the WordPerfect CD-ROM (or other fonts on your hard drive), you can install them instantly by dragging them to your Installed Fonts list, which is the pane on the right side of the window. The lower right shows a sample of the selected font.

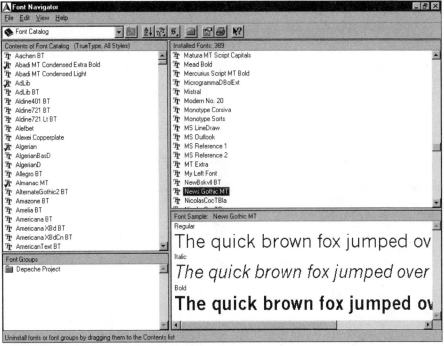

*Figure 11-15: The Font Navigator window.*

## Making a Font Catalog

If you didn't use the Wizard at the beginning, you can still make a font catalog of all the fonts found on the WordPerfect Suite 8 CD-ROM. Here's how:

1. Make sure the WordPerfect 8 CD is in your CD-ROM drive.

2. Select File | Find Fonts, and click the plus sign next to the CD-ROM symbol in the Find Fonts dialog box.

3. Now click the plus sign next to Core, then click next to AppMan, then click Wkswpi8, then click Fonts.

4. Place a check by Corel and CorelReq.

5. Click OK, and Font Navigator will begin cataloging the fonts. This may take a few minutes, depending on the speed of your computer.

## Installing & Uninstalling Fonts

You'll now have over a thousand fonts to choose from. You can make font groups or simply drag to install a font (see Figure 11-16). As you install fonts, notice that the number on the Installed Fonts pane tells you how many fonts are installed on your system. To uninstall a font, drag it from the Installed Fonts pane to the Contents of Font Catalog pane.

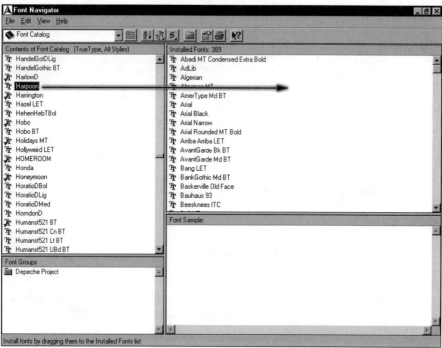

*Figure 11-16: The process of installing a font, dragging from left to right.*

## Creating Font Groups

Font Navigator allows you to *group* fonts. You can categorize fonts, including those that are not loaded on your computer, and place them in viewing folders, using any criteria you want. You could, for example, group decorative fonts, professional boardroom fonts, brochure and newsletter fonts, and load these font groups only for projects that call for them.

To create a font group, do the following:

1. Click File | New Font Group. A folder is displayed in the Font Groups pane, on the lower left of the window.

2. Name your group.

3. Drag fonts from either the Font Catalog pane or the Installed Fonts panel into the Font Groups folder (see Figure 11-17).

You can uninstall and reinstall fonts whenever you want, but make sure that you load the right fonts before opening any document.

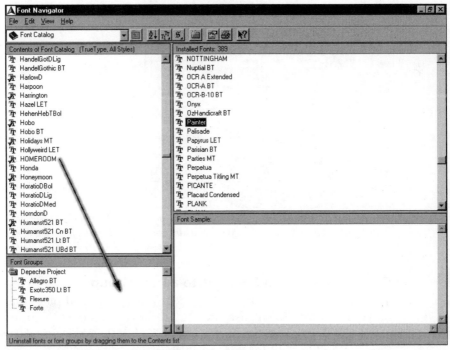

*Figure 11-17: Adding fonts to a font group.*

## Automatically Loading Font Groups

You can load a font group automatically whenever you start a certain program. For example, you might have a group of fonts that you always use with WordPerfect, and a more decorative set you use in your desktop publishing application. Here's how to set up a font group for automatic loading:

1. Right-click on the Font Group folder, and select Properties. Make sure the General tab is selected (see Figure 11-18).

2. In the Association field, specify the executable file or document that you want to associate this group with.

3. You can use the Browse button to search for a file, or type in the path and filename if you know it.

4. Click OK. The next time you launch the associated application or document, the fonts in this group are loaded automatically.

*Figure 11-18: The Font Group Properties dialog box. This allows you to associate a font group with a particular program so the fonts load automatically when the program opens.*

## Creating a Desktop Shortcut to a Font Group

You can create a shortcut to a particular font group, and place that shortcut on your desktop. To create a shortcut, right-click on the font group, and select Properties from the pop-up menu. Select the Shortcut tab, and check the Create a Shortcut for this group check box.

Once you have a shortcut, you can click on it, and select Install (see Figure 11-19). This gives you a quick way to install and uninstall fonts.

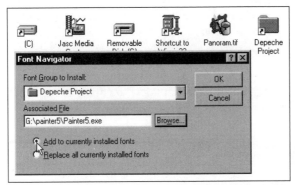

*Figure 11-19: Activating a font group shortcut on the desktop.*

## Uninstalling All the Fonts in a Group

When you install a font group, they are displayed in that group's folder in the Installed Fonts pane of Font Navigator. To uninstall the group, right-click on its icon, and select Uninstall Fonts from the pop-up menu (see Figure 11-20).

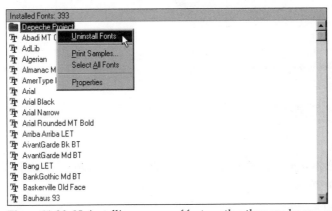

*Figure 11-20: Uninstalling a group of fonts, rather than one by one, which is a real time-saver.*

## Deleting Duplicate Fonts

If you have lots of fonts on your computer, you may have noticed that many look very similar. Bitstream Font Navigator can help you identify these fonts to limit redundancy. Here's how:

1. Right-click on any font, and select Properties from the pop-up menu.

2. Select the Analog Names tab. (Only fonts for which there are known duplicates have this tab.) This displays the names of identical or nearly identical fonts (see Figure 11-21).

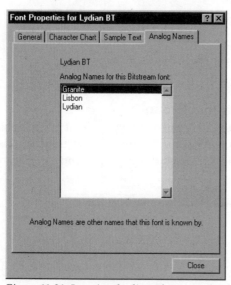

*Figure 11-21: Locating duplicate fonts. Analog fonts are fonts that are very similar or identical to the font you have clicked on.*

3. You can now search your installed fonts to see whether you have any of the duplicates installed.

4. If you locate a redundant font, right-click on it, and select Delete.

**Tip**

*Type the first letter of a font to jump to that letter in the Installed Fonts pane.*

## Envoy 7

Envoy 7 allows you to share documents with people who don't have WordPerfect. Envoy 7 is a portable viewing and editing platform that works even with non–Windows 95 computers, which lets your colleagues edit documents and return them to you. Graphics, advanced formatting, tables, and OLE objects are preserved in your Envoy document. Most WordPerfect Suite applications can create Envoy documents, and the recipient only needs the Envoy Viewer to read them (see Figure 11-22). To publish an Envoy document, you use the WordPerfect Suite application; for example, in Quattro Pro, you select File | Publish to Envoy.

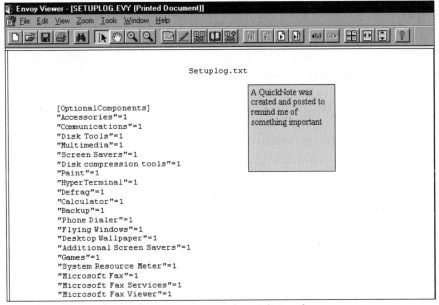

*Figure 11-22: A text document in Envoy. Envoy's QuickNotes lets you create notes to yourself (and others) and 'post' them.*

## Publishing to Envoy

Envoy converts any document to a universal format that can be opened and viewed on any Mac OS, Windows 3.11, Windows 95, or Windows NT-based computer. You can create Envoy documents from Word, WordPerfect, Lotus, and many other types of word processing, graphic, and spreadsheet-based documents. Once you create the Envoy document, distribute it along with the compact Envoy viewer (you have Corel's express permission to do so), and the file can be read just about anywhere, even if the person you are sending it to does not have the host application. If you are transferring an Envoy document to a system other than Windows 95, contact Corel for a correct version of the Envoy Viewer.

Envoy 7 is available to any application on your computer that you can print from. Although the Envoy 7 driver appears in the list of printers, it has nothing to do with creating a paper document. Envoy "prints" your document to an Envoy file, not to a printer. You can, however, print the Envoy document itself.

To publish to Envoy in a WordPerfect Suite application, select File | Publish to Envoy. Note that once you create an Envoy file, you cannot make any major changes to it, so make sure you're happy with your document before you create the Envoy file. After a few moments, the document loads in the Envoy Viewer. Select Save to save a copy of the new Envoy document. Your WordPerfect (or other source) document is unaffected. You can now distribute your Envoy document with the Envoy Viewer.

### Printing any Windows-Based Document to Envoy

To use Envoy from a non-WordPerfect Suite application, open the Print dialog box of the application and select Envoy as the printer. This method provides you with many more options that using File | Publish to Envoy. For example, some options allow the recipient to see your document without installing the Envoy Viewer. Select Properties from the Print dialog box to display the Envoy options:

- The Destination tab determines the type of output for your document. Should it be sent as e-mail, or sent as a spooled printing job, which is a very flexible way of sending your data but results in a large file? Should it be saved to disk as a standard Envoy document, and distributed later at your leisure, or would you rather make such decisions with each print job?

- The Paper tab determines the size of "paper" that your document should appear on when it's viewed on the recipient's screen.

- The Resolution tab lets you set the resolution for your document. The higher the resolution, the bigger the file. Unless you are sending a document that contains photographs or other artwork that requires many colors, try to limit the number of colors.

- The Font tab allows you to embed the fonts used in the document in the Envoy file, so that the recipient sees the document with the same fonts. Embedding a large number of fonts will make your file extremely large.

## Distributing the Envoy Viewer

To distribute Envoy Viewer to others and thus allow them to read and work with your Envoy documents, select Start | Corel WordPerfect Suite 8 | Setup & Notes | Distribute Envoy 7 Viewer.

After installing on your computer, you can distribute the Envoy Viewer to others. You'll need to compress it to fit it on a floppy disk. Once installed, others can use the Viewer to view your work, add comments or bookmarks, and highlight portions of it.

## Working With an Envoy Document

When you open your document in the Envoy Viewer, here's what you can do:

- Attach comments, notes, bookmarks, and highlight text.
- Attach hyperlinks to other portions of the document, or to other documents.
- Zoom in to any portion of the page, or switch to other pages.
- Insert objects like pictures, tables, sounds, or other OLE objects from other applications.
- Attach new pages to the Envoy document.

After converting a document to Envoy, you *cannot* do the following:

- Type in new text.
- Edit existing text.
- Delete text.

### Adding QuickNotes

You can add a QuickNote, which is WordPerfect's computerized version of the little yellow sticky notes, right on to your document. Just click the QuickNote icon on the toolbar. These notes can be short or long, and will be sent with the document to the new location.

## Adding Highlights

Click the Highlight tool on the toolbar and underline any portion of a document you like. After you save, your new highlighting will be part of what you send. The default Highlighting color is neon green. To edit a highlight, right-click on any highlighted portion of your document, and select Highlight Properties. At the resulting dialog box, you can:

- Change the highlight color.
- Type in the name of the author for the highlighted comment.
- Specify the style of highlight demarcation.

## Adding Bookmarks

Bookmarks help viewers navigate large documents, and make it easy for you to direct their attention to the really important parts. To add a bookmark to an Envoy document, select Tools | Bookmark. Your cursor becomes a small book icon. Select the text that you want viewers to see when they activate the Bookmark, and the Bookmark Properties dialog box is displayed (see Figure 11-23). You can select the text when the bookmark is activated or just place the cursor at that point. You can name the bookmark; if you do not, the selected text becomes the bookmark's name. To make the marked text fill almost the entire window when the viewer moves to the bookmark, select the Fit Bookmark to window radio button.

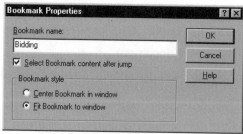

*Figure 11-23: Creating bookmark options.*

## Adding Hyperlinks

In Envoy, it's very easy to create a hypertext link, which moves the viewer to a new segment of your document when clicked. To do so, follow these steps:

1. Select Tools | Hyperlink.

2. The cursor becomes a Hyperlink Selector icon. Choose the phrase you want the visitor to click on, which will take them to a new location. (This is called the **source link**.)

3. Next, click the target text link, which is where the viewer will go to.

4. Double-click on the target after you select it.

5. A dialog box offers the same choices as when creating a bookmark. Make the appropriate selection.

6. From now on, whenever the cursor passes over the source text (the first portion of text you selected), it turns into a hand. When clicked, the linked text is displayed onscreen.

### Comparing Two Versions of an Envoy Document

If you send out multiple copies of a document, you might end up with two versions, each one annotated by a different reviewer. You can import the annotations from one Envoy document into another by selecting File | Import | Annotations. In the Browse dialog box, select which Envoy document to import the mark-ups from. Click OK, and the imported annotations are displayed onscreen along with the ones already in the document. If the source document is longer than the target document, then annotations on the left-over pages are not imported.

# QuickView Plus

One special program included on the WordPerfect CD-ROM is QuickView Plus. You use QuickView Plus to quickly look at text-based or graphic files, instead of opening the native application. This helps you quickly identify whether the file is really the one you're looking for.

## Installing QuickView Plus

To install QuickView Plus, do the following:

1. Put the WordPerfect Suite 8 CD in your CD-ROM drive.

2. When the Setup screen appears, click QuickView Plus.

3. Follow the onscreen instructions.

If AutoPlay is disabled on your computer, then do the following:

1. Place the WordPerfect Suite 8 CD in your CD-ROM drive.

2. Right-click on My Computer, and select Explore.

3. Locate the CD, and click on it.

4. Locate and open the folder "QvPlus4."

5. Click the Setup Icon inside the QvPlus4 folder.

6. Follow the onscreen instructions.

## Using QuickView Plus

QuickView Plus adds a QuickView Plus option to the pop-up menu that is displayed when you right-click a file. If you want to "peek" at a file, click QuickView Plus. See Figure 11-24 for an example of a graphic file viewed in QuickView Plus. Click the push-pin icon to temporarily fasten the viewer to the border of Explorer while you open another file.

You can print from QuickView Plus, and specify that you want a picture to become Windows wallpaper. You can also open more than one file at a time, including online documents.

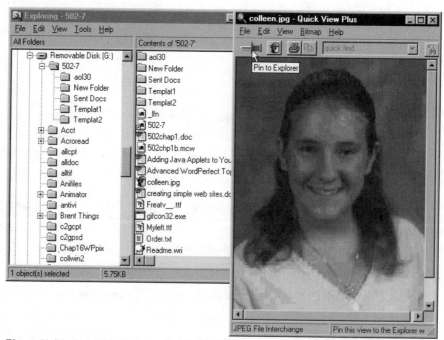

*Figure 11-24: A graphic file opened with QuickView Plus. "Pinning" a picture to Explorer keeps it anchored there.*

# Corel Memo

You can use Corel Memo to attach quick notes to any document, not just WordPerfect Suite documents. You can access this feature by selecting Insert | Object. It places a small memo of adjustable size on your document.

A Corel Memo is saved with its host document, but can be opened as a Corel Memo file, edited, and saved again. In a sense, it is separate from the document, because you can keep opening it and changing it, even after the main document itself is no longer being changed. Corel Memo is perfect for leaving yourself (and other people) notes, and for bits of information that change frequently.

If you send someone else a document with a Corel Memo attached, they'll need Corel Memo installed to view it. Many Corel applications install Corel Memo automatically.

Corel Memos are objects, which are accessible by selecting Insert | Object. You cannot open the Corel Memo application directly. To insert a Corel Memo into any application, do the following:

1. Select Insert | Object, to display the Insert Object dialog box.

2. Select the Create New radio button and select Corel Memo in the list.

3. Click OK.

The Corel Memo window appears in your document.

A Corel Memo has two sections, the header (heading) and the body. To create your Corel Memo, follow these steps:

1. Place your cursor in the small single-line segment at the top and type a heading.

2. Click in the body area and type your message. (For example, "Wash the car and buy concert tickets.")

3. To change the color of the heading and main body text, select the Color menu.

4. To change the font size and font type for both the heading and the message, select the Font menu.

5. To change the color of the memo paper itself, choose Color | Paper.

6. To change the small picture in the upper left corner of the memo, select Edit | Memo Picture. Click the Browse button to search your hard drive for another .BMP file. Keep in mind that a file larger than 100K will cause problems.

Figure 11-25 shows a memo in a document.

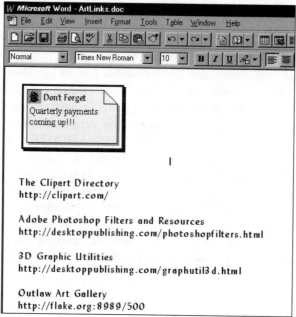

*Figure 11-25: A memo embedded in a document. Notice that a border is applied.*

# TrueType Fonts

If you want to install the TrueType fonts that are included with WordPerfect, you have two choices:

- Use Bitstream Font Navigator. See the section earlier in the chapter for details.

- Install the fonts manually.

To install the fonts manually, follow these steps:

1. Put the WordPerfect CD-ROM in the drive and wait for the installation screen to appear.

2. Select Custom Installation from the Installation Type dialog box. Select Bonus Applications. WordPerfect Setup begins.

3. You'll see the list of programs you can choose to set up. Select only TrueType Fonts before proceeding (see Figure 11-26).

4. Click the Components button, and a list of TrueType fonts is displayed (see Figure 11-27). By default, all the fonts are selected.

5. Select the fonts you want to install and deselect the fonts you don't want.

6. Click OK, and WordPerfect Setup installs the fonts you selected.

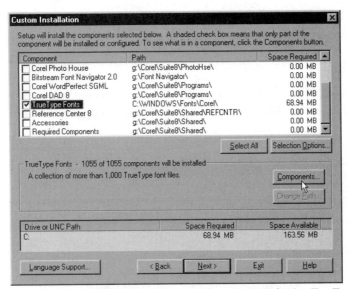

*Figure 11-26: Installing TrueType fonts. The cursor is selecting TrueType Fonts, which lets you choose which fonts to install.*

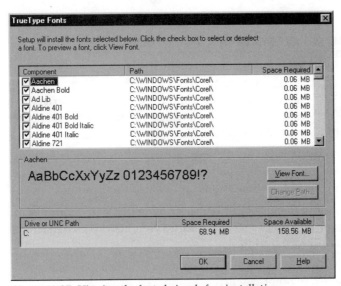

*Figure 11-27: Viewing the font choices before installation.*

## Tip

*Remember that having more than 300 fonts installed on your computer can cause performance problems.*

# PerfectScript

Corel PerfectScript lets you record your actions, save them, and play them back, which means you can automate mundane tasks. The program displays a small "console" on top of any program you are working with at the moment. As a new user, the only buttons of great interest to you are the Record, Stop, and Play command buttons (see Figure 11-28).

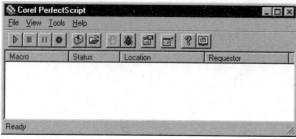

*Figure 11-28: The Corel PerfectScript "console" ready to record any keyboard, text, or mouse-click commands.*

## Creating a PerfectScript (or Macro)

Corel PerfectScript allows you to record any keyboard, mouse, or text creation action in WordPerfect, Quattro Pro, and Presentations 8. PerfectScript is another way for you to record macros, which we discussed in Chapter 6.

To record a script, do the following:

1. Open PerfectScript by clicking the Start | WordPerfect Suite 8 | Tools | Corel PerfectScript. Corel PerfectScript's Record button is available only if WordPerfect, Presentations, or Quattro Pro is open.

2. You'll see a Record and Playback dialog box with Compile and Debug commands. You can start recording your actions as a macro by pressing the red Record button.

3. You are prompted to name your macro (which is saved as a .WCM file, just like any other macro).

4. Perform the actions you want in the macro and save it just like any other macro (see Chapter 6 for details on creating macros).

Later, you can open the script you recorded (called a macro), press Play, and repeat the action you recorded. WordPerfect Suite 8 includes many macros, and provides a macro tool in the three main WordPerfect Suite applications, which we discussed in Chapter 6.

If you know some VisualBasic, you can quickly learn Corel's robust scripting language, and create complicated scripts that function in many other applications. First open the application that you want to record a script in, then select Start | Corel WordPerfect Suite 8 | Tools | PerfectScript.

## Creating Dialog boxes With PerfectScript

PerfectScript provides advanced tools that let you create full-featured dialog boxes. You can include list boxes, drop-down lists, Browse dialogs, OK and Cancel buttons—any of the features you are used to seeing in dialog boxes in Windows 95 programs. You must, of course, know how to associate the elements in the dialog box with the macro script's tasks and procedures. With even a little bit of knowledge of VisualBasic, PerfectScript's Dialog Editor and toolbar can be very helpful to you.

You can use PerfectScript to edit existing scripts and add dialog boxes to them, even when no other WordPerfect Suite 8 applications are open. The macros shipped with WordPerfect Suite 8 are on the CD-ROM, in the Corel\Suite8\Macros folder. To use the Dialog Editor and toolbar, do the following:

1. Select Tools | Dialog Editor.

2. Select a macro that you want to change, or create a new one by typing a name for it in the File Name data box. The Dialog Editor is displayed.

3. Select File | New to create a New Dialog icon.

4. Double-click the New Dialog icon. This displays a toolbar for adding visual elements to your dialog box.

Discussing how to use VisualBasic to create a new dialog box is beyond the scope of this book. But if you know how, you can now create a new dialog box.

Once you've created code in the Dialog Editor, you can copy and paste the code as follows:

1. Right-click on the New Dialog icon, and select Copy from the pop-up menu.

2. Return to the PerfectScript dialog box.

3. Open any script you like, and select File | Paste to paste the code into this script.

# Data Modeling Desktop

Data Modeling Desktop provides a way to create custom reports from Quattro Pro data. It lets you import data from Quattro Pro and present it as a series of movable bars. To work with the Data Modeling Desktop, do the following:

1. Open Quattro Pro, and select the rows and columns of data you want exported to the Data Modeling Desktop.

2. Click Data | Data Modeling Desktop.

3. You'll have to choose where in your spreadsheet you want Data Modeling Desktop to put the results. Specify cells and columns in the Cell For Returned Data field.

4. Specify a Data Exchange Method, such as DDE (Dynamic Data Exchange).

5. Now open the Data Modeling Desktop by clicking Start | Corel WordPerfect Suite 8 | Tools | Data Modeling Desktop.

6. Your Quattro Pro data is displayed in the source window. You can apply the Data Modeling tools to the data to create a report, which is returned to Quattro Pro in the cells you specified.

# SGML Layout Designer

Standard Generalized Markup Language (SGML) is a way to build a document that any computer can read. It is used by large governmental organizations, such as the IRS, NASA, and other institutions in which a document must be readable on many different types of computers and operating systems.

Turning a WordPerfect document into SGML requires several steps. The SGML Layout Designer helps you convert WordPerfect formatting to the structure information in SGML.

SGML is an extremely powerful language, but it's also very difficult to use, and discussing it is beyond the scope of this book. If you need to use WordPerfect's SGML Layout Designer, we suggest that you first become familiar with the concepts of SGML before you dive in.

# Moving On

In this chapter, we covered many of the bonus applications that come with WordPerfect Suite 8: Bitstream Font Navigator, QuickView Plus, Envoy, Corel Address Book, and others. One bonus application deserves a chapter all its own: Corel Photo House. You can use it to edit photographs, paint on them, and add text. After learning to use Photo House, you'll realize that it's unnecessary to spend money on another program to spruce up photos for use in WordPerfect Suite.

# 12

# Working With Corel Photo House

Corel Photo House is an image editing application that is included with WordPerfect Suite 8. Photo House is installed as part of the setup process.

## What is Photo House?

Photo House lets you work with pictures. You can add special effects to a scanned photo or repair a damaged one. You can add blur effects, embossing, and psychedelic lighting, or simply make an old photograph look new again. It's also great for enhancing poor colors and increasing color ranges.

Photo House also includes drawing tools to create bitmaps from scratch. It supplies various paintbrushes to help you draw lines in your graphics.

To work with Photo House, make sure your video card is set to work with 65,000 or 16.7 million colors. Check the Windows Display Control Panel. If your video card is set to work with only 256 colors, your photos will appear grainy. To access controls for changing screen colors, right-click on the Windows desktop, click Properties, and choose Settings. The Palette drop-down menu contains color display options. Consult your Windows 95 manual or video display driver instructions for more details.

# Introducing Photo House

The Photo House window includes the image workspace—where your picture is displayed—the Notebook, the Toolbox, and the toolbars. The Notebook provides project management tools, and the Toolbox provides image editing tools.

## The Notebook

The Notebook, which is located on the left side of the Photo House window (see Figure 12-1), has eight main buttons when you start Photo House. They are grouped into three categories:

- **Making changes**. The Make Changes button lets you edit a photo, for example, by creating special effects or retouching a photo.

- **Starting a project**. These buttons provide ways to start a project: by opening an image on your hard drive, scanning an image, opening an image from the library of photos included with the CD, or starting from scratch.

- **Saving your work**. The Save Image As button is for writing your finished image to disk.

The Notebook changes when you select a tool. Click the Key icon at the top of the Toolbox, and the Notebook enters Interactive mode. Keep your eye on it as you work. Every time you change tools, you'll see an explanation of a tool or a tip for working faster. Figure 12-2 shows the Eyedropper tool hovering over an image. The Notebook explains how to select a paint color or a page color using the Eyedropper tool.

The Return arrow lets you return to whatever task was explained last. This function lets you retrace your steps or repeat procedures without much fuss. The Notebook works similarly to the PerfectExpert.

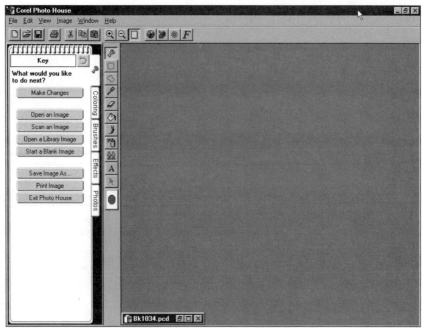

*Figure 12-1: The Photo House Notebook guides you through any procedure.*

*Figure 12-2: The Notebook explains the operation of the Eyedropper tool, which is currently selected.*

## The Image Workspace

The main work area is the image workspace. This is where your images are displayed and where you draw. Once you know your way around Photo House, select View | Notebook to hide the Notebook (see Figure 12-3). (You can always bring it back by selecting View | Notebook again.)

Like any standard window, you have scroll bars and arrows to reposition your image. You can use the zoom tools on the toolbar to zoom and unzoom your image.

*Figure 12-3: Remove the Notebook to free up space for an extra large picture. Click View | Notebook.*

## The Toolbars

Photo House has two toolbars: one at the top of the window, as you would expect, and one along the left edge of the workspace, which provides drawing tools. This vertical toolbar is actually called the Toolbox. Figure 12-3 shows both the toolbar and the Toolbox.

The first four icons on the toolbar are the standard New, Open, Save, and Print icons. The four towards the far right are important, and are not duplicated elsewhere (see Figure 12-4). They are as follows:

*Figure 12-4: The four unique icons on the toolbar.*

 **Coloring dialog button**—opens a dialog box with color swatches that you can apply with one mouse click. The drop-down list lets you apply one color, called the paper color, to the image background and another color to the paintbrush or fill. The selected color swatch has a numeric label which indicates the color's position on the RGB color wheel. For example, a particular shade of blue might be R102 G99 B244, which means that the red component of the color is 102, the green is 99, and the blue is 244. (The maximum value for any color is 255.) If you ever need to reproduce a color exactly, even in another program, you can use the numeric value to do so. Click More to display a dialog box where you can adjust the hue and saturation of a color choice (see Figure 12-5).

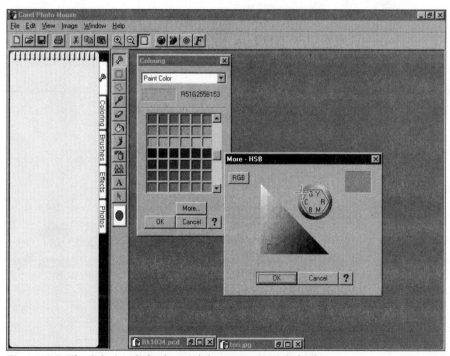

*Figure 12-5: The Coloring dialog box and the More – HSB dialog box.*

**Tool dialog button**—displays the Tool dialog box, where you can select a brush type, which affects the brush size, shape, and pattern (see Figure 12-6). It controls the width of the paintbrush, how "drippy" the painting effect is (the Ink Flow Rate number), and whether the brush has a sharp edge, hard edge, or fades out gradually. You can also control the brush angle; for example, if you want your strokes to have a slanted, calligraphic effect, you could add some angle to a thin, straight brush. And finally, you can affect how transparent your brush is. A high transparency number causes the brush to paint strokes that reveal what's underneath. A low transparency number creates a stroke with a more solid paint color.

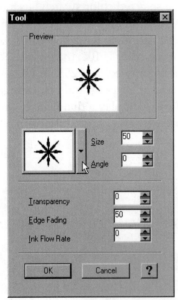

*Figure 12-6: The Tool dialog box. There are nearly a hundred different brush types.*

 **Color Tolerance dialog button**—displays the Color Tolerance dialog box, which determines how precise your fills are (see Figure 12-7). When you are filling an area that is *not* enclosed by a selection tool (meaning you haven't used a tool to mark off a fill area), your fill is applied to a particular color and all the "similar" colors in the area. A lower color tolerance means that, to be affected by the fill, the colors must be very similar; a high color tolerance means that the colors are only somewhat similar. A high color tolerance means that the fill is likely to fill a larger area.

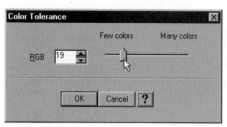

*Figure 12-7: The Color Tolerance dialog box. Moving the slider to the left causes a fill to fill a smaller area.*

**F**    **Text Styles dialog button**—displays the Text Styles dialog box, which you use to add text to your image. You can include a single letter or an entire paragraph of text, and use any font on your system.

The Toolbox has many different tools for you to work with the images (see Figure 12-8).

*Figure 12-8: The Toolbox.*

# Working With Images

When you launch Photo House, the Notebook gives you several options to get started. You can open an image, scan an image, open an image from the Library, or create a blank image. The Library is a collection of photo images organized by category.

## Opening an Image From the Library

To use the Library, you must have the Photo House CD in your CD-ROM drive. Click Open a Library Image to display a list of 50 categories. Double-click a category to see a thumbnail representation of images in that category (see Figure 12-9). To open an image, double-click on any thumbnail.

*Figure 12-9: The Library provides hundreds of pictures for your projects.*

## Opening an Image From Your Hard Drive

Click the Open an Image button from the Notebook, or select File | Open, to display a Browse dialog box that lets you search your hard drive for a picture. Photo House supports lots of different image formats, including complex file types like Photoshop 4 and Corel PhotoPaint.

Instead of opening the entire image, you can open only a part of it by selecting the Crop option (see Figure 12-10). You can also select the Resample option to open a smaller version of the image.

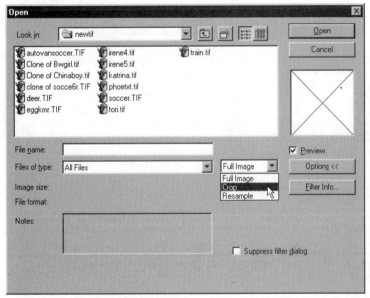

*Figure 12-10: The Open dialog box. The mouse is shown selecting the Crop option.*

Select Crop, and then click Open to display the Crop Image dialog box (see Figure 12-11). Use your mouse to resize and move the cropping square, which is displayed on a preview of the image. When you are satisfied, click OK to open the cropped image.

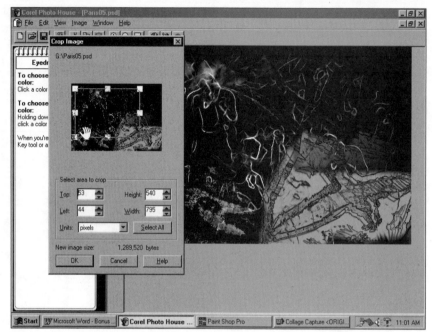

*Figure 12-11: The Crop Image dialog box. You can move or resize the cropping square.*

Select Resample, and click Open to display the Resample Image dialog box, which lets you open a smaller or larger version of the image. You can select a number of pixels or a percentage of the current image. Make sure you check the Maintain Aspect Ratio check box to prevent distortion. Be aware that images with text in them look particularly bad if resampled to more than 15 percent of their original size.

## Creating a New Image

Click the Start a Blank Image button in the Notebook, or select File | New to display the Create New Image dialog box, where you determine the size, page shape, resolution, and paper color of a new image. The dialog box provides predefined sizes for postcards and various folded-card styles. You can also create your own size with the Custom option.

The Color Mode controls allow you to create a 256-color or 16 million-color image. Images with more colors look better onscreen but do not necessarily print at a higher quality. 256-color images take up considerably less disk space, but do not carry the full range of colors found in a photograph. Selecting CMYK mode simulates how an image will look if printed professionally, which can be important if you plan to print your project at a print shop. If you are only concerned about how the image looks onscreen and don't plan to print your work,

72 dpi is sufficient; if you plan to have your image printed professionally, use at least 300 dpi. You can also create 16-color images and images that combine 256 shades of gray, black, and white (called Grayscale images).

## Cloning an Image

The Clone tool lets you paint with an image. That means when you move your brush around the page, you'll start to see portions of your picture being spread around in the shape of your brush strokes. Here are two immediate uses for the Clone tool:

- Airbrushing an image of a person from one picture into a second picture.
- Removing a crease from a picture by dragging your mouse over the creased part and cloning in a part that is not creased.

The Clone tool works in two phases:

1. Click your mouse in the part of your image that you want to reproduce.
2. Click and drag your mouse across a *new* area of your image, and you'll start to see the *first part* of your image appear underneath your brush strokes.

You can also click to clone part of an image, then open a new image, and paint a clone of the first image onto the new image.

Any brush modifications you choose in the Tool dialog box will affect how your strokes appear while cloning. For example, if you choose a high transparency setting, your new brush strokes paint a faded clone of the first image.

Under the Clone tool is the Color Changer (see Figure 12-12), a square icon with a circle inside. Click it to display the Coloring dialog box. You have two choices with the Color Changer:

- To change the color you are painting with, click the circle inside the Color Changer.
- To change the page color (or the background color, if you'd rather think of it that way), click the square area of the icon, outside the circle.

*Figure 12-12: The Color Changer in the Toolbox. Click* inside *the circle to change the paintbrush color, and* outside *to change the page color.*

# Resizing & Cropping an Image

If your image is too big, you can either crop it around the edges, or you can resize the image. When you resize the image, you reduce its width and height.

## Cropping an Image

To crop an image, select the portion of the image you want to keep with the Select tool. To do this, click in the upper left corner of the section you want to select and drag to the lower right. When you've drawn a box around the area you want to select, release the mouse button. Click Image | Crop To Selection (see Figure 12-13) to cut away all the portions outside the selected part of the image. You can save the new image with a new filename or overwrite the original image with this new image.

*Figure 12-13: The Crop To Selection feature.*

## Resizing an Image

To resize an image, select Image | Properties. Type in new numbers in the Width and Height data boxes, and select Inches or Centimeters in the drop-down list. Make sure you check the Maintain Aspect Ratio check box to ensure that your image is not distorted.

Remember that you can resize an image as you open it by clicking Resample in the Open dialog box's drop-down list.

# Painting on an Image

Instead of painting on a blank image, you can also use Photo House's tool to paint on a photograph.

## With a Brush

You can use any brush on an existing image. Using a degree of transparency with a paint color could add a nice touch to a photo. Also, Photo House has many decorative brushes, so you are not limited to painting with regular brush strokes.

## With an Eraser

Painting on an image with the Eraser tool doesn't really erase part of the image. You are merely applying the chosen paper color (most often white) to your image. Erasers have "feathered" edges that fade out gradually, rather than abruptly, to create smoother effects.

# Working With Selections

Selections let you carve out a portion of your image so that you can move it around, copy it, or cut it. After copying or cutting a selection, you can paste it into another image.

## Creating a Selection

You can select part of the image with the Selection tool or the Freehand Selection tool. A red and white striped boundary appears around your selection. Be careful about clicking outside your selection. If you click outside a selection that you haven't moved, you deselect it. If you click outside a selection that you've moved, you paste it where it's now located.

## Creating a New Image From a Selection

To create a new image from a selection, select Edit | Paste | As New Document. Your new selection appears in the image workspace as a complete picture, not a part of any other document.

## Pasting a Selection Into an Existing Image

To paste a selection from one image into another image, cut or copy the selection to the clipboard, and then open the target image. Select Edit | Paste | As New Selection. You may want to feather the selection first.

## Changing the View of Your Image

You can change your view of the image in two ways: you can use the View menu controls or the magnifying glass icons on the toolbar. The toolbar icons zoom in or out one level at a time. Click the View menu to display a list of preset zoom types. They are as follows:

- **Zoom to Fit**—automatically scales your image to fit into the space allotted.

- **Zoom 100%**—shows the image at its actual size.

- **Zoom submenu**—provides nine additional zoom settings.

## Using the Preview Area

Every image editing effects and corrections dialog box has a preview area, which shows the image before and after you make your changes (see Figure 12-14). The preview area lets you see how your settings will look before you apply them to the actual image.

But there's more to the preview windows than meets the eye. Click once on a preview window to zoom in on it. Click again, and you'll zoom in even closer. Drag the mouse cursor inside the image, and the image will move inside the preview window to reveal more of the image.

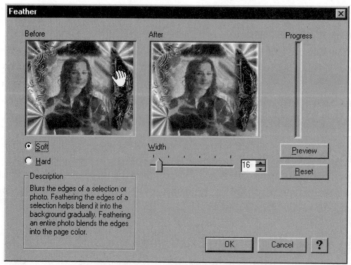

*Figure 12-14: The preview area found in any Effect dialog box.*

# Using Photo House With a Scanner

You can scan an image directly into Photo House by clicking File | Acquire Image | Acquire to access your scanning software's interface. Most scanners provide controls to adjust the scanned image size, resolution, color mode, and any preset filtering (see Figure 12-15). This last option is only recommended if you know your scanner tends to be too dark or too bright or favors one hue over another.

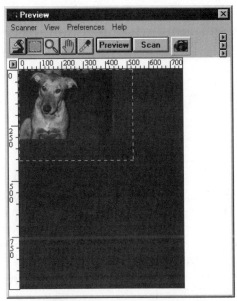

*Figure 12-15: A scanning control. Photo House uses the scanning software that comes with your scanner. You access it by selecting File | Acquire Image | Acquire.*

## Previewing Your Image

Before scanning your image, it's a good idea to use your scanner's preview feature. This lets you set the borders of your scanned image before you scan the final image.

After opening your scanning window, set the picture you want to scan in your scanner and click Preview (or Pre-scan). Your scanner scans the image at low resolution. You can now set the area of the image that you want in your final scan.

## Scanning Your Image

After setting the area of the image that you want to scan, you're ready to do your final scan. The Scanning dialog box tells you how big the scanned image will be. Scanned images can be enormous; reducing the resolution can help make them more manageable. Unless you're planning a professional print job, 200 dpi should be adequate.

Once you've scanned the image, it is opened in Photo House. If the scan settings were set properly, you'll have little to do to fix the scan. In general, you're better off trying to change your scanner's settings to get a high-quality scan than trying to use Photo House (or any other image editing tool) to fix the problems. If your scanner has an "auto-levels" feature, try using it to improve the color balance in your picture. Photo House does not provide this color adjustment feature.

Make sure that you save your image in Photo House. When the scan first appears in Photo House, it is not saved.

## Fixing Damaged Images

Photo House can restore a photograph to its original quality or sometimes to even better quality than the original. You can also use these techniques to improve poorly scanned images. We will be exploring a number of special effects. Note that setting the effect level too high can make the image look worse, not better. In most cases, the default settings work well, and increasing the effect does not necessarily make the photo look better. For example, adding too much sharpness to a photo can make it look as though it's covered with tiny seashells, and overdoing the Dust filter can make a photo's colors look dull and flat.

### Removing Scratches, Speckles, Particles & Red Eye

After opening a scanned image, it's time to survey the damage. Does the image look scratchy? Was it scanned with a fine, unattractive layer of dust on the surface? Are all the principal characters suffering from red eyes? You may have to zoom in fairly close to see some of the damage inflicted by time or poor scanning. Zooming in very close on any image will make it look "pixelated;" you'll see the millions of tiny dots that make up the image. Photo House, however, can help you make images look good enough for normal viewing by removing obvious scars and imperfections.

To remove dust and scratches from your image, select Image | Touch-up Effects | Remove Dust and Scratches. The corresponding dialog box opens with two settings you can change. Increasing the Level setting removes more "image fuzziness;" it's similar to a sharpness control. Increasing Radius makes the Remove Dust and Scratches filter more aggressive, but increases the time it takes to render the effect.

To remove speckles from your image, select Image | Touch-up Effects | Reduce Speckles. The dialog box contains one slider that you can adjust: the Threshold control. Lower values will produce more radical changes in your photo. Apply only the amount of speckle reduction you need (a lower Threshold number means more effect!). Overdoing this filter causes a blurry picture.

To remove red eye from your photo, select Image | Touch-up Effects | Remove Red Eyes. This dialog box gives you access to three tools: Hand, Select, and Eyedropper tool. Use the Hand to zoom in and locate a red eye. Use the square selection box to select the red area. Then, use the Eyedropper tool to select an eye color near the red-eye area (see Figure 12-16). Click the Preview button when you have selected your new color with the Eyedropper to make sure you've chosen the right shade to replace the red. When you are happy with the new color, click OK. Now repeat this procedure with all the red eyes in your image. If you are treating a class photo with 35 red-eyed students, you may want to reconsider this project—you cannot select more than one eye at a time.

*Figure 12-16: Use the Select tool to select the red area and then the Eyedropper tool to select a new, desired eye pupil color.*

## Fixing Creases, Dog Ears & Bends

To fix creases, dog ears, and bends, you need to clone a portion of the image near the damaged section to replace the damaged part. Figure 12-17 shows a dog-eared photograph.

*Figure 12-17: A family photo with a damaged upper left corner.*

Near the damaged area is an undamaged section with exactly the same coloration. Here's what to do:

1. Select the Clone tool and choose a medium-sized square brush with a feathered edge (for natural blending). Click the Brushes tab on the Notebook, and click the very first brush you see. It's a round brush with feathered edges.

2. Reduce the size of the brush to 3, as shown in Figure 12-18. Increase the Edge Fading option to 99.

3. Zoom in to 200% on the image. Click on the damaged area with the zoom tool twice.

4. Now click once on the area that has no damage but has the same coloration as the damaged area. This sets the clone source. The next time you click your brush, you'll be painting with that cloned area.

5. In this image, select a region as close to the top of the photo as you can. We want as much of the picture's own coloration to work with as possible. We will be sweeping downward with the clone, so we'll need the maximum downward area below us with this same off-white coloration.

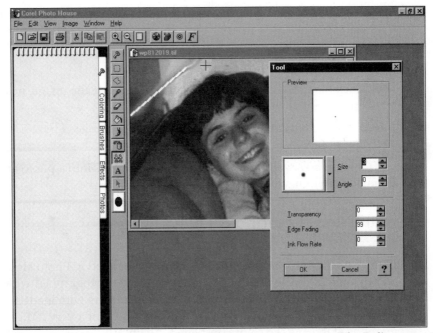

*Figure 12-18: Decrease the size of the cloning brush, and increase its Edge Fading amount.*

6. Position your brush over the damaged, dog-eared area, and click and drag the cursor. You'll see the crease being covered (see Figure 12-19). The feathered brush makes the color change around the brushed area less obvious.

*Figure 12-19: The crease is partially covered by cloning.*

7. To finish, you need to set a new cloning source area, this time near the darker brown area where the crease continues towards the other edge of the photo. This means you'll have to reset the Clone tool.

8. Click any tool besides the Clone tool.

9. Click the Clone tool again, and click once inside the image, near the dark brown, where the crease continues.

10. Click and drag over the crease. The crease is replaced by the original darker brown coloration of the photo.

Cloning works well for bringing missing elements into a photo and for removing anything you don't want.

## Fixing Poor Coloring & Faded Images

If you have images that are faded or whose color is poor, Photo House can work wonders. These might be images that were photographed with bad lighting, bleached in too much sunlight, taken indoors with inadequate flash, or scanned with less than optimal technique. A scan of a very old photograph might need to have the colors freshened. Again, a little correction often goes a long way.

### Brightness/Contrast/Intensity

Your main tools for fixing color-poor images are in the Brightness/Contrast/Intensity dialog box (see Figure 12-20), which you display by selecting Image | Touch-up Effects | Brightness/Contrast/Intensity. These three tools can each help restore your picture.

To begin the process, open a photo, and survey the damage. Is the image too dark? Too bleached? Is it blurry? Is it dull? Is the definition poor? After figuring out the problem, select Image | Touch-up Effects | Brightness/Contrast/Intensity. The Brightness/Contrast/Intensity dialog box is displayed with its three sliders.

Adding a bit of contrast improves almost every image. Contrast and definition are lost in all but the most professional printing processes. Start with a contrast level of 15, and see whether the image looks clearer. If you see little difference, try repeating the process with the same number.

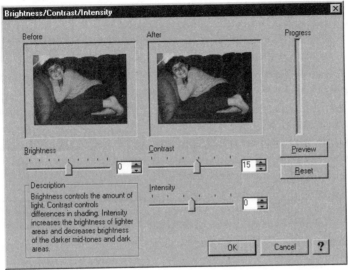

Figure 12-20: The Brightness/Contrast/Intensity dialog box.

If your image is faded, increase the brightness; if it is bleached and color-less, decrease the brightness. Remember that your monitor may not reproduce brightness accurately, so take its bias into account. If your monitor is a bit on the bright side, your printed image will look darker than what's onscreen. If your monitor is dull, don't overcompensate by using too much brightness, or your printed image will look bleached.

Increasing color intensity is helpful for most images that have experienced some color loss. Again, exaggerating the intensity a little won't hurt if your image is destined for an inkjet printer, especially if the image will be reduced significantly from its original size. Increasing intensity helps restore loss of detail in such instances. However, overdoing the effect can cause the image to lose subtle ranges of color, pushing all colors to the extremes, an undesirable result. If an image is dull, start by increasing the intensity by about 9, and repeat if you don't see a real change.

### Restoring Sharpness

The Sharpness command (Image I Touch-up Effects I Sharpen) can restore some definition and "edge" to a dull, flat-looking picture. But this effect is really easy to overdo. Start with 5, and before you repeat the effect, check the image's light areas to make sure you don't see that "crystallizing" look that is charac-teristic of too much sharpening.

# Working With Special Effects

Treating images with special effects and using a little creativity the fun part of Photo House. You can take a standard image and make it more "your own" using some of the techniques here. The effects can be divided up into three categories: photography effects, which you might use in a professional photo lab; brush stroke effects, which re-render your photograph as if it were painted or treated by a traditional artistic process; and distortion effects, which twirl, twist, or reshape the image. All effects discussed in this section are found by selecting Image | Cool & Fun Effects and by selecting the effect you want. Some, but not all, of the effects are also listed in the Notebook.

You can apply an effect to a portion of an image or to the entire picture. If you select a portion of the image and then select an effect, it is applied only to the selected portion of the image.

## Photography Effects

Photographic effects include the Add Light Source effect, which places a "lens flare" ball of light in your image. You can adjust the brightness of the light and the type of photographic lens you are simulating. Creating this special photography effect in a photo lab with real film would take hours.

The Photo Negative effect reverses your photo by switching colors with their opposite on the color wheel. Click Custom Negative to apply the effect with a Threshold slider, which means you can control which colors are reversed.

The Motion Blur effect is very useful to create the illusion of movement in your photo. If you apply it to the entire picture, it often just looks like a mistake. But if you select a portion of the image, feather it (we'll examine feathering below) and then apply the motion blur, it looks as though that portion of the image is moving.

The Vignette effect creates an oval frame around your image, as though you are looking at it through the very end of a tunnel. You can control the color of the walls surrounding your image, how gradually or abruptly the surrounding frame fades into the image, and the size of the frame itself.

The Sketch effect reduces the picture to an outline of its edges. The large structures appear outlined in black, thick lines. It also renders the image in a "thin rainbow" effect of oil floating on the surface of water. This effect is usually called Find Edges in other image editing packages.

Figures 12-21 and 12-22 show the results of some of these special effects.

Here's how to do something similar:

1. Open an image of a picture frame.

2. Type some text large enough to almost fill the frame as shown. Color the text a bright color.

3. Copy the text to the clipboard.

4. Now color the text black. We're creating a drop shadow for the text we've copied to the clipboard.

5. Select Edit | Paste, and position the brightly colored text over the black text as shown for a shadowed appearance.

6. Click Edit | Merge Text with Background.

7. Using the Select tool, create a rectangular selection around the entire text area. We're going to apply a Swirl effect to the selected portion.

8. Select Image | Cool & Fun Effects | Swirl.

9. In the Swirl dialog box, set the number to 90. You'll find that many of the special effect dialog boxes have default settings that exaggerate the effect a bit too much.

The selected text area should resemble Figure 12-22.

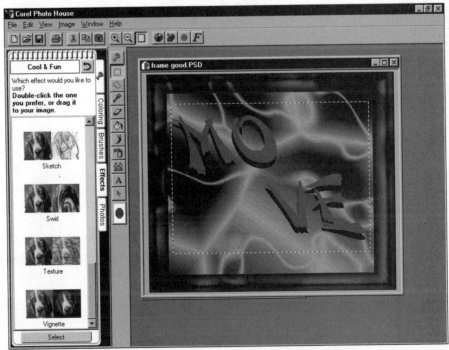

*Figure 12-21: Two text selections pasted together to create a shadow effect.*

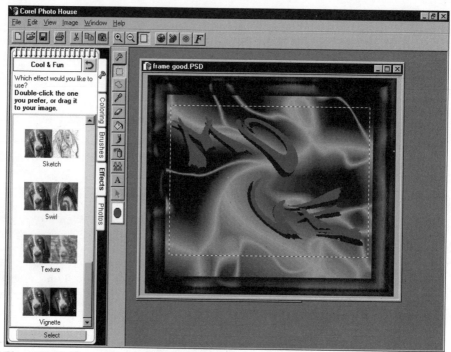

*Figure 12-22: The same text selection treated with the Swirl effect.*

Let's use the Photo Negative effect and feathering, to create a "beveled box" appearance:

1. Using your image that is similar to Figure 12-22, select Image | Crop to Selection. That removes the external frame around the letters, leaving only a small frame around the word itself. The Crop to Select option works only if you have selected a portion of your image.

2. Select Image | Cool & Fun Effects | Photo Negative to apply a photo negative effect.

3. Select Image | Cool & Fun Effects | Feathering. Set the option to Soft, and try 40 as a feathering amount. The result should be similar to Figure 12-23. The coloring will be somewhat removed evenly from all the edges of the image, creating an impression that the center of the image is closer to you than the edges. This gives the image a beveled look. This technique can be helpful for creating buttons for Web pages or other online documents that require user input.

*Figure 12-23: Treating a rectangular image with a large amount of feathering gives it a beveled look.*

## Brush Stroke Effects

Photo House provides several effects that mimic brush strokes:

- **Embossing**—creates raised areas in your photo, based on where light intensity is brightest. This gives your picture a 3D appearance; it looks as though someone pounded it out of a tin plate with an embossing tool. You can choose the image's original color as the starting point for embossing, or select a particular color. If you select another color as your embossing color, all the color data is removed from your picture. You are left only with embossed raised areas. This works if your image is something simple, perhaps an animal standing still or some other single object. The Direction choices allow you to select from where you want the image's light source to emanate. This is important because the light shining on your embossed areas is what causes them to be raised. If you use this effect, take the time to experiment with light source direction. Often light shining from the upper right provides the most realistic results. As for an Embossing setting, try 5 to begin with.

- **Impressionist**—"paints" your photograph, subtly displacing the pixels of your image as it creates brush strokes. The dialog box provides two sliders, which let you control the size of the area affected by each stroke. This effect makes your picture look like an impressionist painting or perhaps as though you were viewing it through a beaded glass window.

- **Psychedelic**—changes the colors of your image to resemble one of those 1967 San Francisco concert posters with lots of eye candy—neon green, yellow, pink, lavender. You have a single Threshold slider to work with. Low numbers apply the effect only sparingly. High numbers make the image unrecognizable, resembling one of the light shows that went along with those concerts.

- **Texture**—superimposes one of four texture patterns over your image: Linen, Marble, Paper, or Rock. In graphic programs, true textures are created by applying "bump maps," which are algorithms that calculate raised and lowered areas, without leaving a picture. When you want a texture, you don't really want a faded image of the texture in the background; you just want the shapes. Unfortunately, Photo House's texture feature creates superimposed images, not true texture maps. To apply a texture to your picture, select one of the four texture types, and chose a level of transparency. Low transparency numbers mean you see more of the texture image itself, colors and all. You can also select an Emboss level. High emboss levels create the appearance of deeper grooves and higher raised areas.

## Distortion Effects

Effects that reshape your image actually twist, twirl, remove edge pixels, and otherwise distort your image; they don't just change the colors. All these effects are available by selecting Image | Cool & Fun Effects, and choosing from the list.

- **Page Curl**—lifts a corner off your page as if it were turning, revealing blank paper color underneath. Page Curl is a nice, clever touch. You can select the corner you want to apply the effect to, and choose the width and height of your curl. You can also determine whether you'd like to see part of the image through the curl or want the curl to appear completely silver.

- **Ripple**—makes your image look like water after a pebble is dropped in it. You have three sliders to control. Strength controls the size of the ripples. Period controls how far apart the ripples are, with higher settings pushing the ripples farther apart. Damping controls how far from the center the ripples extend. A low Damping setting will make it look as though the ripples go on way past the edge of your image.

- **Swirl**—swirls your image, as used to create Figure 12-22.

## Using & Editing Brushes

Click the Brushes tab on the Notebook to choose from over 100 brush shapes. (You can also display the list of brushes by clicking its icon on the toolbar.) Some of these brushes differ only slightly, so you can make subtle changes.

The angled thin brush tips are especially good for calligraphic drawings. You can display the brush editing features (see Figure 12-24) by clicking the Tool Dialog button on the toolbar.

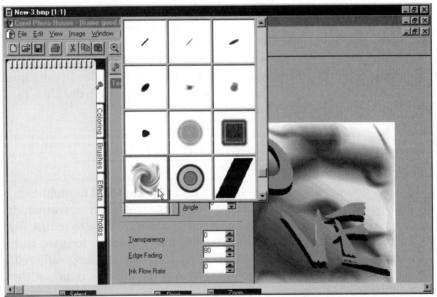

*Figure 12-24: The Tools dialog box lets you edit many aspects of the brush's behavior and properties. The user is selecting a brush shape from the drop-down list here.*

To layer several paint colors over each other with overlapping effects, adjust the transparency setting. Use Edge Fading to create a feather-tip brush. High numbers create gradual blends around the brush edge; low numbers create sharp, often jagged edges.

If you use high Ink Flow Rate numbers, the longer you hold down the mouse the more ink will drip off the edges of the brush. If you use low numbers, the ink will adhere closely to the exact shape of the brush.

## Selecting & Creating Colors

Display the Coloring dialog box by clicking the icon on the toolbar and then clicking the More button. This displays another dialog box where you can create your own color (see Figure 12-5). By default, this dialog box uses the RGB model. Click on the color wheel to select a color. Click on the color triangle to adjust the lightness of the color.

If you want to use the HSB model, click the HSB button. Use the three sliders to adjust the hue, saturation, and brightness of your color choices.

## Saving an Image

To save an image, select File | Save, and choose a folder using the Browse dialog box. Remember, if you began your project with a photo from the CD-ROM, the first folder you'll see when you try to save the file is the CD drive, and you can't save onto the CD.

## File Size & Resolution Considerations

As you work with images, you'll find that they tend to proliferate on your hard drive. Disk space is like a paycheck—you're always wondering "where did it all go?" There are some steps that you can take to reduce the bloat, though. You can save your images in many different formats, and some can compress the image greatly. JPG and TIFF formats can greatly reduce the size of a file. In this section, we'll explore the advantages and disadvantages of the various file types.

### Saving With Compression

When saving your image, use some sort of compression which reduces the size of the file. Saving your file in TIFF format with compression reduces the size of the file without any loss of quality. Choose TIFF format, then click the Compress Type drop-down list, and choose LZW. The only disadvantage to LZW compression is that images may take a little longer to load. If you must save the file as a bitmap (BMP), use RLE compression.

Finally, saving your image in JPEG format will save you a lot of disk space. JPEG is a lossy format, which means that compression does cause some loss of information. You can choose a high degree of compression with a significant reduction in quality or less compression with little loss of quality. I suggest you set the slider to around 8, which reduces file size quite a bit but generally doesn't cause any noticeable loss of quality.

### Reducing Resolution

Reducing the resolution of your image will greatly reduce its size. But it will, of course, also greatly reduce the quality of the image. If you plan to print your images, you'll need a resolution of at least 300 dpi. If your images will be used only online, then 72 dpi is probably sufficient.

## File Format Considerations

There are a few issues to consider when saving your image:

- TIFF files can be opened on both Macintosh and Windows machines. They are very flexible and understood by almost every image processing application.

- BMP format is a Windows native file format. The file size is small and works well for Windows screen savers and wallpaper. Beyond that, there's not much reason to use it.

- PCX file format is very old. If you think you may have to open your image in a DOS-based program like an old version of Harvard Graphics, then you might want to consider saving in PCX format.

- JPG format lets you use the image on the World Wide Web. If you repeatedly save your file as a .JPG, open it and again save it as a .JPG, you will notice a loss in quality. Consider saving your file as a .JPG only after you have finished editing it.

## Moving On

In this chapter, we covered Photo House, a convenient photoediting tool that can bring life and personality to the photos you use in your documents. In the next chapter, we'll discuss how WordPerfect Suite 8's core programs interact with each other and share information.

## Part VI

# Putting It All Together

# 13 Putting It All Together

Worderfect Suite offers excellent integration among the various applications. You can link documents, combine documents, and share information among different document types. For example, you could create one Quattro Pro database and then include information from this database in a WordPerfect document and other information in a Presentations document. To accomplish this, the suite uses Object Linking & Embedding (OLE) technology. In addition to sharing information among the various suite components, you can also include other objects in your documents; for example, video and sound objects. Finally, you can create hyperlinks from one document to another, which can be used to enhance communication in an office or to keep track of data that changes frequently.

## Object Linking & Embedding

When you insert information from one type of document into another type of document, the information is considered an object. For example, if you insert a Quattro Pro spreadsheet into a WordPerfect document, the spreadsheet is considered an object within the WordPerfect document.

Using objects has several advantages. Most importantly, you can still edit your source document (such as the Quattro Pro spreadsheet, in our example). The changes you make will be reflected both in the document (Quattro Pro spreadsheet), and in the document where the information was inserted (the WordPerfect document). The WordPerfect document has a link to the Quattro Pro spreadsheet.

Instead of linking the two documents, you can also embed information from one to the other. When you embed a source document, updating the original source *does not* update the host document. Instead, you have to double-click on the embedded object in your host document to refresh the data. Embedding a document is less automated, but also incurs less system overhead than linking a document.

The Windows environment actually provides three ways to share information:

- **Pasting.** You can cut or copy information from one application and paste it into another application. Pasting does not create a link from the source document to the insertion document. Pasting is fast and convenient, but inflexible. Select Edit I Paste to paste the information on the clipboard into your document. In some cases, you can use pasting and still create objects by selecting Edit I Paste Special.

- **Embedding an object**. When you embed an object, you can double-click the object to reactivate the source application. This means that you could, for example, embed a Presentations slide into a WordPerfect document. To make changes to the embedded slides, double-click them. This launches Presentations. After making your changes, click File I Update (or File I Update and Exit) to return to your host document and update the embedded object. See Figure 13-1. (Embedding an object increases the file size of your document, but you can start the source application just by double-clicking.)

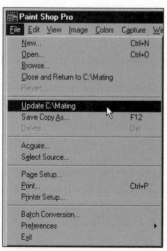

*Figure 13-1: Updating a Paint Shop Pro image that was embedded into a WordPerfect document.*

■ **Linking an object.** When you link an object to your document, any changes you make in the source file for your object are automatically reflected in your host document. Figure 13-2 shows the Insert Object dialog box. Selecting Create from file lets you use an existing file on your hard drive. If you check the Link toggle, the file is linked. If you uncheck the Link toggle, the file is embedded instead.

If you need to include information in your document that changes frequently, linking is a good choice. By linking, you ensure that the document always contains the most recent information. If you embed, you have to remember to update the information, and if you paste, you would have to paste the information again every time it changed.

Unlike embedding, linking does not significantly increase the file size of your host document. Linking does, however, increase the time it takes for your WordPerfect document to load, and you must have the source application in which the linked object was created running on your machine without errors. Also, if you move the file to a new location, your WordPerfect document will not be able to find it. You must again create a link with the file in its new location.

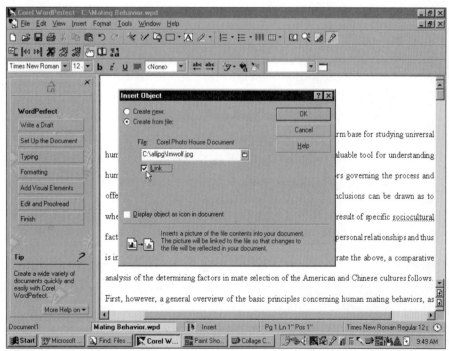

*Figure 13-2: Linking an object to a WordPerfect document. Whenever you edit the Imwolf.jpg file, the linked copy in WordPerfect will reflect the changes.*

## Types of Objects

You can insert many different types of objects into your documents, including Quattro Pro notebooks, charts, and graphics; WordPerfect text files; sounds, such as WAV and MIDI files; tables; videos; or graphics, such as pictures created in CorelDraw or PhotoPaint.

## Pasting an Object

You can use the Paste Special command to insert a simple object into your host document. This is much simpler than using the Insert I Object command; however, Paste Special has some limitations.

Using Paste Special can restrict which of the source application features you can access. When you use Insert I Object, you can use all the features of the source application. In addition, using Paste Special means that the inserted object must be edited with the default associated application. For example, if you have a picture that by default is opened in Windows Paint, but you want to use PhotoPaint to edit it, you'll need to use the Insert I Object command, which lets you choose the source application. Paste Special simply defaults to the application that Windows *thinks* should open the file.

When you paste text using the Paste Special command, you can paste the text either as Rich Text Format (RTF) or without any formatting. RTF preserves much of the formatting of the text, and usually works well with the following source applications:

- DOS-based word processing programs.
- Word processing applications that are not installed on your system.
- Plain text sources, such as Notepad.

If using RTF doesn't work, try pasting in the text using the Paste Special command with the Unformatted Text option selected.

You can maintain a link with the source file for the text. Click the Paste Link radio button in the Paste Special dialog box to do so (as in Figure 13-3).

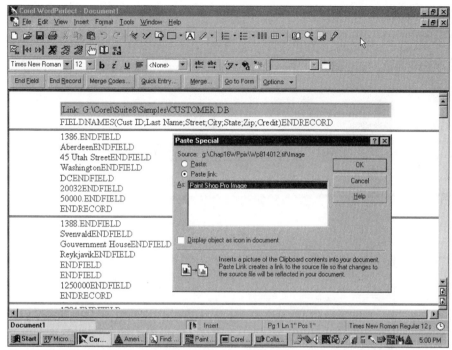

*Figure 13-3: Selecting Paste link lets you double-click the object to open it in the source application. In this figure, a PaintShop Pro image is being pasted.*

## Embedding an Object

To update an embedded object, you double-click it. This launches the source application, where you can make changes to the object. When you are finished, you close the source application, and the updated object is displayed in your host document. For example, you can embed an equation in a WordPerfect document. Here's how:

1. Open any WordPerfect document, and place the cursor where you'd like an equation to appear.

2. Select Insert | Object. This displays the Insert Object dialog box.

3. In the Object Type list, select Corel Equation!2.0. (Corel Equation! is an equation editor that is included with the Suite and is installed automatically.) Click OK.

4. The equation editor is launched. Use its tools to create an equation.

5. After you've created your equation, click File | Update (see Figure 13-4). Then select File | Exit and Return to Document. The equation editor is closed and you return to your WordPerfect document, which is still open.

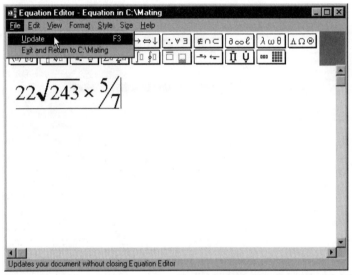

*Figure 13-4: After creating your equation, select File | Update, then File | Exit and Return.*

6. Your new equation appears in the WordPerfect document. Notice that it is surrounded by bounding boxes, which indicate that you can update the object using the source application.

7. You can edit the object in two ways:

   ■ Double-click on the object to open Corel Equation!, where you can modify the object.

   ■ Right-click on the object and select Equation Object | Open. Instead of opening the equation editor separately, this opens the object for editing inside WordPerfect. The toolbars, menus, and other parts of the interface display Equation!'s choices (see Figure 13-5).

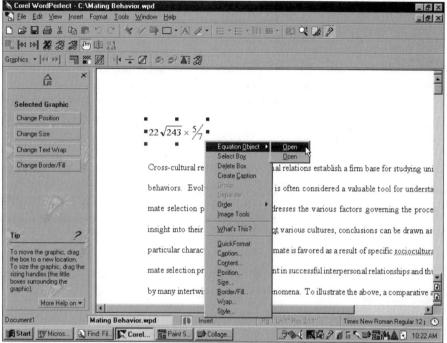

*Figure 13-5: After the equation appears in WordPerfect, you can edit it again in the source application by right-clicking and selecting Equation Object | Open.*

If you pasted the equation into your document instead of inserting it, you would have to return to the equation editor, open the saved equation (assuming that you saved it!), change the equation, then select it and paste it again. You can see that working with objects is much faster.

## Tip

*Instead of selecting Insert | Object and selecting the equation editor, you can select Insert | Equation to accomplish the same thing.*

Once you embed an object, it behaves like any other WordPerfect box. You can right-click on it and make a selection to create a border, provide a caption, or change the fill or text wrap properties.

## Linking an Object

Instead of embedding an object, consider linking it if you have a file that you use in many different documents and that changes frequently. For example, if you have to generate a chart that contains the weekly sales figures, and you use that chart in WordPerfect documents and in presentations, then it would make sense to link the chart to the document and to the presentation. That way, you maintain one copy of the chart, and the document and presentations file are always in sync.

On the other hand, it probably makes more sense to embed a business logo, because it's unlikely to change very often. As we mentioned earlier, linking objects makes your system run more slowly, so you need to consider carefully whether an object really needs to be linked, or whether just embedding it is good enough.

Here's how to link to an object:

1. Click where you'd like the object to appear and select Insert | Object to display the Insert Object dialog box.

2. Select the Create From File radio button.

3. Click the File icon next to the File field. This displays the Insert as Object dialog box.

4. Locate the file to which you want to build a link and select it.

5. Click Insert to return to the Insert Object dialog box. Notice that the File field now lists the path to the file you just selected.

6. Check the Link toggle (refer to Figure 13-3, if necessary).

7. Click OK to insert the object with a link into your document.

If you need to make changes to the linked object, double-click the object to open its source application. You can change the source file, and the changes will be reflected in your host document. Because you are changing the source file directly, any changes you make by opening the source file via this document will also be reflected in any other document that contains links to this source file. That means that you can make a change once, and have it show up in many documents.

## Inserting Presentations Objects Into WordPerfect or Quattro Pro

Many of the elements from Presentations are already available in WordPerfect and Quattro Pro. For example, creating a Draw picture (Insert I Graphics I Draw Picture) or a chart (Insert I Graphics I Chart) actually launches the drawing or charting component of Presentations.

Unfortunately, there isn't an elegant way to place an entire Presentations slide into a WordPerfect or Quattro Pro document. You have to take a screen shot and then paste the screen shot into WordPerfect or Quattro Pro. Here's how to do it:

1. Open the presentation that contains the slide you want in Presentations.

2. Select View I Play Slide Show.

3. Press the spacebar until you reach the slide you want.

4. When the information on the slide is not moving, press the Print Screen (PrtScrn) key on your keyboard. This pastes the contents of the screen into the Windows clipboard.

5. Switch to WordPerfect (or Quattro Pro) and select Edit I Paste to insert the screen shot into your document.

This process does not create a link to the Presentations slide or slide show. To create links, you'll need to use hyperlinks, which are discussed later in this chapter.

## Inserting WordPerfect Documents Into Quattro Pro or Presentations

You can embed or link a WordPerfect document into Quattro Pro or Presentations using the standard embedding and linking procedures. In addition, Quattro Pro and Presentations both offer special features you can use with embedded or linked WordPerfect objects.

## Quattro Pro Features

Once you have inserted the WordPerfect object into your Quattro Pro file, right-click on Object and select OLE Object Properties from the pop-up menu. This displays the OLE Object dialog box, with the following features:

- In the OLE tab, check the Automatic Resizing toggle to specify that the cell in which the WordPerfect document is inserted should resize automatically to accommodate the contents of the inserted object.

- The Border Color tab lets you specify a color for the border around the object.

- The Box Type tab lets you specify the thickness of the box and whether it has a drop shadow or is transparent.

- The Protection tab lets you lock the inserted object. If the Locked toggle is on, and you have set up sheet protection, then you cannot move, change, or delete the object in Quattro Pro. To set up sheet protection, select Format I Sheet to display the Active Sheet dialog box. Click the Protection tab and check the Enable Object Locking check box.

- The Object Name tab lets you give the inserted object a name. The default is Embedded1, which isn't particularly informative. The object name is displayed in the Active Cell Address field in the Quattro Pro toolbar.

## Presentations Features

In Presentations, your inserted WordPerfect object is treated just like any other object; for example, you can specify how long it should remain onscreen, how long to wait before displaying it on the slide, transition effects, and 3D bordering.

To control the amount of delay before the object appears onscreen, right-click on the object and click OLE Play Settings. This displays the OLE Play Settings dialog box (see Figure 13-6). You can set a delay by checking the Begin the action when the transition ends check box and specify the amount of delay, in seconds, in the Delay action data box.

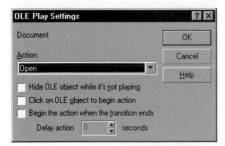

*Figure 13-6: In Presentations 8, linked or embedded objects can have timing parameters attached to them.*

## Inserting Multimedia Elements Into a WordPerfect Document

Most often, you would use multimedia elements in a WordPerfect document that is going to become a Web page, but many offices use online documents to distribute information internally. To make your document more interesting, you could add music, narration, sound effects, and video—it's as easy as adding a table or a chart.

You link and embed multimedia objects, such as sound and video files, in the same way described earlier in this chapter. To edit the objects, double-click them. To play the objects, click them once.

**Tip**

*Instead of trying to creating a multimedia-rich WordPerfect or Quattro Pro document, consider creating a Presentations document. Unlike WordPerfect and Quattro Pro, Presentations is designed for multimedia work.*

### Configuring Your Multimedia Hardware

Your hardware and software configuration are critical to the success of your multimedia project. These configuration issues are beyond the scope of this book, but you should be aware that problems with sound and video playback and applications freezing when a large animation is loaded are generally related to your hardware and driver configuration.

If you are using a low-quality microphone, your sound will sound thin and tinny, no matter how sophisticated the playback software is.

### Dragging & Dropping Multimedia Files

WordPerfect supports drag and drop for most multimedia types. Locate a multimedia file (for example, a QuickTime for Windows file) using the Windows Find feature. Then, drag the file from the Find dialog box directly into your open WordPerfect document (see Figure 13-7). This is equivalent to using the Insert I Object command to create a link.

You can also drag and drop a multimedia object onto a Presentations 8 slide or a Quattro Pro 8 cell.

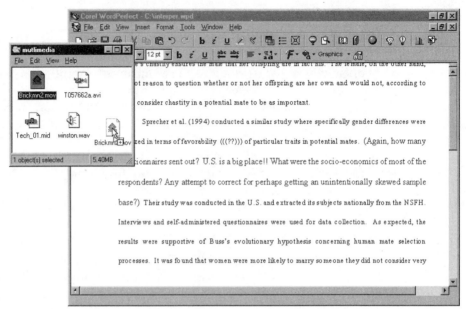

*Figure 13-7: Dragging and dropping a QuickTime movie onto a WordPerfect document.*

### Inserting Sounds

WordPerfect lets you insert WAV format sound files, the most widely used sound format for Windows.

**Tip**

> *The quality of the WAV file is determined by the settings in effect when it is recorded. This is why some WAV files sound excellent, and others sound terrible. (Other factors include your computer hardware, as mentioned above.) None of this affects how you insert the files into your WordPerfect document.*

To insert a WAV file, follow these steps:

1. Select Insert | Sound. The Sound Clips dialog box is displayed.

2. Click the Insert button to insert a new sound into your document (see Figure 13-8).

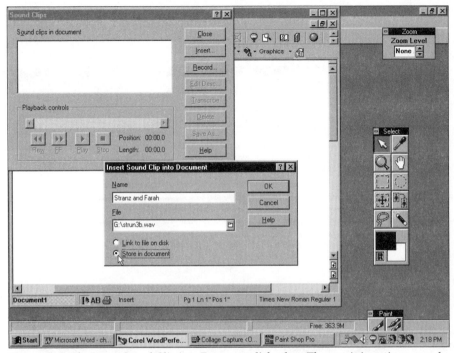

*Figure 13-8: The Insert Sound Clip into Document dialog box. The user is inserting a sound, specifying that it be stored in the document itself.*

3. Type a name for the sound in the Name field. This name will appear in the list of sounds in the Sound Clips dialog box.

4. Click the File icon to the right of the File field. This displays the Select Sound File dialog box.

5. Locate a sound on your hard drive that you want to include and select it. Click Select. The File field now lists that sound's file path.

6. To create a link to the file path, click the Link to file on disk radio button. To embed the sound file in your document, click the Store in Document radio button.

If you store the sound file in your WordPerfect document, you cannot edit the sound in the sound file's native application and your document's size increases greatly.

7. Click OK twice to close the Insert Sound Clip Into Document and Sound Clips dialog boxes.

The speaker icon is your only indication that you've inserted a sound (see Figure 13-9).

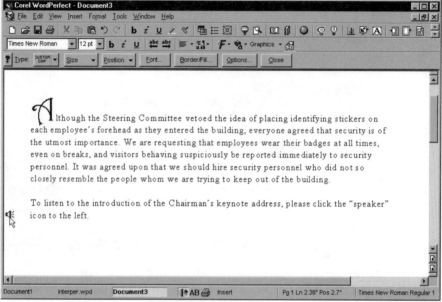

*Figure 13-9: The only indication you'll receive that a WAV file has been inserted into your document is the small speaker icon.*

8. Select Insert | Sound again, and you will see the sound clip you just inserted listed in the dialog box (see Figure 13-10).

- Click **Transcribe** to display playback controls on the WordPerfect toolbar.

- Click **Insert** to add a new sound to your list.

- Click **Edit Desc...** to add a new sound to the list or to save the current sound to a new location.

- Click **Record** to display the Windows 95 recording and sound editing application. You can record using this button, increase or decrease the volume, add an echo, and mix sounds.

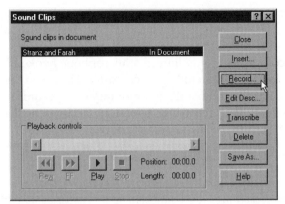

*Figure 13-10: The Sound Clips dialog box, now appearing with a sound file we have inserted. The cursor is selecting the Record feature, which does far more than merely record a new sound.*

**Adding Sounds & Editing With the Record Feature**   Figure 13-11 shows the Sound - Sound Recorder dialog box. Select File I Open to load an existing file for editing here. The controls on this dialog box function like the controls on the front panel of a cassette recorder. The slider bar moves towards the right as the WAV file plays.

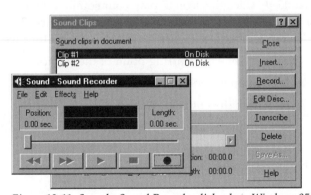

*Figure 13-11: Sound - Sound Recorder dialog box. Windows 95 provides some powerful sound-editing features.*

The Effects menu provides options that let you increase or decrease the volume, speed up or slow down the sound, add an echo, or reverse the sound.

The Mix With File feature lets you combine the sounds of two files. Open one file, and place the slider where you want the second file to chime in. Select Edit I Mix With File and locate the second file. This immediately mixes the two files. You can then play back the combined file.

To insert a second sound file into the current sound, position the slider where you want to insert the new file, then select Edit | Insert File and select the new sound file.

If you want to record sounds, you'll need a microphone hooked up to your computer. Click the Record button to begin recording. The green line shows you the volume of your recording: if it's not moving, your recording is too soft, and if it's maxed out, your recording is too loud and will be distorted.

**Tip**

*Your individual sound card, sound card software, and microphone all have an effect on the quality of your recording. You'll probably need to experiment a bit to achieve satisfactory results.*

Remember that sounds take up lots of memory. If you are thinking about creating a multimedia document with lots of video, sounds, and animation, consider using Presentations instead of WordPerfect.

**Playing Back a WAV File in WordPerfect**   After you insert a sound in WordPerfect, a small icon appears in the margin to show where the sound is located (see Figure 13-9). Click this icon to play your sound. If you want to play only a section of the file, right-click the icon and select Transcribe. This inserts sound controls on your toolbar (see Figure 13-12). Here's how they work:

- Move the slider to change the starting point of the sound.
- Click the Replay button to replay the segment you just played.
- Click Play to play back the entire WAV file.
- The Position number under the slider indicates the current location of the slider.
- The Length number under the slider indicates the total length of the sound.

**Inserting a MIDI File**   A MIDI file is a sound file, but instead of recording and storing the sound the MIDI file contains music commands, such as which note to play and how long to hold it. In general, MIDI files are much smaller than WAV files.

To insert a MIDI file, use any of the methods we described for inserting other multimedia files. The MIDI file is indicated by a small icon with musical notes, as shown in Figure 13-13. To play a MIDI file, double-click on it. To stop playback, click the Stop button on the MIDI toolbar, which appears at the top of the window when you begin playing the file.

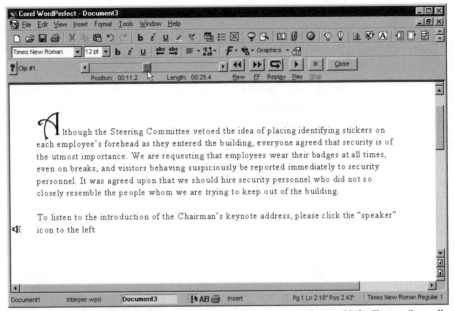

*Figure 13-12: Right-click on the speaker icon and select Transcribe to add the Transcribe toolbar to your WordPerfect window.*

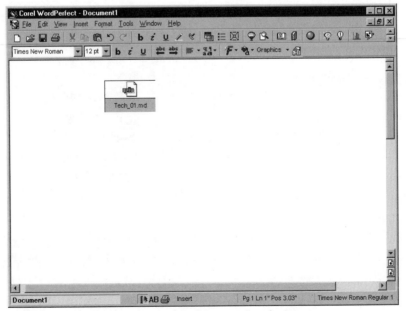

*Figure 13-13: A MIDI music sample as it appears in a document.*

## Inserting Video

The most popular video file type for Windows is AVI. WordPerfect recognizes and can play back AVI video files. To insert an AVI file into your document, do one of the following:

- Locate it on your hard drive and drag it onto your document.

- Select Insert | Object, and click Create From File. Click the File icon at the right side of the File text box and use the Browse dialog box to locate the file you want. Select it, then click Open, then click OK.

- Locate the video file on your hard drive using Windows Explorer, right-click on the file and select Copy. Then return to WordPerfect and select Paste.

To play back the video, click on it.

After you insert the video, you can reposition your video and the text will be displaced to accommodate it. You can put a border around the video by creating a separate box that sits underneath the video (see Figure 13-14).

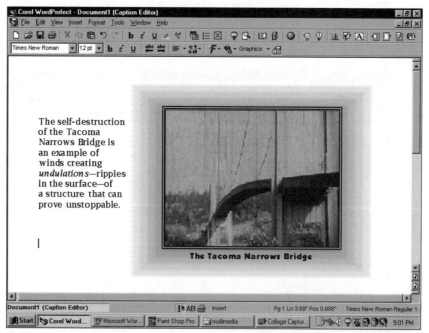

*Figure 13-14: You can place a decorative border around any video by right-clicking on it, and selecting Border/Fill.*

To create the border, follow these steps:

1. Drag to create a box in your document that's large enough to contain the video.

2. Click Custom Box and select Image from the list of box types.

3. Close the Insert Image dialog box that is displayed next.

4. On the Graphics Property bar, select the icon labeled Box Fill (see Figure 13-15). This displays a list of fill styles.

5. Select a fill from the list, and then position the box behind the video.

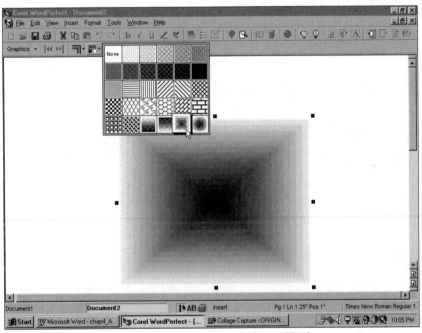

*Figure 13-15: Choosing a fill style that can be applied to a video box.*

**Editing a Video Clip**  Right-click on a video clip, and select Video Clip Object | Edit. A toolbar appears at the top of the window (see Figure 13-16).

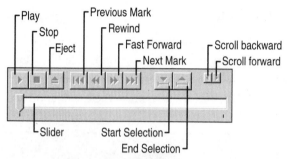

*Figure 13-16: The Video Clip toolbar.*

Like the sound editing toolbar, the video toolbar has a slider that indicates what part of the video is being played. To select a specific section of the video, place the slider where you want to begin the section. Hold down the Shift key and drag the scroll bar forward. A dark blue line marks the section you have selected. Clicking the Play button now plays only the selected part of the video.

You can also mark a section of the video by clicking the Start Selection button. Move the slider to where you want the selection to end and click the End Selection button.

You can use many graphic box features, such as adding captions, on video clips as well. Right-click on the video and select the appropriate item.

**Resizing a Video Clip & Changing the Volume**  To resize a video clip, you need to be in video editing mode. Select the Insert Clip menu, then select a size from the choices.

To change the audio portion of the video, select Insert Clip | Volume Control. The standard Windows volume control dialog box is displayed.

# Inserting Databases Into WordPerfect

If you want to insert a non-Quattro Pro spreadsheet, you can't count on OLE. Instead, select Insert | Spreadsheet/Database | Import to display the Import Data dialog box (see Figure 13-17). This method supports the Open Database Connectivity (ODBC) drivers, which let you access a wide variety of data.

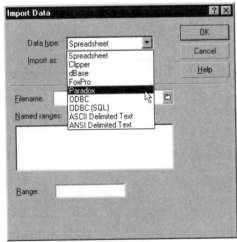

*Figure 13-17: The Import Data dialog box lets you choose what data to import, and how it should appear in your document.*

Importing a spreadsheet means you are bringing the numbers into your document, not creating a link to a spreadsheet. To import a spreadsheet or database, follow these steps:

1. Select Insert | Spreadsheet/Database | Import from the host application (WordPerfect or Presentations).

2. Choose the type of data you'll be using (see Figure 13-17 above).

3. You can import the data as a table, as text, or as a merge data file. Select a choice in the Import As drop-down list.

4. In the Filename field, identify the spreadsheet or database file you want to use.

5. Click OK.

If you choose to import your data as a table, then each field from your spreadsheet will appear as a cell on a table on your WordPerfect page (or Presentations slide).

If you choose to import your spreadsheet data as text, then each row from the spreadsheet is displayed on a single line in your document. The cells are now separated by tabs.

## Working With Merged Data Files

A merge data file contains information that you combine with a form in WordPerfect. Often, this is used to create a form letter and then add individualized name and address information for each letter (the infamous "mail merge"). To import merge data, follow these steps:

1. Select Insert | Spreadsheet/Database, and choose Import or Create Link.

2. Select a data type.

3. In the Import As drop-down list, choose Merge Data File.

4. In the Filename field, specify the data file you want.

WordPerfect supplies some sample database files. They are located in the \corel\suite8\samples directory. Choose one of these to follow along with this example (see Figure 13-18). You do not have to import the entire database.

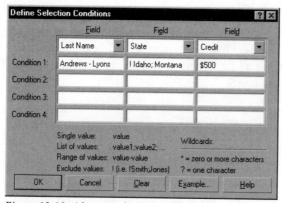

*Figure 13-18: After you choose a database, you can select which field to import from the database.*

5. The database fields appear in the Fields list of the Import Data dialog box. By default, each field is checked, which means that it will appear in your WordPerfect document.

6. To remove a field from the import list, uncheck it.

7. To restrict the values for certain fields (for example, specifying that only customers who live in New York should be included), click the Query button.

8. Three drop-down lists let you determine on which field to set restrictions (for example, Customer ID, Address, or Last Name). Select a field, then type in condition limits in the text area under the list (see Figure 13-19).

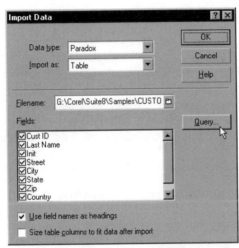

*Figure 13-19: Click Query to limit which portions of the database you want to work with.*

To learn about correct syntax for creating these limits, read the rules at the bottom of the Define Selection Conditions panel, or click Examples.

9. Click OK, and then click OK on the Import Data dialog box as well. Your data will appear record by record in your WordPerfect document. You'll notice codes appear after each entry. The Merge toolbar appears near the top of the WordPerfect window (see Figure 13-20). If you find it irritating to look at the codes, choose Options | Hide Codes.

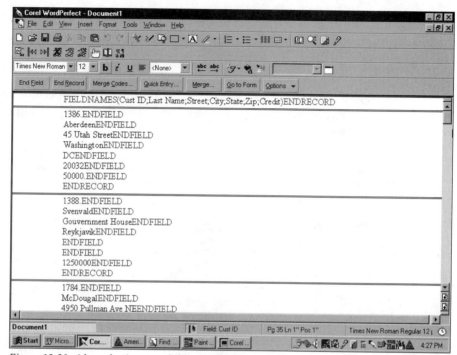

*Figure 13-20: After selecting your fields, use the Merge toolbar to arrange your data on the page.*

Your spreadsheet data has now been converted to a WordPerfect data document. You can save it and then use the new document in a WordPerfect form. (To create a form, select Tools | Merge | Create Document.)

## Linking to a Database

Until now, our database examples have discussed how to import data. Instead of importing, you can create a link to a database by selecting Insert | Spreadsheet/Database | Create Link. You use the same dialog box as above to specify the database information, but when you are finished, you'll have a link to your database. The only visible difference between imported data and linked data is that you see a thin gray bar right before and after the data you've linked. This bar lists the location of the database that you have linked to (see Figure 13-21).

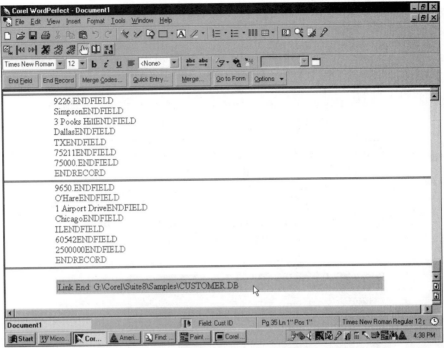

*Figure 13-21: The gray bar at the top and bottom of each linked data file displays its source.*

## Changing Field Conditions & Editing Data

You can edit any database you've linked to your document by clicking Insert | Spreadsheet/Database | Edit Link. This displays the same dialog box you saw when you created the link. You can change the field conditions or change how the data is linked.

## Updating Your Data Manually or Automatically

To update the link between your host document (your WordPerfect page or Presentations slide) and the database, click Insert | Spreadsheet/Database | Update. Remember that the procedures are different for OLE objects.

To choose between allowing WordPerfect Suite to update your host document as soon as it opens, or updating the link yourself, select Insert | Spreadsheet/Database | Options, and check or uncheck the Update When Document Opens check box.

## Database Access & ODBC

To use a database fully in WordPerfect, you need Open Database Connectivity (ODBC) drivers on your system. This is especially true if you are using a Microsoft Access database.

The ODBC drivers are installed and maintained in the Windows Control Panel. If you are experiencing problems, make sure that you have the most recent versions of the drivers installed. Database software generally ships with a set of ODBC drivers.

Make sure that the database you are trying to open is registered properly in the 32-bit ODBC control panel. If you don't see the name of the database source you are trying to use, click Add and select the database source you need (see Figure 13-22). Click Setup and use the Browse dialog box to specify which database you want to make available to all your Windows applications.

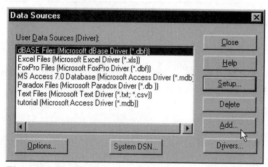

*Figure 13-22: The Data Sources dialog box, accessed by clicking 32-Bit ODBC in the control panel.*

# Creating Hyperlinks Between Applications

You can create hyperlinks among your suite applications. You're probably familiar with hyperlinks in Web pages. In WordPerfect Suite 8, you can set up a hyperlink from one document to another; for example, from a WordPerfect document to a Quattro Pro spreadsheet. Of course, these hyperlinks won't work when you print the document, only when you are using it online. Setting up hyperlinks can be helpful to keep track of related documents.

Each of the three main WordPerfect Suite 8 applications handles hyperlinks in a slightly different way:

- **WordPerfect**. You can create hyperlinks to any Web site, any spreadsheet, and almost any word processing document. WordPerfect's hyperlinks can also open macros. Any section of text, graphic, table cell, or WordPerfect drawing can be made into a hyperlink. You cannot use a hyperlink to launch an application. When you launch a document from a hyperlink, the source document closes.

- **Presentations**. You can create a hyperlink to launch any application or executable file. You can link to a Web site. Presentations remains open when you use a hyperlink.

- **Quattro Pro**. The most sophisticated feature of the three. You can create links to a Web site, an application or executable file, and any word processing file or picture.

The Quattro Pro document remains open when you click a hyperlink.

## Creating Hyperlinks in WordPerfect

In WordPerfect, you can create hyperlinks to Web pages, and to launch other word processing files, spreadsheets, or macros. You cannot link to an application or executable file.

Creating a link to a non-WordPerfect word processing file (like a Word document) converts the linked document to WordPerfect format and then opens the file in WordPerfect. If you create a link to another document, the current WordPerfect document is closed before the new one is opened.

To create a link in WordPerfect, follow these steps:

1. Create and select the object you want to turn into a hyperlink. You might select Insert | Shape | Polygon and create a button, choose a graphic, or select a small section of text.

2. Click Tools | Hyperlink. The Hyperlink Properties dialog box is displayed (see Figure 13-23).

3. In the Document/Macro text box, type in one of the following:

   - A Web URL.

   - A document filename (another WordPerfect project, a Microsoft Word document, or perhaps a graphic, such as a .TIF file).

   - A macro (most of WordPerfect's macros are located in the Corel\Suite8\Macros\WPWIN directory).

   - You could also click the Folder icon and use the Browse dialog box to locate the file, or click the Browse Web button to locate a URL.

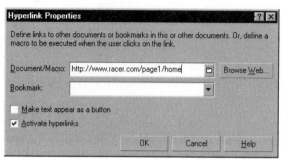

*Figure 13-23: The Hyperlink Properties dialog box. A URL is shown in the Document/Macro text box. This link will activate the specified Web page.*

4. To make the hyperlinked text appear as a gray, raised button, check the Make text appear as a button check box (see Figure 13-24). If you do not check this check box, the text will appear blue.

5. Click OK to close the dialog box.

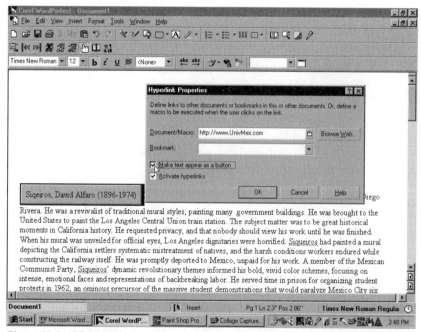

*Figure 13-24: Check Make text appear as a button to change the hyperlink's appearance.*

## WordPerfect Hyperlinks & Web Pages

Please note that the discussion of creating hyperlinks in WordPerfect here does not include working in Web Page view. We're covering hyperlinks placed in standard WordPerfect documents, not using WordPerfect to create Web pages. For that topic, refer to Chapter 14.

To edit your link, right-click on the link and click Edit Hyperlink. This displays the Hyperlink Properties dialog box again. To link to a new document, simply type a new document path into the Document/Macro text box. Check Activate Hyperlinks to make all the links in your document work.

You can make your link activate a bookmark. You must use the Bookmark command (Tools | Bookmark) to *set* the bookmark. This dialog box lets you point this hyperlink to a particular bookmark. See Chapter 6 for a discussion on creating bookmarks.

### Testing & Operating Your Link

If you checked Activate Hyperlinks, your cursor turns into a hand pointer when it is positioned over a hyperlink and a small text box (like a ToolTip) indicates the hyperlink's destination (see Figure 13-25).

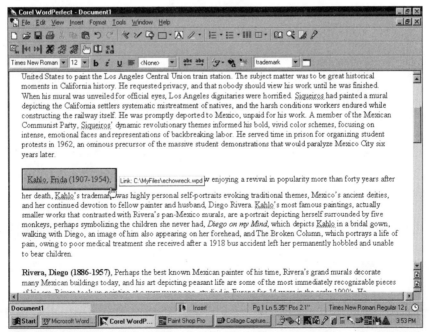

*Figure 13-25: The cursor turns into a hand pointer when positioned over a hyperlink. The target link is also displayed.*

Depending on what action you linked, here's what will happen when you click:

- **Linking to a local document**. If you linked to another document, such as a graphic or a Microsoft Word file, the current document is closed, and the new document opens. If the document is another word processing document, it opens in WordPerfect, not in the source application (in our example, Microsoft Word).

- **Linking to a macro**. If you linked to a macro, the macro is executed. Macros can do all kinds of chores, such as create check boxes, close all open documents, or create a list of all the fonts on your computer. Refer to Chapter 6 for instructions on how to work with macros. The current document is not closed, unless the macro dictates it.

- **Linking to a Web Page**. If you linked to a Web page, your default browser is opened to the URL you indicated. WordPerfect and the current document remain open. Close the browser, and you can return to your document.

### Using the Hyperlink Toolbar

The Hyperlink toolbar gives you easy access to various hyperlink functions (see Figure 13-26). To display the Hyperlink toolbar, right-click on the WordPerfect toolbar and select Hyperlink Tools from the pop-up menu.

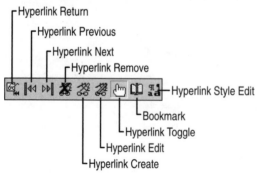

*Figure 13-26: The Hyperlink toolbar.*

Working with the Hyperlink toolbar can save time, because you don't have to right-click on a link before you make changes.

### Deleting a WordPerfect Link

To delete a link, but not the underlying image or text, select the hyperlinked object and then click on the Hyperlink Remove button on the Hyperlink toolbar.

## Creating Hyperlinks in Presentations 8

In Presentations, hyperlinks are called QuickLinks. Most often, you'll use QuickLinks to provide a link on one slide that displays another slide. For example, you can have several different text boxes that represent different options on a slide; clicking a choice displays a slide specific to that choice. You can use QuickLinks to create hyperlinks to two types of documents:

- Web pages
- Executable files

Instead of selecting another slide as the target of the link, select a Web page or an executable file to create a hyperlink.

You can hyperlink any graphic, draw picture, or text box. Follow these steps:

1. Select a clickable object—a shape, graphic, or text box—in Slide Editor mode.

2. Right-click on the object and select QuickLink (see Figure 13-27). This displays the Object Properties dialog box with the QuickLink tab selected (see Figure 13-28).

3. Click the Action radio button. In the Action drop-down list, select one of the following items:

    - **Browse Internet**. The Location text box is displayed. Type a URL or use the Browse Web button to open your Web browser and search for the site you want.

    - **Launch Program**. The Program dialog box is displayed. Type the filename for an executable file or click the Folder icon to browse your hard drive and select a file.

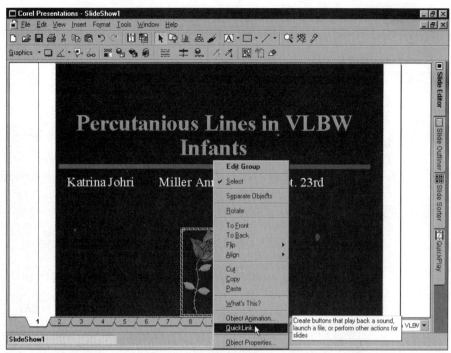

*Figure 13-27: To create a hyperlink, right-click the object and select QuickLink.*

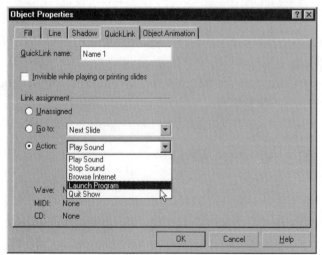

*Figure 13-28: Click the Action check box to assign a URL or any executable file to this hyperlink.*

### Testing or Operating Your Presentations Link

To test your Presentations 8 hyperlink, you'll need to run the slide show. Follow these steps:

1. Select View | Play Slide Show.

2. Click on the hyperlink object to open the link (see Figure 13-29).

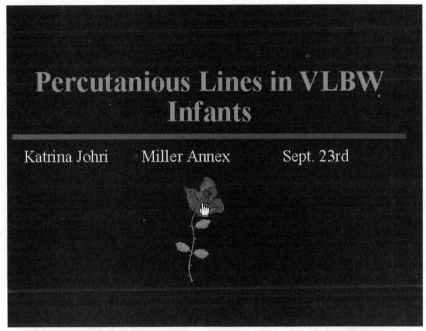

*Figure 13-29: The cursor changes to a hand when positioned over a hyperlink.*

3. Close the target program or leave the Web site to return to Presentations.

4. To exit the slide show, press the Esc key.

## Creating Hyperlinks in Quattro Pro

In Quattro Pro, you must assign the hyperlink to a cell instead of a drawn object or graphic. Quattro Pro hyperlinks can open Web pages and other documents, but you cannot link a program to a Quattro Pro cell. When you activate a link, Quattro Pro remains open.

To create a hyperlink in Quattro Pro, follow these steps:

1. Select a cell for your hyperlink.

2. Select Insert | Hyperlink. The Edit Hyperlink dialog box is displayed.

3. Type in the filename for a document, or the URL for a Web site.

You can use the Folder icon to browse your hard drive for a file, but this dialog box does not provide a way to browse the Web. You must know your URL.

4. Click OK to close the Edit Hyperlink dialog box.

## Testing Your Quattro Pro Hyperlink

As soon as you create your link, it is active (see Figure 13-30). Once you've created a link, you can't select the cell for editing, because selecting it activates the link. Therefore, it's advisable that you wait until your spreadsheet is finished before creating any Quattro Pro links.

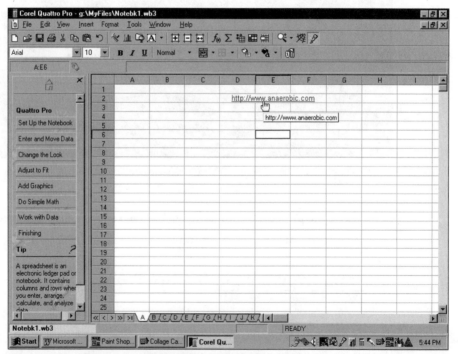

*Figure 13-30: After creating a hyperlink of a cell in Quattro Pro, it is immediately active. Notice in this case, the hyperlink is created from three joined cells.*

If you need to remove a hyperlink, use the Remove Hyperlink button in the Edit Hyperlink dialog box.

Activate any Quattro Pro hyperlink by clicking it, and the target file will open. Quattro Pro is unaffected. Close the target URL or document to return to Quattro Pro.

## Moving On

In this chapter, we explored the ways that you can create links in WordPerfect Suite documents. These include using OLE objects or creating a hyperlink. We learned how to link a Quattro Pro notebook to a WordPerfect document, and how to insert multimedia objects into any WordPerfect Suite 8 document. We learned the techniques for creating OLE links, hyperlinks, embedding objects, and how these techniques vary from application to application. In our next and final chapter, we'll explore creating Web pages with WordPerfect Suite 8.

# 14

# Creating Web Pages With WordPerfect 8

In this chapter, we'll discuss how to create Web pages with WordPerfect, both by creating them from scratch and by converting existing documents. WordPerfect does a lot of work behind the scenes to get your document ready for the Web. If you want to use graphics on your Web pages, there are some format limitations and file size issues to consider. You can also create tables, lists, hyperlinks, and use a simple outline form for your pages.

To add some pizzazz to your pages, you can add Java applets. WordPerfect Suite 8 also includes Corel Barista, which lets you display almost any Windows-based document on your computer.

When you've finished designing your pages and are ready to upload them to your Web server, WordPerfect supplies a Web Publishing wizard that takes you through the process step by step.

## Preliminary Considerations

If you decide to publish a term paper or a working document to the Web, WordPerfect can accommodate you. But a little planning for your Web pages will make the process much easier and the results much better—Web pages and paper documents have different requirements.

## Understanding HTML

HyperText Markup Language, or HTML, forms the backbone of Web pages. You don't need to learn HTML to work with WordPerfect's Web design tools, but understanding how HTML works can help you see how your Web pages are assembled.

HTML uses a simple tagging structure, where commands are placed inside angle brackets (<>). There are only a few basic rules to which all the features adhere. With a good book, an enthusiastic computer novice can learn HTML in about 20 hours of hands-on practice. One good choice is *Official HTML Publishing for Netscape, 2nd Edition*, published by Ventana.

HTML documents are text documents, so you can create them in any text editor, like Windows Notepad. All you have to do is type in a few lines of HTML code and then save your file with an .HTM extension instead of a .TXT extension, and you then have a Web page. All Web browsers recognize the standard HTML codes, so once you create a simple HTML document, any browser will display the file appropriately.

To create a simple HTML document, type the following into an empty Notepad file. Press Enter at the end of every line.

```
<html>
<head>
<title>My Thoughts on Furniture</title>
</head>
<body>
<h1>Furniture</h1>
There are many different kinds of furniture; take chairs, for example.
<h2>Chairs</h2>
Chairs come in all shapes and sizes. They have been with us for many
millennia. The first chair in history was used by Gilgamesh, a pseudo-
legendary character of about 3,000 BC.
</body>
</html>
```

Save your Notepad file with an .HTM extension, and you've created a short Web page.

If HTML is this easy, why does WordPerfect provide Web page creation tools? WordPerfect's tools are faster and more flexible than hand-coding HTML, and they support content beyond simple HTML. But since some of WordPerfect's more advanced tools will require you to insert a bit of HTML code into your document, it's useful to have a basic understanding of HTML.

## Putting Graphics on the Web

World Wide Web graphics come in many flavors, but the two most popular and widely supported are the CompuServe Graphics Interchange Format (GIF) and the Joint Photographic Experts Group (JPEG) format. The differences between the two revolve mainly around their ability to hold color information. GIF files are quite small (always a consideration on the Web, where speed is a premium), but they don't hold color information very well. Use GIF files when your artwork is black and white or when your graphics contain large, flat areas of color. Also, GIFs can be saved with a transparent background, so if you need something to show through your graphic, GIF is the way to go.

JPEG files, while a bit larger and not able to hold transparency information, are still fast and hold up to 16 million colors. This means that artwork where color data is vital, such as photographs and paintings, will be rendered more faithfully if you use JPEG files.

One final consideration is image size. If your graphic is smaller than two inches on a side, use GIF. The extra color from a JPEG won't show up, so you'll be wasting bandwidth using the larger file.

When you are creating your Web page in WordPerfect, you can import files from many formats. When you save your Web file, WordPerfect converts the artwork to one of those two appropriate file types. Therefore, when creating a Web page in WordPerfect, you need not worry about the file type of your picture. WordPerfect takes care of that for you.

When creating an image that you know will be used in a Web page, try to make it as small as possible. Your image resolution need not be any higher than 72 dpi. (When editing or saving a file in any good graphic design program, you'll always have an opportunity to adjust image resolution.) The lead graphic (usually called the banner graphic) of your Web page should not be any larger than 150K. The width of your image should be no more than 550 pixels. When creating small buttons as clickable objects for your Web page, you should make them no larger than 10 X 10 to 10 X 30 pixels. Keeping image size down enables your page to load faster. Try to keep your image size not much larger than 50K.

## Setting Up a Web Site

Setting up a Web site is not a solo performance. The files you create will be uploaded to your Internet Service Provider (ISP) according to specific guidelines dictated by their Web Administrator and support staff. Start preparing now by saving all your Web-related files in one folder. Before you create a Web site, designate one particular folder for all HTML files, pictures, tables, and other related material. WordPerfect will create subfolders within this main folder you designate. Remember not to move files out of those folders until it comes time to upload everything to your ISP.

Commit your ISP to providing no less than five megabytes of hard drive space for your Web files. Find out from them how and when you can log on and update your files, add new features to your Web pages, check links for validity, and purge information that's no longer valid.

As far as the actual uploading of your Web site files, you have WordPerfect's Web Wizard to guide you through that task.

# Creating Web Pages With WordPerfect

There are two ways to create Web pages in WordPerfect 8. One option is to convert your existing document to a Web page. The other is to change your View to Web Page View and work from scratch, directly adding components with a Web page in mind.

What follows is the creation of a sample Web page. Then we'll look at each step individually.

## Creating Your First Web Page

Let's start by discussing how to create a Web page from scratch. We'll be creating the page shown in Figure 14-1.

1. Create a folder for all the Web-related files in this project. I created one called Barbena.

2. Open WordPerfect.

*Figure 14-1: A Web page created in WordPerfect.*

3. Change your view of your new document to Web Page view (View | Web Page).

4. Create a background for your Web page by selecting File Properties. Select the Text/Background Colors tab. In the Background Wallpaper field, type in this path: C:\Corel\Suite8\Graphics\Textures\Nature\ Sand.bmp. Click OK to close the dialog.

5. Place your cursor at the upper left of the page. Click the Font/Size button on the Property bar. This is where you choose a heading style for your page, and subheading styles for text beneath the main heading. Click Heading1 from the menu.

6. Type in "Barbena County Beach" as shown. Press Enter.

7. Return again to the Font/Size selector on the Property bar. Select Heading2.

8. Type "For a Summer You'll Never Forget" as shown.

9. Select the text you just typed, and choose the Justification tool on the Property bar. Center the heading.

10. Type in the bullets as shown at the left of the Web page, pressing Enter after each. Start with "Hotel Reservations," and end with "AAA Web Site."

11. Press Enter after "AAA Web Site," and then click the Horizontal Line tool, found on the middle of the WordPerfect toolbar. This inserts a horizontal rule after the final bullet entry.

12. Make sure your WordPerfect CD-ROM is in the CD-ROM drive.

13. Press Enter. Select Insert | Graphics | From File.

14. In the Look in dialog box, locate the file X:\Photos\Nature\347041.JPG (substitute the letter of your CD-ROM for the X). Click OK.

15. After the picture appears on your Web page, right-click on it, and select Position.

16. From the Attach Box To list, select Paragraph. In the drop-down menu below that, select Right Margin. Click OK to close the dialog box.

17. Right-click again on the image and choose Size. Click the top Set radio button. Type in 5 inches.

18. Click the bottom Set radio button. Type in 3.15 inches. The image should be about the same size as shown in Figure 14-1, approximately half the width of the page. Click OK to close the dialog box.

19. Again right-click on the picture, and select Border/Fill. Choose the green and black border. It's the second row, second border from the left. Click OK to close that dialog box. Your picture now has a border.

20. The bullets will appear to the left and the picture on the right.

We've added some important elements to our page: a banner graphic, main and secondary headings, a background graphic, and five text bullets we can convert to hyperlinks. These bullets are our links to other pages in the site. Below, we'll discuss in detail each component we've created, and later, we'll create another page, linking both pages together. For now, let's give our page a title and add some body text.

To add a title to your page, select File | Properties, and click the Title tab. Click the Custom Title radio button. Type in "Barbena County Beach Tourist Association."

To type in body text, position your mouse cursor right below and to the left of the horizontal line you created, below the text bullets on the left of the page. Simply type text as shown in Figure 14-1. When you are done typing, select the text, and make it bold, using the Bold button on the Property bar.

Save your Web page in the folder you've created for this project.

## Creating a New Web Document

To create a new Web document, you can open WordPerfect, and change to Web Page view (View | Web Page). The PerfectExpert Help System, at the left of the screen, can guide you step by step through the process of adding each element. Please remember that turning on the PerfectExpert Help System will cost you about a third of your screen space on the left side of the screen. So your Web elements (Headline, main graphic) will appear squeezed towards the right as long as the PerfectExpert Help System is open.

You can also begin by opening WordPerfect, selecting File | Internet Publisher, clicking New Web Document, and selecting Create a Blank Web Document. Using these two methods makes the same options and menus available.

## Adding Text

In our example above, we added two types of headings, body text near the bottom of the page, and five short lines of text that will be converted to hyperlinks, leading to other pages. So we can see that adding text is simply a matter of typing where you want text to go. To add headings, click the large "A" on the far left of the Property bar (see Figure 14-2). As mentioned previously, this is the Font/Size tool. You'll see a drop-down menu of heading levels and sizes. Other text format options such as Addresses and Definition Lists are available here as well.

To apply such formatting to text, type the text, select it with the mouse, then click the tool on the Property bar, and select your formatting type.

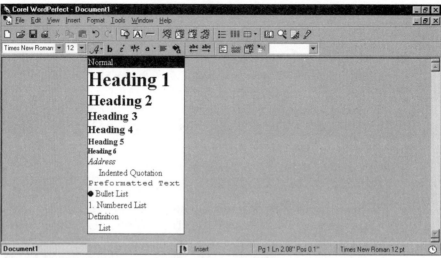

*Figure 14-2: The text styles that are standard on the Web.*

## Giving a Title to a Page

It's easy to mix up a Web page title and its filename. The title is what the visitor sees in the Title bar of the browser window. More importantly, the title is the first item that a Web browser reads when determining if it will include your page in a return list of "found matches" with what a browser user has suggested. Therefore if your Web site has something to do with helping people with their taxes, for example, make sure the word "taxes" appears in the title of your home page and in other "deeper" pages within your site as well.

When a person searches the Web for a particular topic, the browser first looks at the title of every page it searches to determine if that page is to be included in the "finds" that it returns to the searcher. As a further example, if your Web page involves advertising chamber music at a venue in Santa Fe, make sure *several* appropriate words are included in the title. That way, if a person searches for "Classical" or "Santa Fe" or "Chamber Music," for example, they would find your page in each case.

The filename, on the other hand, is the eight-character name of the computer file and will always end with an .htm or .html file extension. Filenames may be important to you for organizing Web pages on your computer, especially if you have several Web sites running that you need to maintain regularly. And filename conventions will likely be important to the service provider hosting your Web site. So remember, a Web page title is not the same as the filename (for example, chamber.htm is the filename, but the page title could very well be "Fall Schedule for Sandia Music Society Chamber Concerts").

To add a title, click Format I Text/Background Colors (see Figure 14-3). You'll see five tabs. Choose the Title tab, and place a check by Custom title. Type in your own title, up to 256 characters. If you check the First Heading radio button, then your title will be whatever you've typed for your first heading in your document. We'll explore the other tabs later in this chapter.

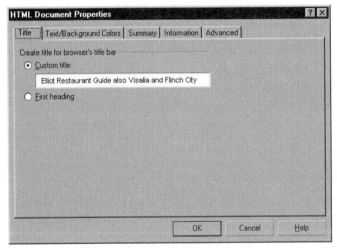

*Figure 14-3: Adding a title to your Web page.*

## Adding Graphics

Your home page's central graphic should be something memorable. It is worth the investment of time or money to make this central graphic look quite special. Whether you take the time to create something special yourself or get someone else to do it for you, having a nice central graphic entices visitors to stay long enough to find out if what your Web site offers appeals to them. On a Web page, graphics position themselves according to the text that surrounds them. It's often best to add graphics after much of the text is in place, as we did with our example above.

To add WordPerfect clip art to your Web page, do the following:

1. Click the Clipart icon on the standard toolbar. Holding your mouse over it reveals the ToolTip "Clipart." It opens the WordPerfect Scrapbook, allowing you to search the various folders for a picture.

2. Drag and drop a picture onto the page.

3. As we discovered above with our example, you can right-click on the graphic, select Position, and determine where on the page you'd like your graphic to appear.

After positioning your clip art, right-clicking on it reveals the standard WordPerfect options, plus the menu item HTML Properties.

### Adding Photos to Your Document

To add photos and other graphics not found in the WordPerfect Clipart Scrapbook, do the following:

1. As with our example above, Select Insert | Graphic, making sure the WordPerfect CD is in the CD-ROM drive. The Insert Image dialog box appears.

2. In the Look In data box, locate the folder D:\Photos, and search the subfolders for the picture you'd like to use.

3. Click on it, and choose Select. The image will appear in your document.

If you'd like to use a picture not included on the WordPerfect CD-ROM, simply locate the picture's folder on your hard drive.

Although only GIF and JPEG graphics are widely viewable on the Web, you may include pictures of other formats since, as part of the Web Publishing Wizard process, all graphics that are not GIFs are converted to JPEGs anyway.

You may edit your graphic and graphic box using tools identical to WordPerfect's word processing graphic tools. Graphics and graphics boxes are edited the same way. You can add captions, create a border and fill, and resize your picture using the bounding boxes around the image, just as you would in a standard WordPerfect document.

## Adding Lists

The five short lines of text we added to our page above are an example of a list. Lists are often short text entries such as those that will be converted to hyperlinks to other pages. Adding bullets to your page helps make your list appear well organized. Especially if a list is going to be more than four or five entries long, you should consider adding bullets.

Bullets, which are markers that highlight sequential lists, are a mainstay on the Web. You can add animated bullets, bullets that change colors, or just regular, standard black spheres. To add a standard HTML bullet sequence, do the following:

1. Click the Font/Size icon on the toolbar, and select • Bullet List from the drop-down menu.

2. Begin typing your line of text.

3. Press Enter to move to a new line and create the next bullet.

4. Repeat for as many bullets as you'd like.

5. To break the numbering or bulleting and return to normal text entry, press Enter while depressing the Control Key.

Your bullets may not appear exactly the same to every visitor, depending on the browser, but the effect will be the same.

To include a new level of entries in your list, bulleted or numbered, type your final entry under the first level, and then, rather than pressing Enter to continue, click the button or numbered list icon on the toolbar. You'll see the beginning of a secondary level list appear under your final level one entry.

You may add decorative bullets to your page. These are actually small graphics (perhaps 10 x10 pixels in size). Some are included on the WordPerfect CD-ROM, and others are available from other Web graphic sources. These are added as graphics. To add a graphical bullet list to your page, insert them as you would any other picture, and then begin writing a sentence immediately to the right of the bullet. Start with the following steps.

1. Place your mouse cursor where you want your bullet to appear.

2. Select Insert | Graphic | From File.

3. In the Insert Image dialog box, locate the bullet you'd like to use.

4. Click Select. The bullet will appear on your page.

5. Begin typing your row of text.

6. Repeat the above to create your entire list.

## Adding a Table

To add a table to a Web page, let's create another page for our Barbena County Beach site. The finished page will look something like Figure 14-4.

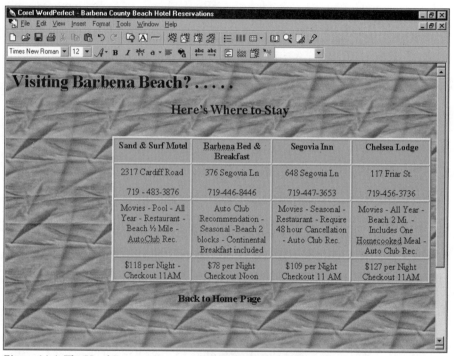

*Figure 14-4: The Hotel Reservations page, which includes a table.*

We'll quickly review the steps we used, right up to where we add the table:

1. Start a New Web page, and add a background graphic by selecting File | Properties and choosing the Text\Background Colors tab.

2. In the Background Wallpaper field, click the small folder to locate the following folder and file: C:\Corel\Suite8\Graphics\Textures\Fabrics\Blue Wrinkled.BMP.

3. Click Select, and then click OK to close the Insert Graphic dialog box. The new background appears on the page.

4. Click the Title tab, select Custom title, and type in "Barbena Beach Hotel Reservations."

5. Type in text and the level one and two headlines, as shown in the above figure.

6. Now let's create our table: Select Insert I Table. The HTML Table Format dialog box appears.

7. In the Table Size area, type in 4 for both numbers. Our table will be four columns across and four rows deep.

8. Click the Background color button, and choose the flesh-tone color, the first row and the second color box from the right. This gives your table a different background color than the page itself.

9. In the Table Position on Page drop-down menu, select Right.

10. In the Vertical Alignment of Cell Contents, select Center.

11. Click OK to close the dialog box. Your blank table appears on the page.

12. Simply click in any cell, and begin typing, creating a table as shown in the above figure.

13. Use the Bold tool on the Property bar to create bold text. Do not press Enter to create a new line unless your intention is to skip a line. This type of table has automatic word wrap.

14. When you are done adding text to your table, click outside and below the table.

15. As shown in the figure above, type the phrase "Back to Home Page."

16. After typing the phrase, select it with the mouse, and, using the Property bar, center the phrase. Later, we'll turn this phrase into a hyperlink to lead back to the home page.

17. Later, we'll explore how to turn the text in any table cell into a hyperlink, which, in this case, could be a link to a particular hotel's Web page.

18. Save this Web page as "Hotel.htm," taking care to save it in the same folder (Barbena) that you've used for other Web files for this project.

## Creating Hyperlinks

Hyperlinks are clickable objects that open other documents or Web pages when the visitor clicks them. With WordPerfect, you can create text and text box hyperlinks, and hyperlinks from graphics or from cells of a table. Open the first page we created, so we can turn a couple of those list items on the left of the page into hyperlinks.

1. Select the phrase "Hotel Reservations," and click Tools I Hyperlink. The Hyperlink Properties dialog box appears.

2. In the Document field, type in Hotel.htm. This links the text to the other Web page we just created, the one with the table of hotel reservations. Since this Web page is saved in the same folder as the first, we simply type in the name of the document itself (Hotel.htm) not the entire path (C:\Barena\Hotel.htm).

3. Make sure there's a check by Activate Hyperlinks, and close the dialog box.

4. The phrase Hotel Reservations will appear in blue because it has now become a link. Holding your mouse over the phrase turns the mouse cursor into a hand, and a ToolTip appears, indicating the destination of the link. Click OK to close the dialog box.

5. You may repeat this process for the entire list although we only created one page to set up an actual link.

Please note that you can create links to pages that you have yet to create. Also, when creating a link to a WWW site, be sure to double-check that your information is accurate. Notice the Browse Web button in the Hyperlink Properties dialog box. This allows you to quickly check your link for validity.

### Creating a Hyperlink From a Graphic

You can also create a hyperlink from a graphic. For example, in our first Web page, you could turn the picture of the beach into a hyperlink, so that when it's clicked on, a map with directions appears. To create a hyperlink from a graphic, do the following:

1. Right-click on the graphic, and select HTML Properties. You'll see a dialog box with three text areas (see Figure 14-5).

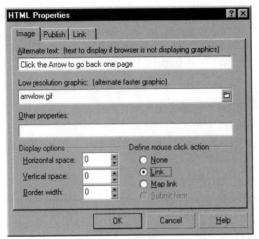

*Figure 14-5: The graphics HTML Properties dialog box.*

- Alternate text allows you to type something in for people to read who are unable to see graphics when viewing your page. Some Web surfers will turn off graphics in order to speed page transmission times. (It's much faster to view only text than wait for the picture to load as well.) For such a visitor to your page, they will see what you have written in the Alternate text area, rather than the graphic you've included.

- Low resolution graphic allows you to include a smaller picture, replacing your larger, main graphic choice. Visitors may have configured their browsers to load graphics only up to a certain size. Selecting a lower resolution picture allows the viewer to make such a choice.

- Placing numbers in the Horizontal and Vertical space fields allows you to position the graphic a specified number away from the margin you've aligned the picture *to*. For example, if you've set the picture for left alignment, and then set the Horizontal and Vertical spaces for 20 and 30 respectively, your graphic will appear 20 pixels to the right and 30 pixels above the left alignment position.

2. Turn your attention to the Define mouse click action area at the bottom of the dialog box.

3. To make this a hyperlink, you must toggle the Link radio button on. You'll see a new tab appear as part of this dialog box called Link. Click it, and type in a URL that specifies what file or Web page will open when the visitor clicks your link (see Figure 14-6).

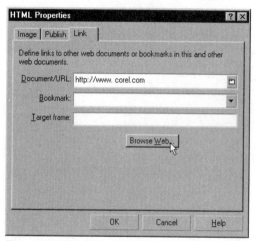

*Figure 14-6: The Link tab of the HTML Properties dialog box.*

4. If you are linking the visitor to another one of your own Web pages, simply type in its name.

5. If you are linking to a site or page elsewhere on the WWW, use the Browse Web button to search for one if you haven't set aside a choice already. To create a link to a page in your own site, make sure the HTML document you are creating a link to is found in the *same folder* as your current page.

- The Bookmark feature allows you to link the visitor to a specific line of text in that target document, rather than open at the top of the page.

- If the target document has frames, you may use the Target Frame field to create a link to a specific frame, rather than a link to the top of the chosen page.

## Adding Forms

WordPerfect 8 gives you tools for adding forms to your page. You can add labeled text boxes, "submit" buttons, check boxes, password entry boxes, and many other form-type objects.

Forms are used, for example, to allow visitors to leave address data, fill out questionnaires, take quizzes online, or submit personality profiles. Figure 14-7 shows a typical Web page form created in WordPerfect. Let's see how to create one:

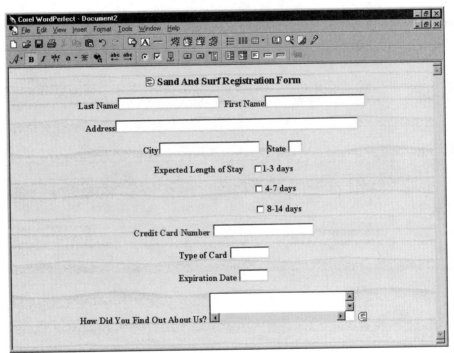

*Figure 14-7: A Web page with a form created in WordPerfect.*

1. Click the New Form button on the Web toolbar.

2. Type a heading for your form, as shown in the figure.

The most standard form elements, such as text lines, should be labeled. Following this example, to add name and address text lines to your page, do the following:

3. Type Name, and then click the Text Line icon on the Property bar (Figure 14-8).

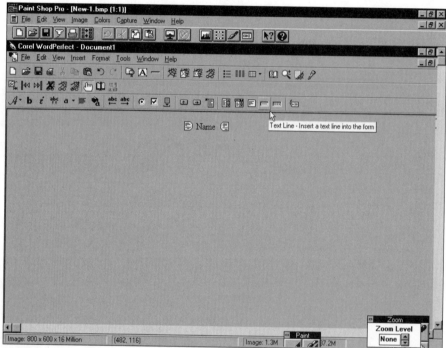

*Figure 14 -8: The Text Line icon, used for creating a single line of text in a form.*

4. A box for visitors to type in their names will appear. You can place a space between the end of the word Name and the text line area itself. Just use the spacebar to do this.

You may also have noticed that the Property bar changes when you create the beginnings of your form. As long as the blinking cursor is in between these two markers, the Property bar will display a dozen tools and actually form elements, that you can add merely by clicking.

5. Press the Enter key to start a new line, and add an Address text line.

6. Use the same method to label your Address area: type the word Address, press the spacebar, and then select Text Line from the Property bar. A new text line element will appear after the word Address.

7. Repeat with City and State.

8. Now how do you make the space for City and State shorter? After you make a Text Line, right-click on it. Select Properties, and type in a new, smaller number for the Width specification. Twenty is the default. For City, usually eight will do fine, and for State, four will do.

9. When right-clicking on the Text Line box and clicking Properties, you'll also see a parameter called "Max Char" (see Figure 14-9). You need to specify the maximum number of characters allowed in your Text Line. Make sure a check is placed by Normal and not by Password. Checking Password causes asterisks to be displayed on the screen, rather than the text itself.

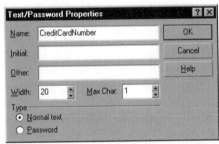

*Figure 14-9: The Text/Password Properties dialog box.*

10. Use the spacebar and the Enter key to align the form items to your liking.

## Adding Check Boxes

There are parameters you may choose for check boxes as well (check boxes are the small squares filled with a check symbol when selected). In our example, check boxes are used in the "Expected Length of Stay" area. First insert a check box, then select it, right-click, and choose Properties. You'll see the Check Box Properties dialog box (see Figure 14-10).

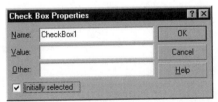

*Figure 14-10: The Check Box Properties dialog box. Notice that "Initially selected" is chosen. When this button appears on your page, it will first appear selected.*

You may name your check boxes and define a parameter. (Specifying a parameter value involves knowing CGI scripting language. You need not enter anything here for your box to work.) Click the Initially selected check box if you want the check box to appear selected when the visitor first sees the form. The Property dialog for radio buttons works the same way as for check boxes.

### Adding Drop-Down Menus & List Boxes

WordPerfect allows you to make forms with drop-down menus (here called comboboxes) and selection lists, for allowing the visitor to make selections from a list. In our example, a selection list was used for the "How Did You Find Out About Us?" segment.

After inserting a combobox or drop-down menu into your form, reposition and label them as you would the check boxes and text lines we discussed earlier. Double-click on the box, and select Add to add an entry to the box. In our example, such entries are "Barbena Beach Web Page," "Magazine Ad," and so forth.

You can also add parameters and specify if you'd like visitors to be able to make multiple selections from the list. Here is where you come to add items to your list of choices for visitors to see online.

Right-click on the box to access the Properties dialog box. From here you can also name your combobox or menu. This can be very helpful if you build a complex form with many elements included. This is not the same as providing a label for your combobox in the text of the Web page itself. This feature is a personal naming system to help you to keep track of everything in your form.

### Adding Submit & Reset Buttons

You can include Submit and Reset buttons with your form. Visitors would click Submit at the very end of the process, which would record the information on the form for you to work with later. The Reset button is used to clear the form should the visitor want to re-enter the results from scratch. To insert a Submit or Reset button, make sure the blinking cursor is where you want the box to appear, and then click the Submit or Reset button on the toolbar. Your button will appear. Again, right-clicking on your button and selecting Properties gives you access to editing features.

To make your form work, select either of the small "bookend" markers at the end or very beginning of the page. Make sure the cursor turns into an arrow. Double-click on Select marker and select Properties. The Form Properties dialog box appears (see Figure 14-11). Specify an Action URL or MIME script to activate the form. Let's look at the meaning of those terms:

- **Action URL**. In order for your form to truly process data, it must be powered by a CGI script. (CGI stands for Common Gateway Interface, and is a small program that facilitates sorting names, searching databases, and delivering e-mail.) The type of CGI scripting tool used is selected or developed by your Internet Service Provider. In other words, it's up to them to tell you how to access this script because it's on their computer. As part of the process of posting your Web site, the Web server's technical support staff will tell you the URL of the script. Type the Address into the Action URL data area.

- **MIME Script**. If, in the Method panel of the Form Properties dialog box, you select Post (which allows users to send e-mail and post messages), you must specify a type of special script set aside just for this purpose. This is called a MIME script. MIME stands for Multipurpose Internet Mail Extensions and allows visitors to download files and send e-mail. Again, check with your Internet Service Provider to determine the type of MIME script employed for this purpose.

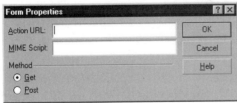

*Figure 14-11: Determining how the form will behave in operation.*

## Adding a Spreadsheet

Figure 14-12 shows a spreadsheet as a Web page, listing recent visitors to Barbena County Beach. This Web page can be saved as an active, updatable spreadsheet using Corel Barista, which we'll discuss later.

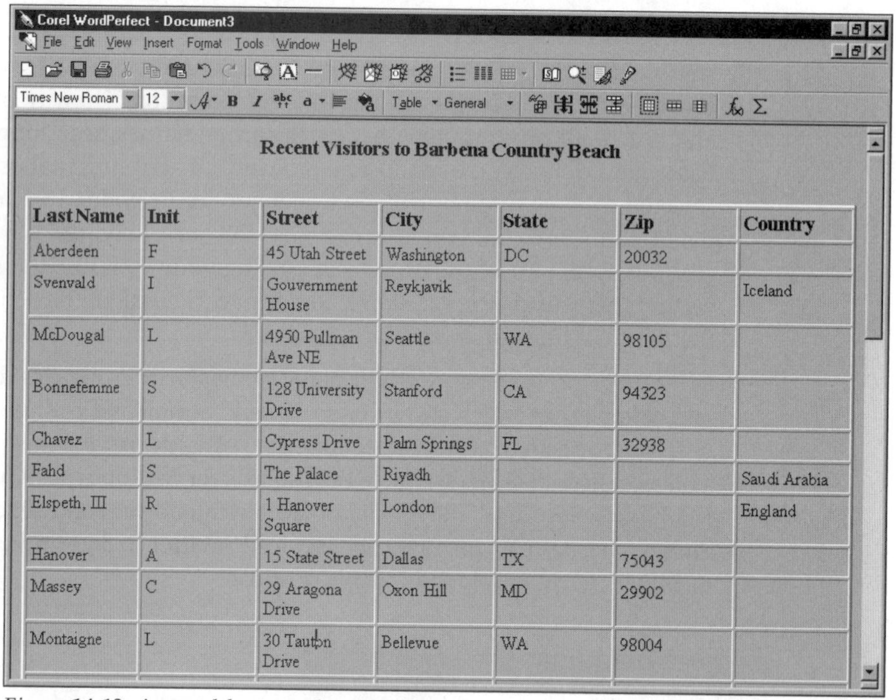

| Last Name | Init | Street | City | State | Zip | Country |
|---|---|---|---|---|---|---|
| Aberdeen | F | 45 Utah Street | Washington | DC | 20032 | |
| Svenvald | I | Gouvernment House | Reykjavik | | | Iceland |
| McDougal | L | 4950 Pullman Ave NE | Seattle | WA | 98105 | |
| Bonnefemme | S | 128 University Drive | Stanford | CA | 94323 | |
| Chavez | L | Cypress Drive | Palm Springs | FL | 32938 | |
| Fahd | S | The Palace | Riyadh | | | Saudi Arabia |
| Elspeth, III | R. | 1 Hanover Square | London | | | England |
| Hanover | A | 15 State Street | Dallas | TX | 75043 | |
| Massey | C | 29 Aragona Drive | Oxon Hill | MD | 29902 | |
| Montaigne | L | 30 Tauton Drive | Bellevue | WA | 98004 | |

Recent Visitors to Barbena Country Beach

*Figure 14-12: A spreadsheet saved as a Web page.*

You may import spreadsheet or database information to your Web page just as you would to a word processing document. Don't create a table first. Simply do the following:

1. Select Import | Spreadsheet/Database | Import.

2. Select the database file you want to import (see Figure 14-13).

3. Choose to import it as a table. Click OK. The new data will appear as a table in your Web page, specifically at the point where the blinking cursor was located when you began importing.

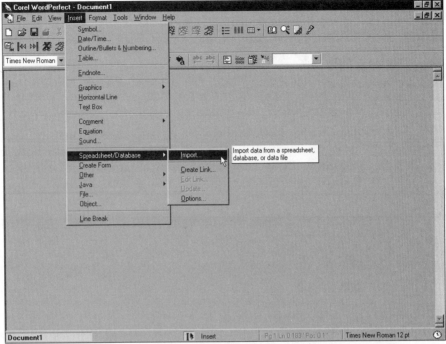

*Figure 14-13: Importing a database to appear as a table in your Web page.*

You can quickly create a hyperlink of any table cell data by doing the following:

1. Select the cell you want to convert by selecting the text inside it.

2. Choose Tools | Hyperlink.

3. Click Create on the resulting toolbar that appears near the top of the screen.

4. Specify or choose a filename to link to. Click Close, and the Hyperlink toolbar disappears.

5. The number in the cell you chose to convert to a hyperlink now becomes a hyperlink. Test it, and operate it as you would any hyperlink.

To insert a linked database, meaning a table that has a link to a database in another program besides WordPerfect, perhaps Quattro Pro for example, do the following:

1. Select Insert | Spreadsheet/Database | Create Link.

2. Just as with WordPerfect, a table will be created showing the data. In the future, you may update this table as it appears in the Web view of this page by clicking Insert | Spreadsheet/Database | Update (see Figure 14-14).

3. Answer Yes when the Update All Links? prompt appears. This way, you are updating a living link between your Web page and the database program, rather than importing a table from scratch each time.

4. For a true link to exist between your spreadsheet and this Web page, bring this issue up with your ISP support staff for specific instructions regarding file location and scripting organization. You must publish a linked WordPerfect spreadsheet Web page as a Corel Barista document.

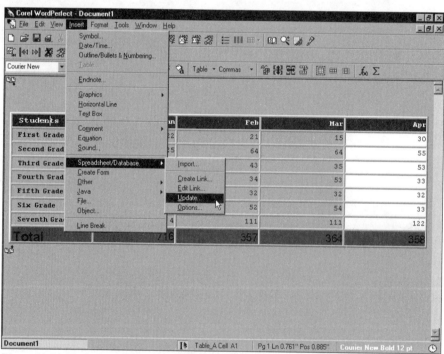

*Figure 14-14: Updating a link to a linked database imported as a table.*

## Adding Java Applets to Your Page

Java applets are small programs that are created with a fairly simple computer lingo, and these mini-programs can be included in Web pages to perform various tasks, such as show the date and time on the page or calculate the value of an equation based on numbers the visitor provides. In short, Java applets make your Web page *do* things. Java applets require the placement of a few files in the same directory as your other Web-related files and the knowledge to specify, for example, how fast a button should display its rainbow of colors or how often to update chart values. Java applets can do simple jobs, like display the time or make a picture move, on up to executing complex formulas in online databases. Properly configured Java applets can function in almost any Web page that has appropriate content; for example, a user can indicate that a particular chart be updated from a database at regular intervals, or that a clock display local or Greenwich time. Lots of people program Java applets, with uses ranging from the cute and facile to the genuinely useful. It is very simple to place and position Java applets in your Web page.

By selecting Insert | Java | Create Applet, you can insert a Java applet into your Web page (see Figure 14-15). The applet will appear at the position of the blinking cursor, using the default size as indicated in the Properties dialog box. (As usual, once you've inserted the Java applet, right-click on it, and select Properties.)

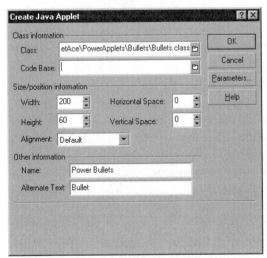

*Figure 14-15: The Create Java Applet dialog box.*

Since there are as many types of Java applets as there are flowers, it's hard to predict how large a Java applet should be. If you are importing a hit counter (a small number gauge that reports how many people have visited your site—it looks like an odometer), then a size of 30 pixels high X 90 pixels wide would be sufficient. If you are importing a "marquee" banner (a phrase of text that moves across the screen like a ticker tape), then your Java applet may need to be 90 pixels high X 320 wide. So the size and alignment parameters you set here really depend on the type of applet you are importing. The Horizontal Space and Vertical Space numbers work the same as inserting Web graphics. You are essentially adding to the margin between your applet's chosen alignment setting (Top, Middle, Absolute Bottom, for example) and the applet itself. For example, adding 20 pixels to the applet's vertical spacing would position the applet 20 pixels farther towards the top than it normally would be.

The Code Base field allows you to draw Java data from another folder, rather than moving and including the Java code with the page itself. The trouble with this approach is that, for a novice, it's really easy to forget where all the relevant data is stored. Then, when it's time to upload your final site with all its pages, Web data has not been stored in one easy location, and confusion can ensue.

Type text into the Alternative Text area so that viewers who are unable to see your applet are at least told that something is amiss. For example, if a particular visitor doesn't see the Java applet, they could see a text phrase such as, "You need a Java-enabled browser to see this applet."

Typing a name for your Java applet allows you to keep track of all the applets you may be using in your site. It is a personal name you choose for your own references purposes. It does not appear in the browser or on the Web page.

## Adding Parameters to Your Applet

You can add parameters to your Java applet by right-clicking the applet and then selecting Properties | Parameters. Then choose Add, and type in an appropriate name and value (see Figure 14-16). To work with Java parameters, you must understand something about the applet you are adding and be able to work with its code, assigning appropriate values. Parameters for each type of applet will be different. Some relate to border thickness or background color for the applet, and others relate to how fast "ticker tape" text moves across the screen. These are just three examples. Java applet parameters are as varied as the applets themselves. (Figure 14-16 shows parameters chosen for a moving text marquee, similar to what was just described. The marquee itself is displayed in Figure 14-17.) Happily, for many applets, you need not manipulate the default parameters to make them work.

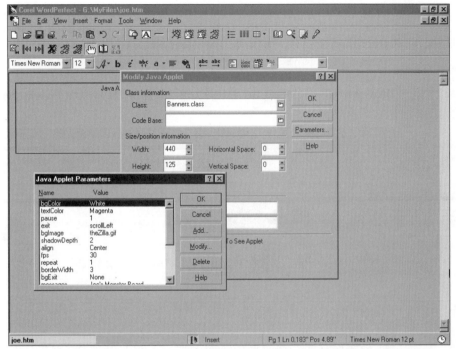

*Figure 14-16: Parameters specify how fast this text marquee moves across the screen, the font used, and other display qualities. Access this dialog box by right-clicking on the applet and selecting Properties.*

### A Java Applet Example

Figure 14-17 shows how the applet itself would appear in a browser. For an applet of this nature to display properly, here are the files that would have to be present in the default C:\MyFiles folder (which is where WordPerfect stores its Web-related files).

- The graphic file, in this case Godzilla.GIF.
- The Banner.CLASS files. .CLASS files are needed to run any Java applet.
- The HTML document itself. In this case, Joe.HTM.

The Click Here to See Applet panel (right-click on the applet, and select Properties) will show you a still, non-animated version of the applet. Sometimes, you must be online to see the animation of a Java applet in action. For example, if your applet is of a butterfly flying around within a square boundary, clicking this preview panel may only show the butterfly as a still graphic, not its movement. Figure 14-18 shows the Joe's Monster Board applet in action. Since it's a very simple applet that performs one action, WordPerfect's applet viewer displays it quite well, except for the fact that the applet itself is obviously larger than the viewing area. This idiosyncrasy has no effect on how the applet appears in a browser. In Figure 14-18, notice also the alternate text provided, "You need a Java-Enabled Browser." Alternate text is what the visitor's Browser will display if the visitor is unable to display the Java applet itself.

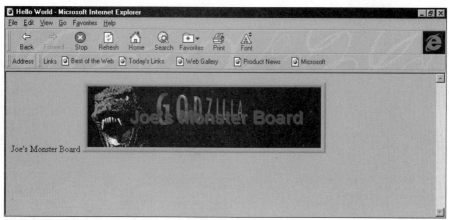

*Figure 14-17: A Java Applet in action. A simple moving marquee such as this can be checked and displayed offline in your browser. You can specify how fast the text moves across the banner graphic, the size of the font, and other parameters.*

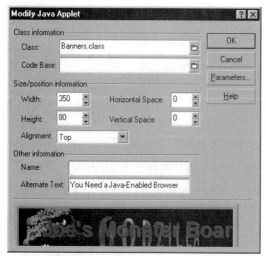

*Figure 14-18: Viewing an applet's Properties. A simple applet such as this can be viewed by clicking on the bottom panel of the Modify Java Applet dialog box, as shown.*

## Testing Your Page Offline

In the sample Web pages we created, there are a number of features we want to test. Will our graphics appear when we open the pages in a browser? Will the text and tables be aligned the way we want them to be? When we click the "Hotel Reservations" hyperlink found on the first page we created, will it open the Hotel Reservations Web page?

To test your Web page locally, click the View in Browser icon near the middle of the WordPerfect Internet Publisher toolbar. This opens the Web page in your default browser. It does not save the page to HTML; it quickly creates a temporary HTML document of the file and posts it in your browser. When you close the browser, that file goes away.

You can view your page locally in a browser other than your default. For example, if Netscape Navigator is set up as your default browser, but you'd like to view your Web page locally in Internet Explorer, it can be done. This is actually advisable. Testing your page in various browsers will save you from having to fix things later, after your project is supposed to be well under way. To test locally using any browser, do the following:

1. Save your document as an HTML file. Select File | Internet Publisher | Publish to HTML. Take note of the folder that the file is being saved to. It must be in the same folder as your other Web-related files, such as graphics, sounds, .CLASS files for Java applets, and so on.

2. Now open the Web browser you want to use. Don't maximize the browser view to take up the entire Windows screen because you'll be using Explorer onscreen to actually drag the icon of your new HTML file onto the empty browser page. (Unless, of course, you prefer to open it using the browser File | Open menu.)

3. Next, open Windows Explorer and locate the folder where your new .HTM file was saved. Don't double-click it to open it. Just drag it as an icon to the open browser (see Figure 14-19). The page will open visible in the browser. Rather than use Windows Explorer, you can simply use the Browser's File | Open menu to locate the new .HTM file you made and open it that way.

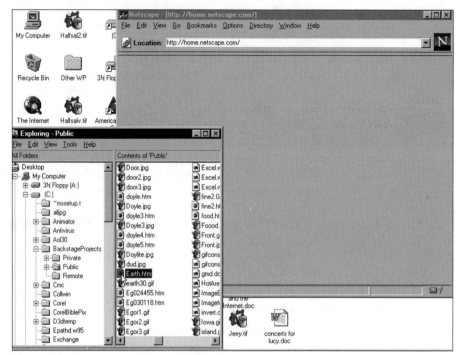

*Figure 14-19: Dragging an HTML file from Windows Explorer onto an open Web browser.*

Java applets may or may not work in local page testing.

# Converting Existing WordPerfect Documents to Web Pages

There are three ways to convert an existing WordPerfect Document to a Web page: using Corel Barista (which will convert just about any Windows-based document to a Web page), using WordPerfect's Internet Publisher, and using Web Publishing Wizard.

## Publishing to Corel Barista

Publishing a document to Corel Barista allows a Web page to retain the look of your original WordPerfect document. This includes tables, charts, pictures, fonts, and headings; all will be reproduced faithfully (when possible) as they appear on your WordPerfect page. If you have components on your page that don't transfer well when you attempt to convert it straight to HTML (File | Internet Publisher | Publish to HTML), then this document should be published or printed to Barista. Barista is a Java-based technology from Corel that facilitates accurate text formatting, table, graph, and frame arrangement in Web pages. So when your Web site needs to look *exactly* like your WordPerfect document, use Barista.

To publish your document to Barista, select File | Send to | Barista. You'll see a dialog box prompting you to specify if you'd like your document published as one single file (remember, a Web document need not be saved as a different file for each literal word processing page) or each page in a separate file. In a Barista site, documents longer than one literal page will appear with a page jump button at the top.

When uploading your Web site later, take special note of the extra files that have been created through the Barista process. There will be additional .HTM documents, as well as the necessary .CLASS files. All .CLASS files must be transferred with your own Web pages and graphic files. Visitors to your site will see your Barista documents appear in a Java window. Therefore, only people with Java-enabled browsers will see your work.

The feature Printing to Barista (File | Print, and set your printer to Corel Barista) is more flexible and powerful than Publishing to Barista. Printing to Barista allows you to create a simple online slide show of your WordPerfect document. This Web-based page-by-page slide show can include an audio narration and special transitional effects in between slides. This feature is covered below.

## Publishing With Sound Using Barista

Your Web page can play sounds saved in the .au file format. When you Print to Barista rather than Send to Barista, sound files in your page will be converted to this format. This language use—"printing" to Barista is a bit confusing—implies that the end result will somehow be a paper product. This is not the case. What is meant by the term "printing" is that the final product will not require WordPerfect's involvement in any way, but will still have the exact look of your paper-based WordPerfect document (similar to the concept "printing to Envoy").

## Creating an Online Slide Show

WordPerfect files printed to Barista are viewed online as a slide show. Each page of your WordPerfect document will become a slide. After the time indicated, one page (slide) segues into the next.

To print to Barista, select Print, and choose Corel Barista from the list of printers. Click Properties. You'll open to the Destination tab of the Barista Driver Properties dialog box (see Figure 14-20). You'll need to run through the entire process twice.

1. Select Open in Browser from the Destinations tab. After setting your specifications and clicking OK, the Barista file will open in your chosen browser.

2. Close the browser, returning you to WordPerfect Web Page view.

3. Click File | Print | Properties. The Driver Properties dialog box opens. Again view this same Destination tab.

4. Click Save to Disk.

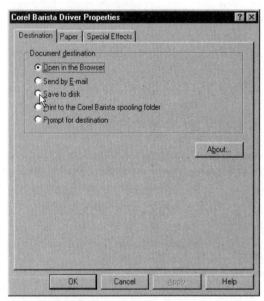

*Figure 14-20: The Barista Driver Properties box.*

## Setting Transitional Effects for an Online Slide Show

Select File | Print | Properties, and click the Special Effects tab (see Figure 14-21). Make sure your printer is set to Corel Barista. This is where sounds are added. One important change you may want to make is allowing the visitor to scroll through the pages themselves, rather than viewing them passively as a slide show. To do so:

1. Click the Transition drop-down menu from the Special Effects tab, and select User Input, rather than Time.

2. If you *do* decide to use a timed sequence, and do *not* require user input to switch between pages, you'll notice the Time text area (the fifth from the top) becomes active. It will default to the number 1000. This number represents the amount of time in milliseconds that each slide will stay on the screen before changing to the next slide.

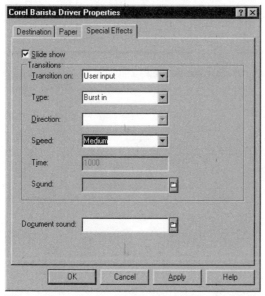

*Figure 14-21: The Special Effects tab of the Corel Barista Driver Properties dialog.*

There are two instances for including sounds:

- First, Barista will facilitate a sound to be played throughout the entire document, like narrative music. At the bottom of the Special Effects tab, you'll see a text box labeled Document Sound. This is where you'd include some type of narrative music or voice-over to be played throughout the entire "show."

- Secondly, another sound can be specified for slide transitions. To insert a sound to be played with every page transition, type a filename and path in the text box labeled Sound, or use the browse menu to locate one.

If you intend to work a lot with sounds in your Web pages, you may want to invest in a CD-ROM of .AU sounds and music, such as Jawai's Java Beat, among others.

## Publishing With Internet Publisher

With a document already open, select File | Internet Publisher. Your workspace changes to Web view (the same as if you had selected View | Web Page from the WordPerfect menu). Although not yet saved as such, your document will appear as if it were in HTML. This Web view has its own toolbar. Take a minute to hold your mouse over each tool button for a ToolTip, explaining the unique purpose of the new tools provided for this job.

You'll find four specific "Web tools" for creating hyperlinks, launching your browser, or temporarily converting your document to HTML and viewing it in a browser (see Figure 14-22). You'll see a button for creating a form, inserting bulleted lists, and creating a table. And by the way, Web documents are very table-friendly. If you can reorganize some information so that it appears neat and tidy in a table, your visitor's Web browser will know just what to do with it, and your meaning will not be lost.

*Figure 14-22: The four specific "Web tool" buttons on the WordPerfect Internet Publisher toolbar.*

The first thing you may notice after converting your document to a Web page is that the text formatting will be different. You will probably lose any special fonts. That's because most often, it's better to allow the visitor's Web browser to select the fonts from the visitor's own computer. If you try to impose your own font choices for your Web page, you may be "locking out" visitors who don't have them. Although a visitor can view your page, any specialized fonts you used to create the page must be found on the visitor's computer as well. If not, the visitor's browser will substitute a more standard font to replace your decorative one.

Also, the placement of pictures and headlines in your Web page may be positioned differently on your new HTML page. HTML documents have their own alignment commands that are universally understood by all Web browsers. Page numbering, paragraph indentations, headers, and footers may not look the same. Also equations placed in your document, double-underlining of text, and text boxes will probably not appear at all. (To publish a document with equations on the Web, use Corel Barista. We'll explain that shortly.) WordPerfect will strive to keep your Web page looking as closely as possible to its word processing counterpart, but *do* expect a few differences.

### Repositioning Text & Graphics

After converting your page, you may need to move things around a bit to retain the appearance you desire. You can actually select a graphic on your page and move it just about anywhere you want, and the visitor's browser will see it in the same place. (To move a graphic, select it with your mouse, and drag it to a new location, just as you would in a normal WordPerfect document.) When you save this Web document as HTML, WordPerfect takes pains to calculate the exact positioning of objects on your page. Please note that advanced text formatting, like expanding the space between letters and lines of text, will be ignored.

You may use the spacebar, tabs, and the Enter key to reposition text the way you like it. Unlike some Web publishing software, WordPerfect doesn't ignore these basic text operations.

### Advantages to Using an Outline Form

As alluded to earlier, a Web-friendly document will make generous use of bulleted and numbered outlines. See if you can reorganize your information to be presented in this way. For one thing, Web browsers can load this type of page very quickly. For another, information presented this way is very easy for Web visitors to understand. They are used to it, since many sites are created this way. And finally, there are lots of interesting bullets and other visual enhancements available that can quickly spruce up an outline-based Web page.

So now we have your information from your WordPerfect document ready to be saved as a Web page. Below, we will discuss saving your Web page. Please note, however, that your document thus far is not saved in HTML form. If you close WordPerfect now, you'll lose your changes. Before long, you should save what you have so far as an HTML document by choosing File | Send to | HTML (see Figure 14-23). Graphics used for your page will automatically be relocated to the same folder.

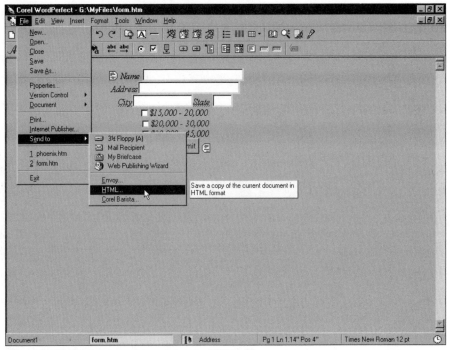

*Figure 14-23: Saving your document as an HTML file.*

## Quickly Checking Your Work

Before jumping ahead too quickly, it's important to check your work as you go along. WordPerfect's Web toolbar provides a single-click method for opening your document locally in a browser (or you can even be online while doing this). Note the four "Web icons," all next to each other on the Internet Publisher toolbar you are now working in. The second one from the left, "View in Web Browser," will quickly open your current page in your default browser (see Figure 14-24). Closing the browser returns you to WordPerfect in the Web view of your document, as you are now.

*Figure 14-24: Using View in Web Browser to quickly open your document locally in your Web Browser.*

## Converting a Document With Web Publishing Wizard

The Web Publishing Wizard (see Figure 14-25) takes you step by step through the entire process of setting up a simple Web page. It converts elements of your document to components that can be viewed correctly on the Web, and—here's an important point—discards those that cannot be converted to a usable format. It also guides you through the process of setting up a server and going online.

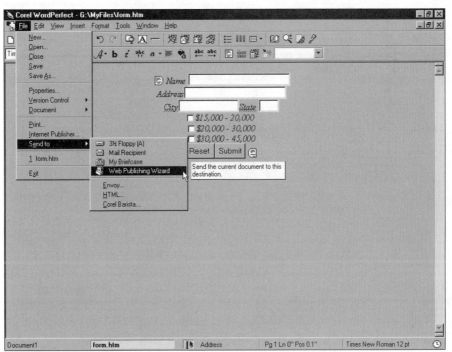

*Figure 14-25: Web Publishing Wizard launches your Web page, as well as converting it to HTML.*

One quick point regarding the Web Publishing Wizard—at the end of the process, it uploads your files to your chosen server. You still must have rights and permissions cleared with your Internet service provider to upload to that chosen site. WordPerfect simply uploads the files to that site if you've received proper authorization and understand in what directories your files belong.

Using the Web Publishing Wizard actually takes you online with your document (see Figure 14-26). Use this method to move from working in WordPerfect one minute to posting your work online in a very short time.

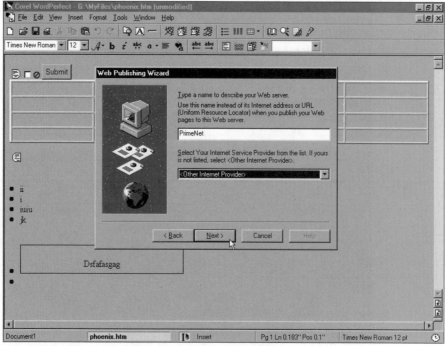

*Figure 14-26: The Web Publishing Wizard at work.*

The Web Publishing Wizard converts your document to HTML and then allows you to choose a Web server with which to work. You may type in the URL (the Internet address) of the server to which you have agreed to send files. They will have specified a folder (or folders) on their host computer to which you may upload your files. Web Publishing Wizard will then upload the current document to that online site. Web Publishing Wizard also helps make sure that any graphics, sound files, or extra files related to your site are found in the correct folder, before uploading them all at once. Your Web server may have set some specifications for uploading of which WordPerfect Web Publishing Wizard may not be aware. Make sure you follow those specifications.

When the Web Publishing Wizard first begins, it will ask to convert the current document to an HTML file; if it isn't one already, then it will ask for a folder where such files should be saved. If you have not set aside a folder on your computer for all your Web-related files for this current project, now is the last time to do so gracefully. Simply use Windows Explorer to make a folder, and, when prompted by Web Publishing Wizard, direct these Web-related files to be placed in that folder. Web Publisher may create a subfolder for graphic and sound files relating to this project. Allow it to do so. Just make sure your Web server's technical staff is aware of this arrangement. They may have some comment or request adjustments. Follow them closely.

## Saving a Copy of Your Document as a Web Page

You may save a copy of your word processing document as a Web page by selecting File | Send to | HTML. This process converts as much of your document as possible to a proper HTML page. Features and formatting that can't be converted will be modified or left out entirely. Note that simply saving it as HTML using this command does not open a preview screen to see exactly what you are saving.

The other method, already discussed above, is to select File | Internet Publisher. This opens the Web View, allowing you to make and oversee changes to your file. Then you can save it to HTML and feel a bit better about knowing what you are really saving.

The process discussed previously, selecting File | Send to | Web Publishing Wizard, is really more like launching a Web page, rather than saving one. The end result is a Web page posted to your chosen ISP, not an HTML file saved to your hard disk.

## Testing Your Web Page Online

Opening your Web page online while it is still local (while the files are still found on your own computer and not uploaded yet to your server) can allow you to test frames, scrolling bars, and most Java applet functionality. To do this, log on to your ISP and open your browser. Rather than browsing for an HTTP site on the Web, type in your own local address for the Web page you want to test (for example, C:\myfiles\Webstuff\Home.htp). Your page will open and behave somewhat as if it were online as a truly functioning Web page.

However, you won't really know how the more sophisticated features of your page will operate until the files are up and running with your ISP. When testing your Web page after it has finally been launched, be sure to use a variety of browsers since they each behave a little differently. Also, test you Web page with your graphics viewer disabled. That way, you can double-check the Alternate Text you included with your graphics. (Right-click on the graphic, and type a text entry into the Alternate Text area.) Every place a graphic would normally appear, there should be a text entry indicating what the graphic represented.

## Posting Your Web Site

Actually posting your Web site (making it available to the world) requires that all your Web-related files be uploaded to a **server**. A server is a computer configured to receive a high volume of Internet traffic. The Internet Service Provider you choose for posting your Web site will offer some services for facilitating your site.

In selecting an Internet Service Provider, find out how much space you can use for your Web site. Also, inquire about choosing your own Domain name, which would make the URL for your Web site much shorter, and thus, easier for others to remember. Find out if they will help you set up scripts. These are often needed for such features as creating Page Hit Counters and keeping track of the date and time that people access your page. As mentioned earlier, you'll need time during the month to update your Web site and add new features. You should not be charged for this time. Make sure the server you choose uses high-speed modem connections and doesn't have lots of "down-time." Also, if your site becomes very popular, your ISP may begin charging you for exceeding a preset amount of traffic allotted for each customer. Before you proceed, make sure these charges are not excessive.

Finally, after choosing an ISP, you'll need to upload your files to their server. For this, you'll need a small FTP program (File Transfer Protocol) which allows you to upload. Your ISP may provide or at least recommend one. One simple program for transferring files via FTP is called WS_FTP and is available for download on the Web.

Before uploading, your ISP will inform you where to transfer your files, giving you specific directories to which to send your files. To find out more about posting and maintaining your Web site, I'd recommend *HTML Publishing on the Internet, Second Edition*, published by Ventana.

## Moving On

WordPerfect Suite 8 is a multi-faceted program that has profited from many upgrades, additions, and improvements over the years—a software developer's job is never done! WordPerfect Suite 8 represents a long history of reading the "wish lists" and accumulated suggestions of users, and has evolved into a versatile and powerful office suite. In this book, we've acquainted you with WordPerfect 8, Presentations, and Quattro Pro 8, as well as the bonus applications, and have explored how they all can work together to make your documents look (and sound) their best. These could be paper documents, or increasingly, Web sites or online documents that never come in contact with ink or real paper.

As you work with WordPerfect Suite 8, you'll inevitably discover faster and more intuitive ways of getting your work done and discover techniques and methods that this book only mentions briefly. In a program as vast as this one, there is always more to explore. But if you ever get lost, you can always use this book to point you north again.

## Part VII

# Appendices

**Appendix**

# A

# Installing
# WordPerfect Suite 8

Wreceive ordPerfect Suite 8 is a huge program. It requires some thought and
planning to determine how much of the software you will use. Remember that
installing programs you are not using can waste hard drive space, and in
certain situations, can cause your computer to run sluggishly. WordPerfect
Suite 8 has a very convenient setup program that leaves nothing to guesswork.
It allows you to keep track of exactly which programs you are installing, as
well as the components within a program itself. Installing WordPerfect Suite 8
will require around an hour of your time and between 60 and 400 megabytes
of hard drive space.

## Beginning the Installation Process

To begin installing WordPerfect Suite 8, do the following:

1. Close any open programs on your computer.

2. Place your WordPerfect Suite CD in the CD-ROM drive. You need not
   click any icons just yet.

3. You'll see the initial Setup screen, as pictured in Figure A-1. Click Corel
   WordPerfect Suite Setup.

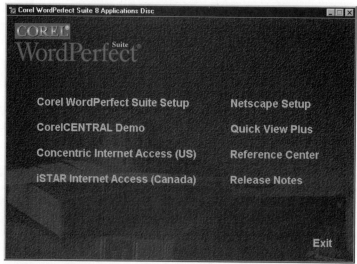

*Figure A-1: The Setup screen.*

**Tip**

*If AutoRun is disabled on your computer, you must place the CD in your CD-ROM drive, right-click on the drive's icon in Windows Explorer, select Explore, and click the Setup icon. Then return to step 3 in the directions.*

4. You'll then see the Welcome screen. If you'd like to find out any late-breaking information about WordPerfect Suite 8 before installing the program, click the Release Notes button at the lower left of the screen.

5. Read and click past the Licensing Agreement. Wait momentarily while WordPerfect places setup files into a temporary folder on your computer.

6. You'll then see the Registration Information dialog box (see Figure A-2). Type in the required information. Note that the serial number lettering must be capitalized, and be careful not to use zeroes for the letter "O" (or vice versa).

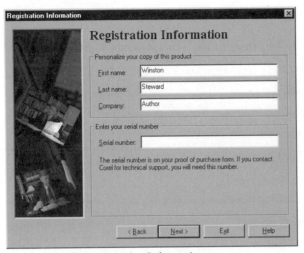

*Figure A-2: The Registration Information screen.*

## Choosing a Type of Installation

At long last, you'll see the Installation Type dialog box, as shown in Figure A-3.

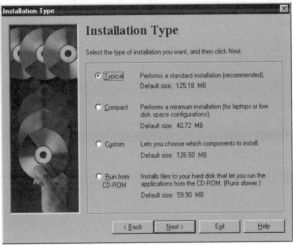

*Figure A-3: The Installation Type dialog box.*

There are four basic installation choices. They are Typical, Compact, Custom, and Run from CD-ROM. The following are the 3 "core" applications that will be installed in any case, unless you go out of your way to leave them out:

- WordPerfect 8

- Presentations 8

- Quattro Pro 8

These are the bonus applications:

- Bitstream Font Navigator

- Corel Photo House

- Envoy 7

- Corel Address Book

- Corel QuickFinder

QuickView Plus must be installed separately—it is a separate procedure from installing WordPerfect Suite 8 as a whole. Accessories such as the Data Modeling Desktop will not be installed if you don't install Quattro Pro. If you choose not to install the Scrapbook, you can still access WordPerfect Suite 8 artwork, but you'll have to use the application's Browse menu. You will not have the benefit of the visual preview.

You can also cut down on installation disk space requirements by not installing all the templates for each application. You'll still have access to those templates. You just won't have the benefit of the visual preview and easy categorization. You'll have to use the Browse menu.

## Typical Installation

Typical installation provides many of the components WordPerfect users will enjoy. It is the fastest way to get the process over and done with. However, Typical Installation will leave out the following programs:

- Envoy 7

- Photo House

- Bitstream Font Navigator

These are nifty programs that even a novice WordPerfect Suite user may miss. Before leaving these programs out of the picture, quickly browse through Chapters 11 and 12 of this book, which will acquaint you with the three missing programs. With typical installation (see Figure A-4) you can choose to install a particular program or not, but you cannot "fine-tune" an installation, specifying which components of a program to install or not.

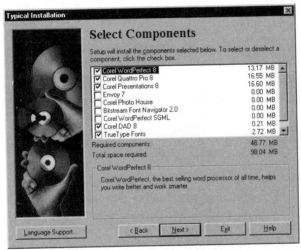

*Figure A-4: The Typical Installation dialog box.*

## Tip

*Only a handful of the fonts included with WordPerfect Suite 8 are installed with the Typical installation. That may or may not be a good thing. To fully inform yourself regarding your choices for installing fonts, read the section of Chapter 12 on Bitstream Font Navigator. Please be sure to read this if you intend to install more than 150 fonts at this time.*

## Compact Installation

Compact installation installs every component of the three "core" WordPerfect Suite 8 applications. None of the bonus applications are installed. If you are working with a notebook computer or have limited free hard drive space, this option may suit you fine. If you want to "fine-tune" your compact installation, for example including Bitstream Font Navigator in your choice, then choose a custom installation, as explained below.

## Custom Installation

Choosing Custom Installation gives you total control over which WordPerfect Suite programs and components are installed (see Figure A-5.) Check Custom Installation, then click a program; for example, WordPerfect. Now click the Components button. Doing so displays a check list of individual components. This lets you choose which WordPerfect features to include. The Components button is available for all WordPerfect Suite 8 applications. Figure A-6 shows the components list for WordPerfect 8. Notice that WordPerfect Macro Help and Java Applet Support are not included at all. Place a check by any component to include it with your installation.

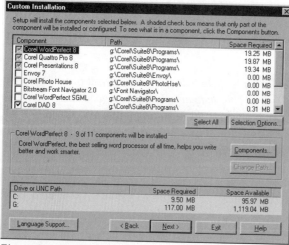

*Figure A-5: The Custom Installation dialog box.*

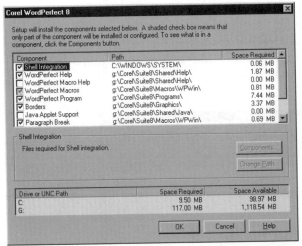

*Figure A-6: The Custom Installation dialog box for WordPerfect.*

## Options With a Gray Checkmark

Obviously, then, it's possible to install a program, such as Presentations, but not install every component of that program. For example, you could install Presentations, but not include all the slide show masters. This saves disk space, and you can access the masters from the CD anyway.

The Setup program indicates that a program is going to be partially installed by placing a gray check next to it. In Figure A-7, the installation option TrueType Fonts has a gray check by it. That means some TrueType fonts are going to be installed, but not all of them.

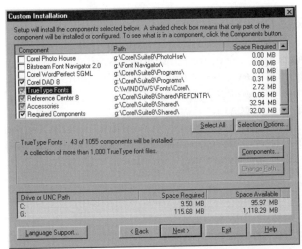

*Figure A-7: Installing only a few of the TrueType fonts.*

Clicking Components reveals a lists of all the fonts that can be installed (see Figure A-8). Placing a check by one selects it for installation. But notice that additional information is provided. In Figure A-8, the font Aldine 401 Italic is selected. To the right, we are told that this font requires .06 megabytes of hard drive space for installation.

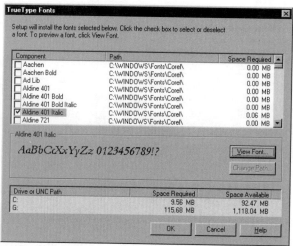

*Figure A-8: Showing which component will be installed. The disk space requirement is also reported.*

Although we've used fonts as an example here, any application that is destined for partial installation will appear with a gray checkmark, rather than a white or black one.

## Keeping Track of Disk Space Usage

All the dialog boxes involving custom installation have an area near the bottom that reports Space Required and Space Available (see Figure A-8, above). These figures tell you how much space the component you've just checked requires (this number is at the upper right of the screen). You're also told how much total space your WordPerfect installation will take up, and how much disk space will remain free on your computer when you are finished installing. Keep an eye on these numbers. Installing WordPerfect can eat up more disk space than you'd think.

### Changing Your Custom Installation Choices

If, when working with a custom installation, you made installation choices you are not happy with, and would like to undo them, click Select Options (see Figure A-9) on the Custom Installation screen, and choose Typical installation. This is like a "reset button." Now you can build your choices again.

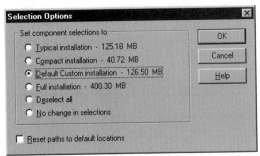

*Figure A-9: The Select Options dialog box.*

If you decide you want "the works" and you have 400 megabytes of hard drive space to spare, click Select Options and choose Full installation.

## Run From CD-ROM

Choosing Run From CD-ROM installs fewer files on your hard drive than Typical or Custom Installation. It does, however, give you access to every feature of the Suite. But you will need to have the CD-ROM in the drive, even to do something as simple as write a letter. Also, even with a high-speed CD-ROM drive, running WordPerfect Suite from a CD-ROM is much slower than from your hard drive.

## Finishing the Installation

After you've selected your components and Suite programs, the Ready to Install screen appears. This is your last chance to exit gracefully and change your mind about a feature or component. Make sure you've kept a close eye on how much hard drive space remains on your computer after your installation choices. Extra-crammed hard drives can be very unforgiving.

The setup program will then update the installation profile, which means it lays out on your hard drive where each component is going to go. This takes a couple of minutes.

Finally, at long last, installation itself will begin. A blue progress bar at the bottom of the screen appears (see Figure A-10). Go get some coffee. Installation can take up to 45 minutes. Can you work on your computer at the same time? Sort of. You can type a short document, but performance will be sluggish. Do not turn off your computer, go online, or save a particularly large file to disk during installation.

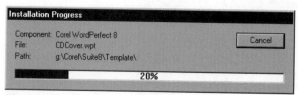

*Figure A-10: The blue Installation progress bar.*

After installation, WordPerfect directs you to restart your computer. It's a good idea to do this now, and not try to carry on with your work and restart later. WordPerfect has made many changes to your system. Installation is not over until WordPerfect restarts your computer. Even after restarting, you will still hear a good deal of whirring and chattering before you can work with your machine again. Please be patient. WordPerfect is now installed. Enjoy.

# Introducing CorelCENTRAL

CorelCENTRAL is an address book and schedule manager that connects directly to the Internet through your desktop. The Internet connection not only allows you to instantly send e-mail to anyone you choose, but to have an online conference with several people at once, no matter where in the world they are. You can include artwork and Java applets in your e-mail and conferencing messages.

With CorelCENTRAL you can schedule your appointments, group all your contacts according to any criteria, send e-mail, and manage a multiparty Internet conference, all from the same interface. During this conference, all participants can view the same information on a markable "whiteboard" in which participants can make changes and pass these revisions around online, while keeping track of who suggested what.

We're going to take a quick look at the version of CorelCENTRAL that is available today. Keep in mind that CorelCENTRAL is brand-new technology. Corel might improve on the features shown here, and what you see in your version of the product might look slightly different. Figure B-1 shows CorelCENTRAL's main features.

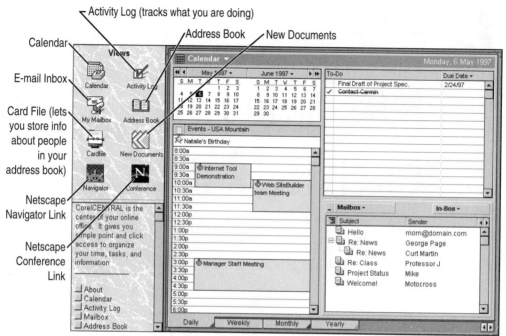

*Figure B-1: The CorelCENTRAL Calendar window.*

Notice the four main components shown in Figure B-1: a small two-month calendar appears at the upper left, below it is an hourly calendar, and to the right is a to-do list and an e-mail in-box. At the bottom are tabs that expand the calendar into weekly, monthly, or yearly formats. The links to CorelCENTRAL's other features are always present onscreen.

Let's look more closely at CorelCENTRAL's calendar and scheduling components.

# Calendar & Scheduling

CorelCENTRAL lets you create appointments and set up schedules and to-do lists. You can view these as a daily, weekly, or monthly calendar, and as a "day planner" list of scheduled activities. It's easy to switch back and forth between these views. You can also assemble the schedule as a time management–oriented "task list" to see more accurately how you are spending your time.

The interactivity between the scheduling features of CorelCENTRAL and its message-sending power is very powerful. You can send a message to anyone whose name appears in an appointment from the same interface you use to build your schedule. Information about any name or company you have built into your CorelCENTRAL Address Book or Card File system is always available with a click.

Figure B-2 shows the CorelCENTRAL Appointment maker. Appointments are scheduled with others via e-mail, and appear in your own scheduler. Notice the icons on the appointment maker interface. You can quickly open any Calendar or Address Book view, attach another document to this message, and use the standard cut, paste, and print functions.

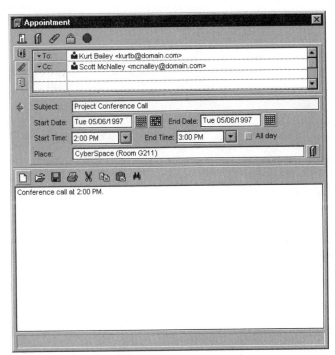

*Figure B-2: CorelCENTRAL's Appointment maker.*

# Mail & Newsgroups

CorelCENTRAL's Mail and Newsgroup feature lets you interact with colleagues through private intranet discussion groups and post and receive Internet newsgroup messages, all from the same interface. With CorelCENTRAL, it's very easy to share newsgroup information, send a Web page link, or keep track of a multilevel conversation with your colleagues. You can do this with the same interface you'd use to send a simple e-mail message.

Figure B-3 shows the My Mailbox window. Here you can review mail you've received, respond to any message, and view Internet newsgroup information. Mail you send (or discussion group responses you post—it's all the same to CorelCENTRAL) can include artwork and Java applets. URL text you type is instantly converted to a clickable link. Notice the Explorer-like tree for viewing lists of messages, which can be expanded or compressed, depending on how much detail you want to see.

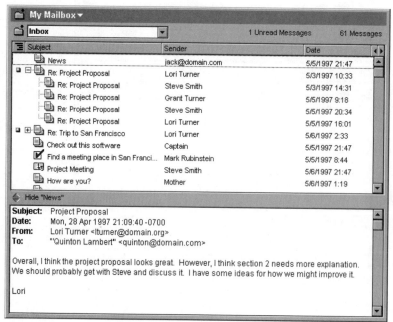

*Figure B-3: The My Mailbox window.*

In the Subject area of the Mailbox window, each message type is represented by an icon. This could include a scheduled to-do item, an e-mail message, or a referral to the Activity Log, for example. All these messages and reminders can be linked and managed from this same interface. To gather more information and respond appropriately, you can quickly open any CorelCENTRAL component with a click.

# CorelCENTRAL Address Book

CorelCENTRAL Address Book links address information to any sort of grouping you designate. A particular address can be linked to other names in a company, family, or list of conference attendees, for example. Dialing an addressee's phone number or e-mail address is always just a click away. Address Book information can be instantly applied to an e-mail message, an online conference invite, or a cc:list or newsgroup routing list. Figure B-4 shows the user looking up a member of the Aagard family. From there, just one more click opens a list of other members of that family (notice the pointing hand in the figure).

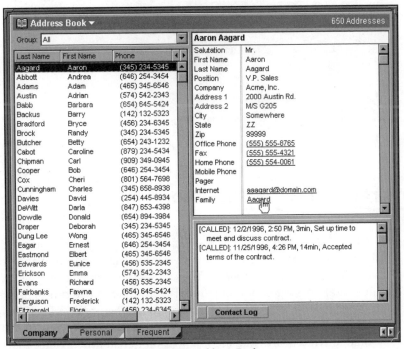

*Figure B-4: Using the CorelCENTRAL Address Book.*

CorelCENTRAL Address Book allows you to access other address lists on the same office intranet. This makes it easy to share contacts. At the bottom right of the Address Book is a Contact Log, which keeps track of who you've contacted and when (see Figure B-4). CorelCENTRAL comes with a rather nifty phone dialer feature (see Figure B-5). Notice the Call Note feature in the right panel, the History list at the bottom left, and the button for saving a record of your call to the Contact Log.

*Figure B-5: The many-featured Phone Dialer.*

## Conferencing & Collaboration

CorelCENTRAL includes Netscape Conference, with which you can conduct a fully interactive conference call using your Internet connection and your computer's speaker and microphone. You can send documents (see Figure B-6), type online 'chat' messages, and talk over the Internet in real time. Also, all collaborators can work with a shared 'whiteboard' (see Figure B-7). Capture any image on your computer screen, and send it to others. It can be viewed instantly on the shared whiteboard, and commented on in real time. Notice that the whiteboard has drawing tools for making impromptu diagrams and highlighting important content.

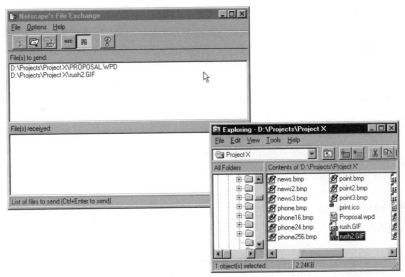

*Figure B-6: Sending a document to an online colleague in real time.*

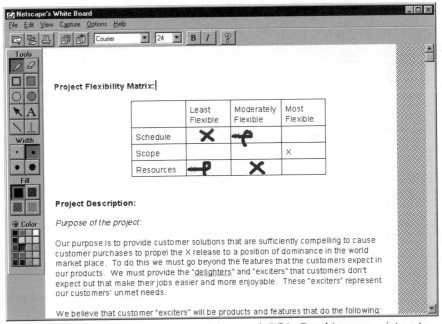

*Figure B-7: Sharing group information over Netscape's White Board (a common intranet workspace).*

Using Netscape Conference, you and your colleagues can all visit the same Web page as you talk. The online chat tool lets you keep a record of your conference; later, you can refer to the chat notes and other content from your conference in a message to your colleagues, as you summarize and evaluate your collaborative work.

## CorelCENTRAL Card File

CorelCENTRAL Card File lets you create 'cards' that contain any kind of information you want on any topic. You can quickly create, for example, a family physician list, linked to information on medical conditions, as well as a quick link to place an emergency call (see Figure B-8). You can create a card with personal information that contains a link to a spreadsheet, for example, or an important family document such as a will (see Figure B-9). Personal belongings, such as household valuables, can be cataloged, along with relevant insurance or tax-related links.

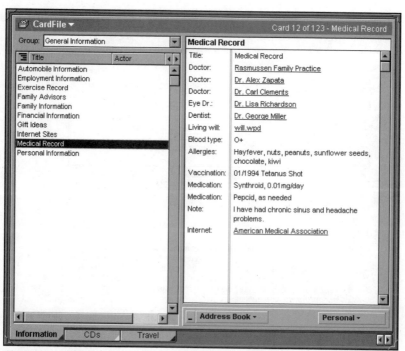

*Figure B-8: Placing links to all relevant personal medical information on a card file.*

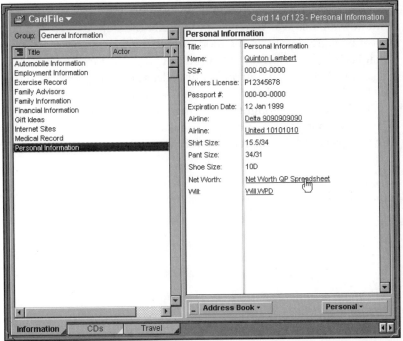

*Figure B-9: A card file can link you to any URL, document, or executable file on your computer.*

Card files can be linked to other cards, or to any document on your computer or any URL. For example, you can use a card file to keep track of all WordPerfect Suite projects on your computer related to a particular client, including links to how to contact that client, and personal information about them. Of course, information on a card file can be included in a CorelCENTRAL note or message to a colleague. Think of CorelCENTRAL CardFile as an information centralizer that helps you keep track of all related documents and URLs for a particular person, group of people, or project.

## Summary

Imaginative use of CorelCENTRAL can truly break the barrier between your personal computer and the world of the Internet and intranets. With CorelCENTRAL, any information on your computer can be presented to others creatively. You can elicit real-time comments from your collaborators, keep track of the course of a project easily, and update everybody involved.

CorelCENTRAL means you'll never again have to wait for the mail to find out how an idea was received, or whether the steps agreed to in a conference meeting were clearly understood. And using CardFile, you need not worry that last week's inspirational outburst will get lost in the shuffle of this week's deadline. Everything you and your colleagues have worked on together can be fittingly evaluated and developed as a team.

This is a fitting thought for closing this book, because WordPerfect Suite 8 gives you tools for creating individually expressive and unique documents, and helps you share them effectively with others.

# Index

# X

# Y

# Z

# VENTANA

## Official Netscape Communicator Book

*$39.99, 800 pages*
*Beginning to Intermediate*
*Windows Edition: part #: 1-56604-617-3*
*Macintosh Edition: part #:1-56604-620-3*

The sequel to Ventana's blockbuster international bestseller *Official Netscape Navigator Book*! Discover the first suite to integrate key intranet and Internet communications services into a single, smart interface. From simple e-mail to workgroup collaboration, from casual browsing to Web publishing, from reading text to receiving multimedia Netcaster channels—learn to do it all without leaving Communicator! Covers:

- All Communicator components: Navigator, Netcaster, Messenger, Collabra, Composer and Conference.
- Complete, step-by-step instructions for both intranet and Internet task.
- Tips on using plug-ins, JavaScript and Java applets.

The CD-ROM includes a fully-supported version of Netscape Communicator plus hyperlinked listings.

## Official Netscape Communicator Professional Edition Book

*$39.99, 608 pages, part #:1-56604-739-0*

Windows Edition • Intermediate

**Your Guide to Business Communications Over the Intranet & the Web!** Unlock the immeasurable potential of Web technologies for improving and enhancing day-to-day business tasks. Netscape Communicator and your office intranet provide the tools and the environment. This easy-to-use, step-by-step guide opens the door to each key module—and its most effective use. Covers:

- Navigator 4, Messenger, Collabra, Conference, Composer, Calendar, Netcaster and AutoAdmin.
- Key business tasks: e-mail, workgroups, conferencing and Web publishing.
- Step-by-step instructions, tips and guidelines for working effectively.

# VENTANA

## Microsoft Windows NT 4 Workstation Desktop Companion

*$39.99, 1016 pages, illustrated, part #: 1-56604-472-3*

Workstation users become masters of their own universe with this step-by-step guide. Covers file management, customizing and optimizing basic multimedia, OLE, printing and networking. Packed with shortcuts, secrets, productivity tips and hands-on tutorials. The CD-ROM features dozens of valuable utilities and demos for Windows NT. Innovative web-site designs, reference information, wallpaper textures, animated cursors, custom utilities and more.

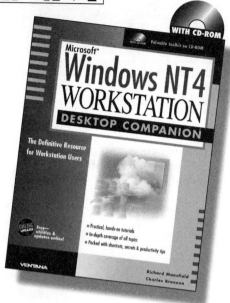

## Microsoft Office 95 Companion

*$34.95, 1136 pages, illustrated, part #: 1-56604-188-0*

The all-in-one reference to Microsoft's red-hot suite is a worthy sequel to Ventana's bestselling *Windows, Word & Excel Office Companion*. Covers basic commands and features, and includes a section on using Windows 95. The companion disk features examples, exercises, software and sample files from the book.

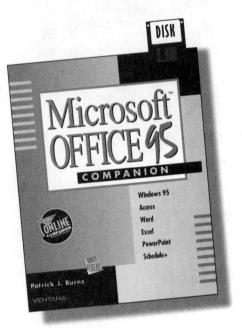

## SmartSuite Desktop Companion

*$24.95, 784 pages, illustrated, part #: 1-56604-184-8*

Here's "Suite success" for newcomers to the critics' choice of business packages. This introduction to the individual tools and features of Lotus' star software packages—1-2-3, Ami Pro, Approach, Freelance Graphics and Organizer—has been updated for the latest versions. Features new enhancements for Windows 95. The companion disk features sample exercises and files that follow the lessons in the book.

## The Comprehensive Guide to SmartSuite 97

*James Meade*
*$34.99, 528 pages, illustrated, part #: 1-56604-651-3*

Here's Suite relief for business users at all levels. Step by step, learn to use applications together, work collaboratively, and maximize Internet and intranet connectivity. Packed with tips and shortcuts.

*For Windows 95/NT • Beginning to Intermediate*

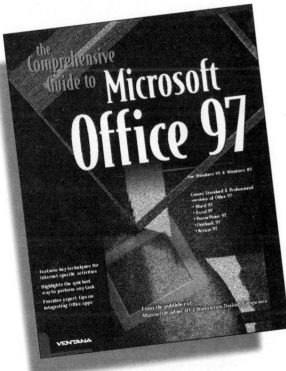

## The Comprehensive Guide to Microsoft Office 97

*Ned Snell*
*$39.99, 848 pages, illustrated, part #: 1-56604-646-7*

The "right-size" guide to the world's hottest suite! Easy enough for beginners, yet in-depth enough for power users. Covers all five applications, plus tips, shortcuts, Internet techniques and more.

*For Windows 95/NT • Beginning to Intermediate*

## Web Publishing With Adobe PageMill 2

*$34.99, 480 pages, illustrated, part #: 1-56604-458-8*

Now, creating and designing professional pages on the Web is a simple, drag-and-drop function. Learn to pump up PageMill with tips, tricks and troubleshooting strategies in this step-by-step tutorial for designing professional pages. The CD-ROM features Netscape plug-ins, original textures, graphical and text-editing tools, sample backgrounds, icons, buttons, bars, GIF and JPEG images, Shockwave animations.

## Web Publishing With QuarkImmedia

*$39.99, 552 pages, illustrated, part #: 1-56604-525-8*

Use multimedia to learn multimedia, building on the power of QuarkXPress. Step-by-step instructions introduce basic features and techniques, moving quickly to delivering dynamic documents for the Web and other electronic media. The CD-ROM features an interactive manual and sample movie gallery with displays showing settings and steps. Both are written in QuarkImmedia.

# VENTANA

## The Comprehensive Guide to Corel WEB.GRAPHICS SUITE

*$49.99, 696 pages, illustrated, part #: 1-56604-614-9*

Create spectacular web pages, incorporating sophisticated graphics and animation! Every component of CorelWEB is highlighted with an introduction, tools, tips and tricks, and a sample project. The Suite features tools for editing web pages, creating animation for web pages, designing 3D worlds and converting word processing files to HTML. Plus an illustration package based on CorelDRAW 5— along with 7,500 Internet-ready clipart images in GIF and JPEG formats. The CD-ROM includes images, textures and shareware for web designers.

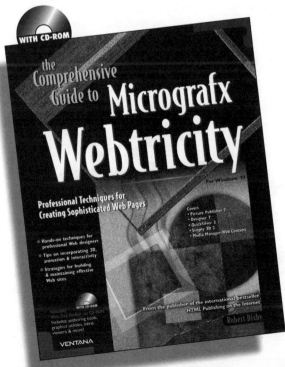

## The Comprehensive Guide to Micrografx Webtricity

*$49.99, 672 pages, illustrated, part #: 1-56604-607-6*

Make your site soar with interactive excitement--and save time and money doing it! Micrografx Webtricity provides the drag-and-drop tool palette--this easy-to-follow, practical guide adds instructions, ideas and professional guidelines. Learn to design sophisticated, eye-catching graphics, optimize your files for the Web, create dazzling 3D effects and animations, catalog the hundreds of graphics files included in Webtricity, and much more. The CD-ROM features in-line viewers for dozens of formats, plus additional web-site utilities and images.

# VENTANA

## Looking Good in Print, Deluxe CD-ROM Edition

*$34.99, 416 pages, illustrated, part #: 1-56604-471-5*

This completely updated version of the most widely used design companion for desktop publishers features all-new sections on color and printing. Packed with professional tips for creating powerful reports, newsletters, ads, brochures and more. The companion CD-ROM featues Adobe® Acrobat® Reader, author examples, fonts, templates, graphics and more.

## Looking Good Online

*$39.99, 384 pages, illustrated, part #: 1-56604-469-3*

Create well-designed, organized web sites—incorporating text, graphics, digital photos, backgrounds and forms. Features studies of successful sites and design tips from pros. The companion CD-ROM includes samples from online professionals; buttons, backgrounds, templates and graphics.

## Looking Good in 3D

*$39.99, 384 pages, illustrated, part #: 1-56604-494-4*

Become the da Vinci of the 3D world! Learn the artistic elements involved in 3D design—light, motion, perspective, animation and more—to create effective interactive projects. The CD-ROM includes samples from the book, templates, fonts and graphics.

## News Junkies Internet 500

*$24.99, 464 pages, illustrated, part #: 1-56604-461-8*

Quench your thirst for news with this comprehensive listing of the best and most useful news sites and sources on the Web. Includes business, international, sports, weather, law, finance, entertainment, politics and more. Plus rated reviews of site strengths, weaknesses, design and navigational properties.

## Internet Business 500

*$29.95, 488 pages, illustrated, part #: 1-56604-287-9*

This authoritative list of the most useful, most valuable online resources for business is also the most current list, regularly updated on the Internet. The companion CD-ROM features a hypertext version of the entire book, linked to updates on Ventana Online.

## Walking the World Wide Web, Second Edition

*$39.95, 800 pages, illustrated, part #: 1-56604-298-4*

Updated and expanded, this bestseller now features 500 listings and an extensive index of servers, arranged by subject. This groundbreaking title includes a CD-ROM enhanced with Ventana's exclusive WebWalker technology; Netscape Navigator; and a hypertext version of the book. Updated online components make it the richest resource available for web travelers.

# VENTANA

## Official Online Marketing With Netscape Book

*$34.99, 544 pages, illustrated, part #: 1-56604-453-7*

The perfect marketing tool for the Internet! Learn how innovative marketers create powerful, effectove electronic newsletters and promotional materials. Step-by-step instructions show you how to plan, deisgn and distribute professional-quality pieces. With this easy-to-follow guide, you'll soon be flexing Netscape Navigator's marketing muscle to eliminate paper and printing costs, automate market research and customer service, and much more.

## Official Netscape Guide to Online Investments

*$24.99, 528 pages, illustrated, part #: 1-56604-452-9*

Gain the Internet investment edge! Here's everything you need to make the Internet a full financial partner. Features an overview of the Net and Navigator; in-depth reviews of stock and bond quote services, analysts, brokerage houses, and mutual fund reports. Plus a full listing of related financial services such as loans, appraisals, low-interest credit cards, venture capital, entrepreneurship, insurance, tax counseling, and more.

## Official Netscape Guide to Internet Research

*$29.99, 480 pages, illustrated, part #: 1-56604-604-1*

Turn the Internet into your primary research tool. More than just a listing of resources, this official guide provides everything you need to know to access, organize, cite and post information on the Net. Includes research strategies, search engines and information management. Plus timesaving techniques for finding the best, most up-to-date data.

# VENTANA

## To order any Ventana title, complete this order form and mail or fax it to us, with payment, for quick shipment.

| TITLE | PART # | QTY | PRICE | TOTAL |
|-------|--------|-----|-------|-------|
|       |        |     |       |       |
|       |        |     |       |       |
|       |        |     |       |       |
|       |        |     |       |       |
|       |        |     |       |       |
|       |        |     |       |       |
|       |        |     |       |       |
|       |        |     |       |       |

## SHIPPING

For orders shipping within the United States, please add $4.95 for the first book, $1.50 for each additional book.
For "two-day air," add $7.95 for the first book, $3.00 for each additional book.
Email: vorders@kdc.com for exact shipping charges.
Note: Please include your local sales tax.

SUBTOTAL = $ _____

SHIPPING = $ _____

TAX = $ _____

TOTAL = $ _____

**Mail to: International Thomson Publishing • 7625 Empire Drive • Florence, KY 41042**
☎ **US orders 800/332-7450 • fax 606/283-0718**
☎ **International orders 606/282-5786 • Canadian orders 800/268-2222**

Name _____

E-mail _____   Daytime phone _____

Company _____

Address (No PO Box) _____

City _____   State _____ Zip _____

Payment enclosed ___ VISA ___ MC ___ Acc't # _____   Exp. date _____

Signature _____   Exact name on card _____

Check your local bookstore or software retailer for these and other bestselling titles, or call toll free:

# 800/332-7450

8:00 am - 6:00 pm EST